CASEY AND KYLE

SO MUCH FOR BEING ON OUR BEST BEHAVIOR!!!

A *Casey and Kyle* Collection by Will Robertson

Contains cartoons from BOOK 1 and BOOK 2

FOR CARTER!!!...
WILL ROBERTSON

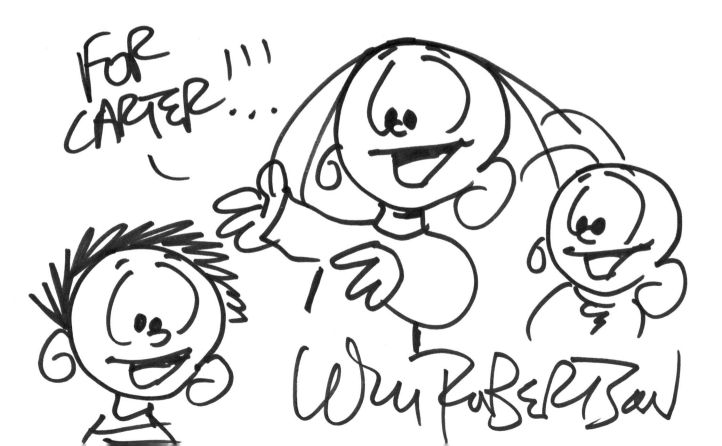

For information, email us at caseyandkylecomics@yahoo.com.

ISBN: 1453844562
EAN-13: 9781453844564

Also By Will Robertson:
Casey and Kyle: BOOK 1 (2009)
Casey and Kyle: BOOK 2 (2009)
So Much For Being On Our Best Behavior (2010)

ATTENTION SCHOOLS AND BUSINESSES
Our books are available at quantity discounts for bulk purchases for educational, business, or sales promotional use. For information, please write to: caseyandkylecomics@yahoo.com

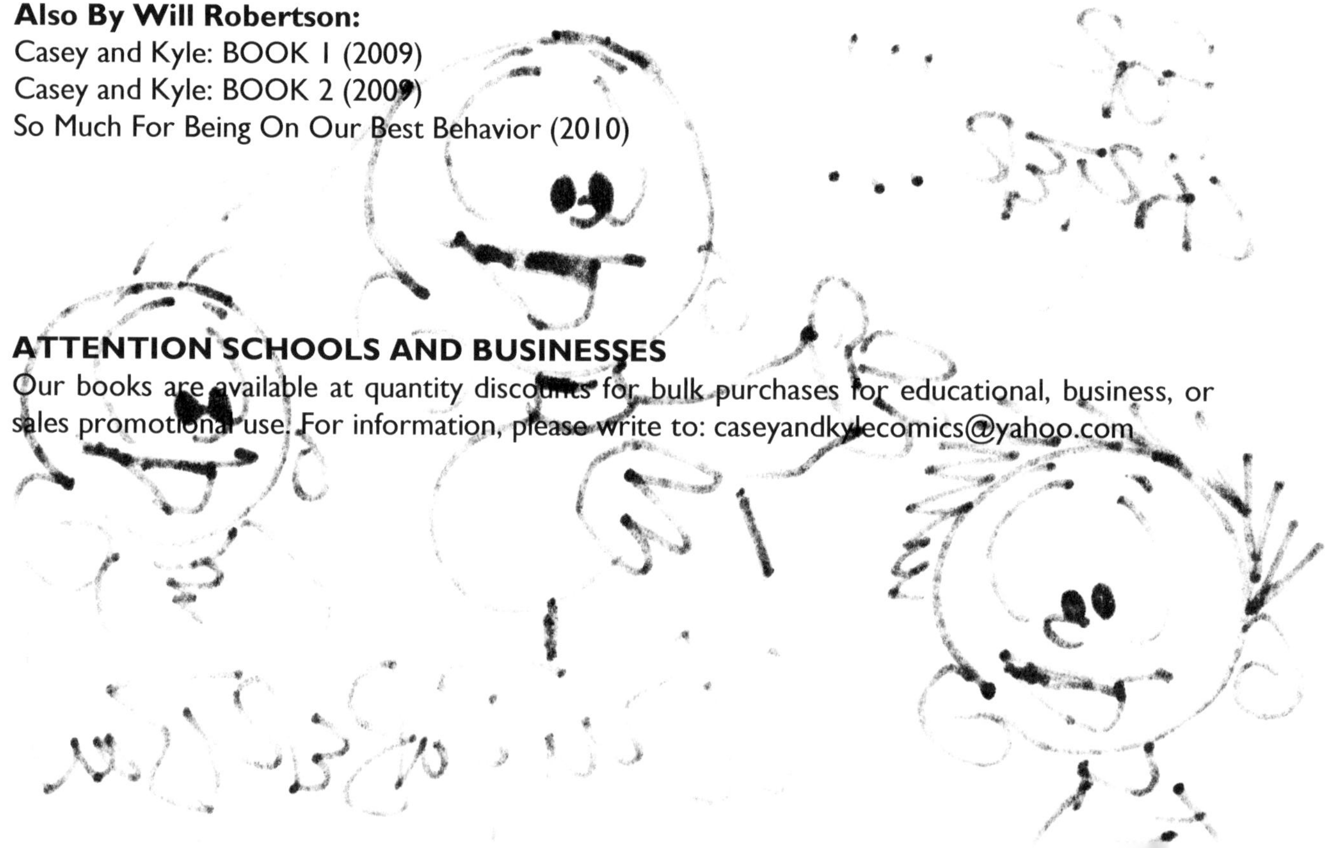

TO MOM, WHO WOULD'VE LOVED THIS...
TO WENDY AND THE KIDS, FOR BEING MY INSPIRATION...
TO DAD, FOR YOUR SUPPORT...
TO JAN, FOR HELPING ME GET STARTED ON THE RIGHT FOOT...
TO ENES, FOR SHOWING ME THE ROPES...
TO MARK AND BETHANY, FOR MAKING IT POSSIBLE...
AND TO CHRISTA AND RYAN FOR PUSHING THINGS FORWARD.

READ NEW COMICS AT:
WWW.CASEYANDKYLECOMICS.COM

QUESTIONS/COMMENTS? E-MAIL WILL AT:
CASEYANDKYLECOMICS@YAHOO.COM

CASEY AND KYLE

OFFICIAL ONLINE DEBUT FEBRUARY 6, 2008

HEY DAD! WANNA PLAY SQUIRT GUNS?
NOT NOW. GO PLAY WITH YOUR BROTHER.
AAARRGHHH! OKAAAAY!!!
DON'T YELL AT ME! THIS WAS DAD'S IDEA!

MOM!! CAN YOU BRING ME A GLASS OF WATER?!!
GO TO SLEEP!!! IF I HEAR YOU ONE MORE TIME, I'M COMING IN THERE!!
WHEN YOU COME, CAN YOU BRING ME A GLASS OF WATER?!

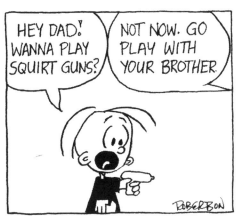

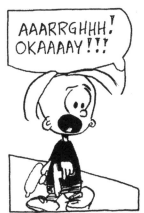

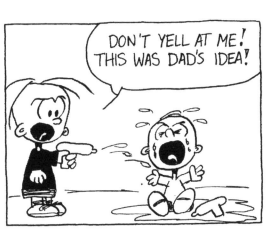

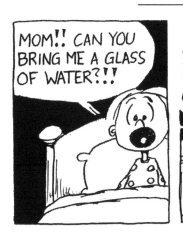

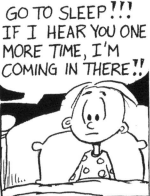

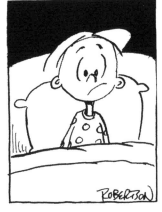

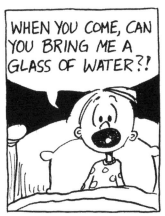

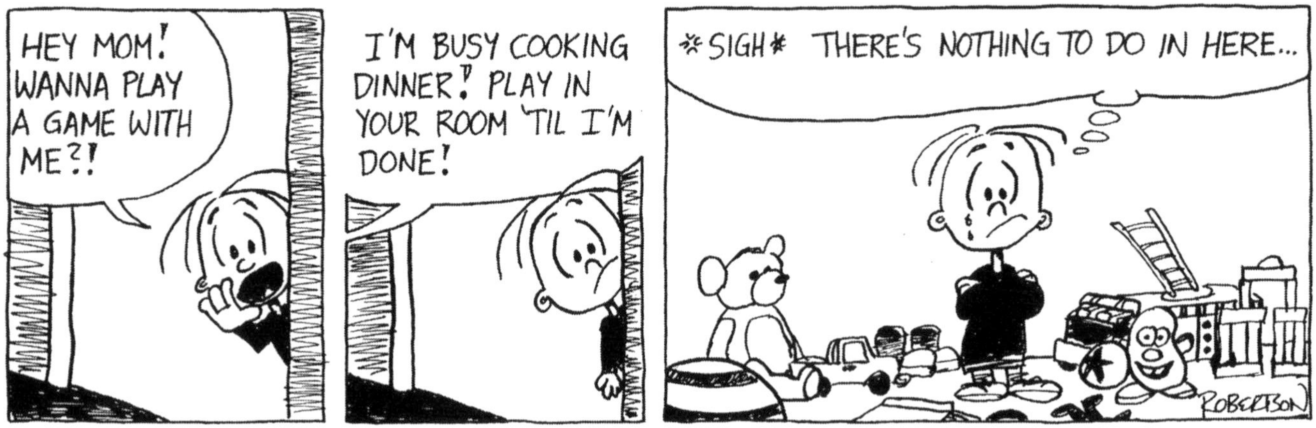
HEY MOM! WANNA PLAY A GAME WITH ME?!
I'M BUSY COOKING DINNER! PLAY IN YOUR ROOM 'TIL I'M DONE!
SIGH THERE'S NOTHING TO DO IN HERE...
ROBERTSON

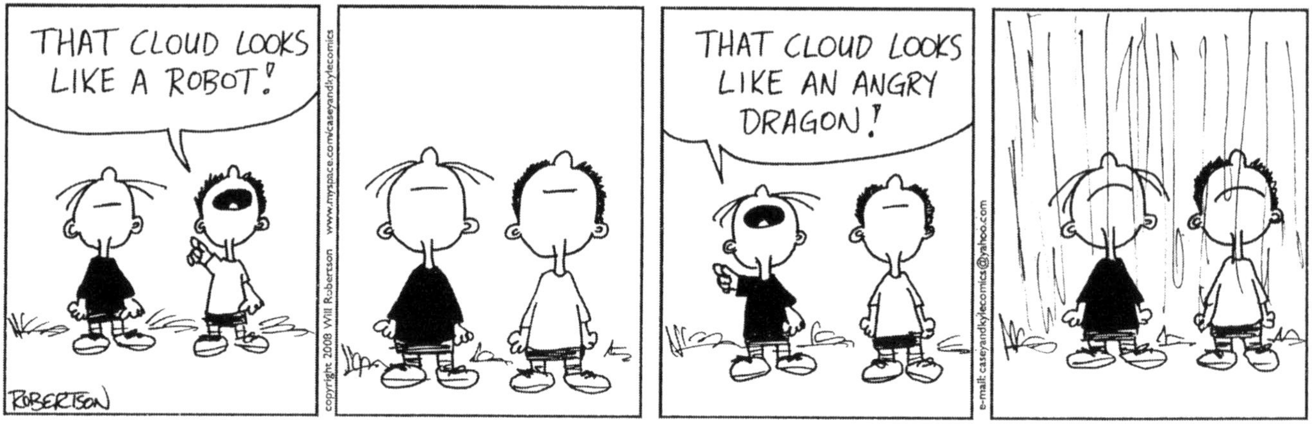
THAT CLOUD LOOKS LIKE A ROBOT!
ROBERTSON
copyright 2008 Will Robertson www.myspace.com/caseyandkylecomics
THAT CLOUD LOOKS LIKE AN ANGRY DRAGON!
e-mail: caseyandkylecomics@yahoo.com

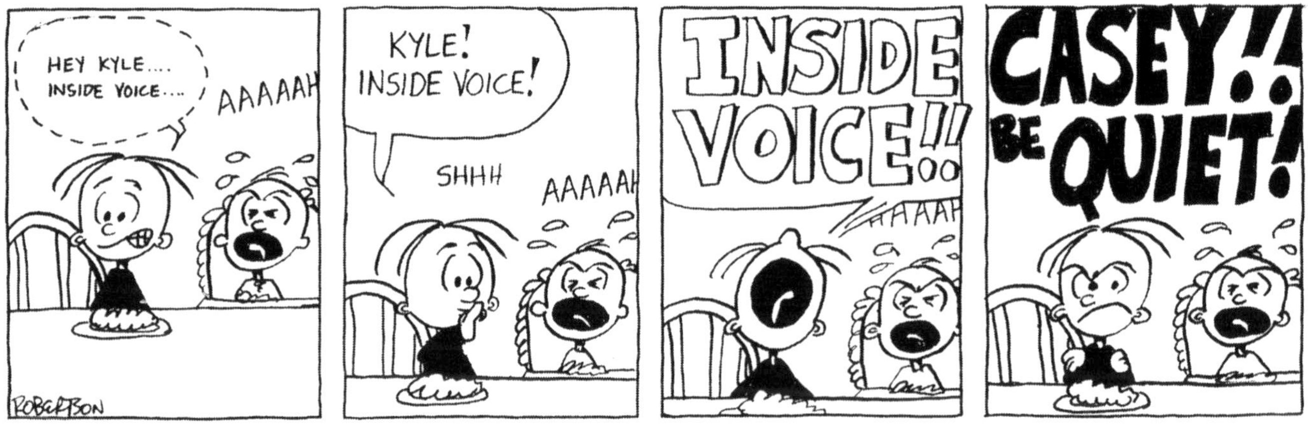
HEY KYLE.... INSIDE VOICE....
AAAAAH
ROBERTSON
KYLE! INSIDE VOICE!
SHHH
AAAAAH
INSIDE VOICE!!
AAAAH
CASEY!! BE QUIET!

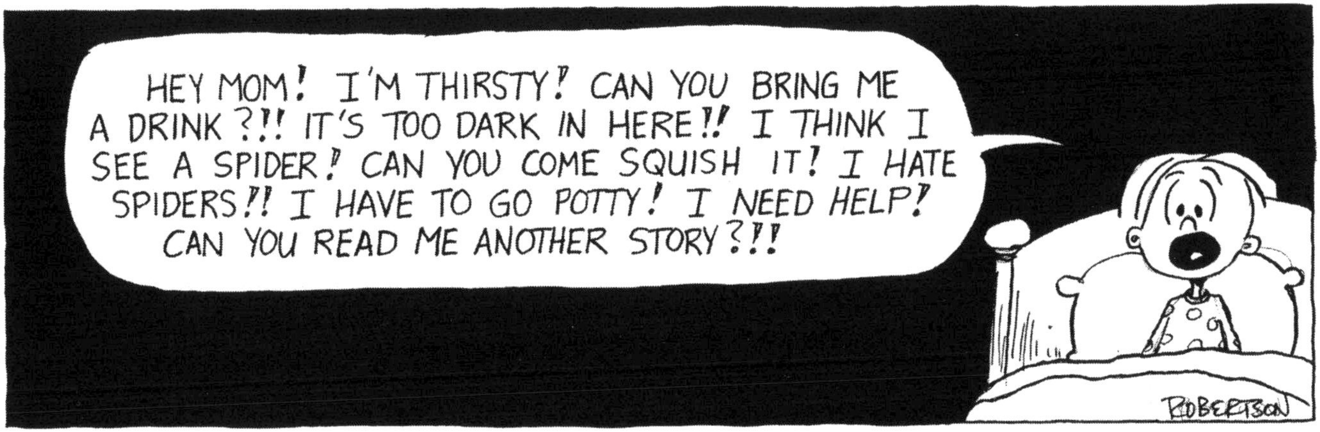
HEY MOM! I'M THIRSTY! CAN YOU BRING ME A DRINK?!! IT'S TOO DARK IN HERE!! I THINK I SEE A SPIDER! CAN YOU COME SQUISH IT! I HATE SPIDERS?! I HAVE TO GO POTTY! I NEED HELP! CAN YOU READ ME ANOTHER STORY?!!
ROBERTSON

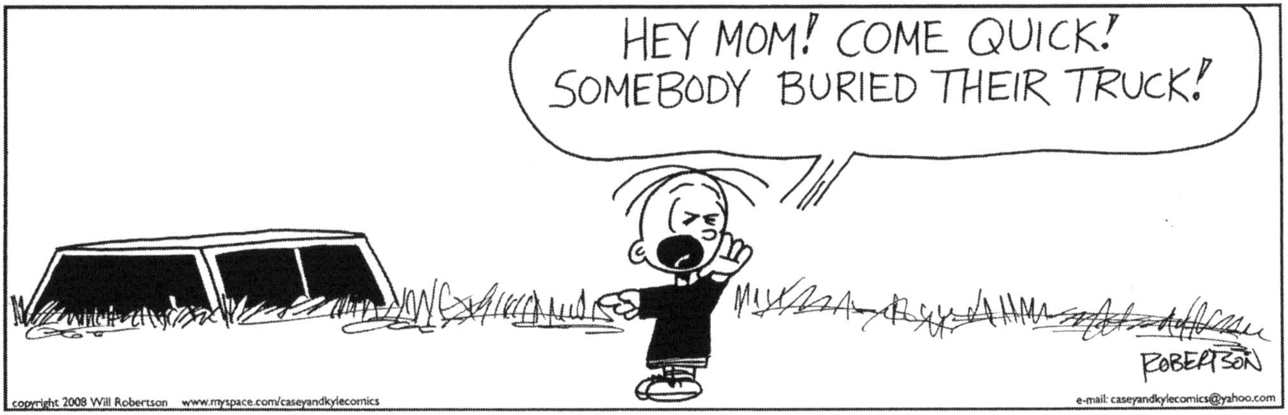
HEY MOM! COME QUICK! SOMEBODY BURIED THEIR TRUCK!
ROBERTSON
copyright 2008 Will Robertson www.myspace.com/caseyandkylecomics
e-mail: caseyandkylecomics@yahoo.com

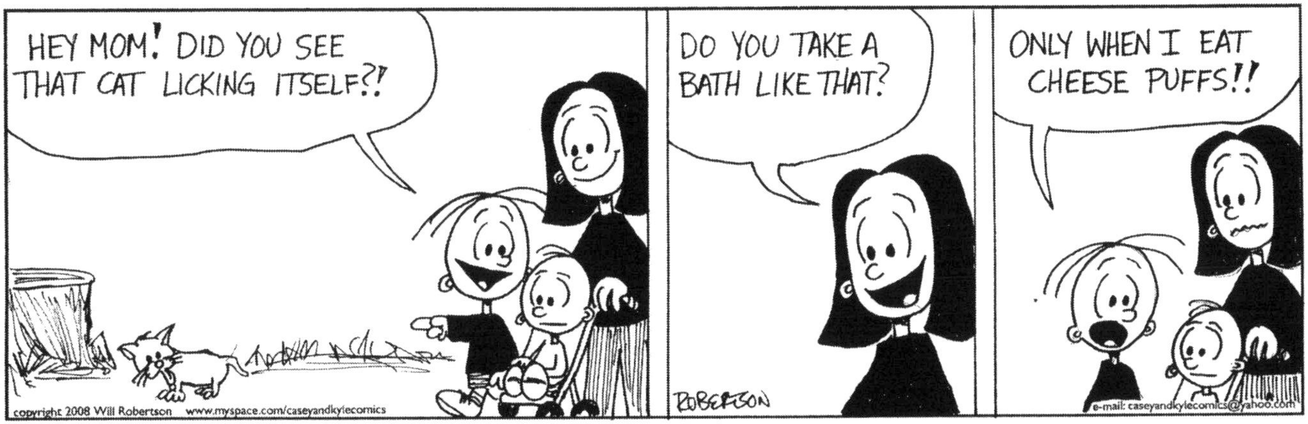
HEY MOM! DID YOU SEE THAT CAT LICKING ITSELF?!
DO YOU TAKE A BATH LIKE THAT?
ONLY WHEN I EAT CHEESE PUFFS!!
ROBERTSON
copyright 2008 Will Robertson www.myspace.com/caseyandkylecomics
e-mail: caseyandkylecomics@yahoo.com

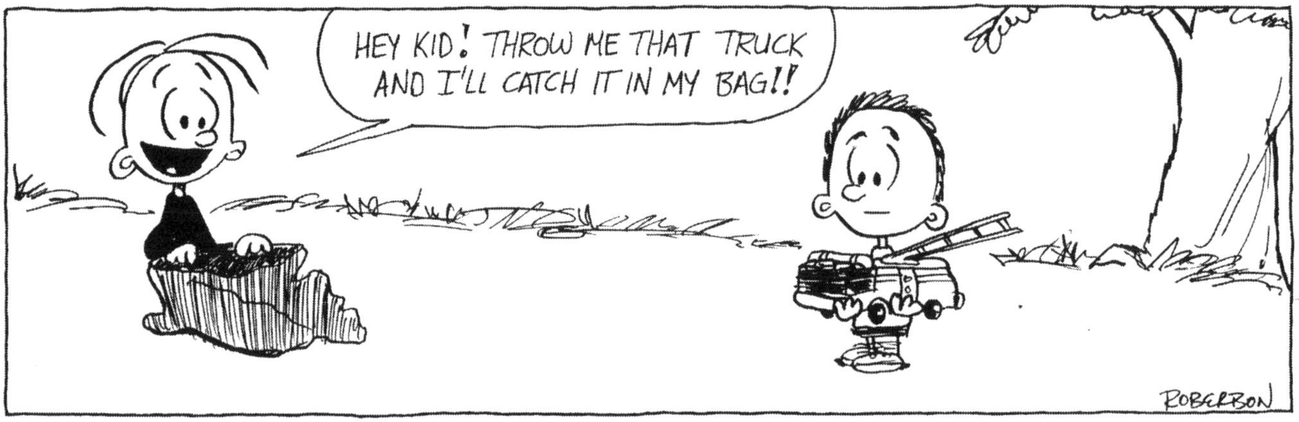
HEY KID! THROW ME THAT TRUCK AND I'LL CATCH IT IN MY BAG!!
ROBERBON

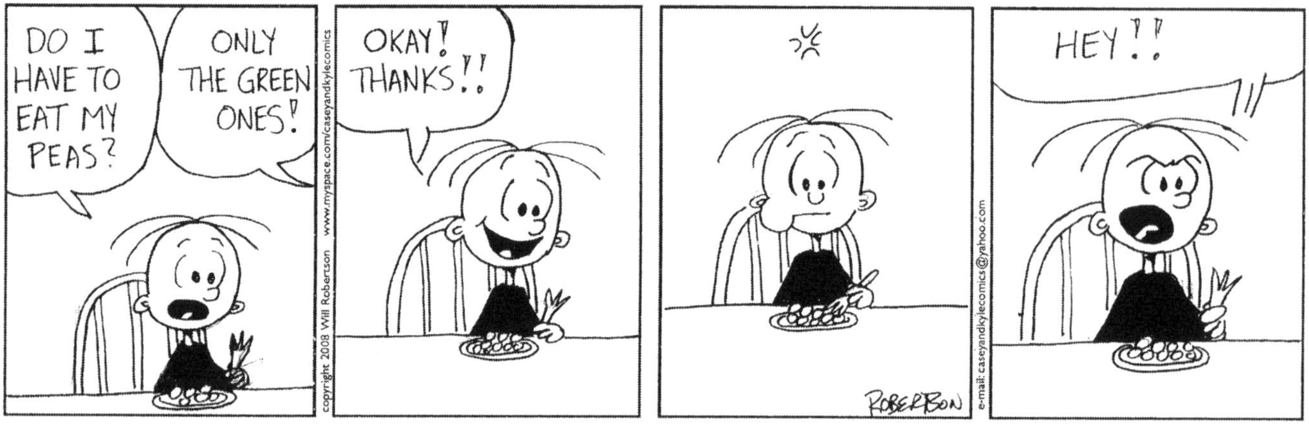
DO I HAVE TO EAT MY PEAS?
ONLY THE GREEN ONES!
copyright 2008 Will Robertson www.myspace.com/caseyandkylecomics
OKAY! THANKS!!
ROBERBON
e-mail: caseyandkylecomics@yahoo.com
HEY!!

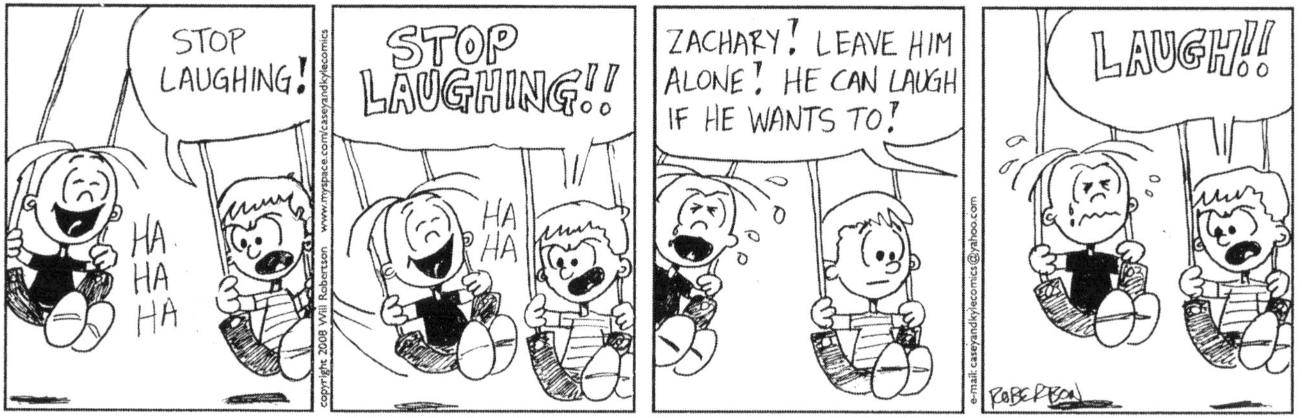
STOP LAUGHING!
HA HA HA HA
copyright 2008 Will Robertson www.myspace.com/caseyandkylecomics
STOP LAUGHING!!
HA HA
ZACHARY! LEAVE HIM ALONE! HE CAN LAUGH IF HE WANTS TO!
e-mail: caseyandkylecomics@yahoo.com
LAUGH!!
ROBERBON

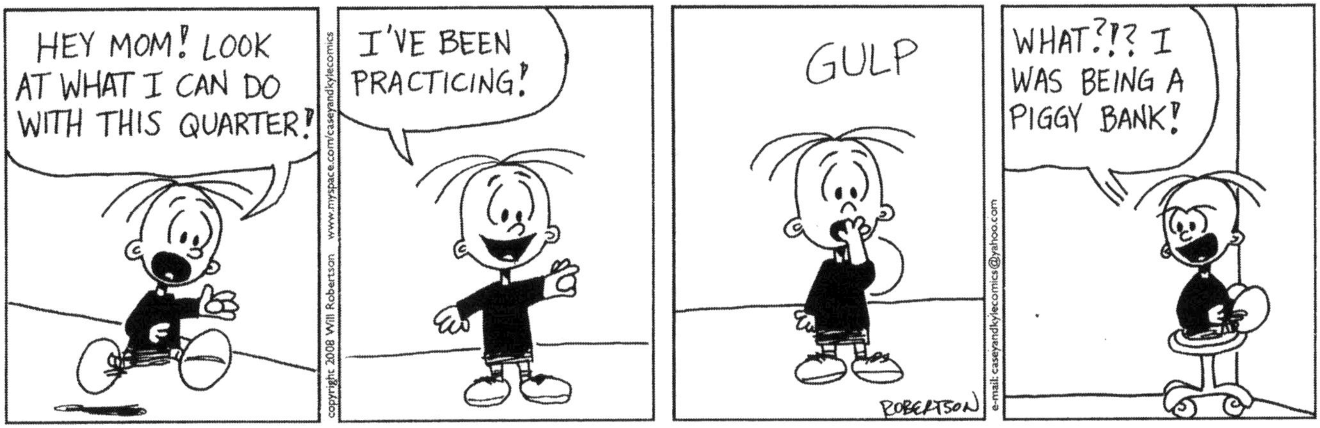
HEY MOM! LOOK AT WHAT I CAN DO WITH THIS QUARTER!
copyright 2008 Will Robertson www.myspace.com/caseyandkylecomics
I'VE BEEN PRACTICING!
GULP
ROBERTSON
e-mail: caseyandkylecomics@yahoo.com
WHAT?!? I WAS BEING A PIGGY BANK!

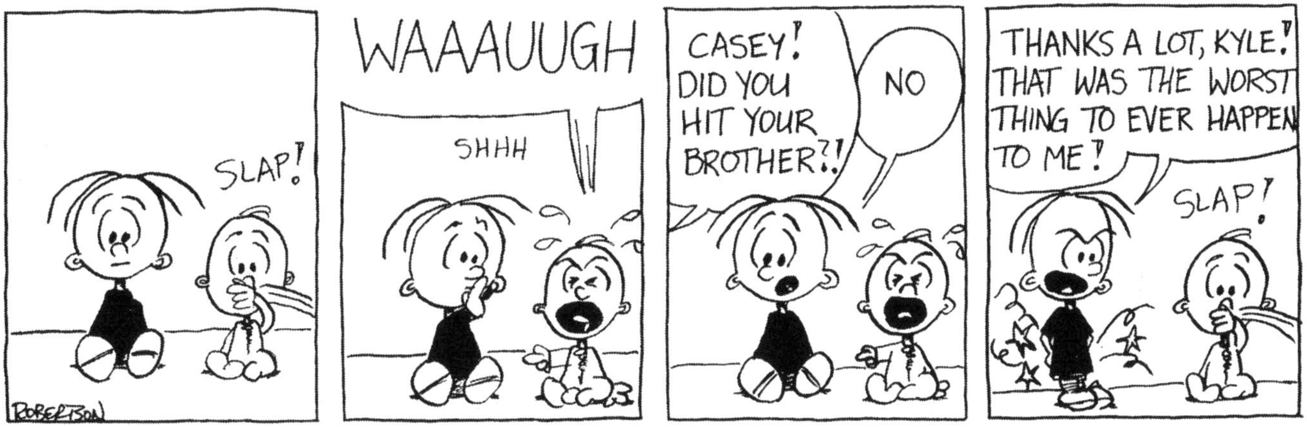
SLAP!
ROBERTSON
WAAAUUGH
SHHH
CASEY! DID YOU HIT YOUR BROTHER?!
NO
THANKS A LOT, KYLE! THAT WAS THE WORST THING TO EVER HAPPEN TO ME!
SLAP!

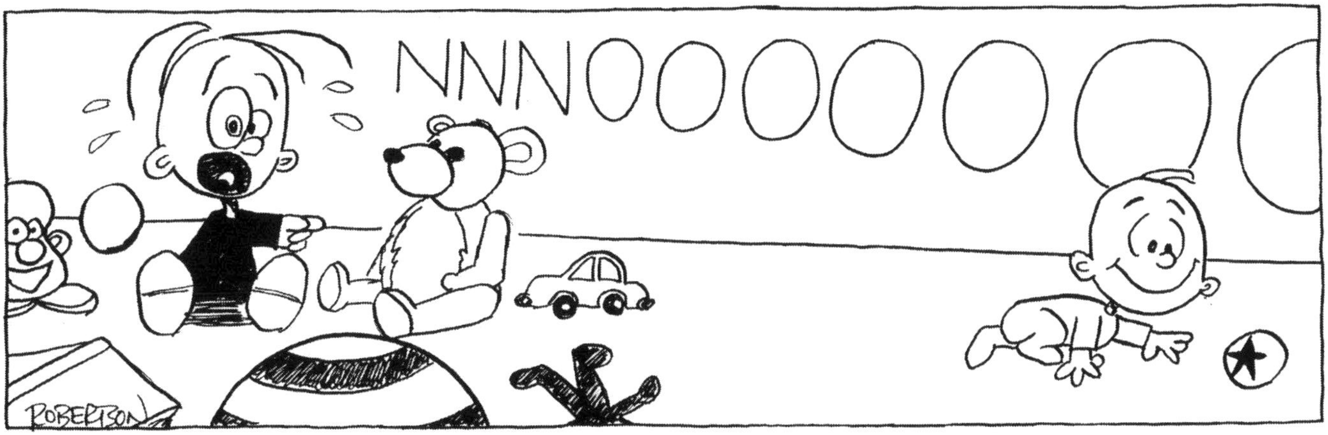
NNNOOOOOOOO
ROBERTSON

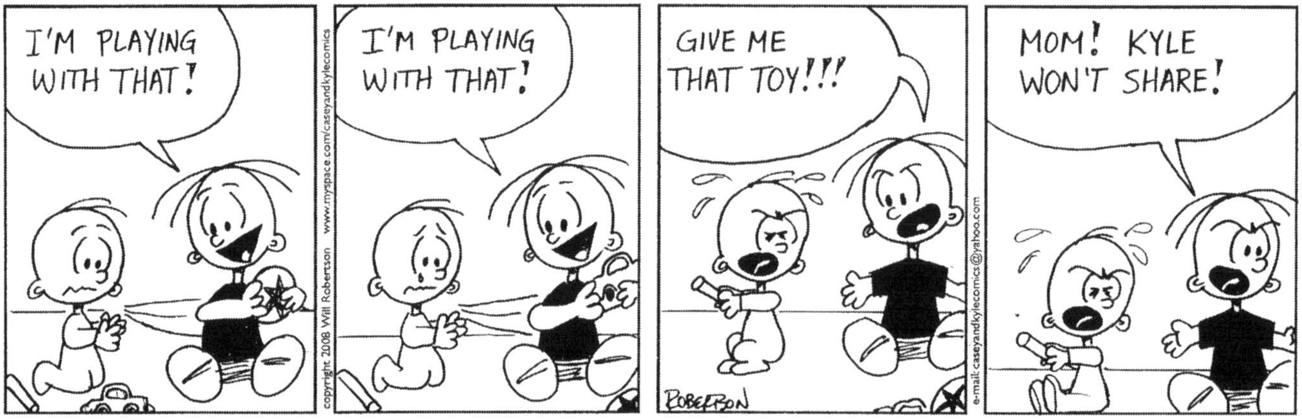
I'M PLAYING WITH THAT!
I'M PLAYING WITH THAT!
copyright 2008 Will Robertson www.myspace.com/caseyandkylecomics
GIVE ME THAT TOY!!!
ROBERTSON
e-mail: caseyandkylecomics@yahoo.com
MOM! KYLE WON'T SHARE!

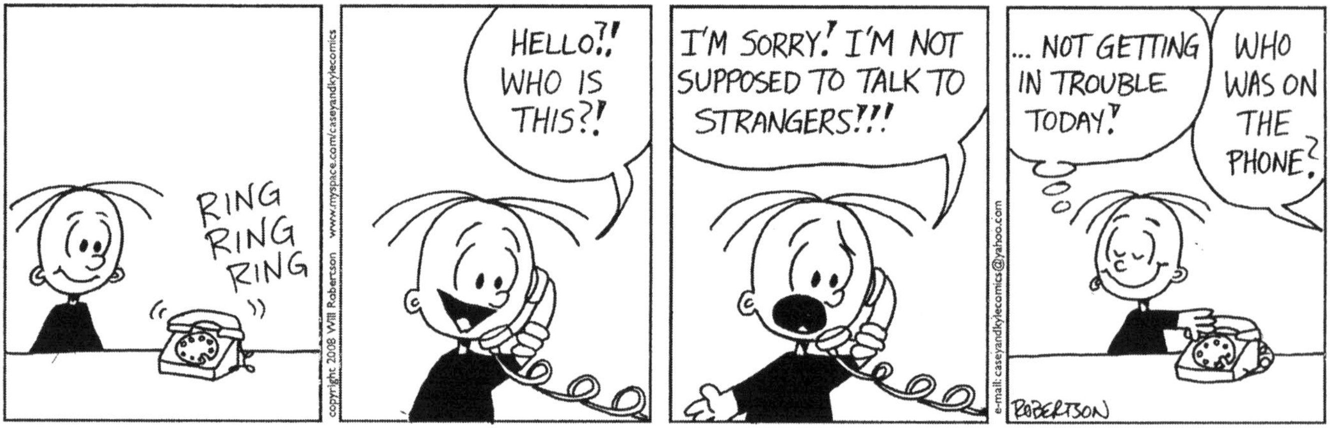
RING RING RING
copyright 2008 Will Robertson www.myspace.com/caseyandkylecomics
HELLO?! WHO IS THIS?!
I'M SORRY! I'M NOT SUPPOSED TO TALK TO STRANGERS!!!
e-mail: caseyandkylecomics@yahoo.com
... NOT GETTING IN TROUBLE TODAY!
WHO WAS ON THE PHONE?
ROBERTSON

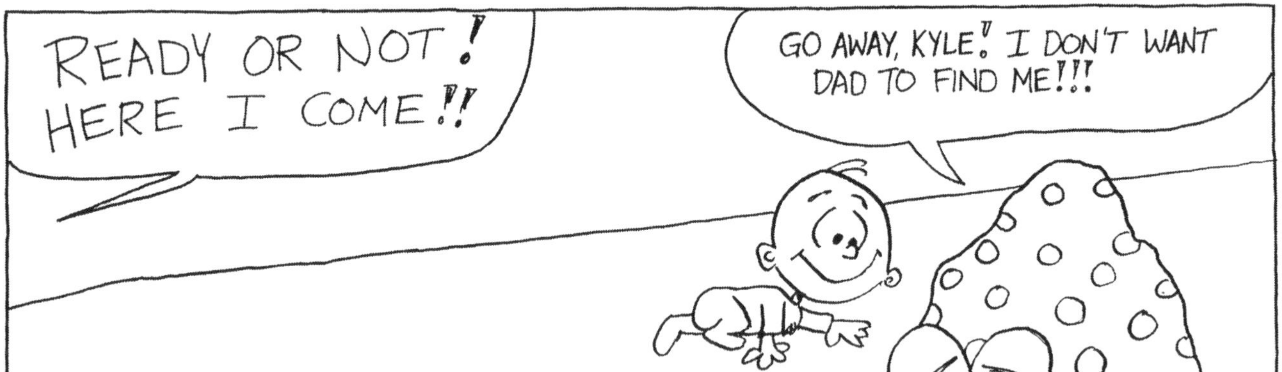
READY OR NOT! HERE I COME!!
GO AWAY, KYLE! I DON'T WANT DAD TO FIND ME!!!
ROBERTSON

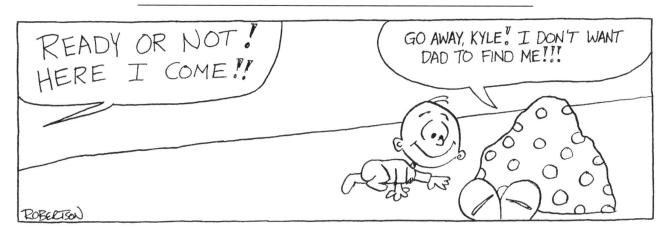

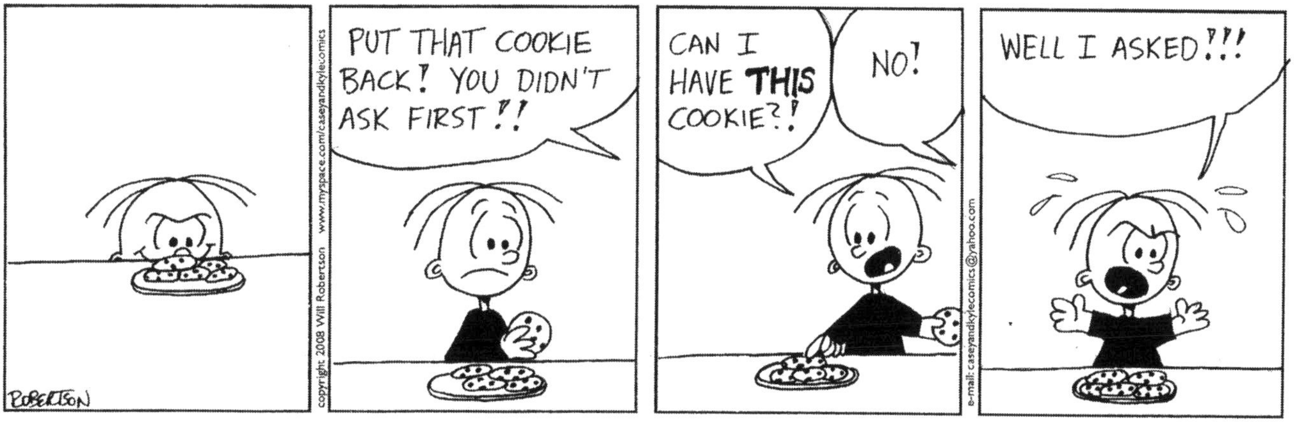
ROBERTSON
copyright 2008 Will Robertson www.myspace.com/caseyandkylecomics
PUT THAT COOKIE BACK! YOU DIDN'T ASK FIRST!!
CAN I HAVE THIS COOKIE?!
NO!
e-mail: caseyandkylecomics@yahoo.com
WELL I ASKED!!!

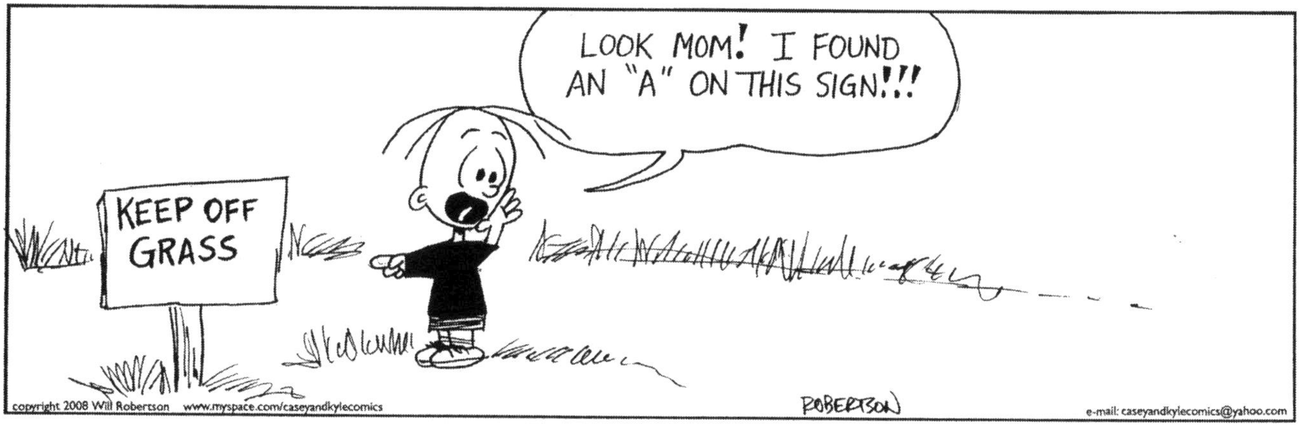
LOOK MOM! I FOUND AN "A" ON THIS SIGN!!!
KEEP OFF GRASS
copyright 2008 Will Robertson www.myspace.com/caseyandkylecomics
ROBERTSON
e-mail: caseyandkylecomics@yahoo.com

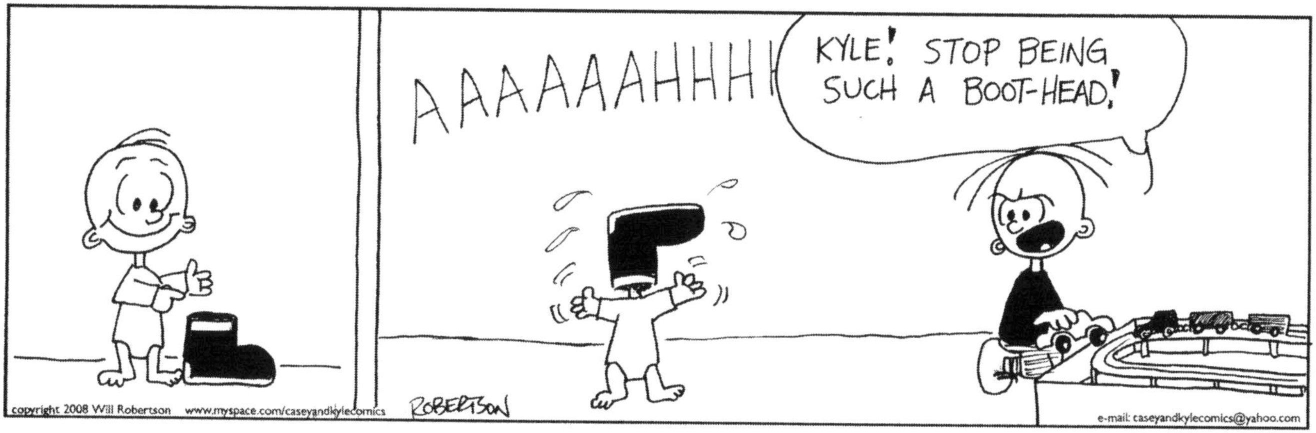
AAAAAAHHHH
KYLE! STOP BEING SUCH A BOOT-HEAD!
copyright 2008 Will Robertson www.myspace.com/caseyandkylecomics
ROBERTSON
e-mail: caseyandkylecomics@yahoo.com

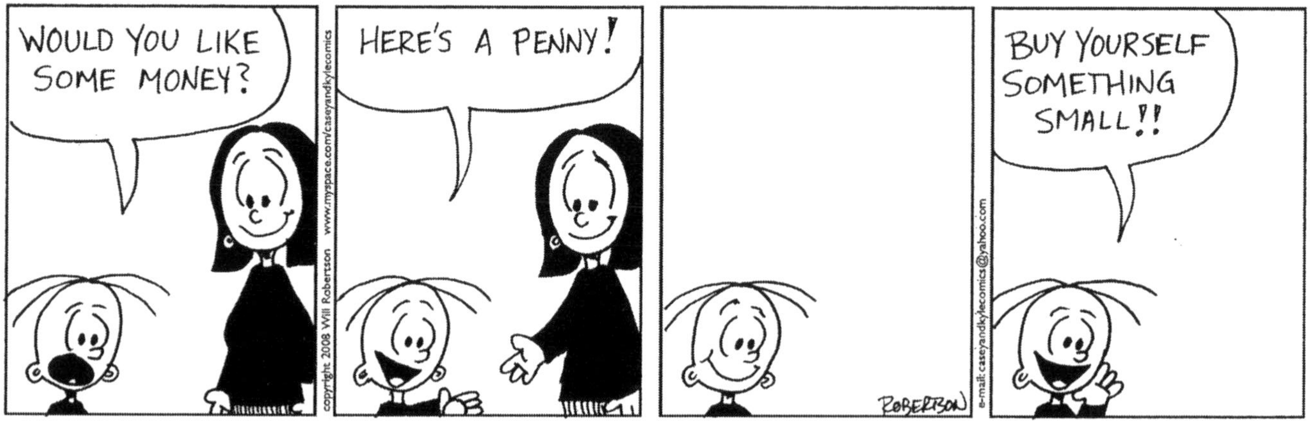
WOULD YOU LIKE SOME MONEY?
copyright 2008 Will Robertson www.myspace.com/caseyandkylecomics
HERE'S A PENNY!
ROBERTSON
e-mail: caseyandkylecomics@yahoo.com
BUY YOURSELF SOMETHING SMALL!!

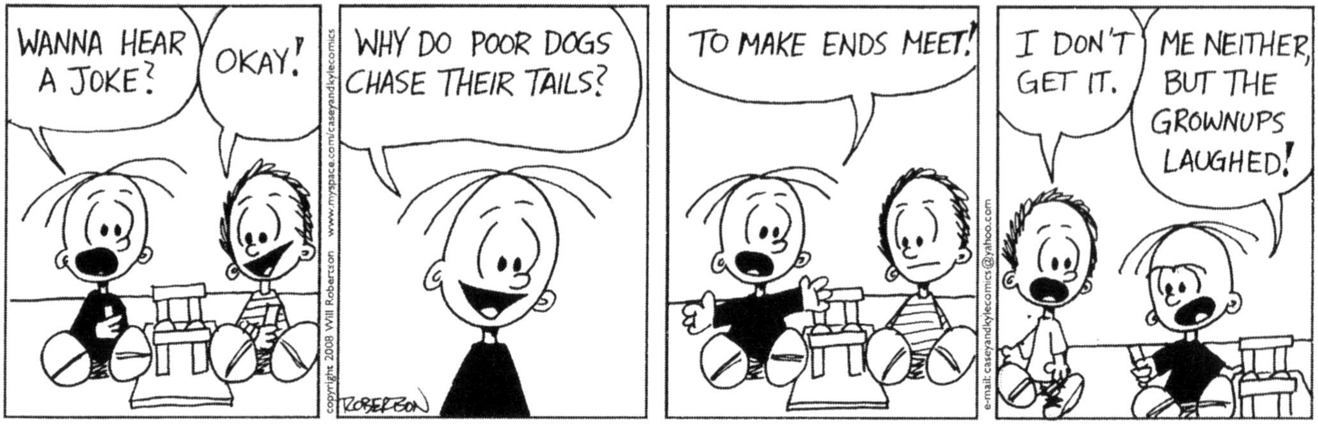
WANNA HEAR A JOKE?
OKAY!
copyright 2008 Will Robertson www.myspace.com/caseyandkylecomics
WHY DO POOR DOGS CHASE THEIR TAILS?
ROBERTSON
TO MAKE ENDS MEET!
e-mail: caseyandkylecomics@yahoo.com
I DON'T GET IT.
ME NEITHER, BUT THE GROWNUPS LAUGHED!

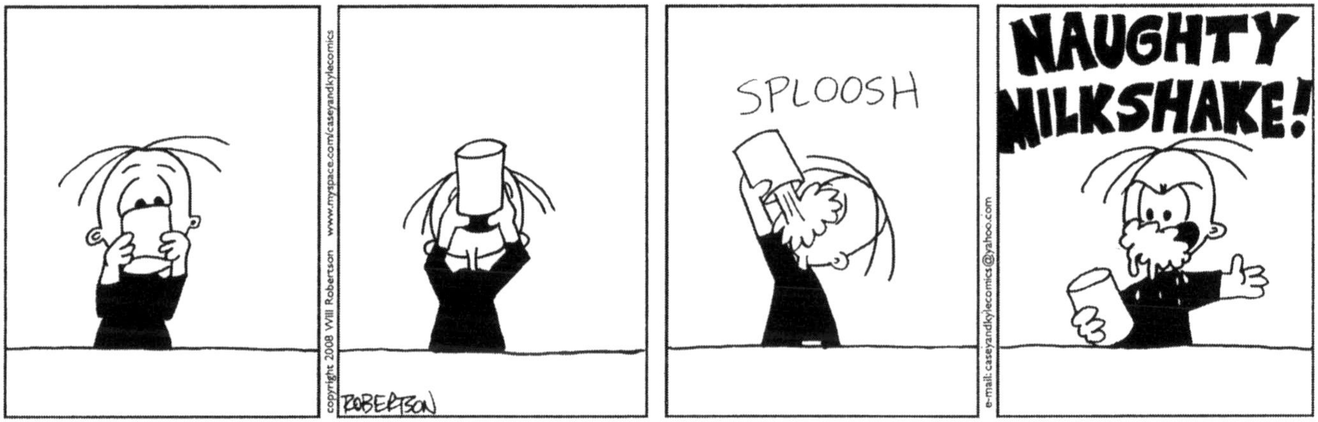
copyright 2008 Will Robertson www.myspace.com/caseyandkylecomics
ROBERTSON
SPLOOSH
e-mail: caseyandkylecomics@yahoo.com
NAUGHTY MILKSHAKE!

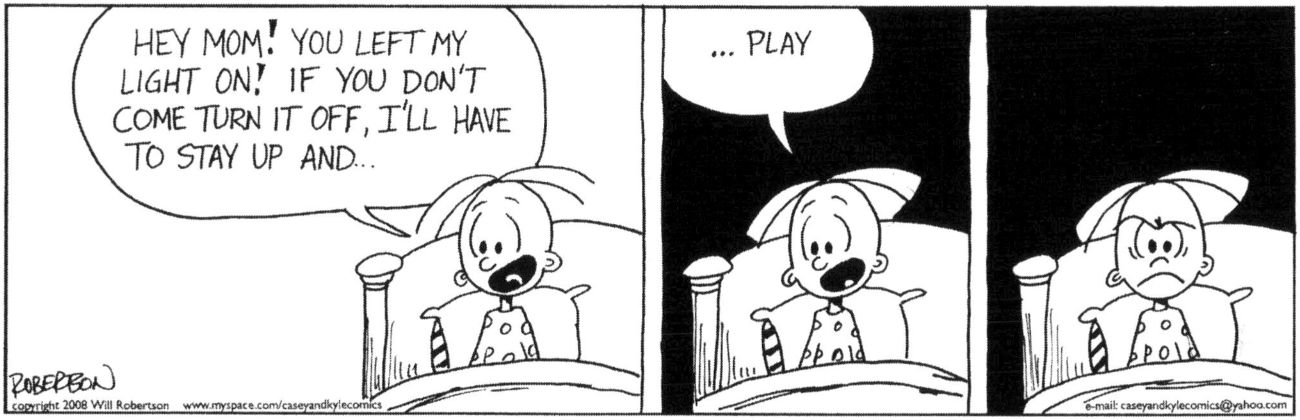
HEY MOM! YOU LEFT MY LIGHT ON! IF YOU DON'T COME TURN IT OFF, I'LL HAVE TO STAY UP AND...
... PLAY
ROBERTSON
copyright 2008 Will Robertson www.myspace.com/caseyandkylecomics
e-mail: caseyandkylecomics@yahoo.com

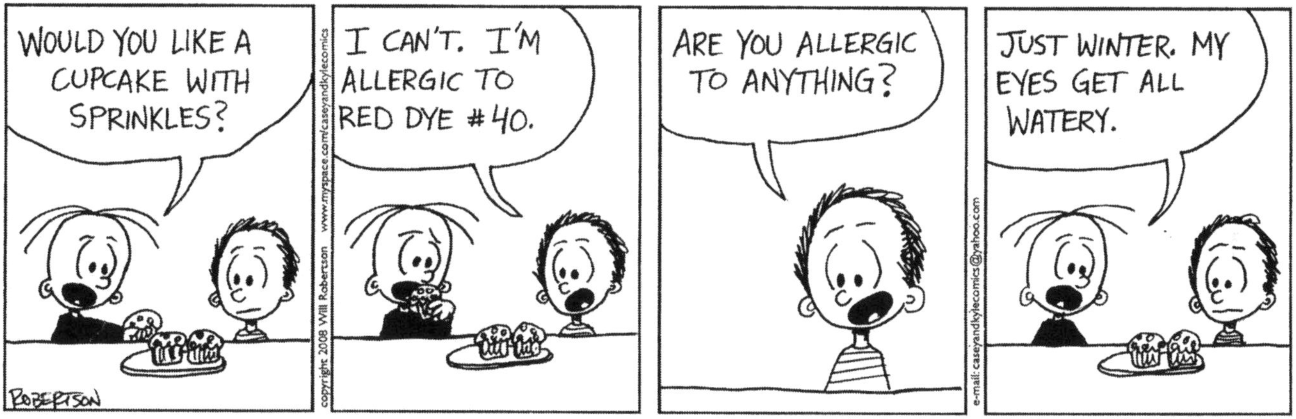
WOULD YOU LIKE A CUPCAKE WITH SPRINKLES?
I CAN'T. I'M ALLERGIC TO RED DYE #40.
ARE YOU ALLERGIC TO ANYTHING?
JUST WINTER. MY EYES GET ALL WATERY.
ROBERTSON
copyright 2008 Will Robertson www.myspace.com/caseyandkylecomics
e-mail: caseyandkylecomics@yahoo.com

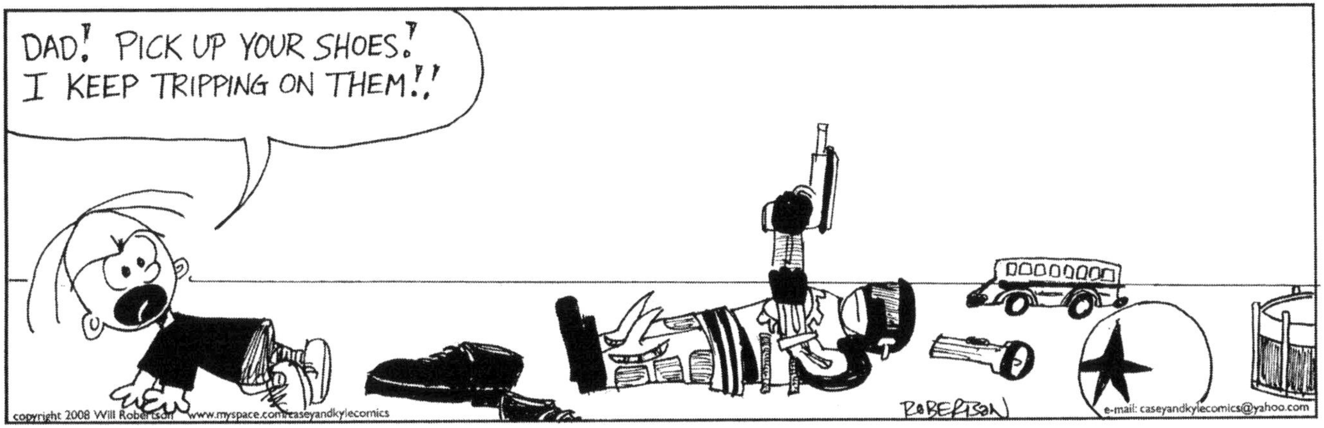
DAD! PICK UP YOUR SHOES! I KEEP TRIPPING ON THEM!!
ROBERTSON
copyright 2008 Will Robertson www.myspace.com/caseyandkylecomics
e-mail: caseyandkylecomics@yahoo.com

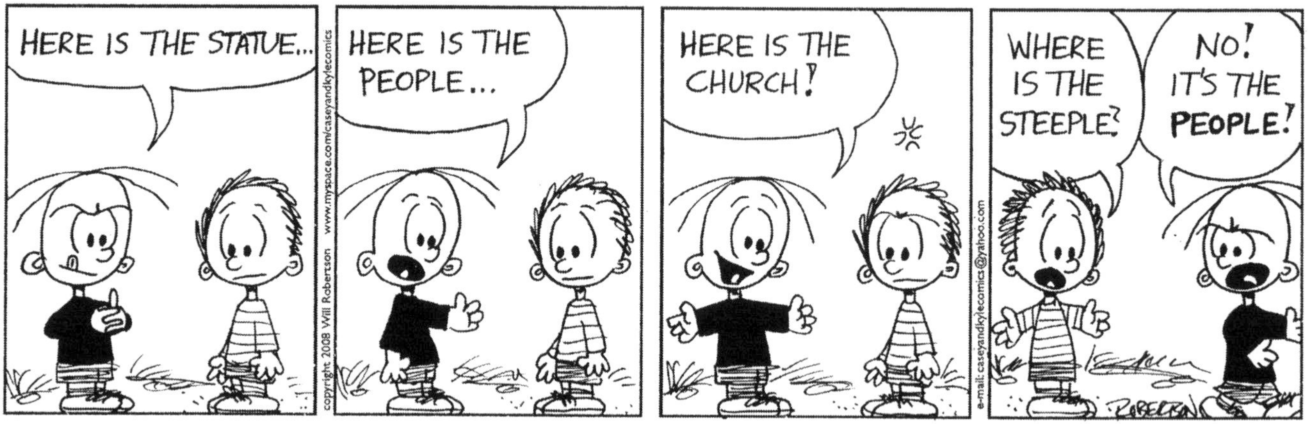
HERE IS THE STATUE...
HERE IS THE PEOPLE...
HERE IS THE CHURCH!
WHERE IS THE STEEPLE?
NO! IT'S THE **PEOPLE**!
copyright 2008 Will Robertson www.myspace.com/caseyandkylecomics
e-mail: caseyandkylecomics@yahoo.com
ROBERTSON

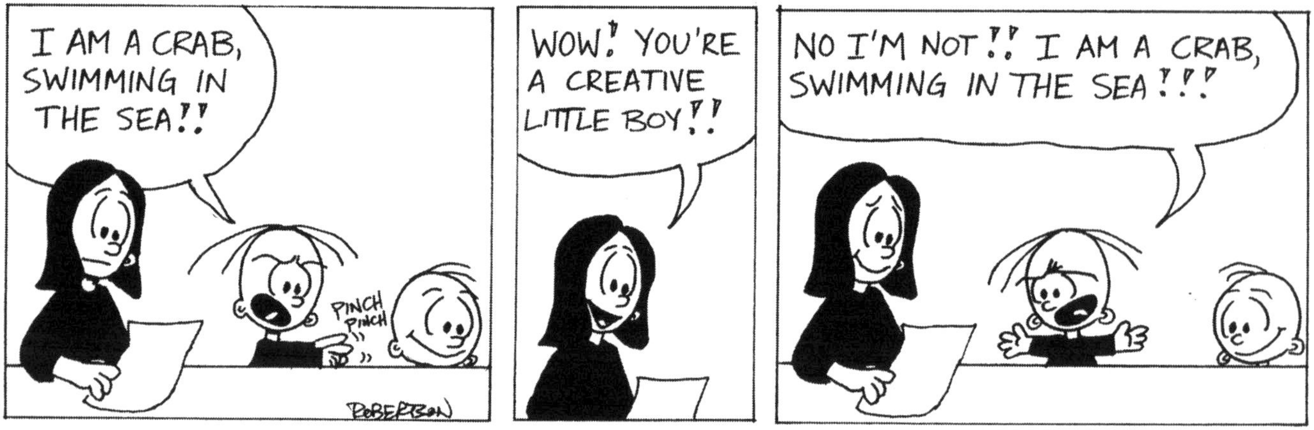
I AM A CRAB, SWIMMING IN THE SEA!!
PINCH PINCH
ROBERTSON
WOW! YOU'RE A CREATIVE LITTLE BOY!!
NO I'M NOT!! I AM A CRAB, SWIMMING IN THE SEA!!!

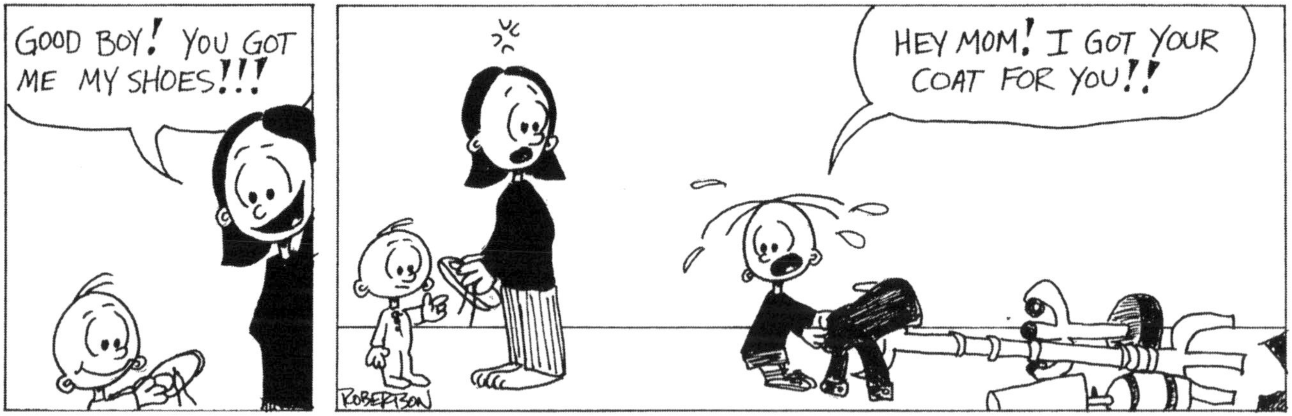
GOOD BOY! YOU GOT ME MY SHOES!!!
HEY MOM! I GOT YOUR COAT FOR YOU!!
ROBERTSON

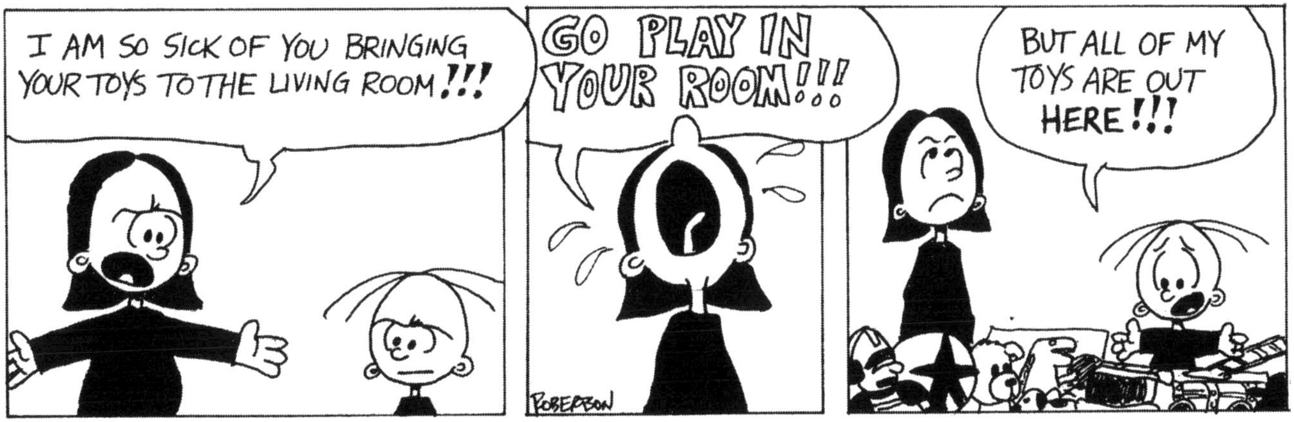
I AM SO SICK OF YOU BRINGING YOUR TOYS TO THE LIVING ROOM!!!
GO PLAY IN YOUR ROOM!!!
BUT ALL OF MY TOYS ARE OUT HERE!!!
ROBERTSON

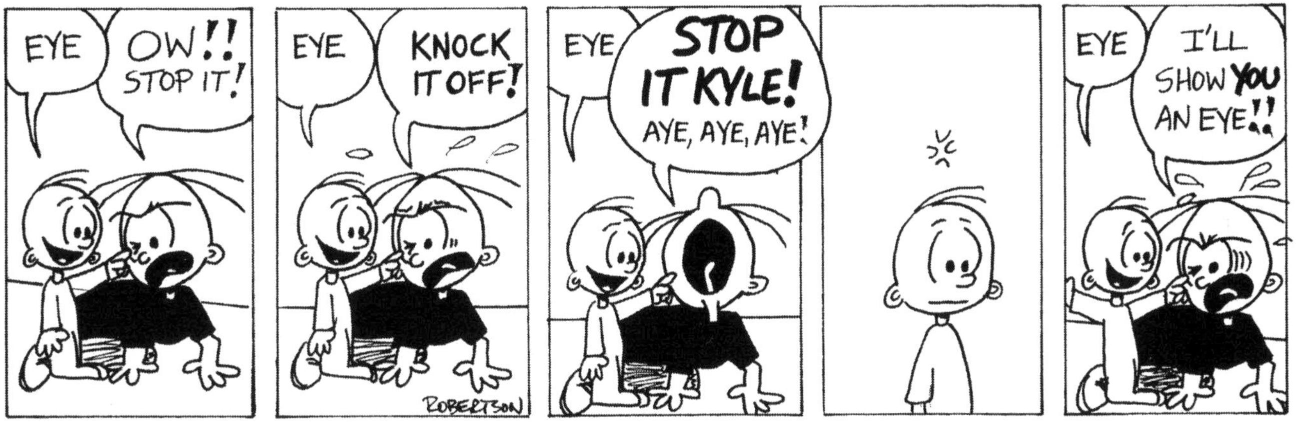
EYE
OW!! STOP IT!
EYE
KNOCK IT OFF!
EYE
STOP IT KYLE! AYE, AYE, AYE!
EYE
I'LL SHOW YOU AN EYE!!
ROBERTSON

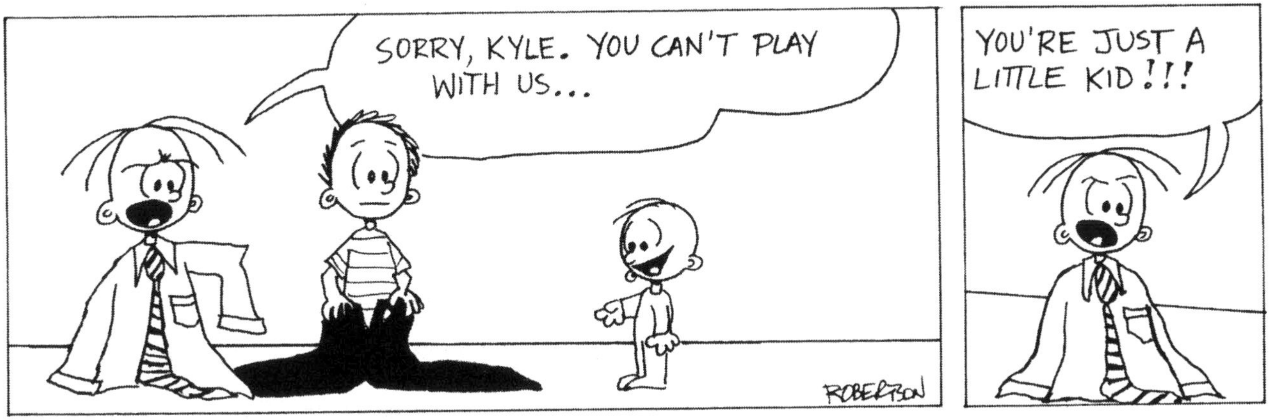
SORRY, KYLE. YOU CAN'T PLAY WITH US...
YOU'RE JUST A LITTLE KID!!!
ROBERTSON

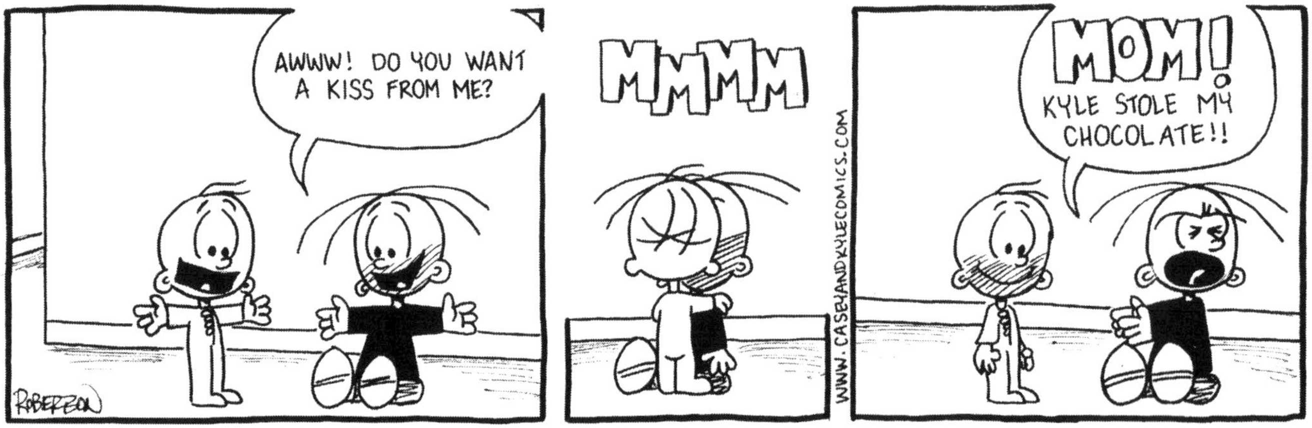
AWWW! DO YOU WANT A KISS FROM ME?
MMMMM
MOM! KYLE STOLE MY CHOCOLATE!!
ROBERSON
WWW.CASEYANDKYLECOMICS.COM

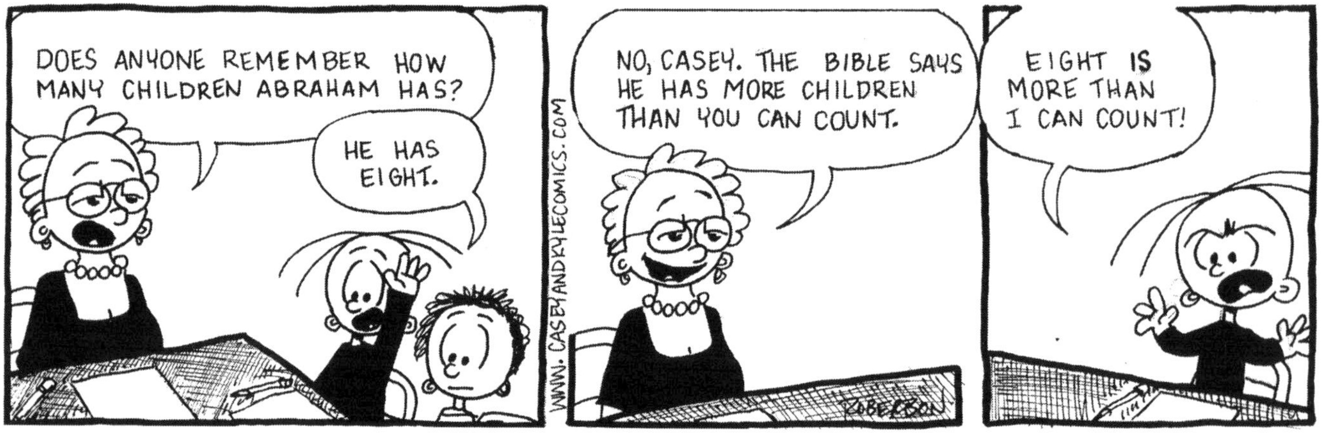
DOES ANYONE REMEMBER HOW MANY CHILDREN ABRAHAM HAS?
HE HAS EIGHT.
NO, CASEY. THE BIBLE SAYS HE HAS MORE CHILDREN THAN YOU CAN COUNT.
EIGHT IS MORE THAN I CAN COUNT!
ROBERSON
WWW.CASEYANDKYLECOMICS.COM

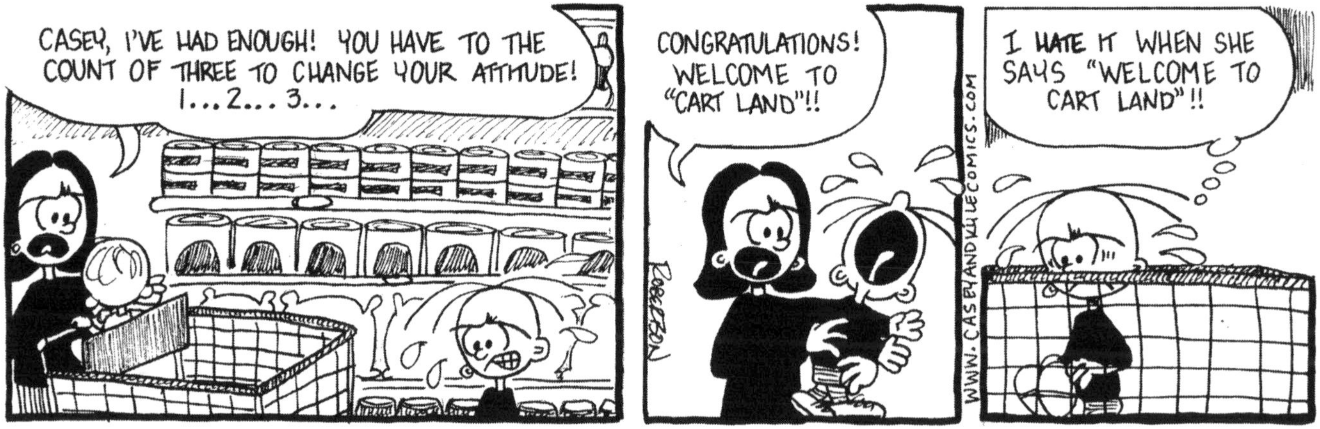
CASEY, I'VE HAD ENOUGH! YOU HAVE TO THE COUNT OF THREE TO CHANGE YOUR ATTITUDE! 1... 2... 3...
CONGRATULATIONS! WELCOME TO "CART LAND"!!
I HATE IT WHEN SHE SAYS "WELCOME TO CART LAND"!!
ROBERSON
WWW.CASEYANDKYLECOMICS.COM

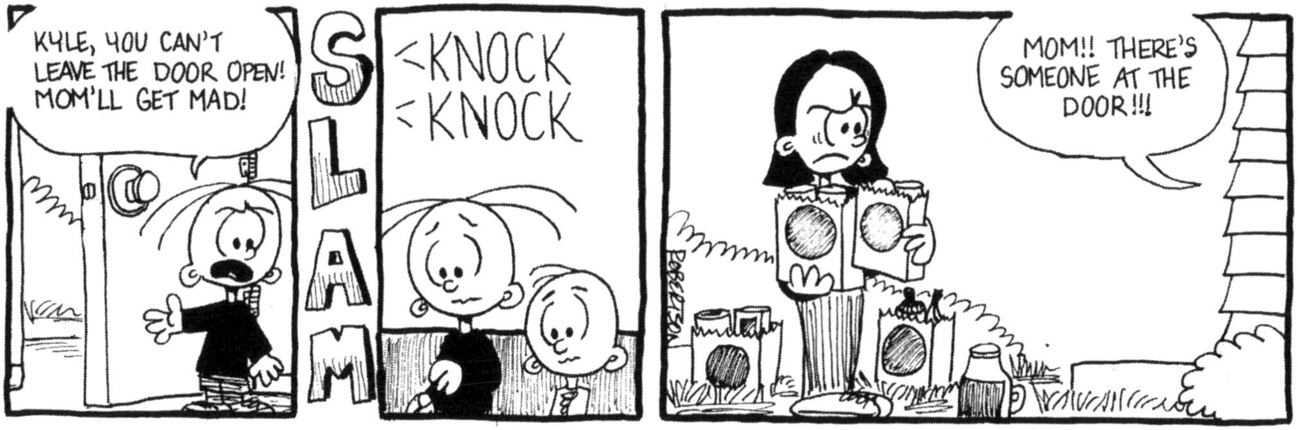
KYLE, YOU CAN'T LEAVE THE DOOR OPEN! MOM'LL GET MAD!
SLAM
KNOCK KNOCK
MOM!! THERE'S SOMEONE AT THE DOOR!!!

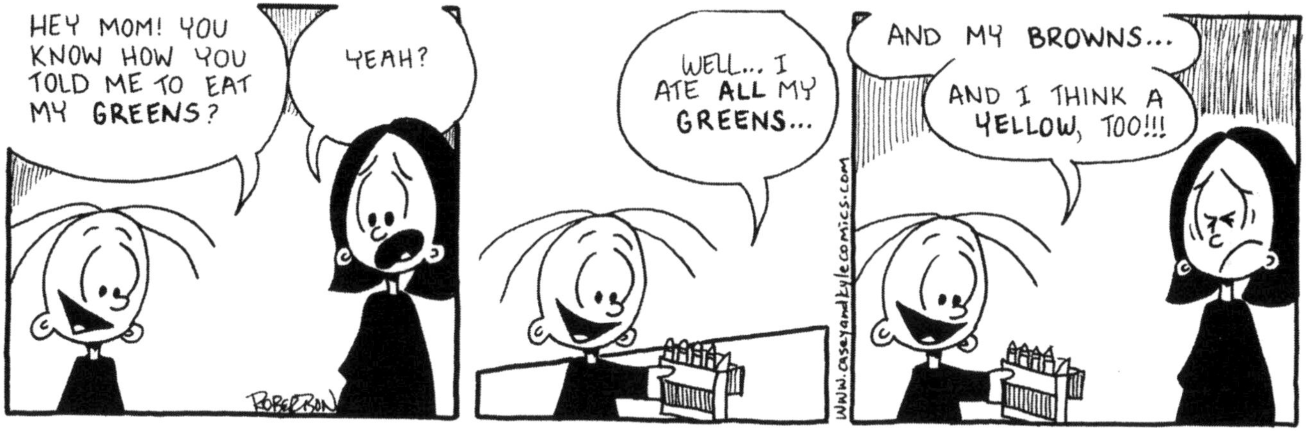
HEY MOM! YOU KNOW HOW YOU TOLD ME TO EAT MY GREENS?
YEAH?
WELL... I ATE ALL MY GREENS...
www.caseyandkylecomics.com
AND MY BROWNS...
AND I THINK A YELLOW, TOO!!!

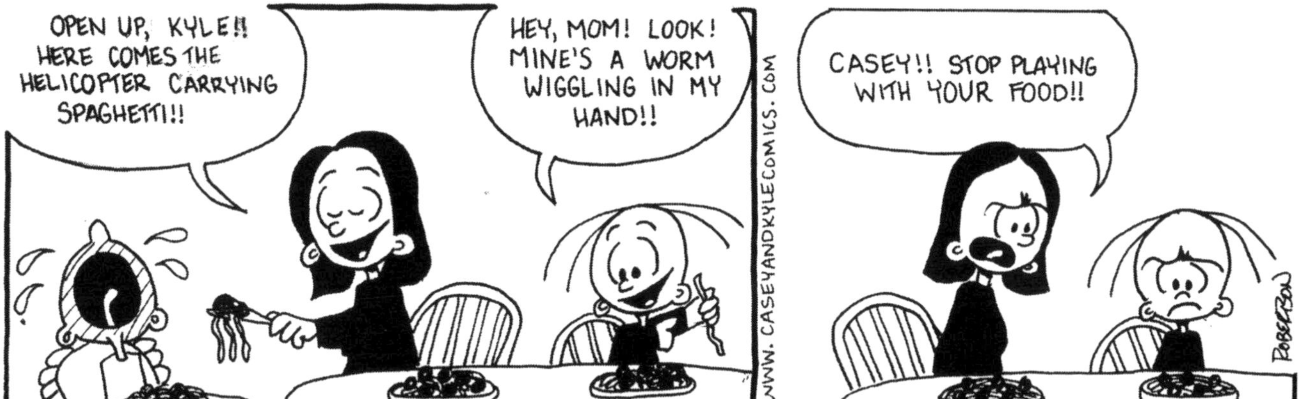
OPEN UP, KYLE!! HERE COMES THE HELICOPTER CARRYING SPAGHETTI!!
HEY, MOM! LOOK! MINE'S A WORM WIGGLING IN MY HAND!!
WWW.CASEYANDKYLECOMICS.COM
CASEY!! STOP PLAYING WITH YOUR FOOD!!

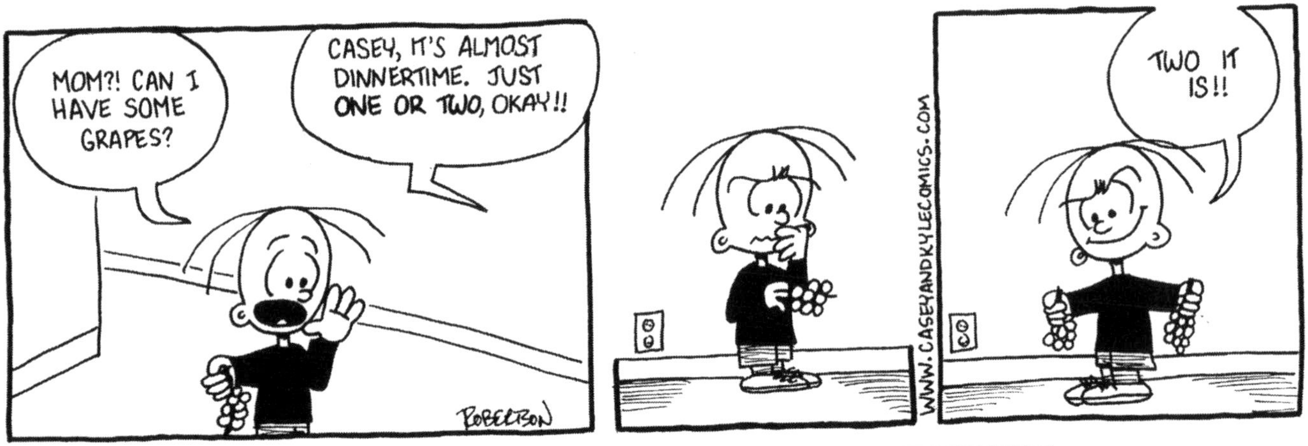
MOM?! CAN I HAVE SOME GRAPES?
CASEY, IT'S ALMOST DINNERTIME. JUST **ONE OR TWO**, OKAY!!
ROBERSON
WWW.CASEYANDKYLECOMICS.COM
TWO IT IS!!

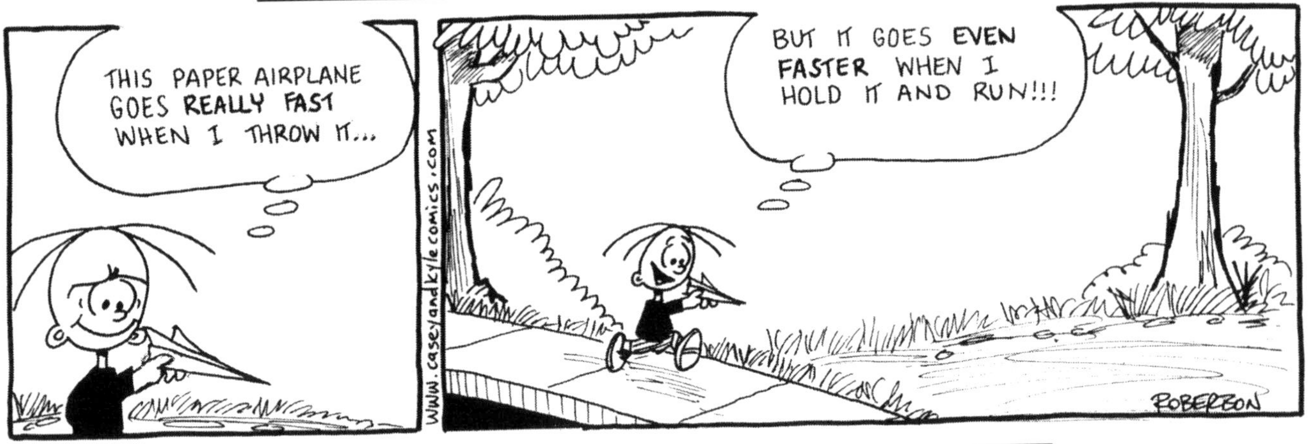
THIS PAPER AIRPLANE GOES **REALLY FAST** WHEN I THROW IT...
WWW.caseyandkylecomics.com
BUT IT GOES **EVEN FASTER** WHEN I HOLD IT AND RUN!!!
ROBERSON

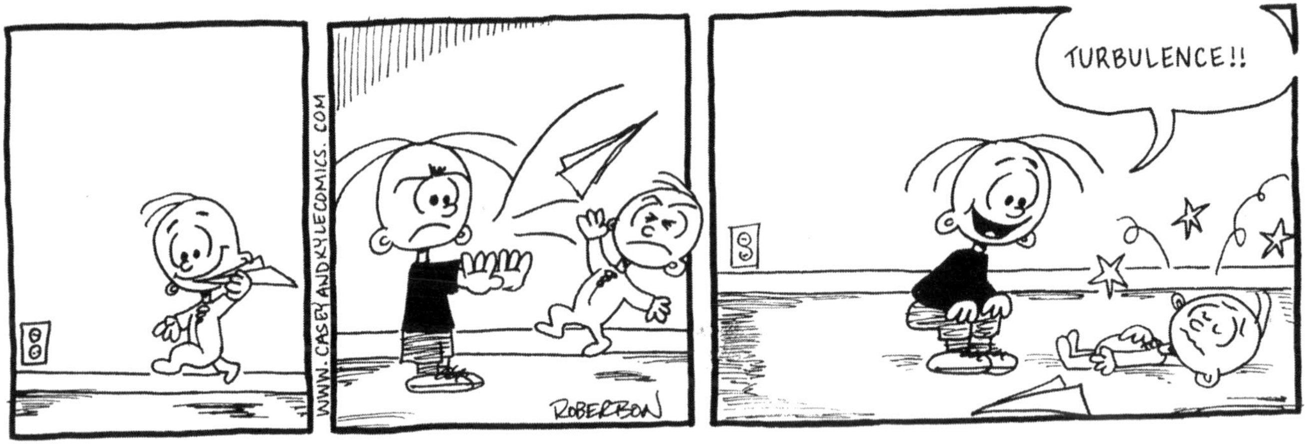
WWW.CASEYANDKYLECOMICS.COM
ROBERSON
TURBULENCE!!

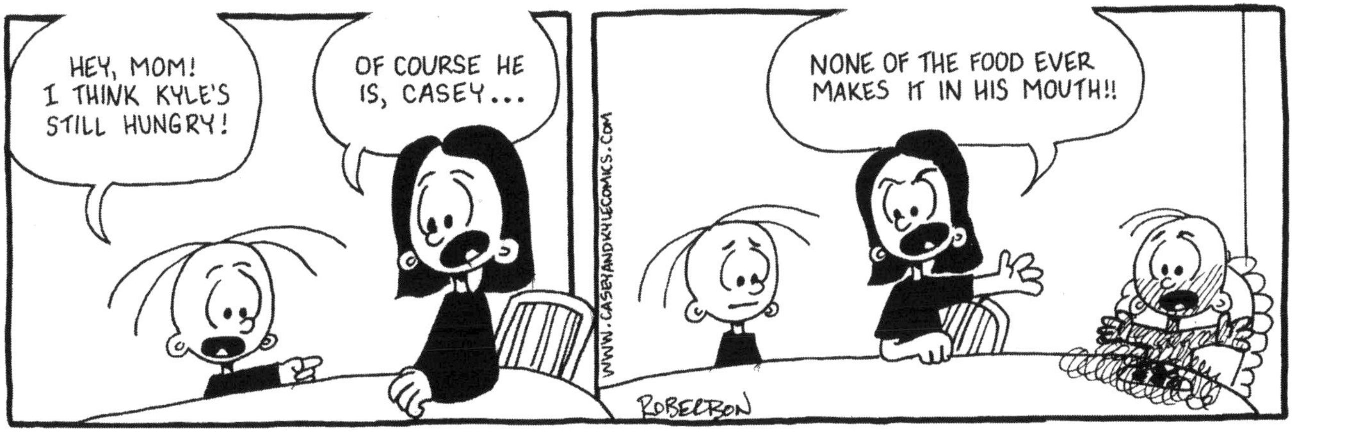
HEY, MOM!
I THINK KYLE'S
STILL HUNGRY!
OF COURSE HE
IS, CASEY...
WWW.CASEYANDKYLECOMICS.COM
NONE OF THE FOOD EVER
MAKES IT IN HIS MOUTH!!
ROBERSON

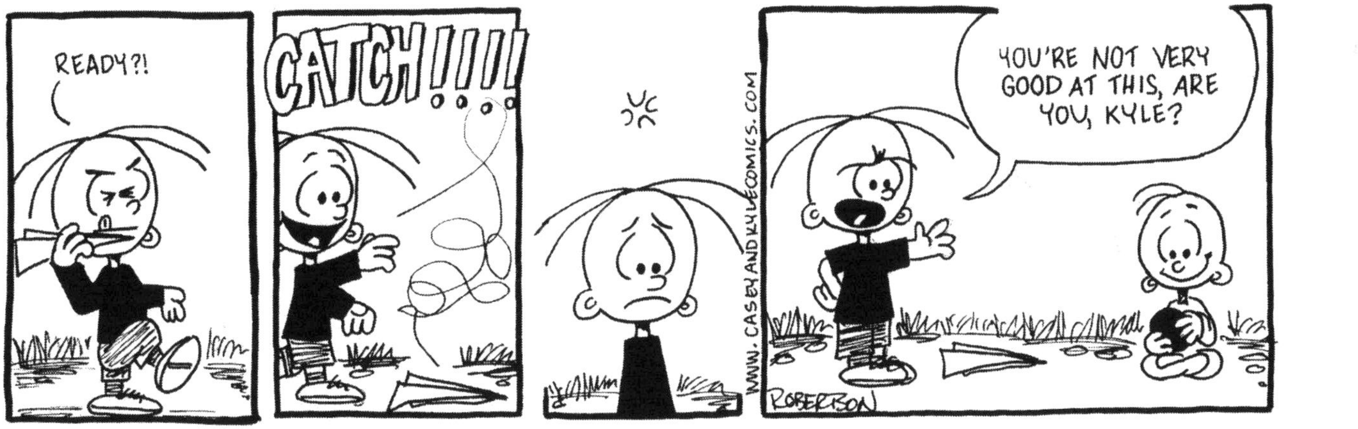
READY?!
CATCH!!!!!
WWW.CASEYANDKYLECOMICS.COM
YOU'RE NOT VERY
GOOD AT THIS, ARE
YOU, KYLE?
ROBERSON

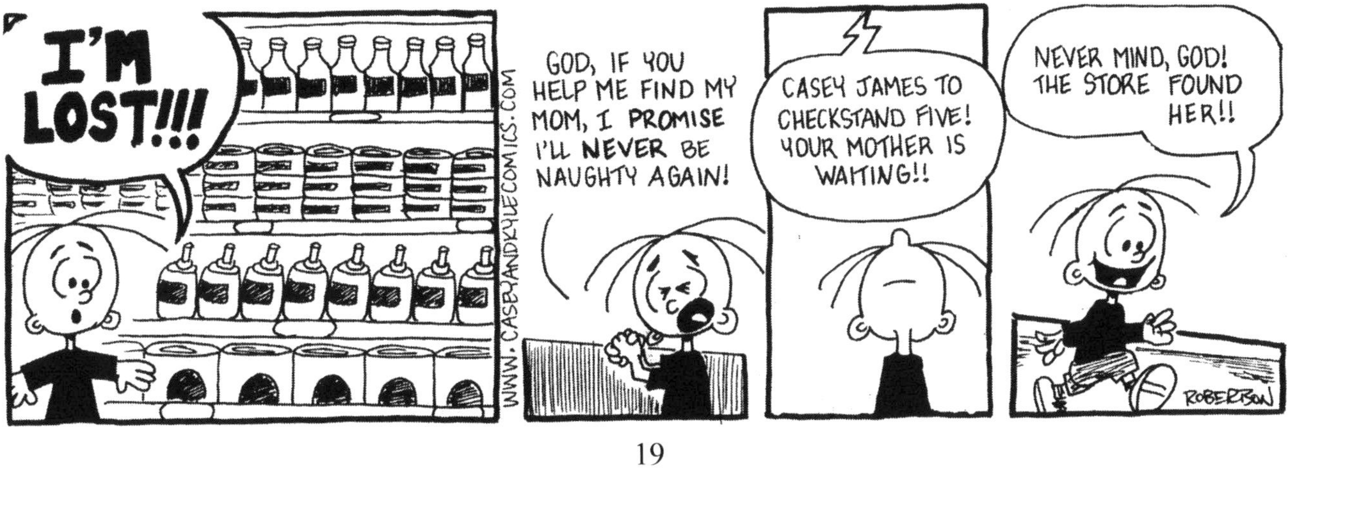
I'M
LOST!!!
WWW.CASEYANDKYLECOMICS.COM
GOD, IF YOU
HELP ME FIND MY
MOM, I PROMISE
I'LL NEVER BE
NAUGHTY AGAIN!
CASEY JAMES TO
CHECKSTAND FIVE!
YOUR MOTHER IS
WAITING!!
NEVER MIND, GOD!
THE STORE FOUND
HER!!
ROBERSON

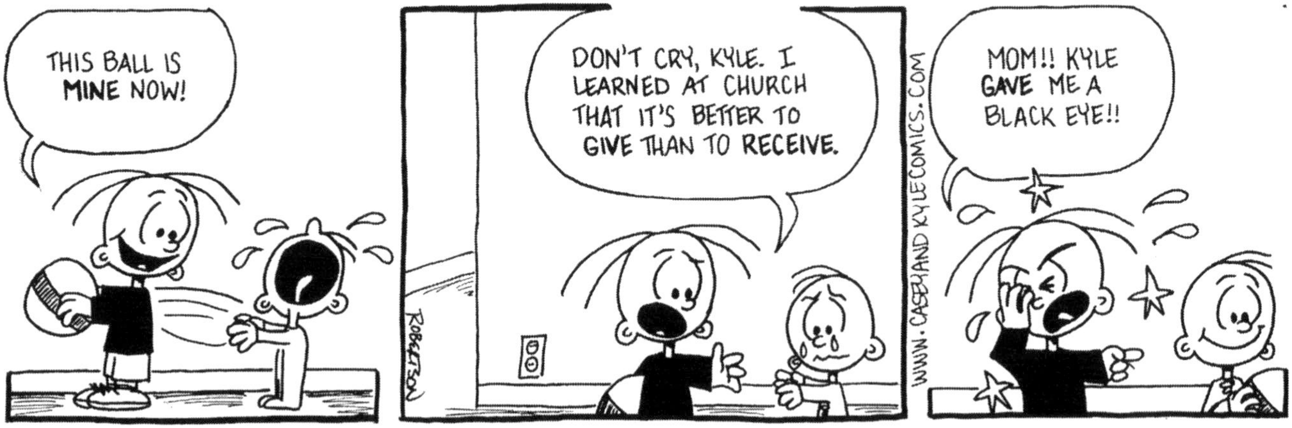
THIS BALL IS MINE NOW!
ROBERTSON
DON'T CRY, KYLE. I LEARNED AT CHURCH THAT IT'S BETTER TO GIVE THAN TO RECEIVE.
WWW.CASEYANDKYLECOMICS.COM
MOM!! KYLE GAVE ME A BLACK EYE!!

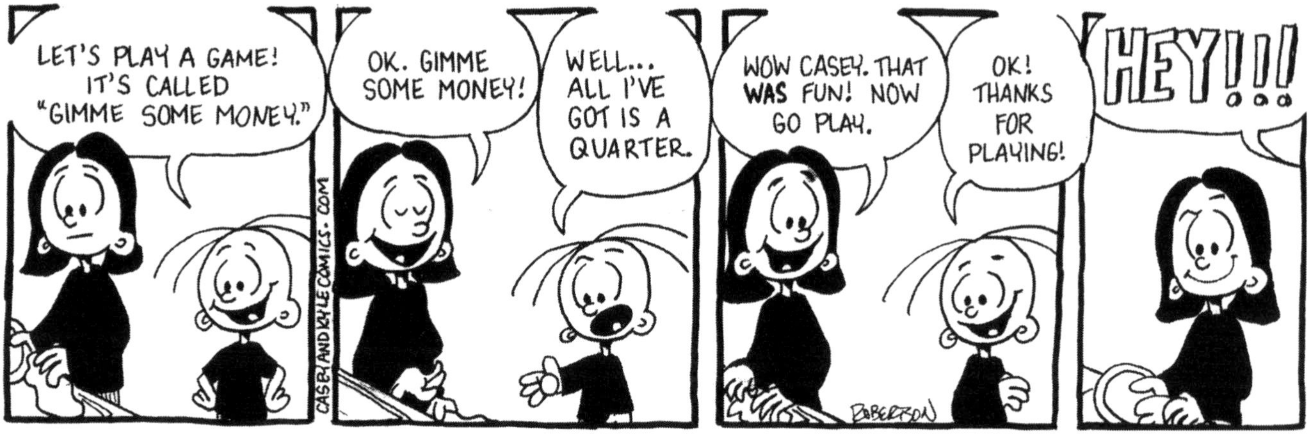
LET'S PLAY A GAME! IT'S CALLED "GIMME SOME MONEY."
CASEYANDKYLECOMICS.COM
OK. GIMME SOME MONEY!
WELL... ALL I'VE GOT IS A QUARTER.
WOW CASEY. THAT WAS FUN! NOW GO PLAY.
OK! THANKS FOR PLAYING!
ROBERTSON
HEY!!!

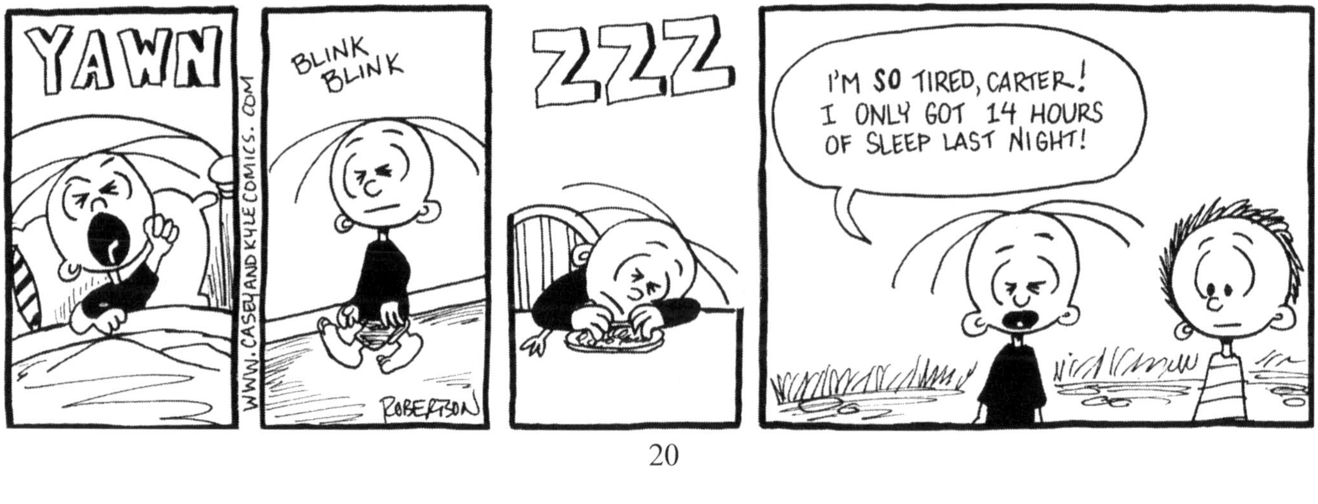
YAWN
WWW.CASEYANDKYLECOMICS.COM
BLINK BLINK
ROBERTSON
ZZZ
I'M SO TIRED, CARTER! I ONLY GOT 14 HOURS OF SLEEP LAST NIGHT!

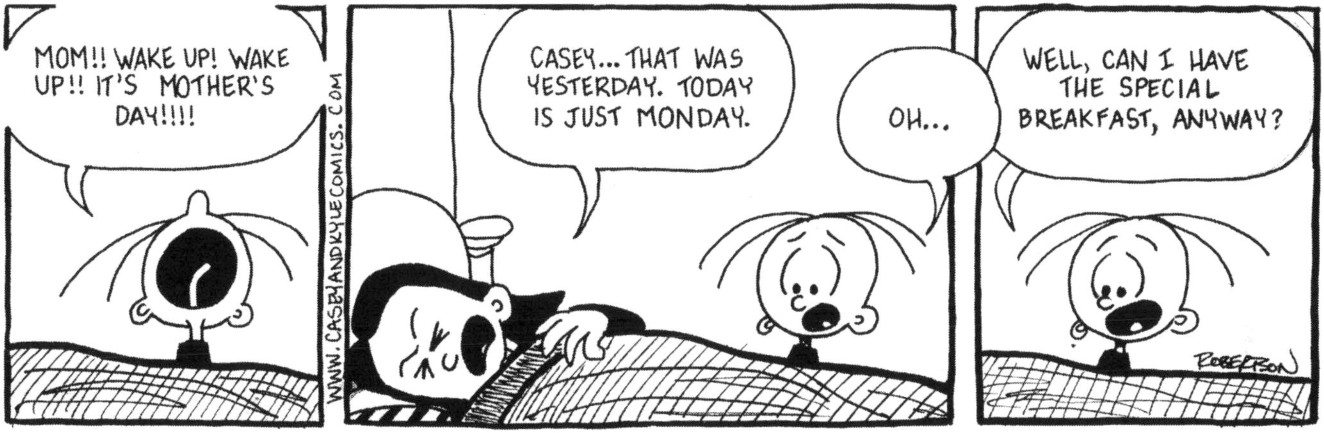
MOM!! WAKE UP! WAKE UP!! IT'S MOTHER'S DAY!!!!
WWW.CASEYANDKYLECOMICS.COM
CASEY... THAT WAS YESTERDAY. TODAY IS JUST MONDAY.
OH...
WELL, CAN I HAVE THE SPECIAL BREAKFAST, ANYWAY?
ROBERTSON

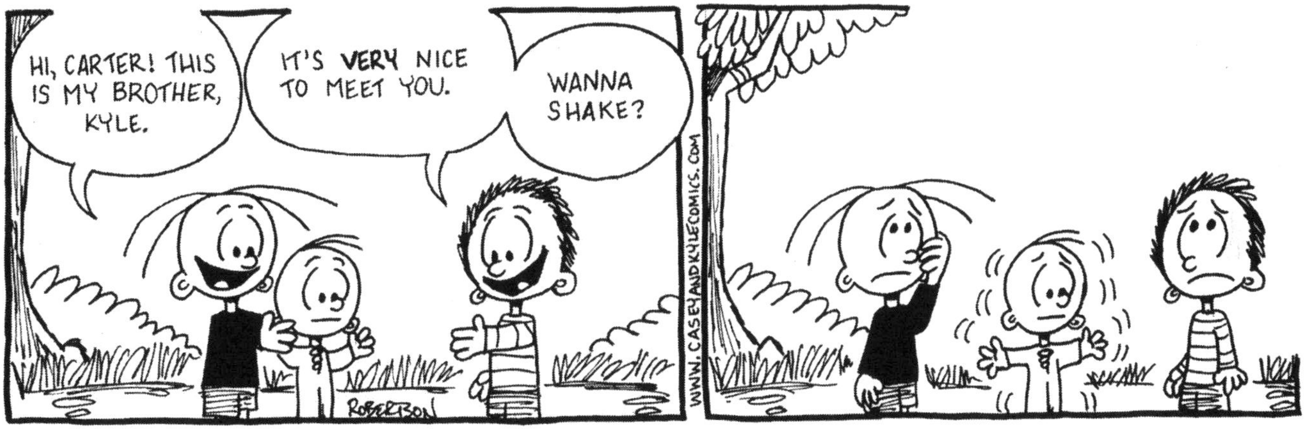
HI, CARTER! THIS IS MY BROTHER, KYLE.
IT'S **VERY** NICE TO MEET YOU.
WANNA SHAKE?
ROBERTSON
WWW.CASEYANDKYLECOMICS.COM

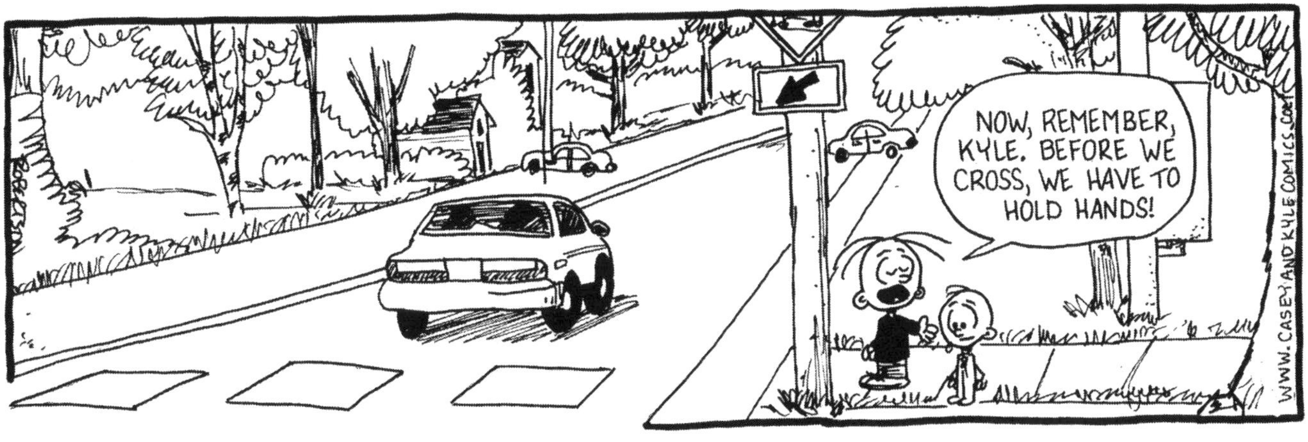
ROBERTSON
NOW, REMEMBER, KYLE. BEFORE WE CROSS, WE HAVE TO HOLD HANDS!
WWW.CASEYANDKYLECOMICS.COM

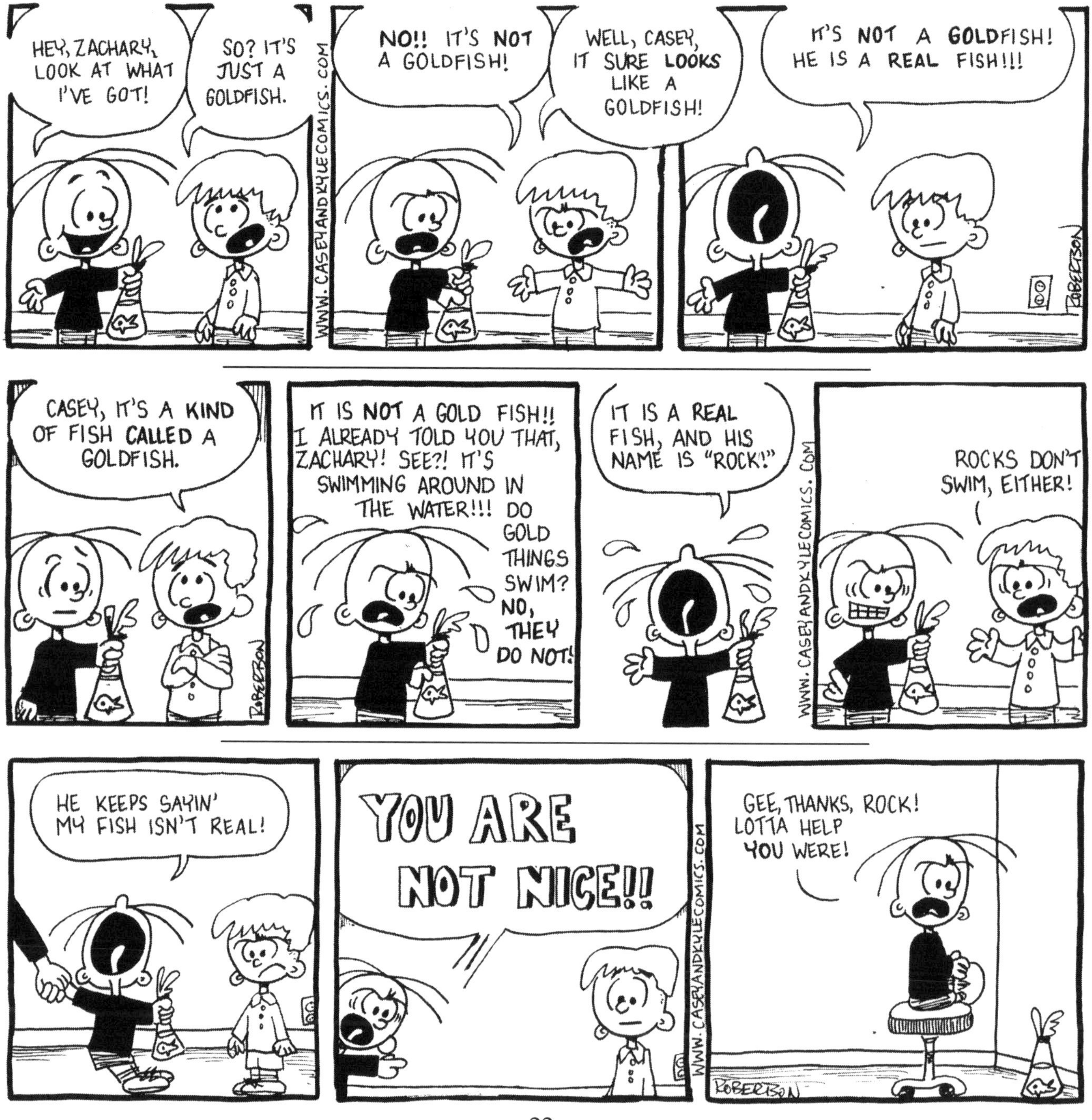
HEY, ZACHARY, LOOK AT WHAT I'VE GOT!
SO? IT'S JUST A GOLDFISH.
WWW.CASEYANDKYLECOMICS.COM
NO!! IT'S NOT A GOLDFISH!
WELL, CASEY, IT SURE LOOKS LIKE A GOLDFISH!
IT'S NOT A GOLDFISH! HE IS A REAL FISH!!!
ROBERTSON
CASEY, IT'S A KIND OF FISH CALLED A GOLDFISH.
ROBERTSON
IT IS NOT A GOLD FISH!! I ALREADY TOLD YOU THAT, ZACHARY! SEE?! IT'S SWIMMING AROUND IN THE WATER!!! DO GOLD THINGS SWIM? NO, THEY DO NOT!
IT IS A REAL FISH, AND HIS NAME IS "ROCK!"
WWW.CASEYANDKYLECOMICS.COM
ROCKS DON'T SWIM, EITHER!
HE KEEPS SAYIN' MY FISH ISN'T REAL!
YOU ARE NOT NICE!!
WWW.CASEYANDKYLECOMICS.COM
GEE, THANKS, ROCK! LOTTA HELP YOU WERE!
ROBERTSON

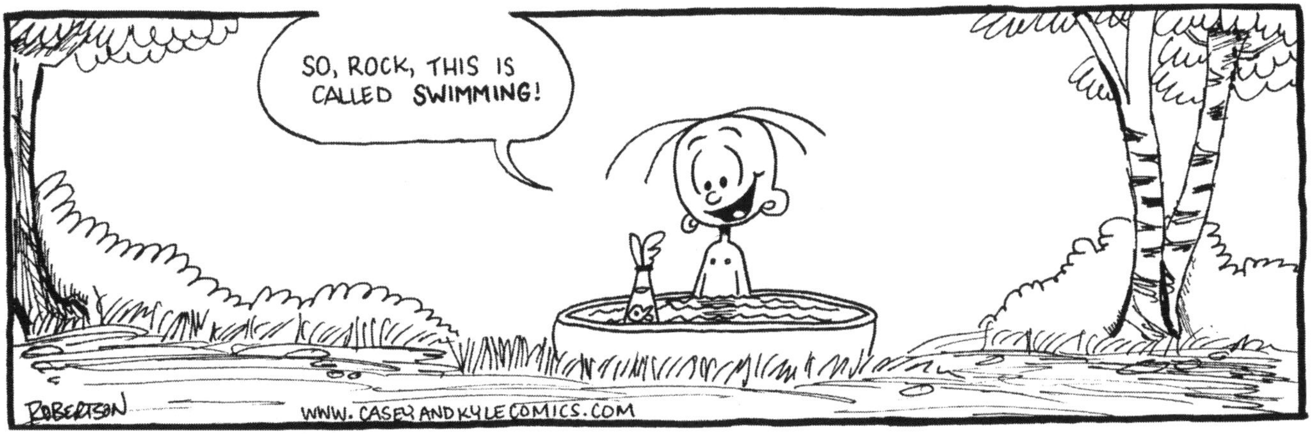
SO, ROCK, THIS IS CALLED **SWIMMING**!
ROBERTSON
WWW.CASEYANDKYLECOMICS.COM

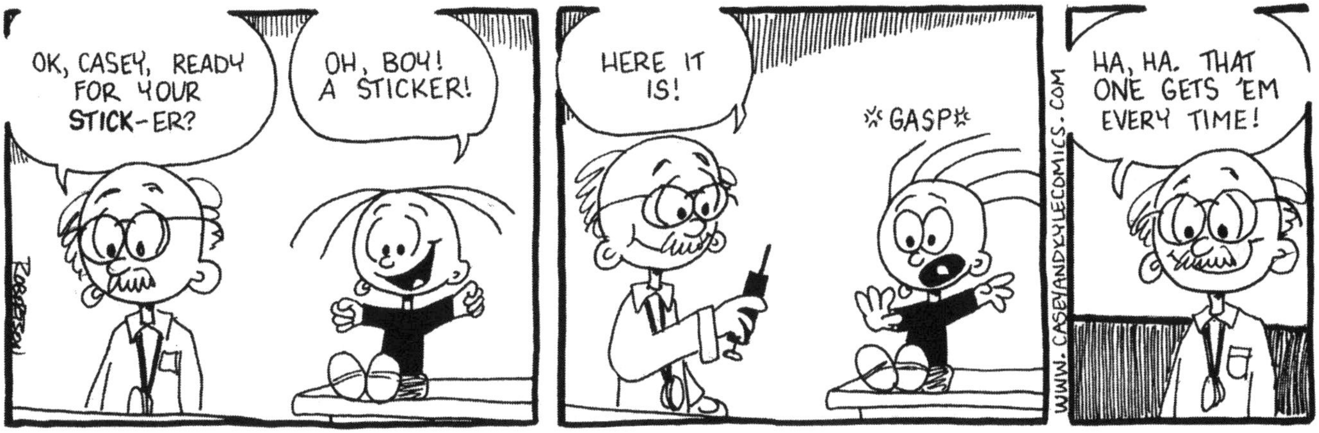
OK, CASEY, READY FOR YOUR **STICK**-ER?
OH, BOY! A STICKER!
ROBERTSON
HERE IT IS!
GASP
HA, HA. THAT ONE GETS 'EM EVERY TIME!
WWW.CASEYANDKYLECOMICS.COM

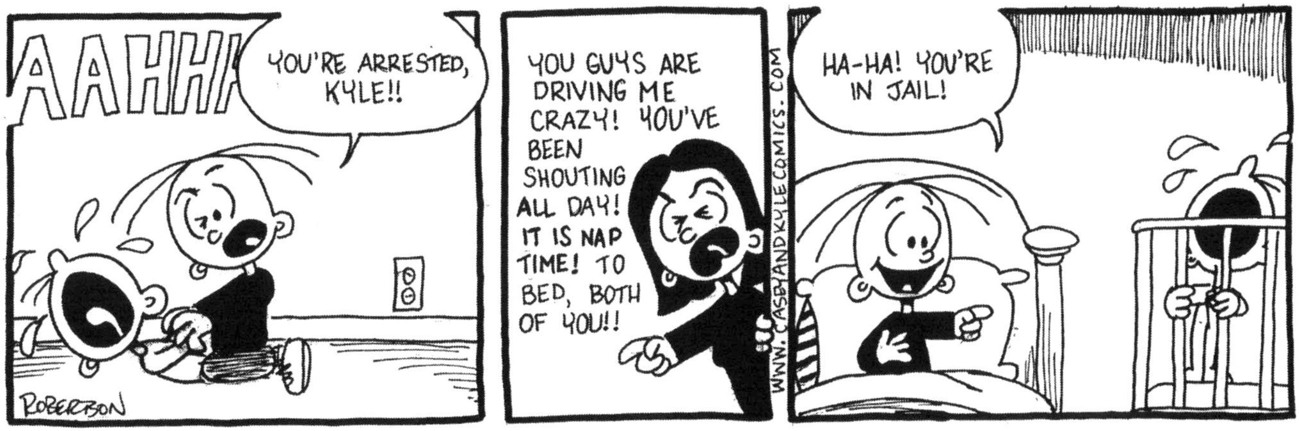
AAHH
YOU'RE ARRESTED, KYLE!!
ROBERTSON
YOU GUYS ARE DRIVING ME CRAZY! YOU'VE BEEN SHOUTING **ALL DAY! IT IS NAP TIME!** TO BED, BOTH OF YOU!!
WWW.CASEYANDKYLECOMICS.COM
HA-HA! YOU'RE IN JAIL!

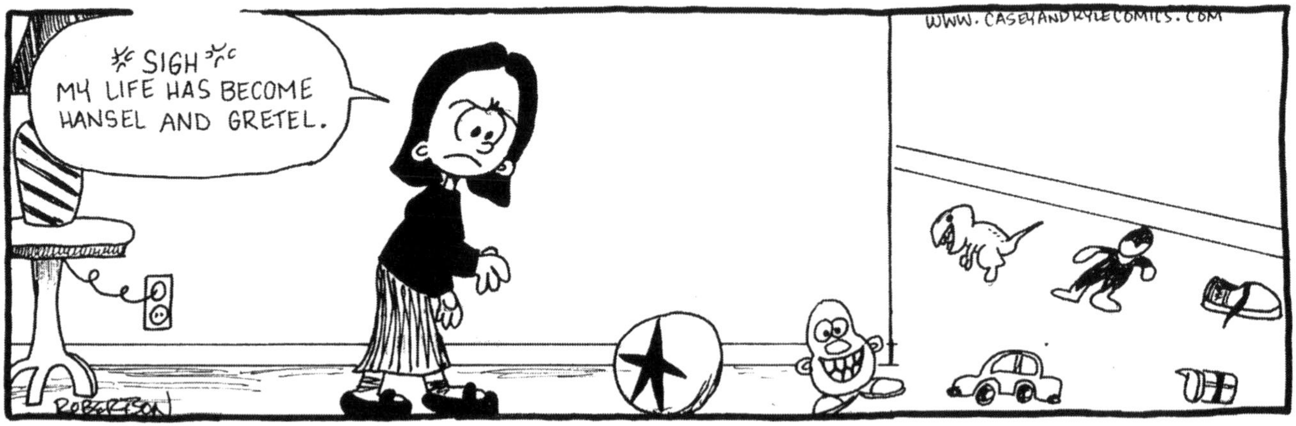
SIGH
MY LIFE HAS BECOME HANSEL AND GRETEL.
WWW.CASEYANDKYLECOMICS.COM
ROBERTSON

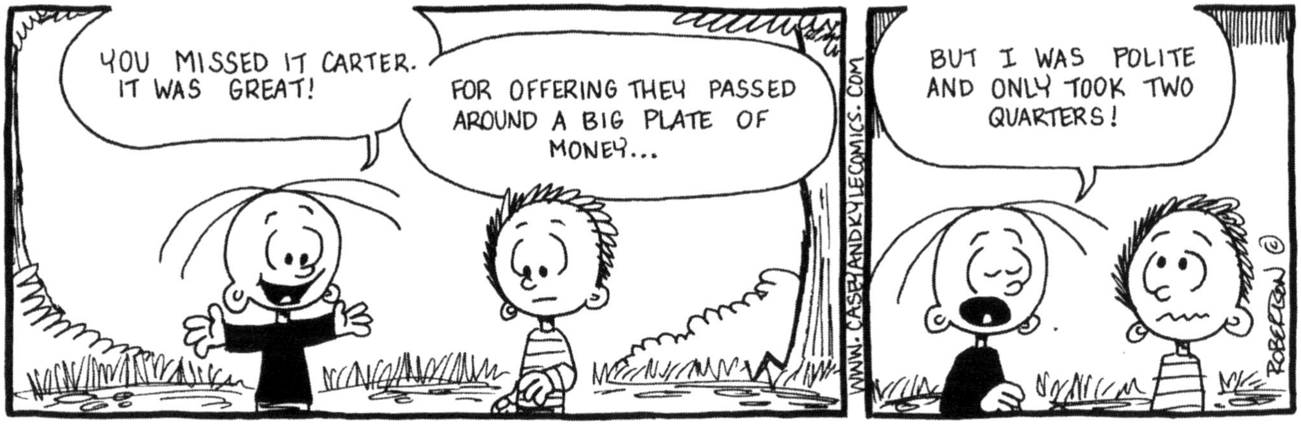
YOU MISSED IT CARTER. IT WAS GREAT!
FOR OFFERING THEY PASSED AROUND A BIG PLATE OF MONEY...
WWW.CASEYANDKYLECOMICS.COM
BUT I WAS POLITE AND ONLY TOOK TWO QUARTERS!
ROBERTSON ©

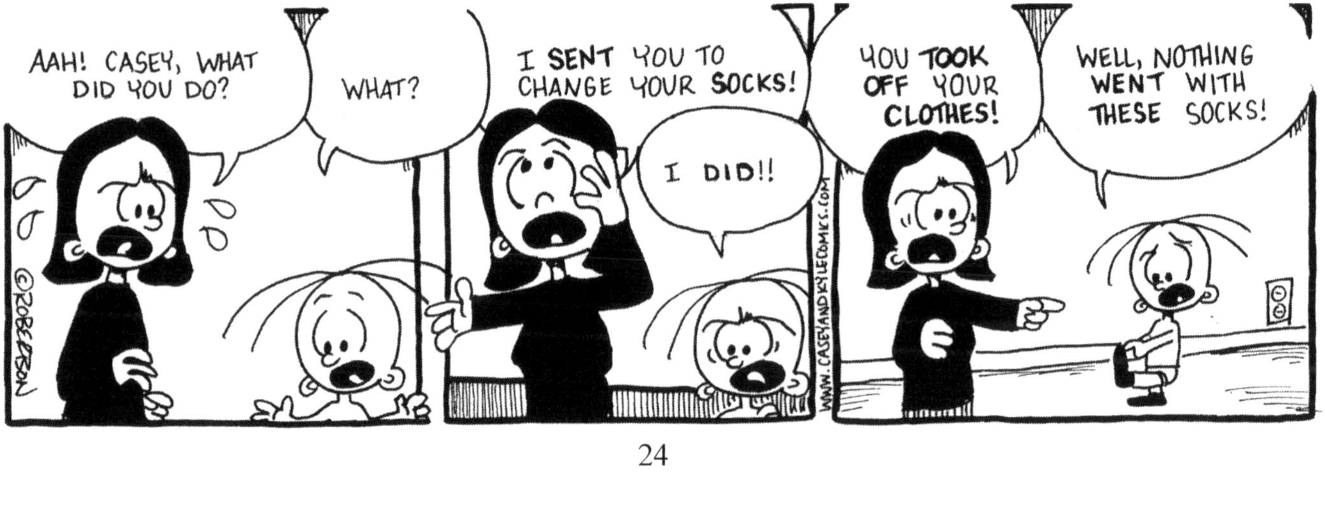
AAH! CASEY, WHAT DID YOU DO?
WHAT?
©ROBERTSON
I SENT YOU TO CHANGE YOUR SOCKS!
I DID!!
WWW.CASEYANDKYLECOMICS.COM
YOU TOOK OFF YOUR CLOTHES!
WELL, NOTHING WENT WITH THESE SOCKS!

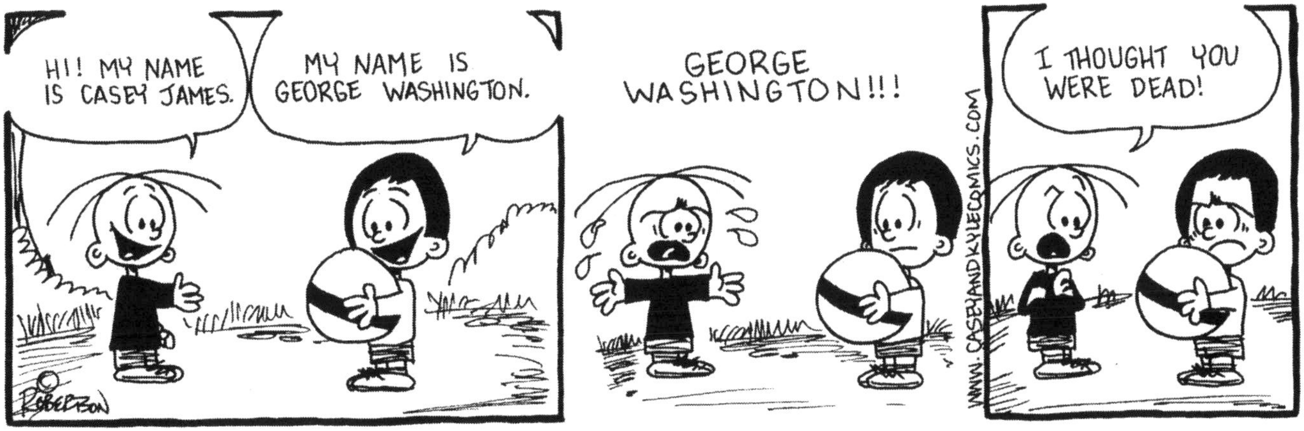
HI! MY NAME IS CASEY JAMES.
MY NAME IS GEORGE WASHINGTON.
© ROBERTSON
GEORGE WASHINGTON!!!
WWW.CASEYANDKYLECOMICS.COM
I THOUGHT YOU WERE DEAD!

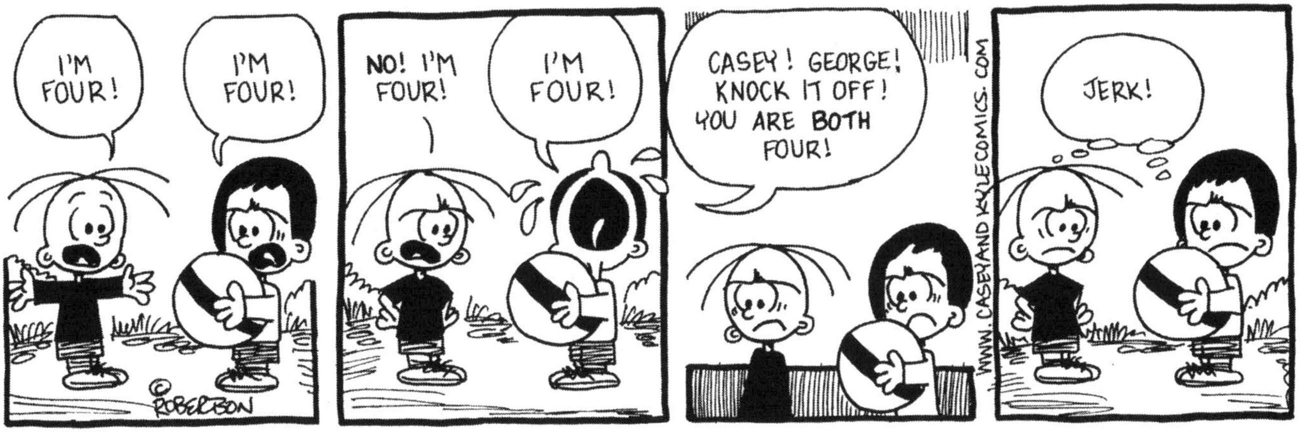
I'M FOUR!
I'M FOUR!
© ROBERTSON
NO! I'M FOUR!
I'M FOUR!
CASEY! GEORGE! KNOCK IT OFF! YOU ARE BOTH FOUR!
WWW.CASEYANDKYLECOMICS.COM
JERK!

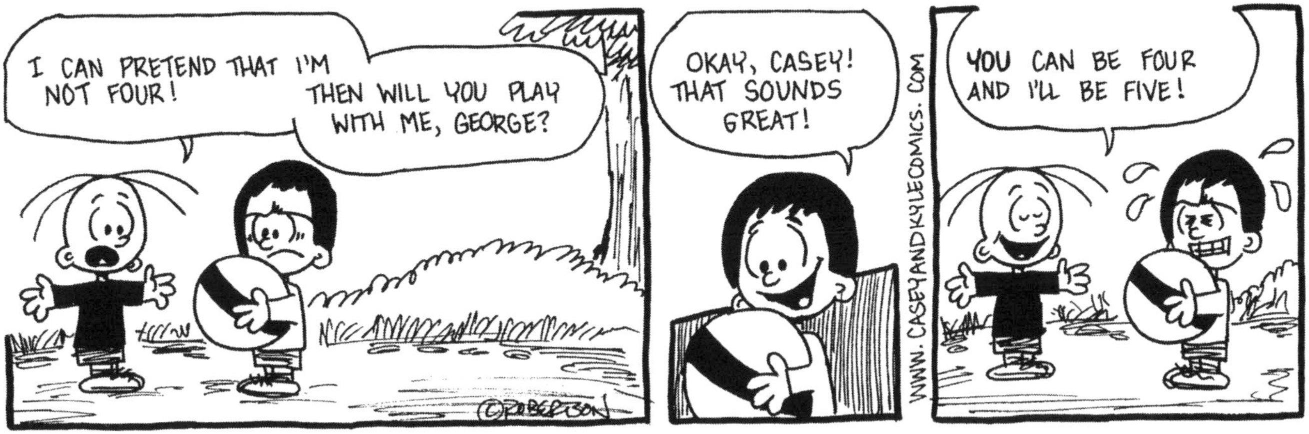
I CAN PRETEND THAT I'M NOT FOUR!
THEN WILL YOU PLAY WITH ME, GEORGE?
© ROBERTSON
OKAY, CASEY! THAT SOUNDS GREAT!
WWW.CASEYANDKYLECOMICS.COM
YOU CAN BE FOUR AND I'LL BE FIVE!

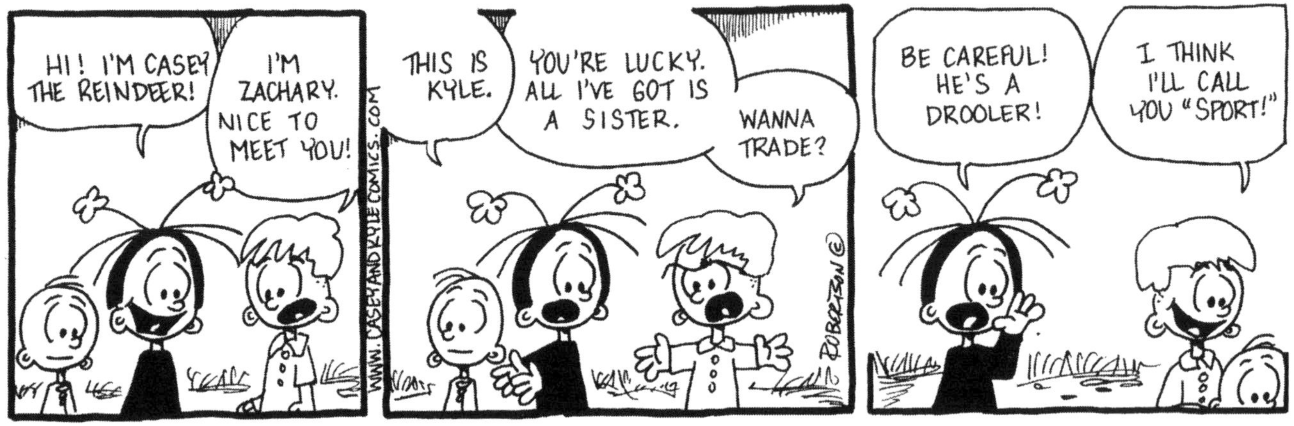
HI! I'M CASEY THE REINDEER!
I'M ZACHARY. NICE TO MEET YOU!
WWW.CASEYANDKYLECOMICS.COM
THIS IS KYLE.
YOU'RE LUCKY. ALL I'VE GOT IS A SISTER.
WANNA TRADE?
ROBERTSON ©
BE CAREFUL! HE'S A DROOLER!
I THINK I'LL CALL YOU "SPORT!"

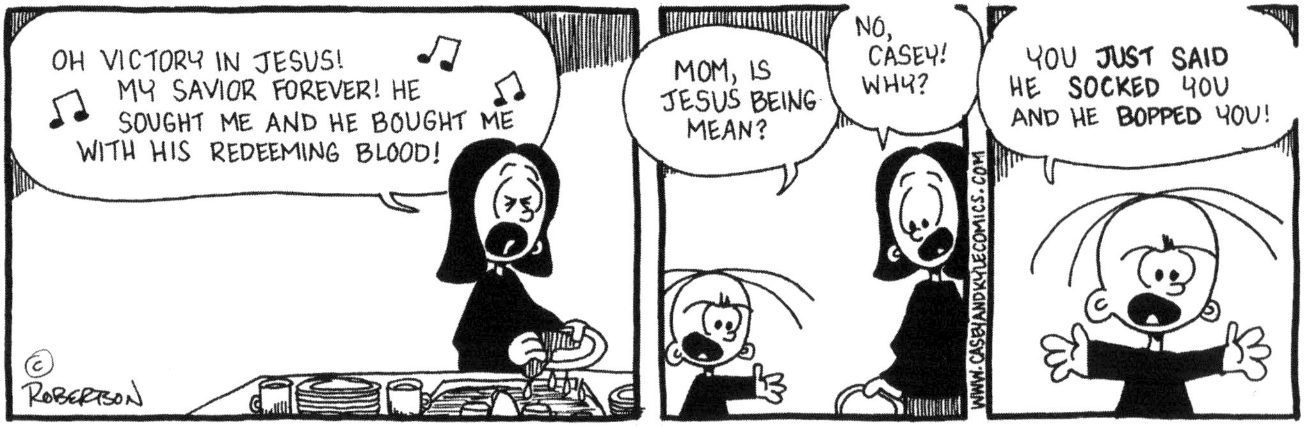
OH VICTORY IN JESUS! MY SAVIOR FOREVER! HE SOUGHT ME AND HE BOUGHT ME WITH HIS REDEEMING BLOOD!
© ROBERTSON
MOM, IS JESUS BEING MEAN?
NO, CASEY! WHY?
WWW.CASEYANDKYLECOMICS.COM
YOU **JUST SAID** HE **SOCKED** YOU AND HE **BOPPED** YOU!

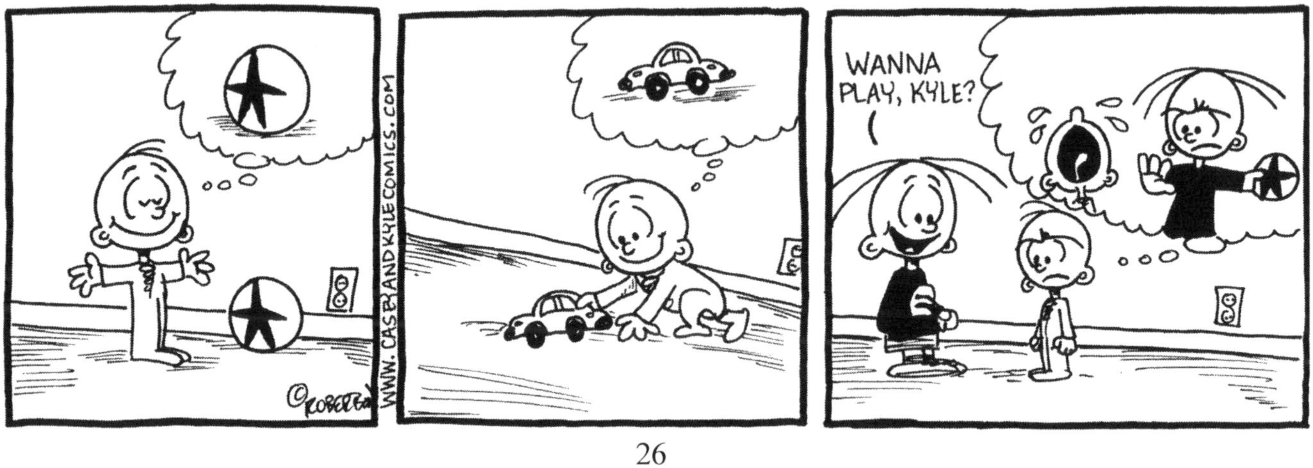
©ROBERTSON
WWW.CASEYANDKYLECOMICS.COM
WANNA PLAY, KYLE?

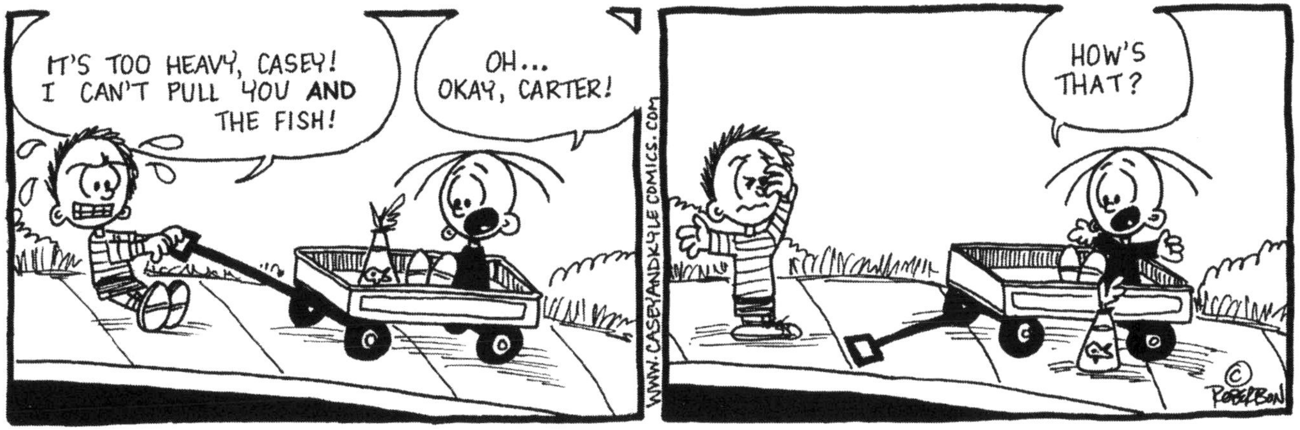
IT'S TOO HEAVY, CASEY! I CAN'T PULL YOU AND THE FISH!
OH... OKAY, CARTER!
WWW.CASEYANDKYLECOMICS.COM
HOW'S THAT?
© ROBERSON

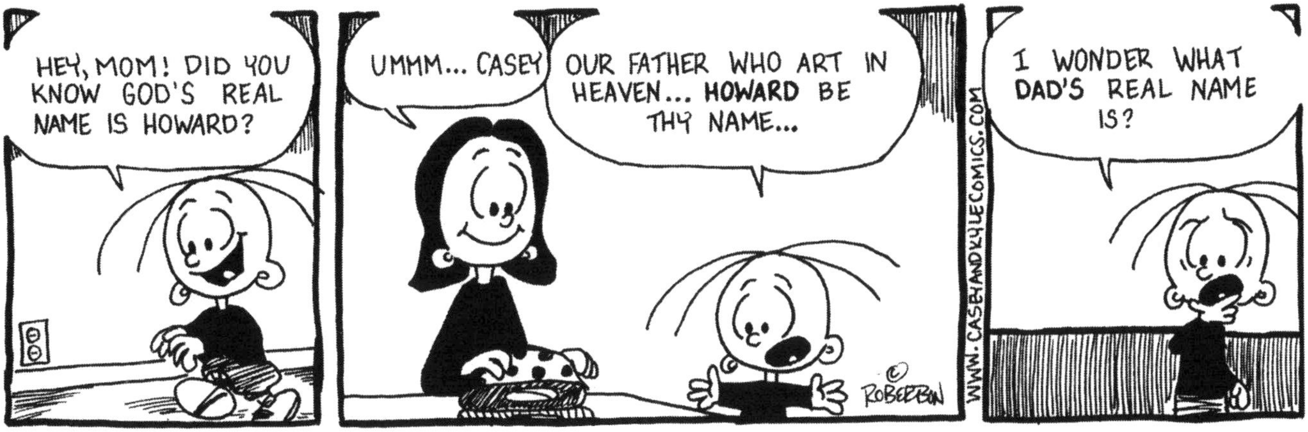
HEY, MOM! DID YOU KNOW GOD'S REAL NAME IS HOWARD?
UMMM... CASEY
OUR FATHER WHO ART IN HEAVEN... HOWARD BE THY NAME...
© ROBERSON
WWW.CASEYANDKYLECOMICS.COM
I WONDER WHAT DAD'S REAL NAME IS?

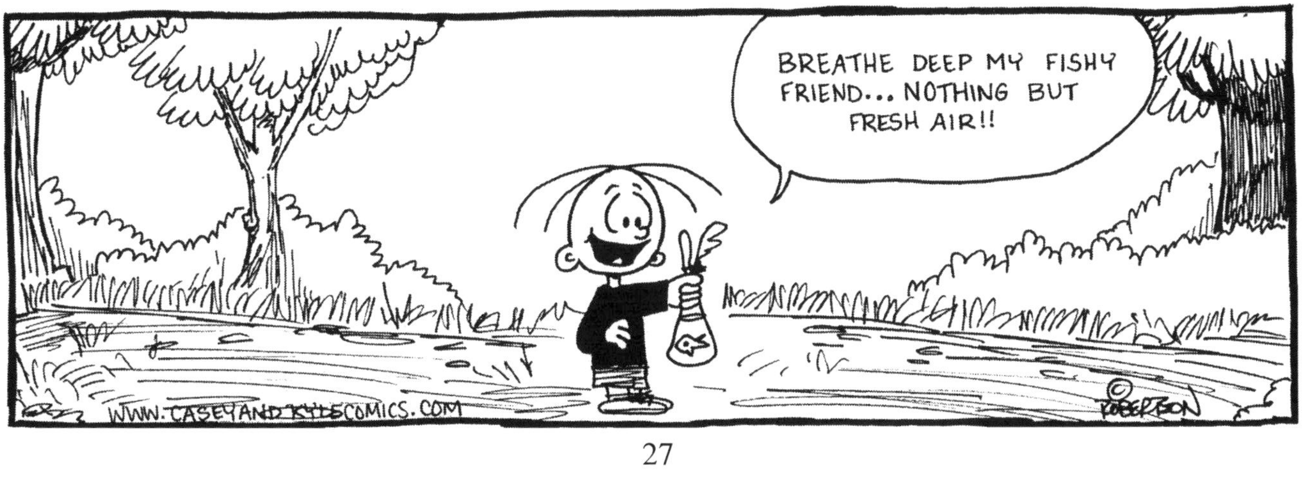
BREATHE DEEP MY FISHY FRIEND... NOTHING BUT FRESH AIR!!
WWW.CASEYANDKYLECOMICS.COM
© ROBERSON

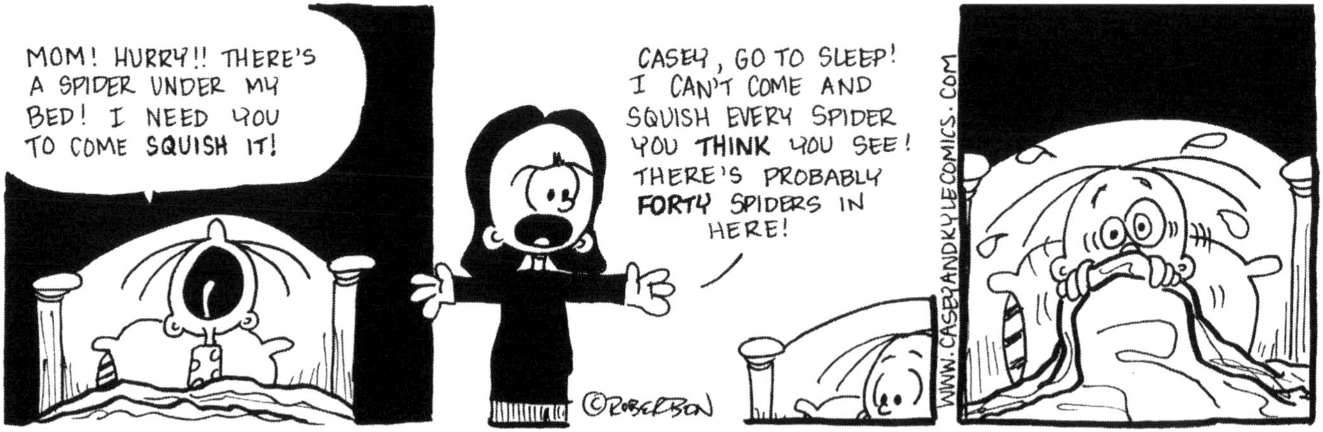
MOM! HURRY!! THERE'S A SPIDER UNDER MY BED! I NEED YOU TO COME **SQUISH IT!**
©ROBERTSON
CASEY, GO TO SLEEP! I CAN'T COME AND SQUISH EVERY SPIDER YOU **THINK** YOU SEE! THERE'S PROBABLY **FORTY** SPIDERS IN HERE!
WWW.CASEYANDKYLECOMICS.COM

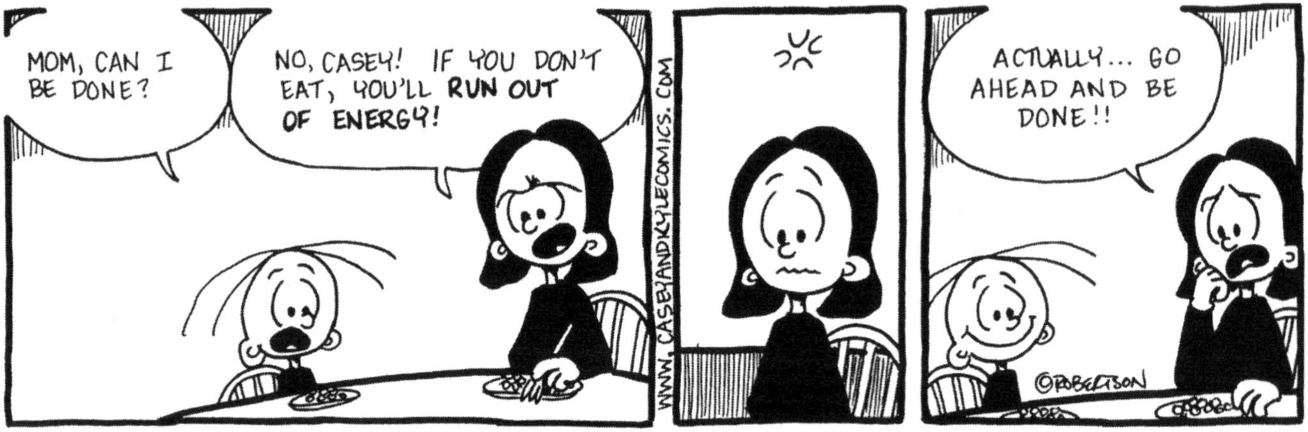
MOM, CAN I BE DONE?
NO, CASEY! IF YOU DON'T EAT, YOU'LL **RUN OUT OF ENERGY!**
WWW.CASEYANDKYLECOMICS.COM
ACTUALLY... GO AHEAD AND BE DONE!!
©ROBERTSON

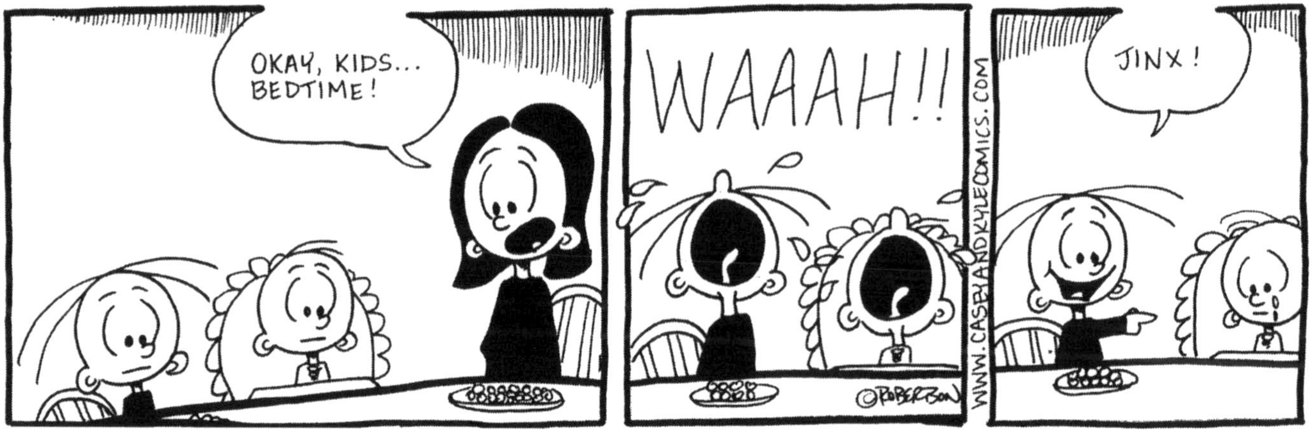
OKAY, KIDS... BEDTIME!
WAAAH!!
©ROBERTSON
WWW.CASEYANDKYLECOMICS.COM
JINX!

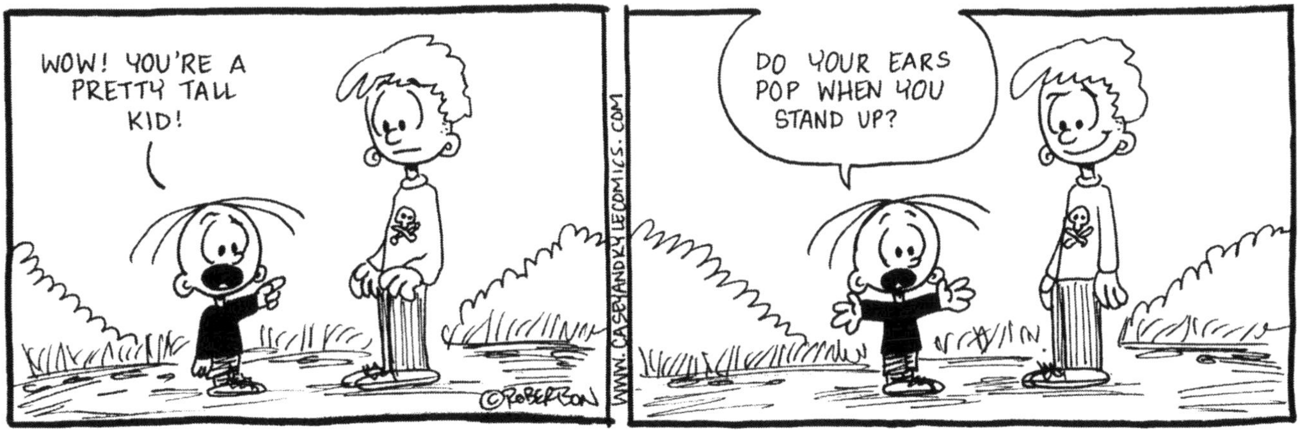
WOW! YOU'RE A PRETTY TALL KID!
©ROBERTSON
WWW.CASEYANDKYLECOMICS.COM
DO YOUR EARS POP WHEN YOU STAND UP?

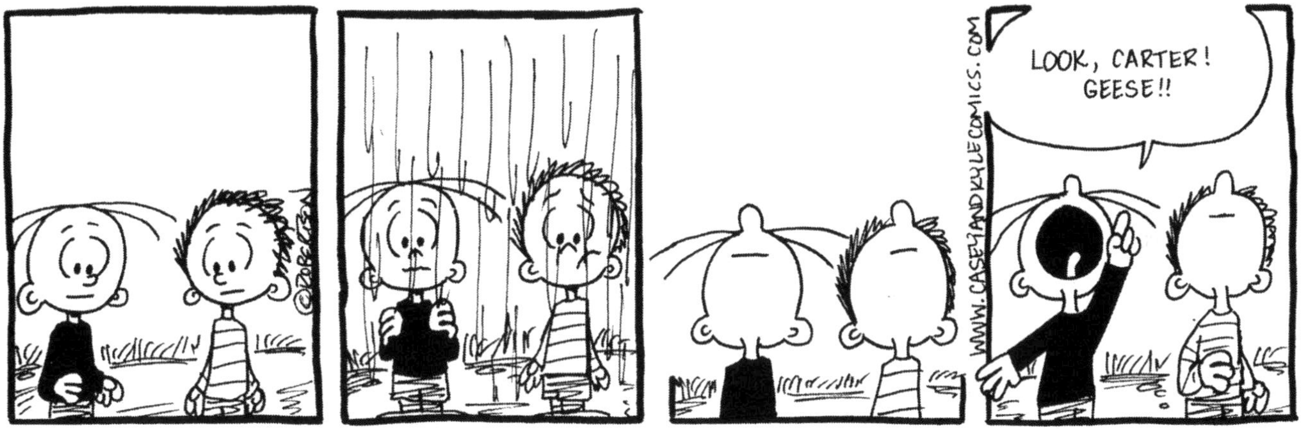
©ROBERTSON
WWW.CASEYANDKYLECOMICS.COM
LOOK, CARTER! GEESE!!

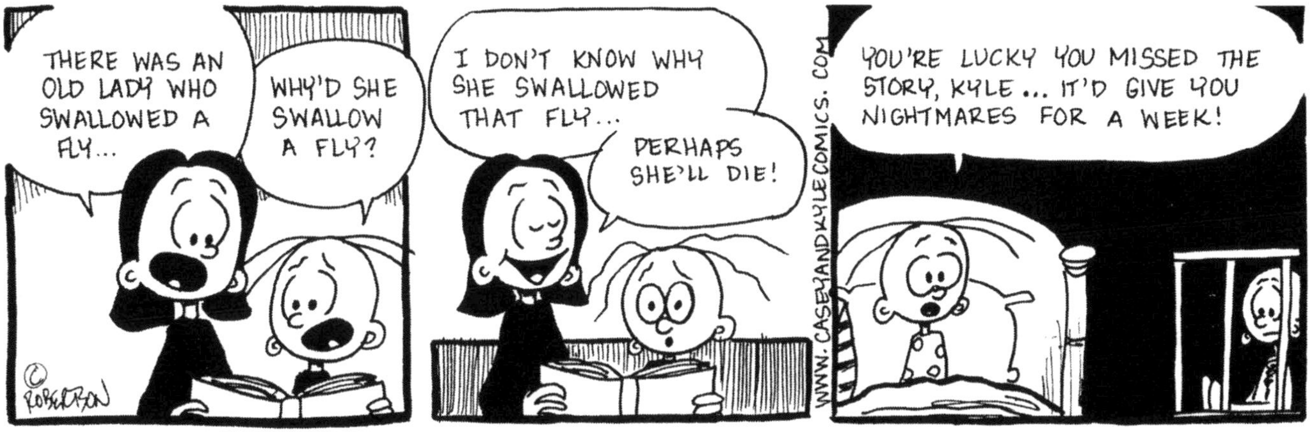
THERE WAS AN OLD LADY WHO SWALLOWED A FLY...
WHY'D SHE SWALLOW A FLY?
©ROBERTSON
I DON'T KNOW WHY SHE SWALLOWED THAT FLY...
PERHAPS SHE'LL DIE!
WWW.CASEYANDKYLECOMICS.COM
YOU'RE LUCKY YOU MISSED THE STORY, KYLE... IT'D GIVE YOU NIGHTMARES FOR A WEEK!

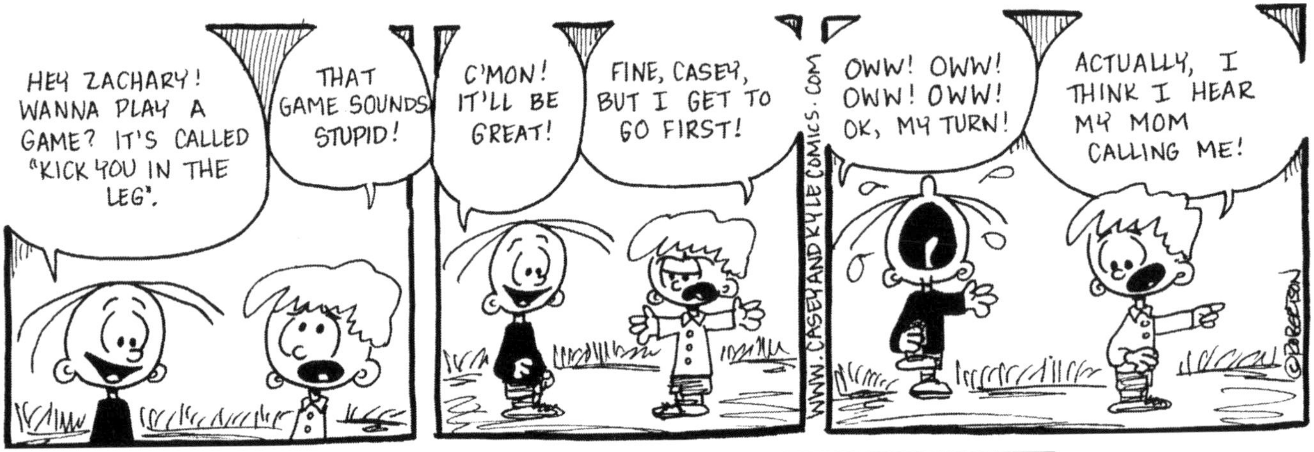
HEY ZACHARY! WANNA PLAY A GAME? IT'S CALLED "KICK YOU IN THE LEG".
THAT GAME SOUNDS STUPID!
C'MON! IT'LL BE GREAT!
FINE, CASEY, BUT I GET TO GO FIRST!
WWW.CASEYANDKYLECOMICS.COM
OWW! OWW! OWW! OWW! OK, MY TURN!
ACTUALLY, I THINK I HEAR MY MOM CALLING ME!
©ROBERTSON

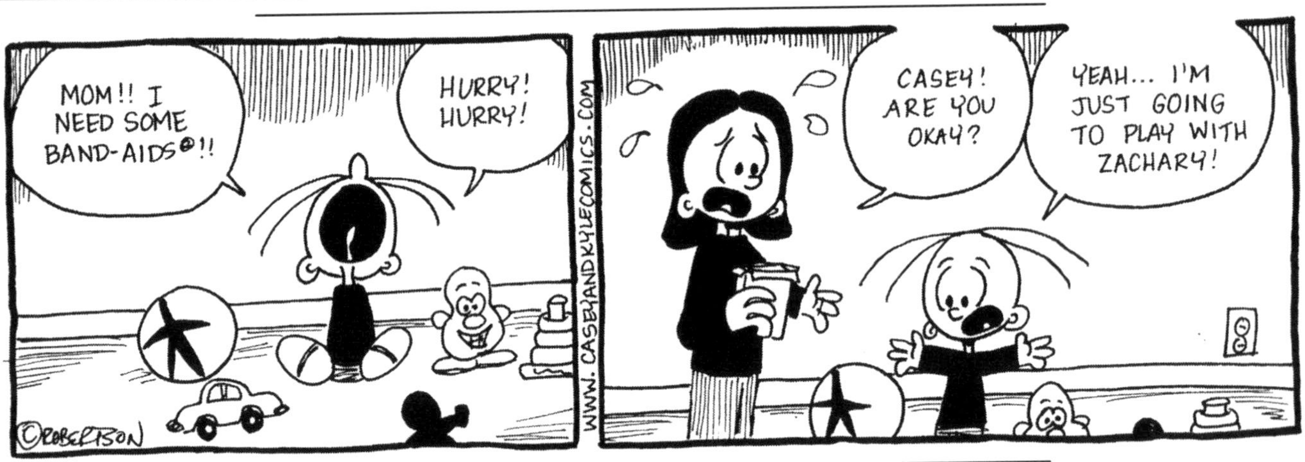
MOM!! I NEED SOME BAND-AIDS®!!
HURRY! HURRY!
©ROBERTSON
WWW.CASEYANDKYLECOMICS.COM
CASEY! ARE YOU OKAY?
YEAH... I'M JUST GOING TO PLAY WITH ZACHARY!

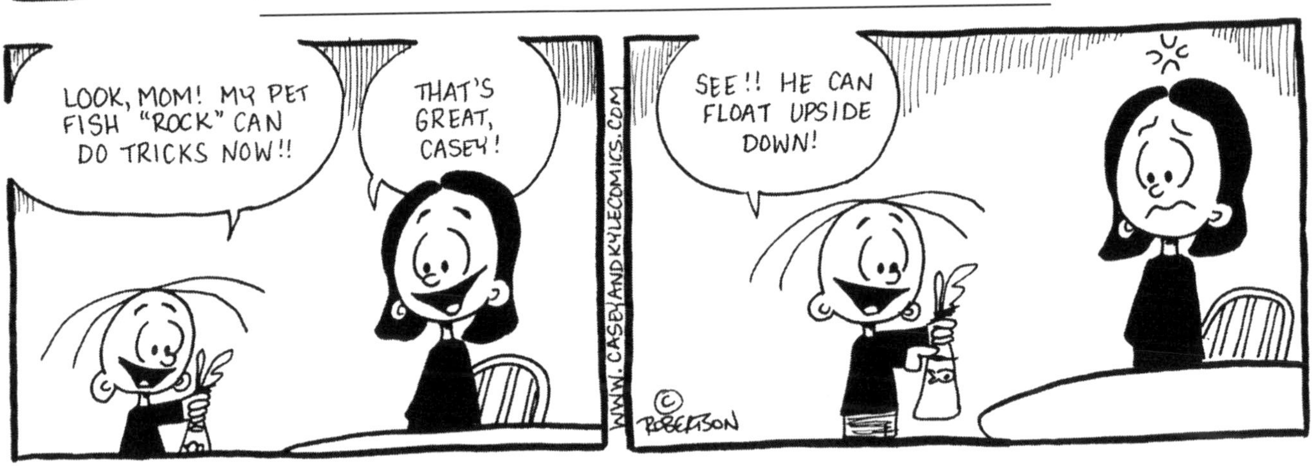
LOOK, MOM! MY PET FISH "ROCK" CAN DO TRICKS NOW!!
THAT'S GREAT, CASEY!
WWW.CASEYANDKYLECOMICS.COM
©ROBERTSON
SEE!! HE CAN FLOAT UPSIDE DOWN!

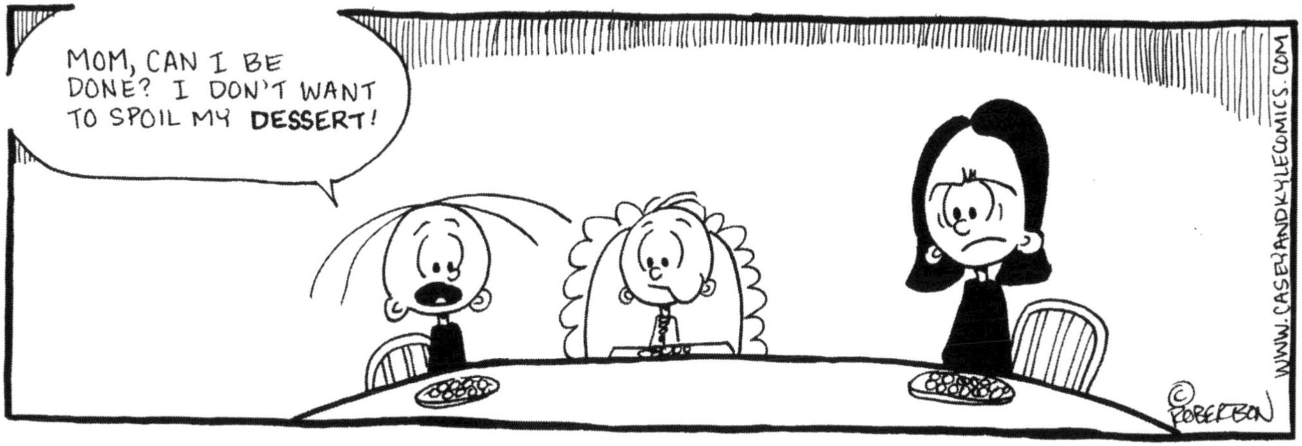
MOM, CAN I BE DONE? I DON'T WANT TO SPOIL MY DESSERT!
WWW.CASEYANDKYLECOMICS.COM
© ROBERTSON

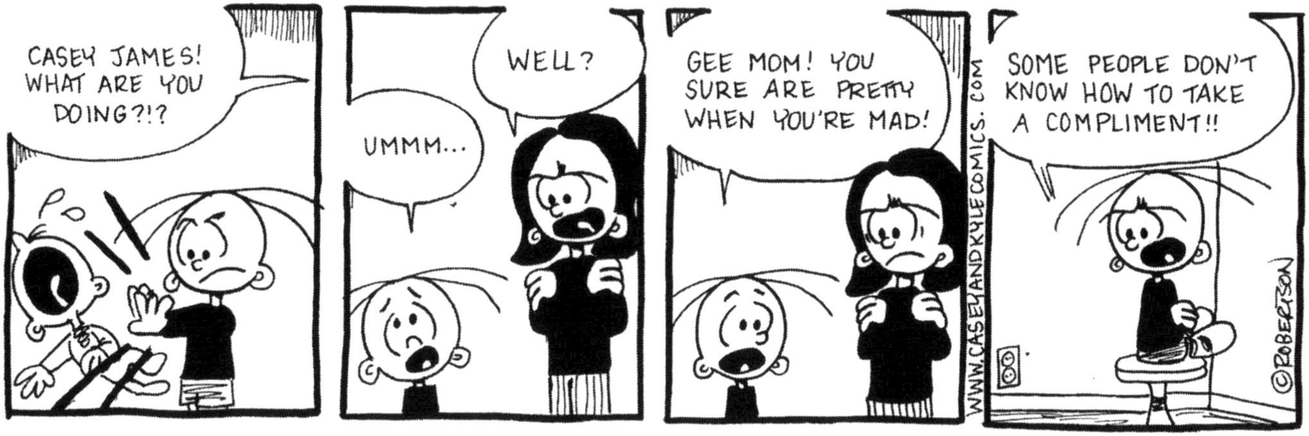
CASEY JAMES! WHAT ARE YOU DOING?!?
WELL?
UMMM...
GEE MOM! YOU SURE ARE PRETTY WHEN YOU'RE MAD!
WWW.CASEYANDKYLECOMICS.COM
SOME PEOPLE DON'T KNOW HOW TO TAKE A COMPLIMENT!!
©ROBERTSON

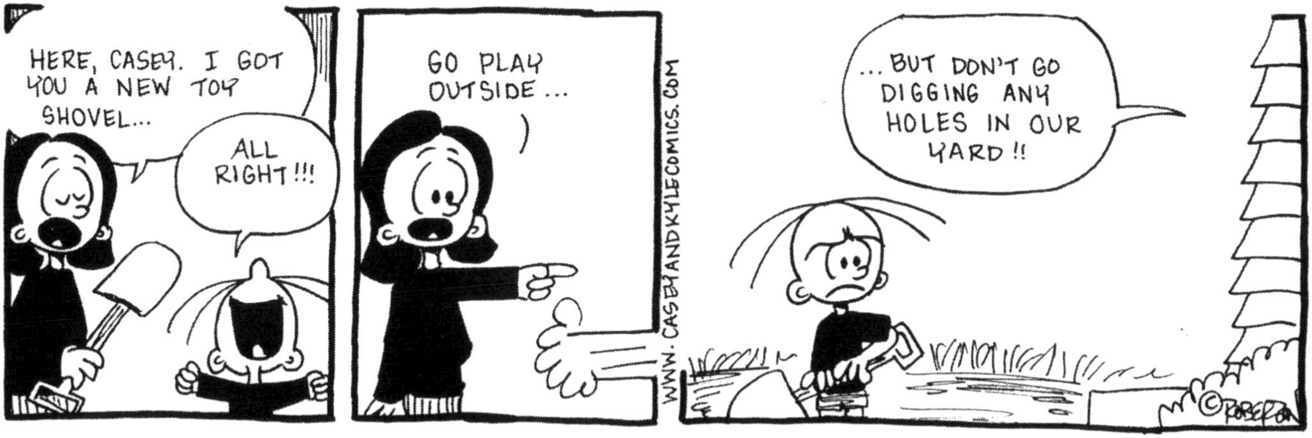
HERE, CASEY. I GOT YOU A NEW TOY SHOVEL...
ALL RIGHT!!!
GO PLAY OUTSIDE...
WWW.CASEYANDKYLECOMICS.COM
...BUT DON'T GO DIGGING ANY HOLES IN OUR YARD!!
©ROBERTSON

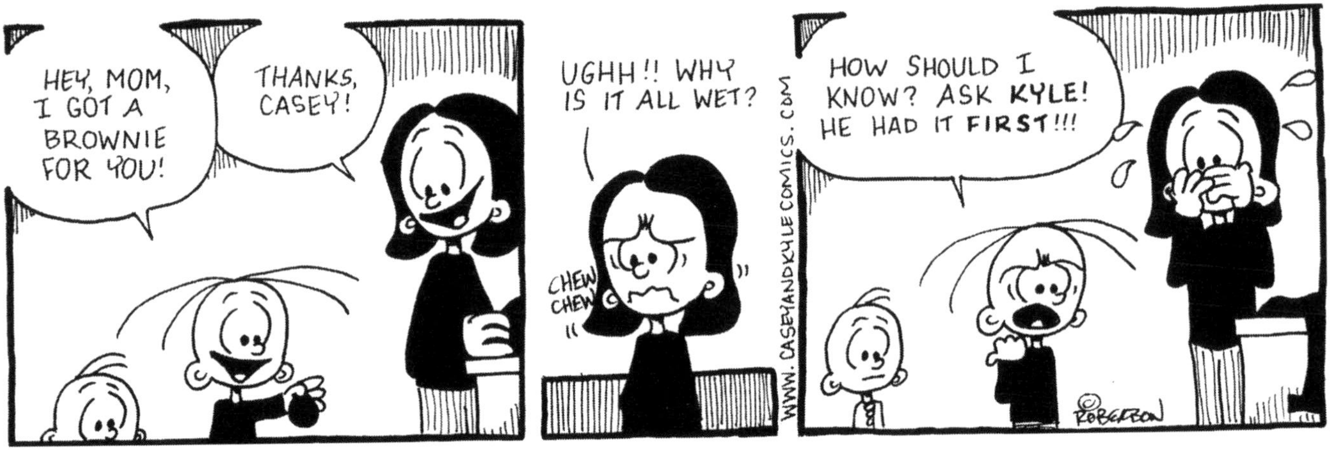
HEY, MOM, I GOT A BROWNIE FOR YOU!
THANKS, CASEY!
CHEW CHEW
UGHH!! WHY IS IT ALL WET?
WWW.CASEYANDKYLECOMICS.COM
HOW SHOULD I KNOW? ASK KYLE! HE HAD IT FIRST!!!
©ROBERTSON

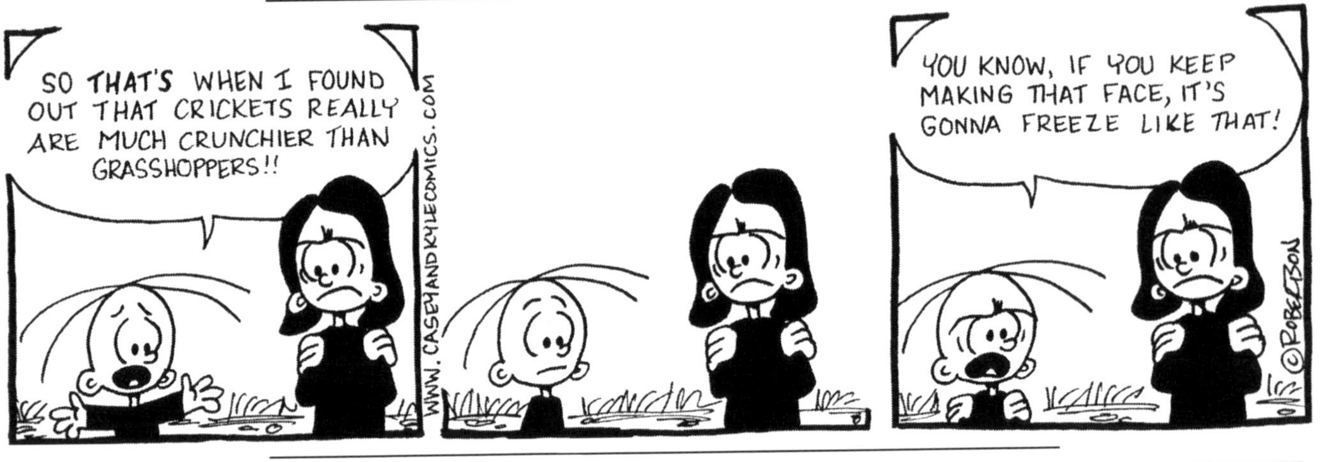
SO THAT'S WHEN I FOUND OUT THAT CRICKETS REALLY ARE MUCH CRUNCHIER THAN GRASSHOPPERS!!
WWW.CASEYANDKYLECOMICS.COM
YOU KNOW, IF YOU KEEP MAKING THAT FACE, IT'S GONNA FREEZE LIKE THAT!
©ROBERTSON

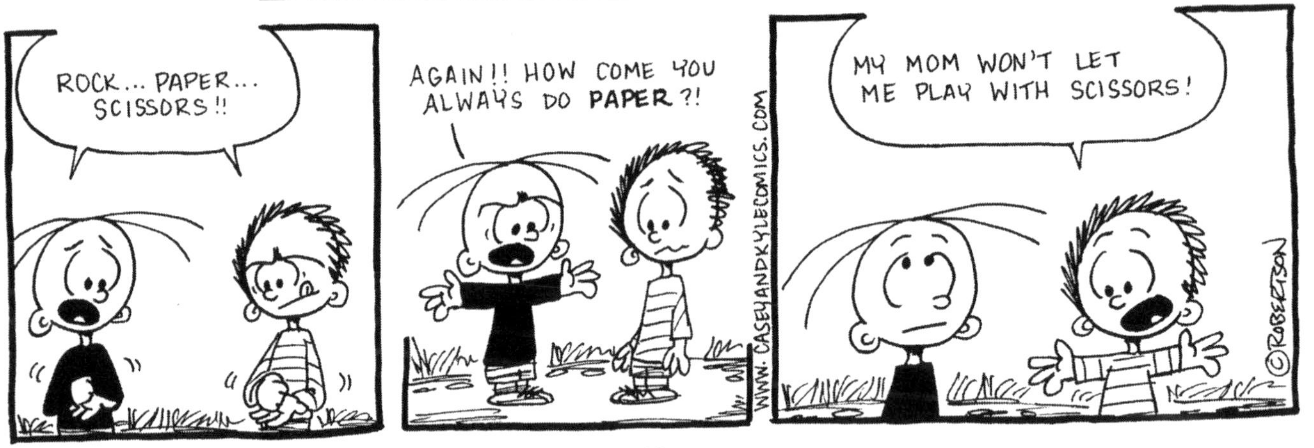
ROCK... PAPER... SCISSORS!!
AGAIN!! HOW COME YOU ALWAYS DO PAPER?!
WWW.CASEYANDKYLECOMICS.COM
MY MOM WON'T LET ME PLAY WITH SCISSORS!
©ROBERTSON

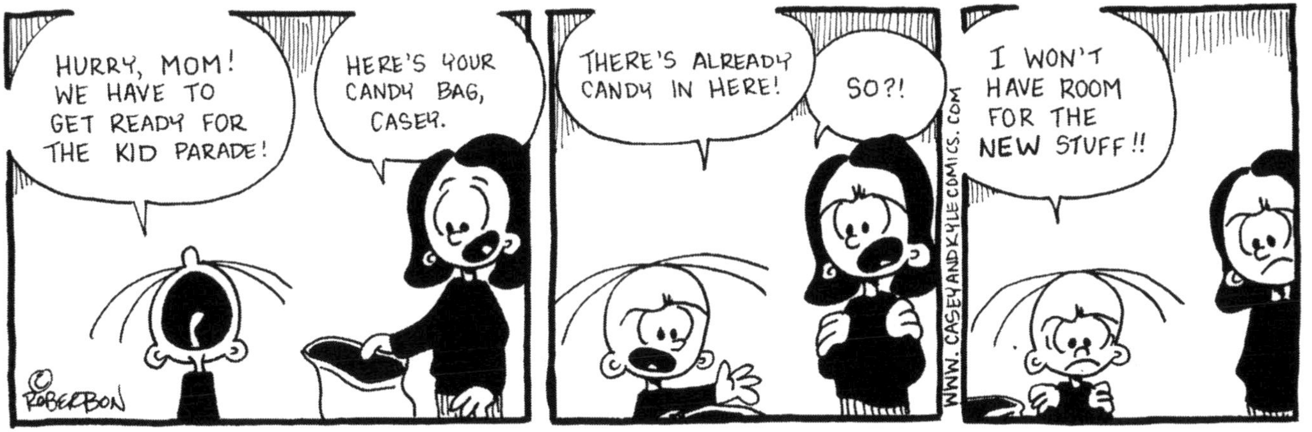
HURRY, MOM! WE HAVE TO GET READY FOR THE KID PARADE!
HERE'S YOUR CANDY BAG, CASEY.
THERE'S ALREADY CANDY IN HERE!
SO?!
I WON'T HAVE ROOM FOR THE NEW STUFF!!
WWW.CASEYANDKYLECOMICS.COM

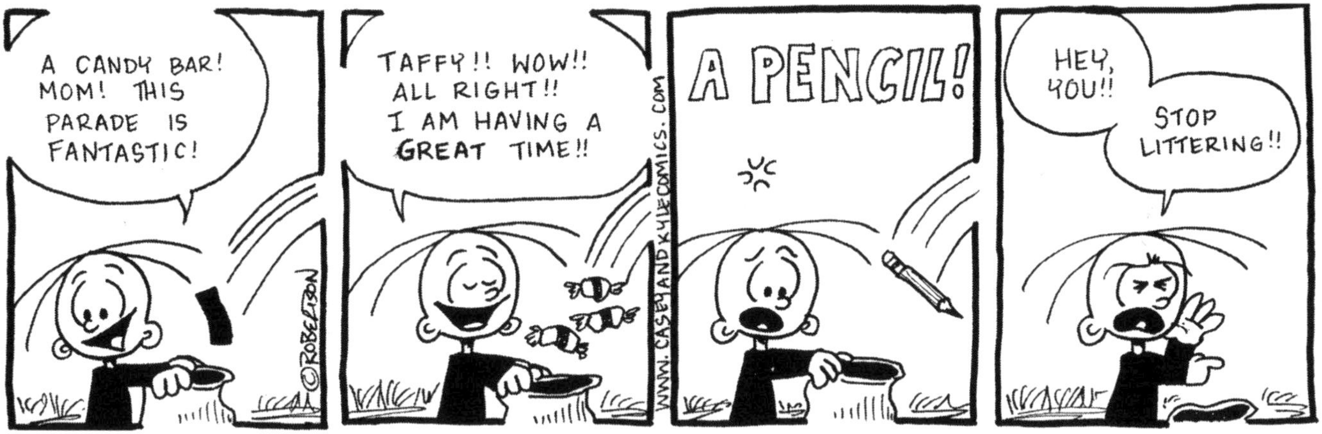
A CANDY BAR! MOM! THIS PARADE IS FANTASTIC!
TAFFY!! WOW!! ALL RIGHT!! I AM HAVING A GREAT TIME!!
WWW.CASEYANDKYLECOMICS.COM
A PENCIL!
HEY, YOU!!
STOP LITTERING!!

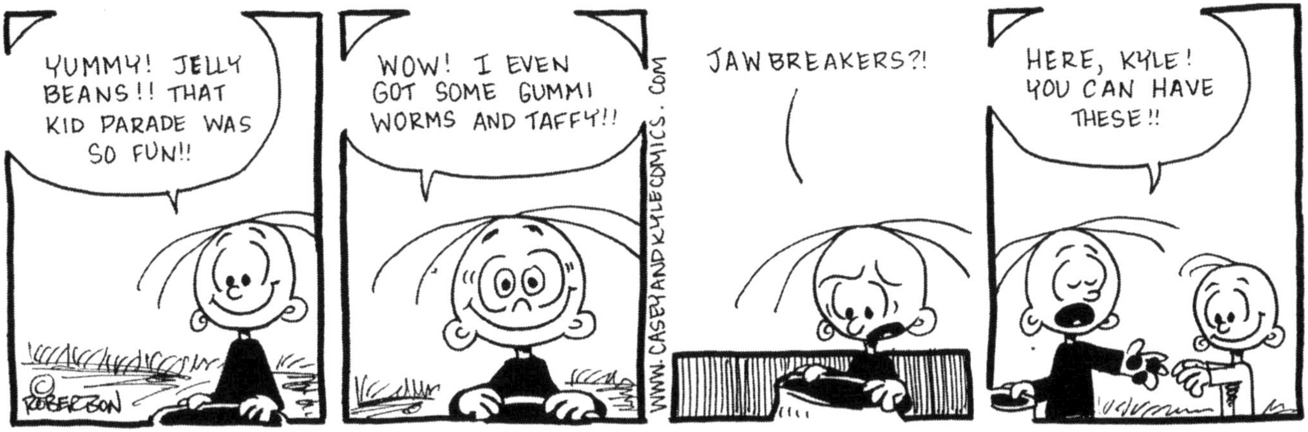
YUMMY! JELLY BEANS!! THAT KID PARADE WAS SO FUN!!
WOW! I EVEN GOT SOME GUMMI WORMS AND TAFFY!!
WWW.CASEYANDKYLECOMICS.COM
JAWBREAKERS?!
HERE, KYLE! YOU CAN HAVE THESE!!

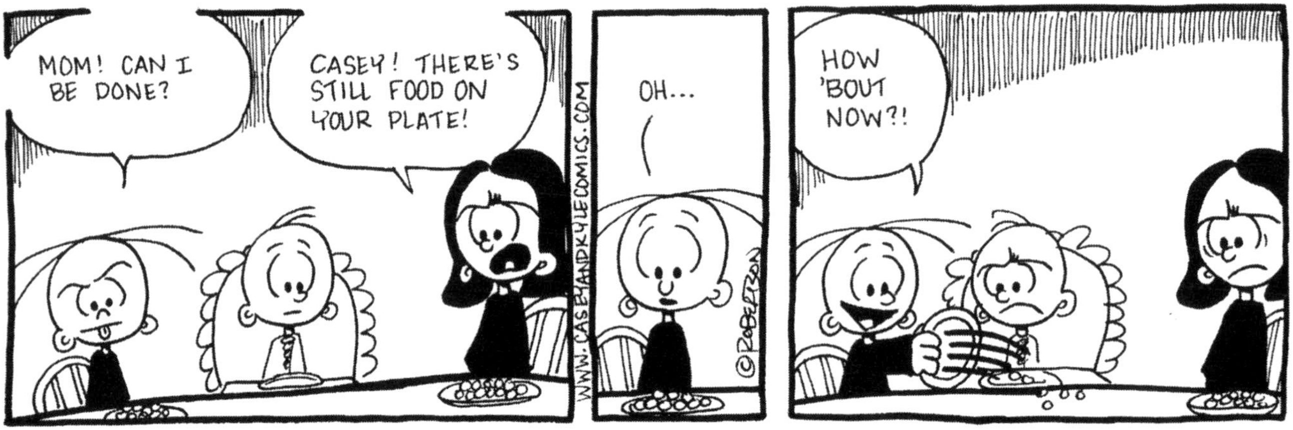
MOM! CAN I BE DONE?
CASEY! THERE'S STILL FOOD ON YOUR PLATE!
WWW.CASEYANDKYLECOMICS.COM
OH...
©ROBERTSON
HOW 'BOUT NOW?!

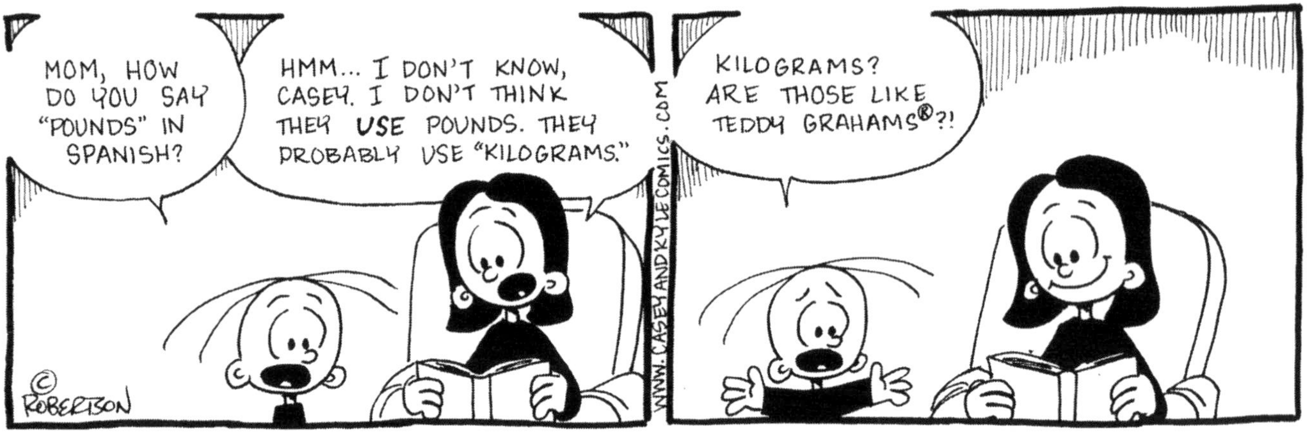
MOM, HOW DO YOU SAY "POUNDS" IN SPANISH?
HMM... I DON'T KNOW, CASEY. I DON'T THINK THEY **USE** POUNDS. THEY PROBABLY USE "KILOGRAMS."
©ROBERTSON
WWW.CASEYANDKYLECOMICS.COM
KILOGRAMS? ARE THOSE LIKE TEDDY GRAHAMS®?!

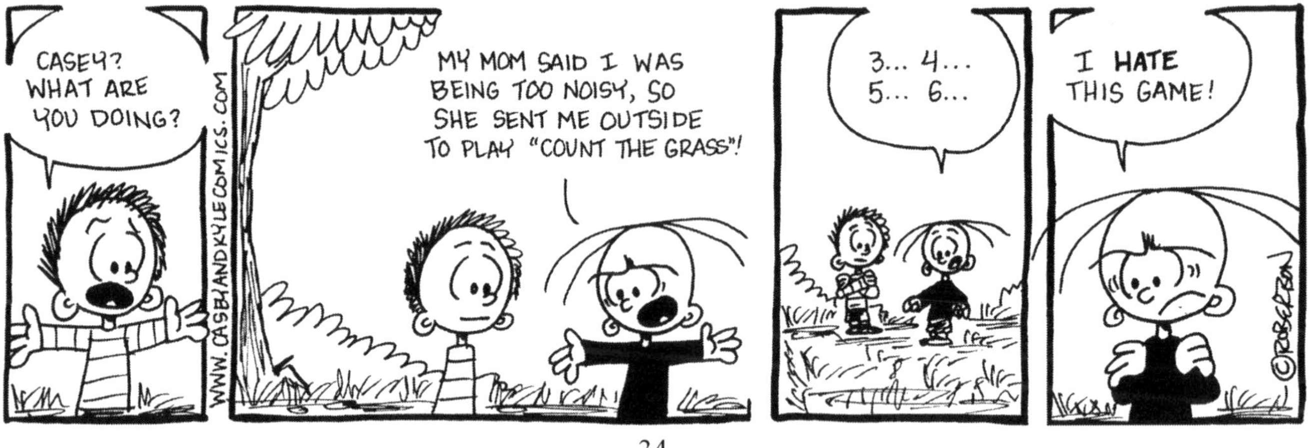
CASEY? WHAT ARE YOU DOING?
WWW.CASEYANDKYLECOMICS.COM
MY MOM SAID I WAS BEING TOO NOISY, SO SHE SENT ME OUTSIDE TO PLAY "COUNT THE GRASS"!
3... 4... 5... 6...
I **HATE** THIS GAME!
©ROBERTSON

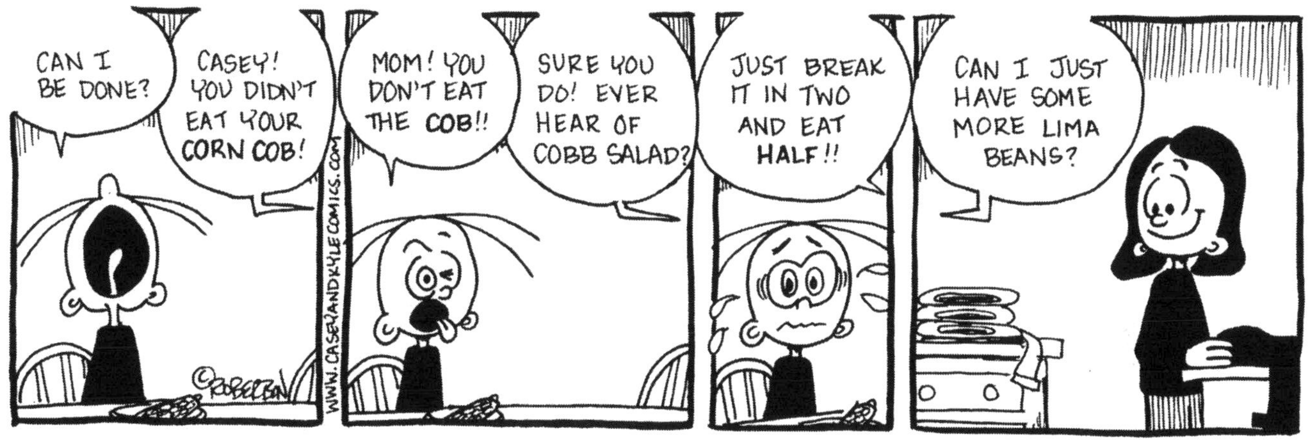
CAN I BE DONE?
CASEY! YOU DIDN'T EAT YOUR CORN COB!
©ROBERTSON
WWW.CASEYANDKYLECOMICS.COM
MOM! YOU DON'T EAT THE COB!!
SURE YOU DO! EVER HEAR OF COBB SALAD?
JUST BREAK IT IN TWO AND EAT HALF!!
CAN I JUST HAVE SOME MORE LIMA BEANS?

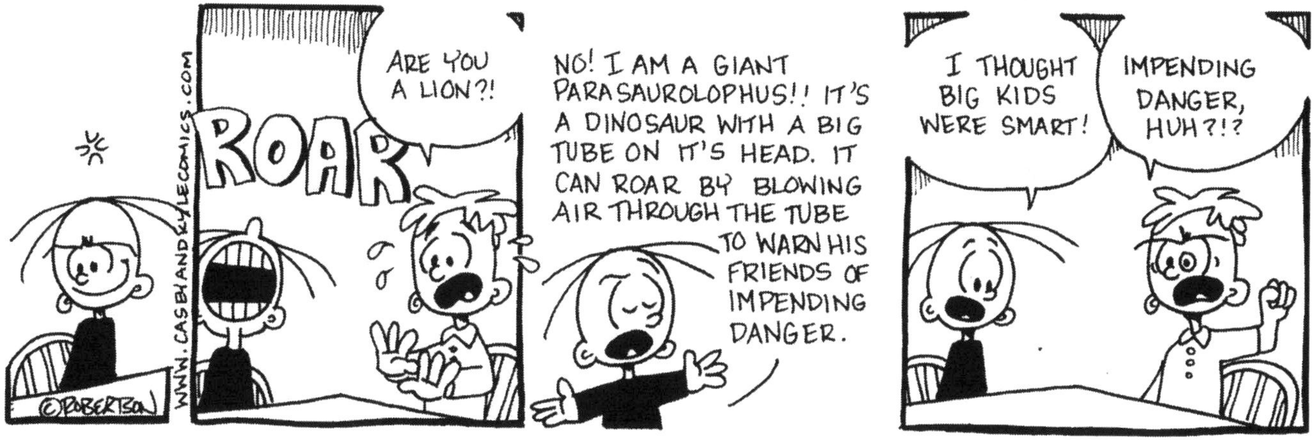
©ROBERTSON
WWW.CASEYANDKYLECOMICS.COM
ROAR
ARE YOU A LION?!
NO! I AM A GIANT PARASAUROLOPHUS!! IT'S A DINOSAUR WITH A BIG TUBE ON IT'S HEAD. IT CAN ROAR BY BLOWING AIR THROUGH THE TUBE TO WARN HIS FRIENDS OF IMPENDING DANGER.
I THOUGHT BIG KIDS WERE SMART!
IMPENDING DANGER, HUH?!?

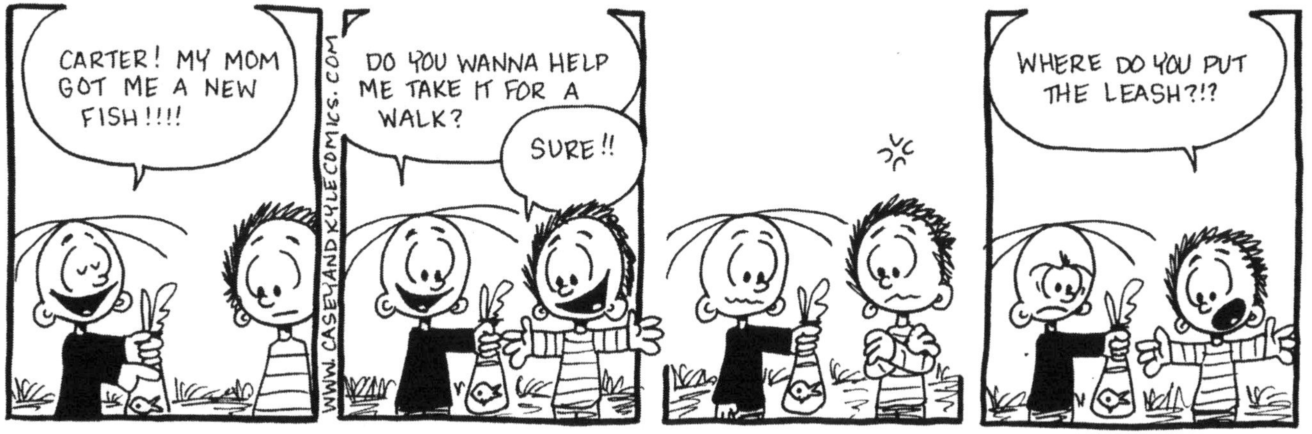
CARTER! MY MOM GOT ME A NEW FISH!!!!
WWW.CASEYANDKYLECOMICS.COM
DO YOU WANNA HELP ME TAKE IT FOR A WALK?
SURE!!
WHERE DO YOU PUT THE LEASH?!?

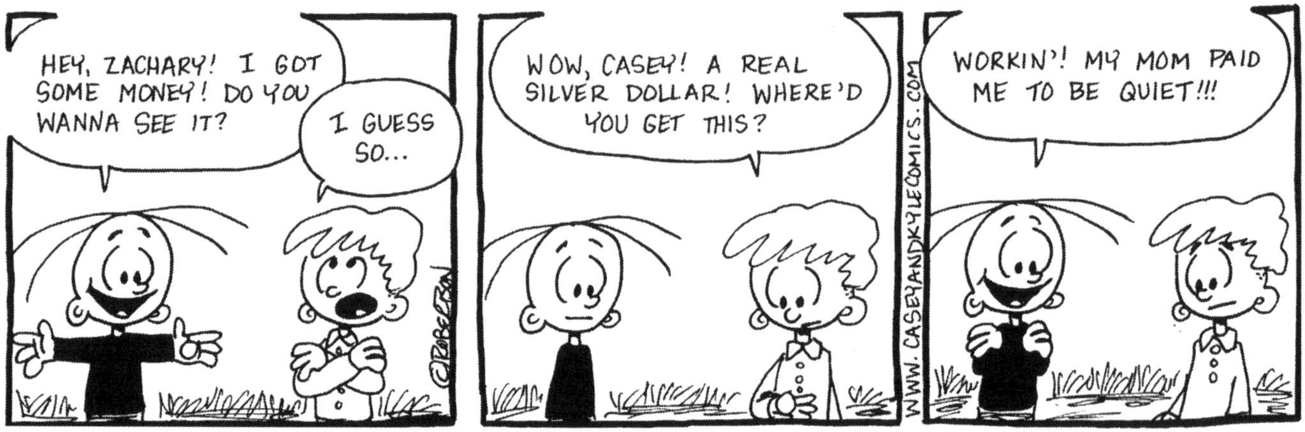
HEY, ZACHARY! I GOT SOME MONEY! DO YOU WANNA SEE IT?
I GUESS SO...
WOW, CASEY! A REAL SILVER DOLLAR! WHERE'D YOU GET THIS?
WWW.CASEYANDKYLECOMICS.COM
WORKIN'! MY MOM PAID ME TO BE QUIET!!!

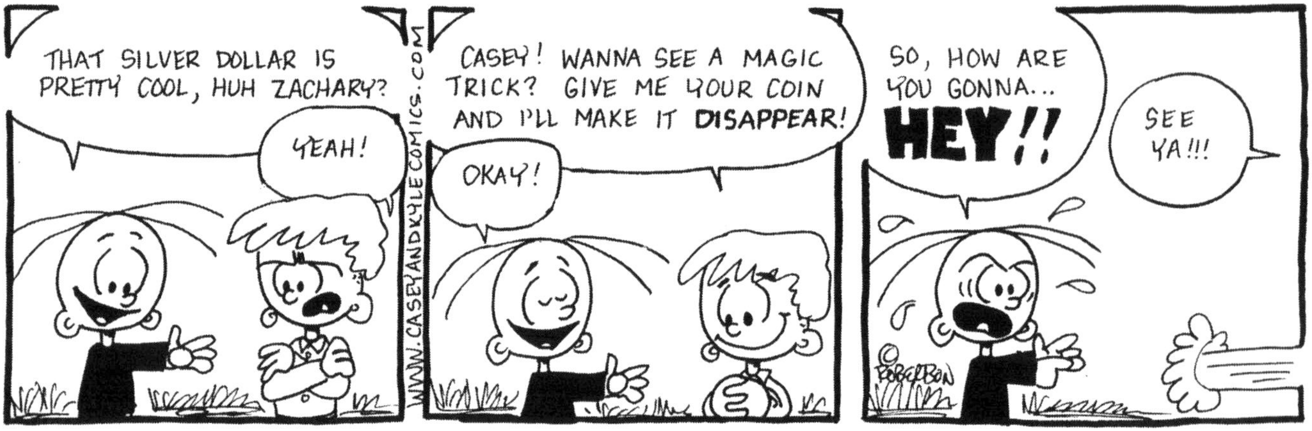
THAT SILVER DOLLAR IS PRETTY COOL, HUH ZACHARY?
YEAH!
WWW.CASEYANDKYLECOMICS.COM
CASEY! WANNA SEE A MAGIC TRICK? GIVE ME YOUR COIN AND I'LL MAKE IT **DISAPPEAR**!
OKAY!
SO, HOW ARE YOU GONNA...
HEY!!
SEE YA!!!

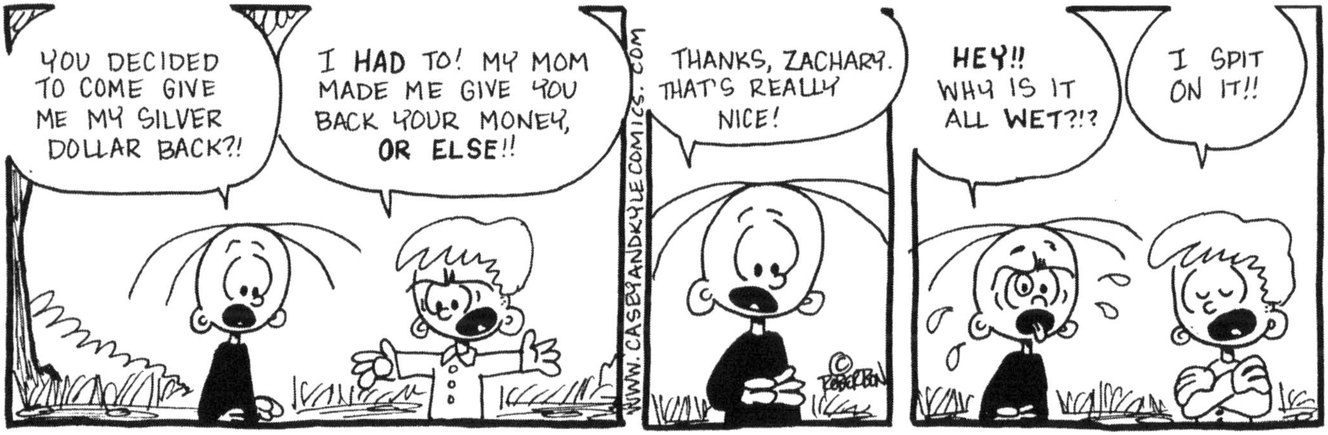
YOU DECIDED TO COME GIVE ME MY SILVER DOLLAR BACK?!
I **HAD** TO! MY MOM MADE ME GIVE YOU BACK YOUR MONEY, **OR ELSE**!!
WWW.CASEYANDKYLECOMICS.COM
THANKS, ZACHARY. THAT'S REALLY NICE!
HEY!! WHY IS IT ALL **WET**?!?
I SPIT ON IT!!

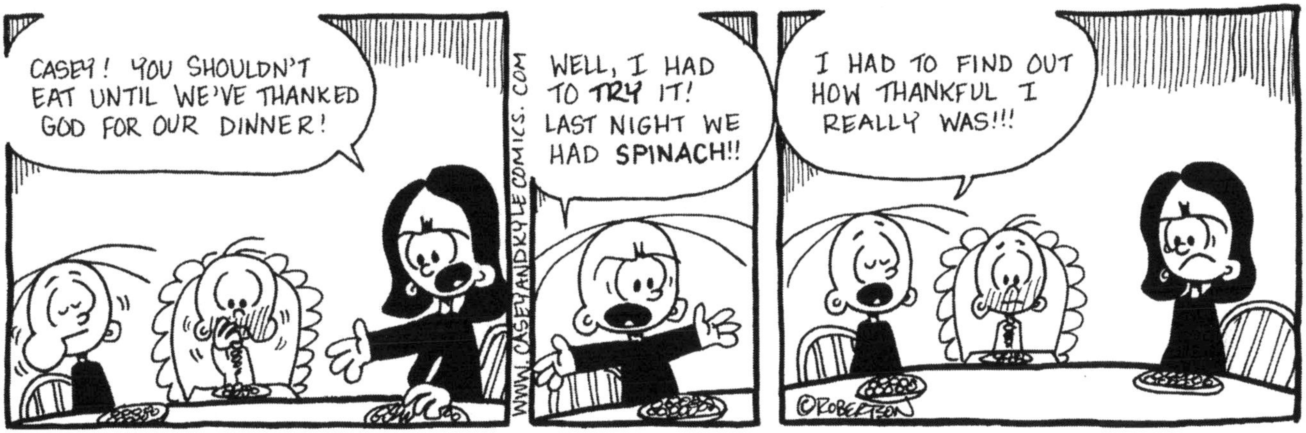
CASEY! YOU SHOULDN'T EAT UNTIL WE'VE THANKED GOD FOR OUR DINNER!
WWW.CASEYANDKYLECOMICS.COM
WELL, I HAD TO **TRY** IT! LAST NIGHT WE HAD **SPINACH**!!
I HAD TO FIND OUT HOW THANKFUL I REALLY WAS!!!
©ROBERTSON

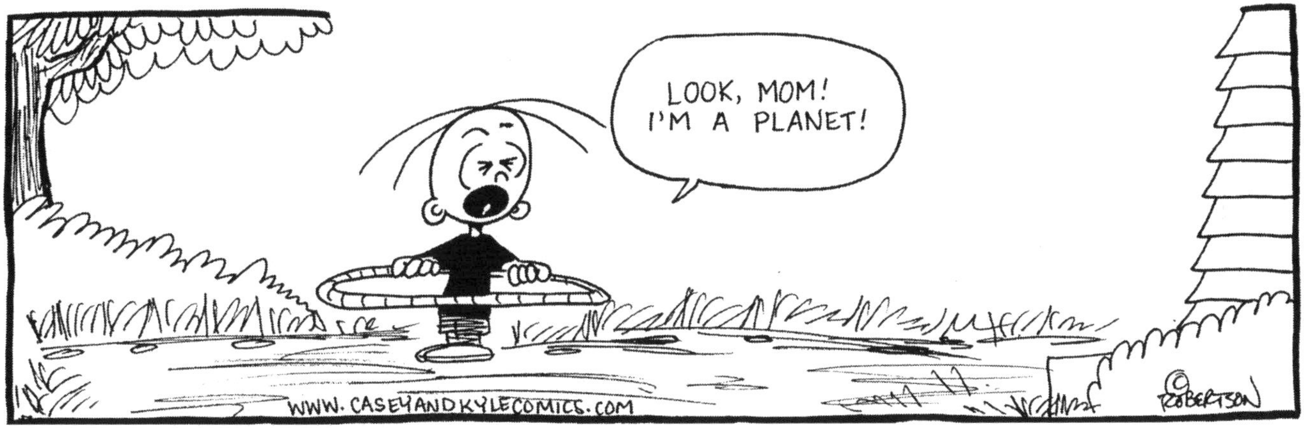
LOOK, MOM! I'M A PLANET!
WWW.CASEYANDKYLECOMICS.COM
©ROBERTSON

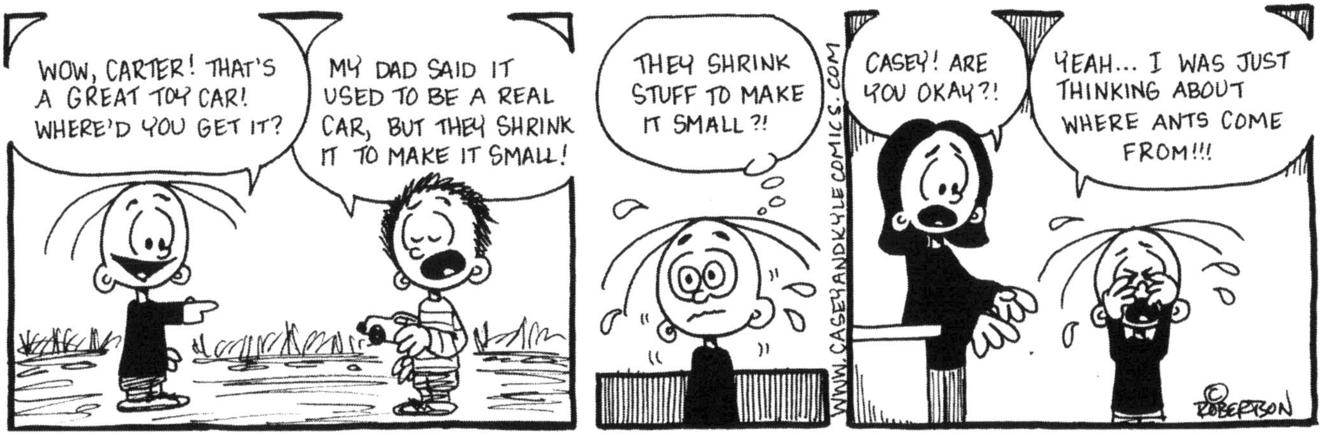
WOW, CARTER! THAT'S A GREAT TOY CAR! WHERE'D YOU GET IT?
MY DAD SAID IT USED TO BE A REAL CAR, BUT THEY SHRINK IT TO MAKE IT SMALL!
THEY SHRINK STUFF TO MAKE IT SMALL?!
WWW.CASEYANDKYLECOMICS.COM
CASEY! ARE YOU OKAY?!
YEAH... I WAS JUST THINKING ABOUT WHERE ANTS COME FROM!!!
©ROBERTSON

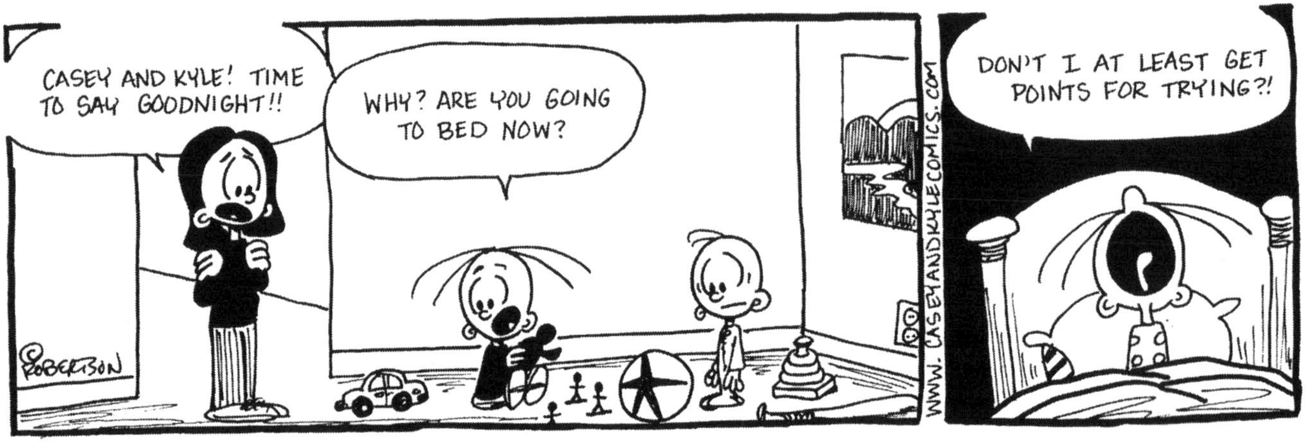

CASEY AND KYLE! TIME TO SAY GOODNIGHT!!
WHY? ARE YOU GOING TO BED NOW?
DON'T I AT LEAST GET POINTS FOR TRYING?!
©ROBERTSON
WWW.CASEYANDKYLECOMICS.COM

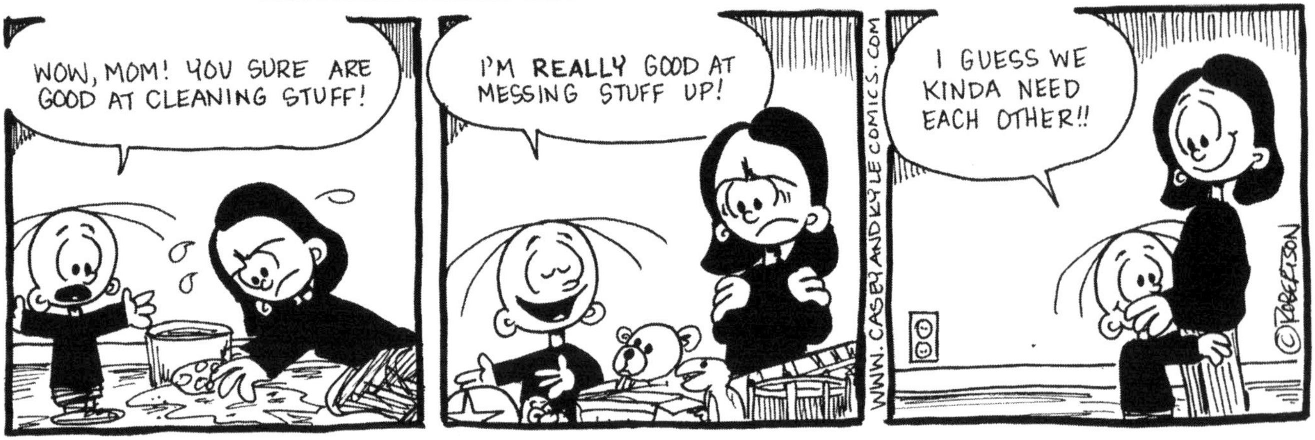

WOW, MOM! YOU SURE ARE GOOD AT CLEANING STUFF!
I'M **REALLY** GOOD AT MESSING STUFF UP!
I GUESS WE KINDA NEED EACH OTHER!!
WWW.CASEYANDKYLECOMICS.COM
©ROBERTSON

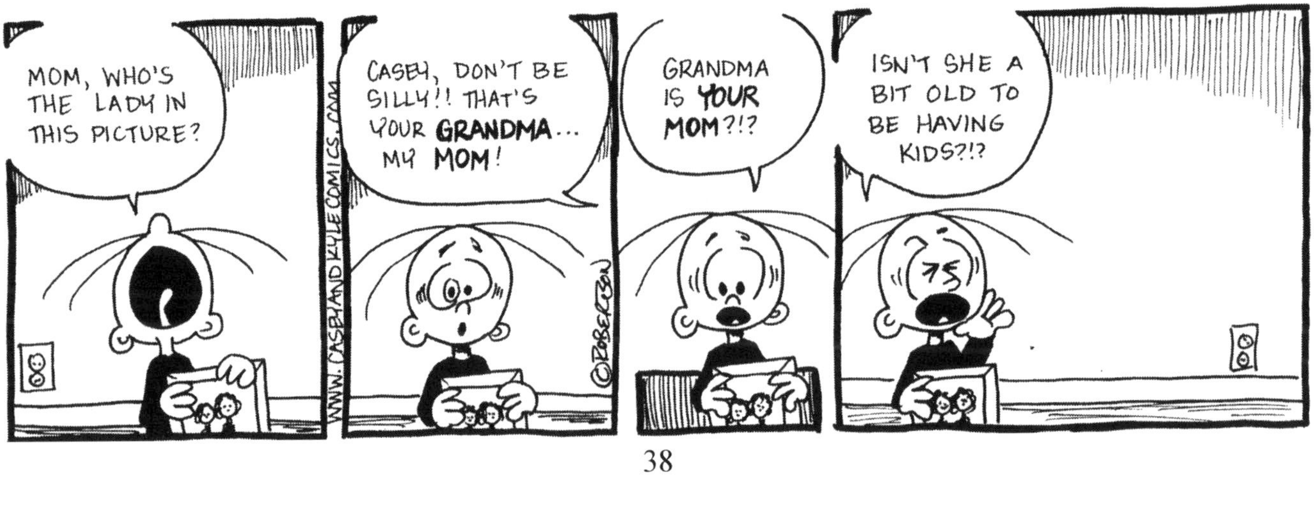

MOM, WHO'S THE LADY IN THIS PICTURE?
CASEY, DON'T BE SILLY!! THAT'S YOUR **GRANDMA**... MY **MOM**!
GRANDMA IS **YOUR MOM**?!?
ISN'T SHE A BIT OLD TO BE HAVING KIDS?!?
WWW.CASEYANDKYLECOMICS.COM
©ROBERTSON

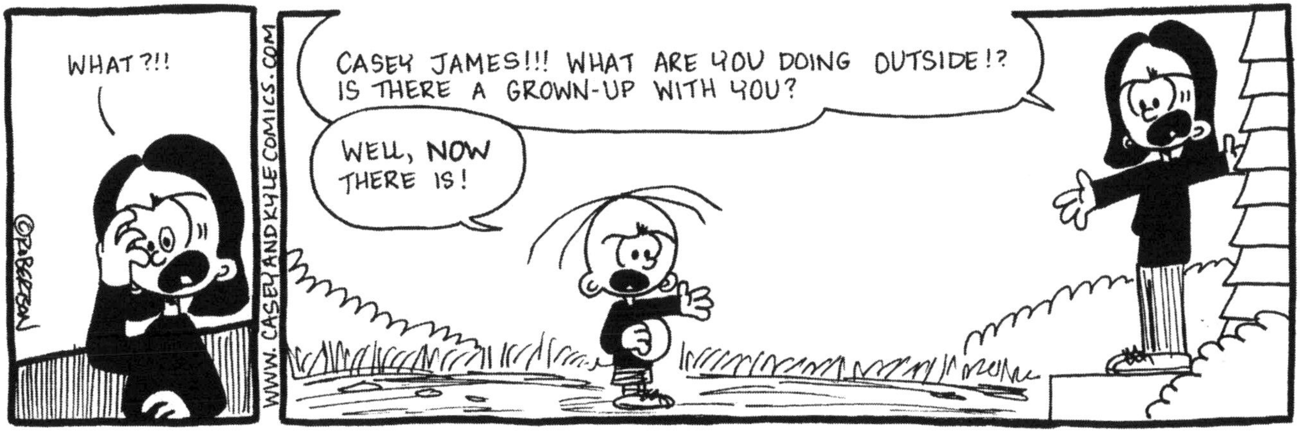
WHAT?!!
©ROBERTSON
WWW.CASEYANDKYLECOMICS.COM
CASEY JAMES!!! WHAT ARE YOU DOING OUTSIDE!? IS THERE A GROWN-UP WITH YOU?
WELL, NOW THERE IS!

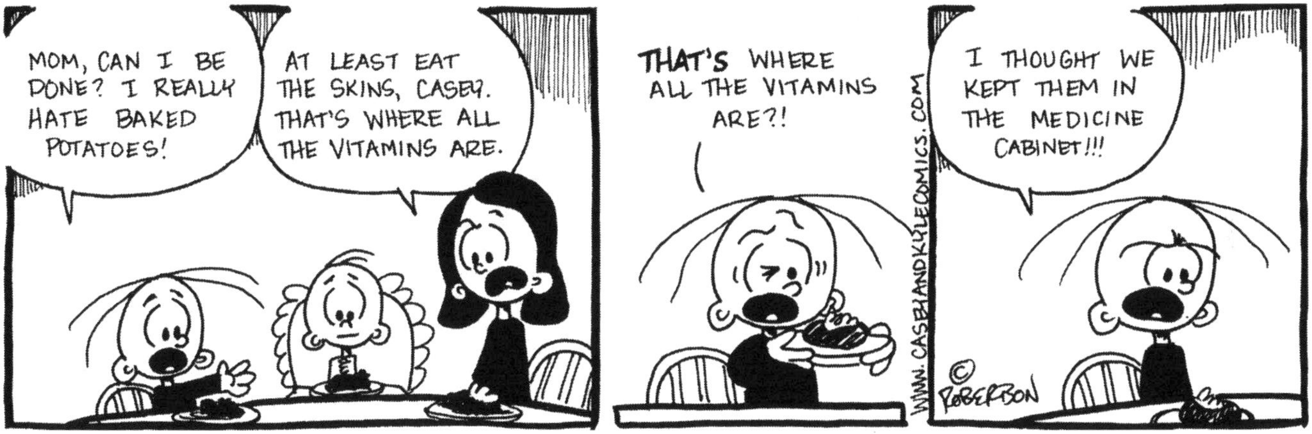
MOM, CAN I BE DONE? I REALLY HATE BAKED POTATOES!
AT LEAST EAT THE SKINS, CASEY. THAT'S WHERE ALL THE VITAMINS ARE.
THAT'S WHERE ALL THE VITAMINS ARE?!
WWW.CASEYANDKYLECOMICS.COM
I THOUGHT WE KEPT THEM IN THE MEDICINE CABINET!!!
© ROBERTSON

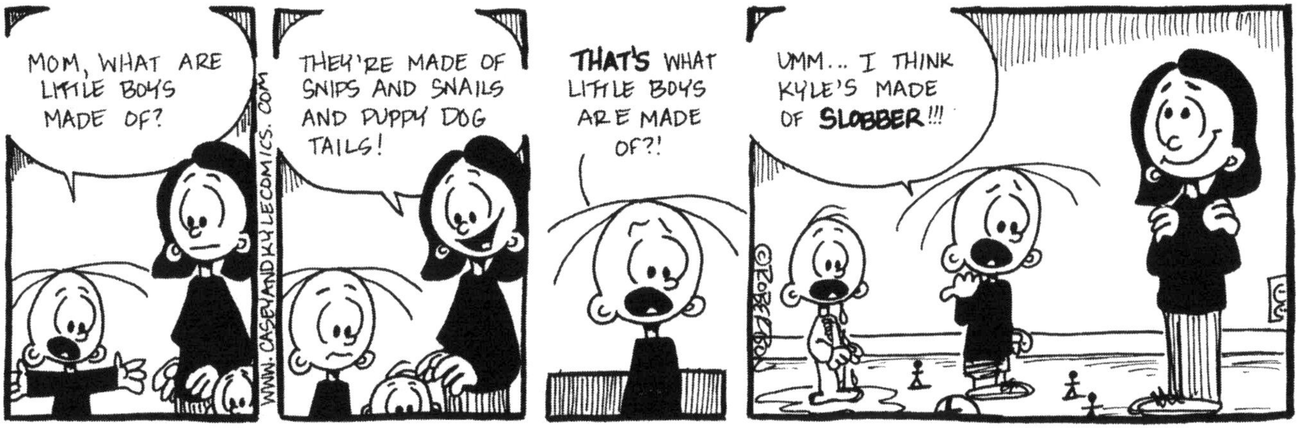
MOM, WHAT ARE LITTLE BOYS MADE OF?
WWW.CASEYANDKYLECOMICS.COM
THEY'RE MADE OF SNIPS AND SNAILS AND PUPPY DOG TAILS!
THAT'S WHAT LITTLE BOYS ARE MADE OF?!
UMM... I THINK KYLE'S MADE OF SLOBBER!!!
©ROBERTSON

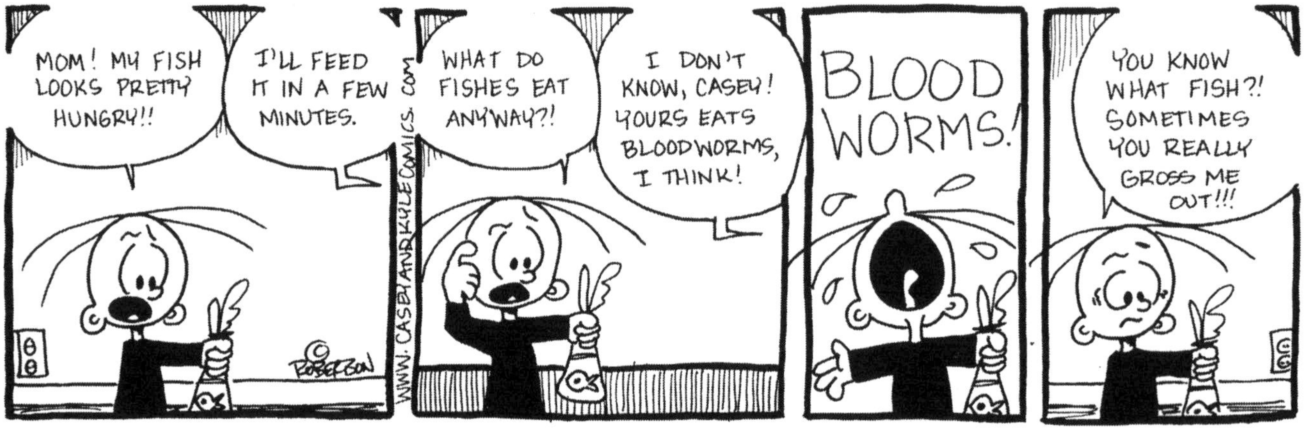
MOM! MY FISH LOOKS PRETTY HUNGRY!!
I'LL FEED IT IN A FEW MINUTES.
©ROBERTSON
WWW.CASEYANDKYLECOMICS.COM
WHAT DO FISHES EAT ANYWAY?!
I DON'T KNOW, CASEY! YOURS EATS BLOODWORMS, I THINK!
BLOOD WORMS!
YOU KNOW WHAT FISH?! SOMETIMES YOU REALLY GROSS ME OUT!!!

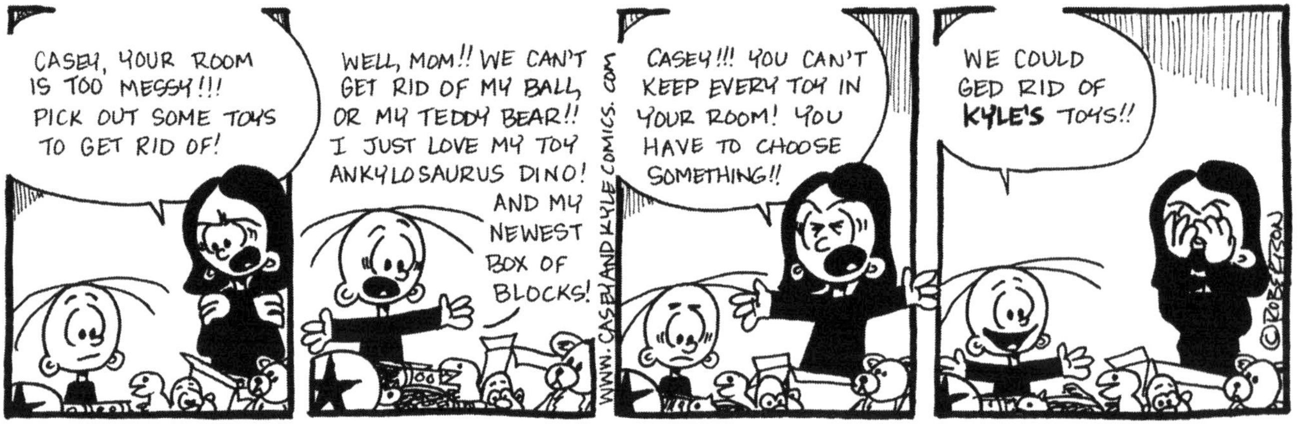
CASEY, YOUR ROOM IS TOO MESSY!!! PICK OUT SOME TOYS TO GET RID OF!
WELL, MOM!! WE CAN'T GET RID OF MY BALL, OR MY TEDDY BEAR!! I JUST LOVE MY TOY ANKYLOSAURUS DINO!
AND MY NEWEST BOX OF BLOCKS!
WWW.CASEYANDKYLECOMICS.COM
CASEY!!! YOU CAN'T KEEP EVERY TOY IN YOUR ROOM! YOU HAVE TO CHOOSE SOMETHING!!
WE COULD GED RID OF **KYLE'S** TOYS!!
©ROBERTSON

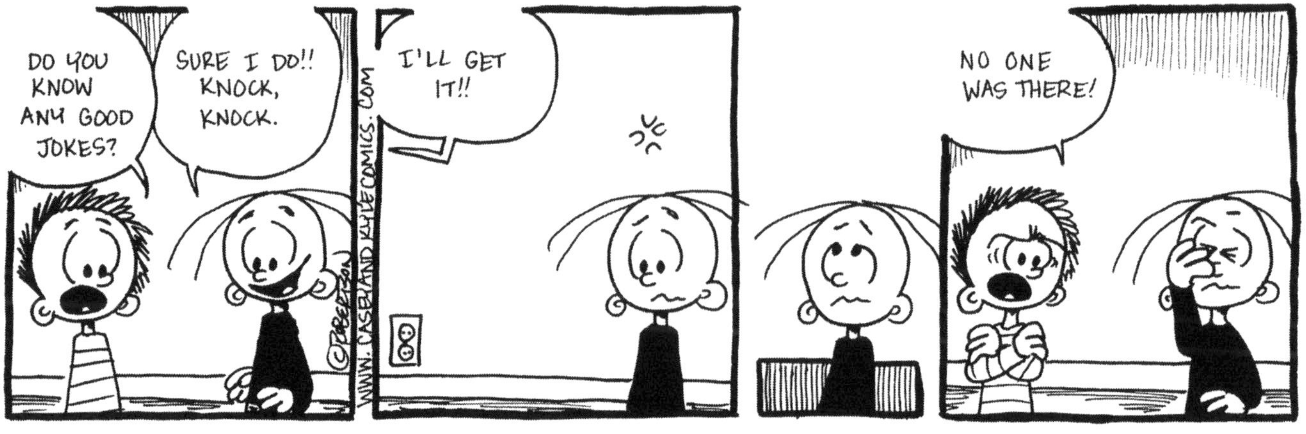
DO YOU KNOW ANY GOOD JOKES?
SURE I DO!! KNOCK, KNOCK.
©ROBERTSON
WWW.CASEYANDKYLECOMICS.COM
I'LL GET IT!!
NO ONE WAS THERE!

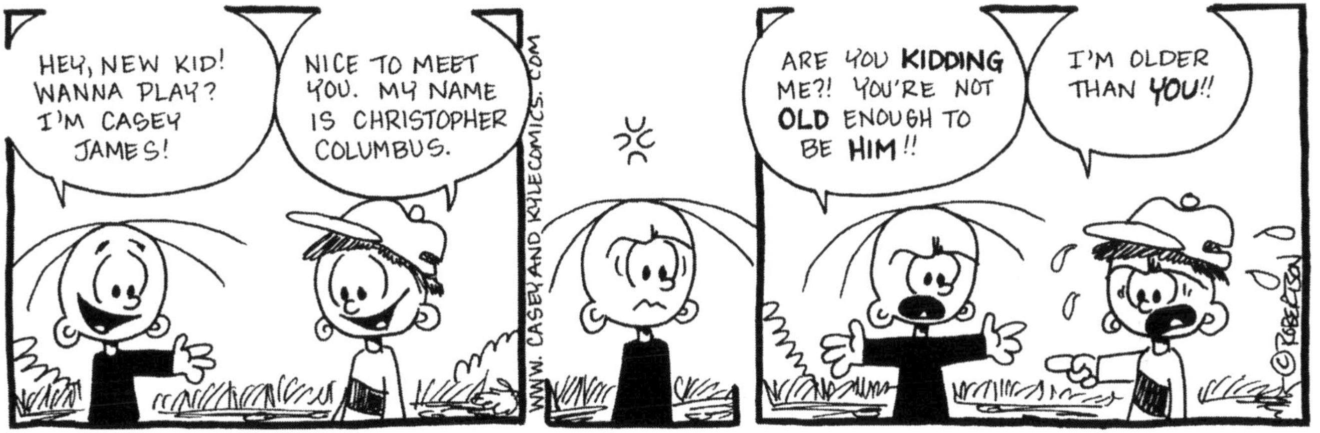
HEY, NEW KID! WANNA PLAY? I'M CASEY JAMES!
NICE TO MEET YOU. MY NAME IS CHRISTOPHER COLUMBUS.
WWW.CASEYANDKYLECOMICS.COM
ARE YOU **KIDDING** ME?! YOU'RE NOT **OLD** ENOUGH TO BE **HIM**!!
I'M OLDER THAN **YOU**!!
© ROBERTSON

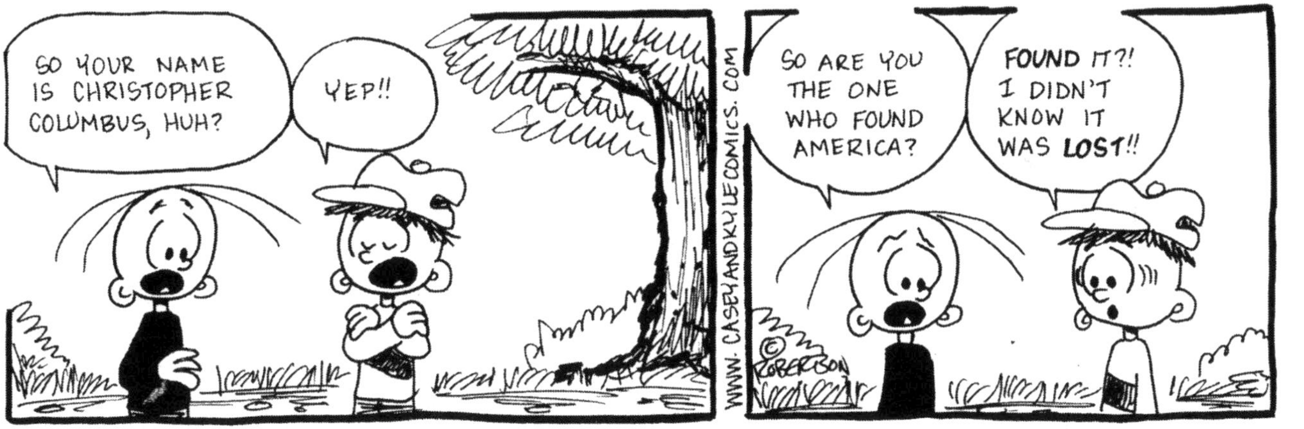
SO YOUR NAME IS CHRISTOPHER COLUMBUS, HUH?
YEP!!
WWW.CASEYANDKYLECOMICS.COM
© ROBERTSON
SO ARE YOU THE ONE WHO FOUND AMERICA?
FOUND IT?! I DIDN'T KNOW IT WAS **LOST**!!

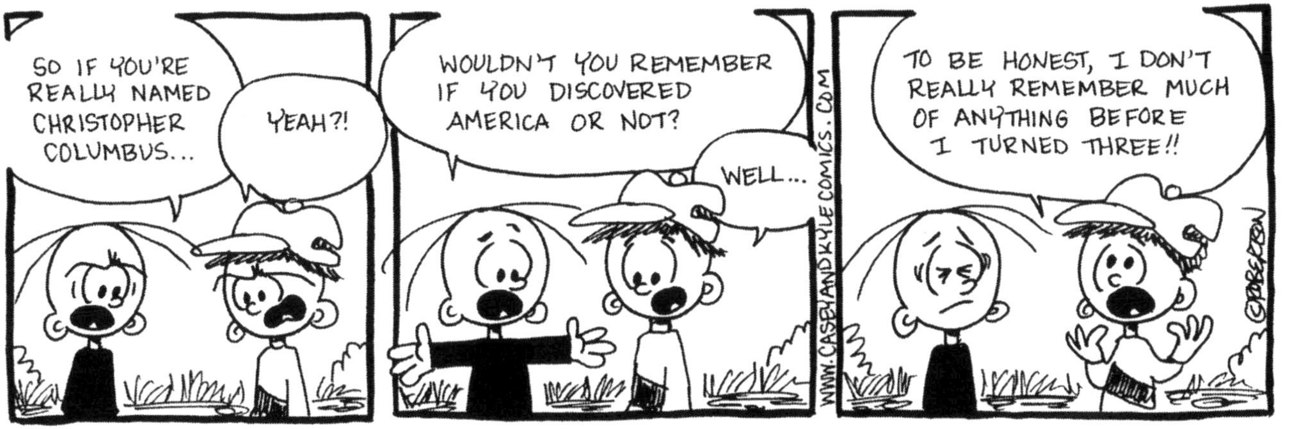
SO IF YOU'RE REALLY NAMED CHRISTOPHER COLUMBUS...
YEAH?!
WOULDN'T YOU REMEMBER IF YOU DISCOVERED AMERICA OR NOT?
WELL...
WWW.CASEYANDKYLECOMICS.COM
TO BE HONEST, I DON'T REALLY REMEMBER MUCH OF ANYTHING BEFORE I TURNED THREE!!
© ROBERTSON

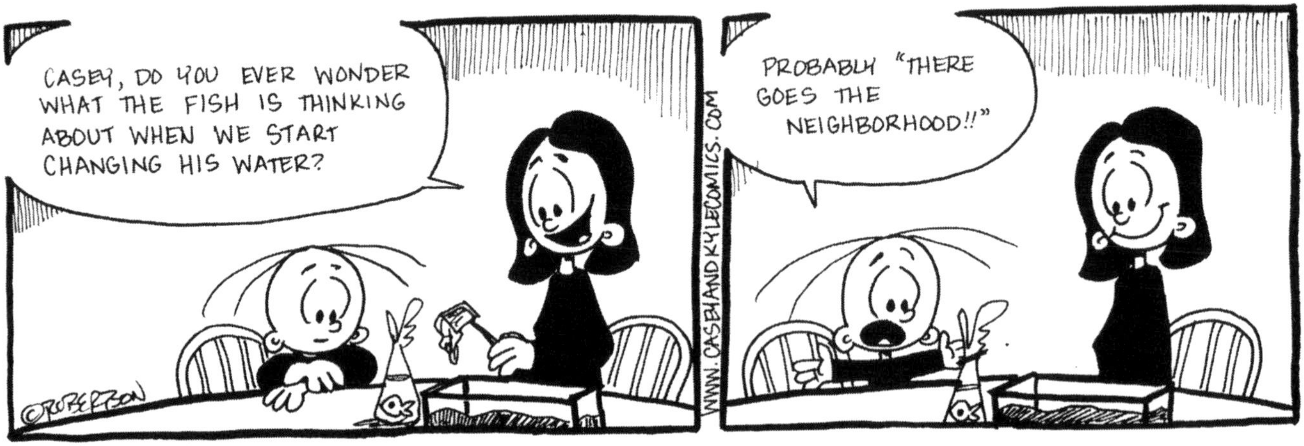
CASEY, DO YOU EVER WONDER WHAT THE FISH IS THINKING ABOUT WHEN WE START CHANGING HIS WATER?
©ROBERTSON
WWW.CASEYANDKYLECOMICS.COM
PROBABLY "THERE GOES THE NEIGHBORHOOD!!"

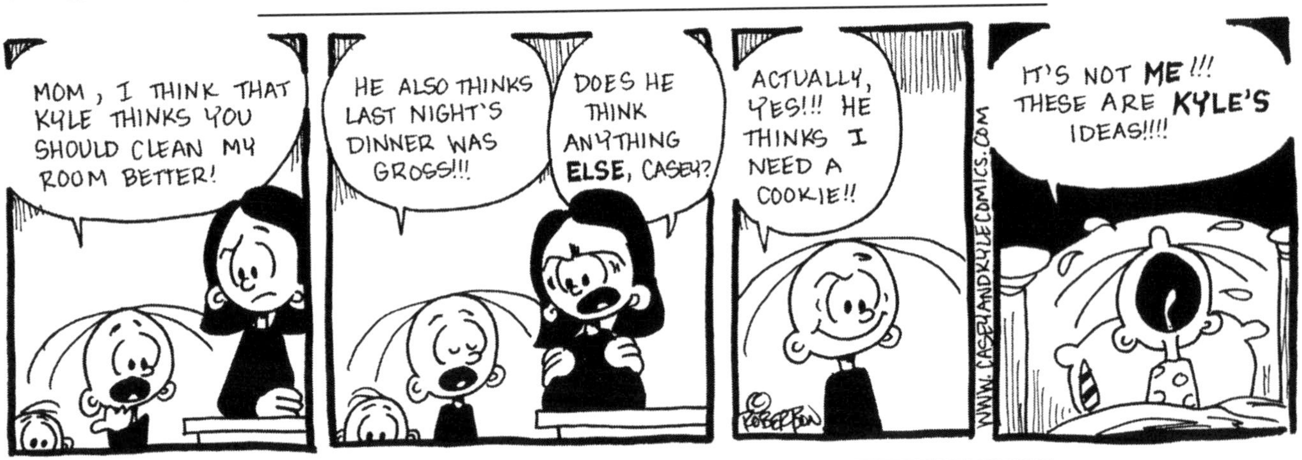
MOM, I THINK THAT KYLE THINKS YOU SHOULD CLEAN MY ROOM BETTER!
HE ALSO THINKS LAST NIGHT'S DINNER WAS GROSS!!!
DOES HE THINK ANYTHING ELSE, CASEY?
ACTUALLY, YES!!! HE THINKS I NEED A COOKIE!!
©ROBERTSON
WWW.CASEYANDKYLECOMICS.COM
IT'S NOT ME!!! THESE ARE KYLE'S IDEAS!!!!

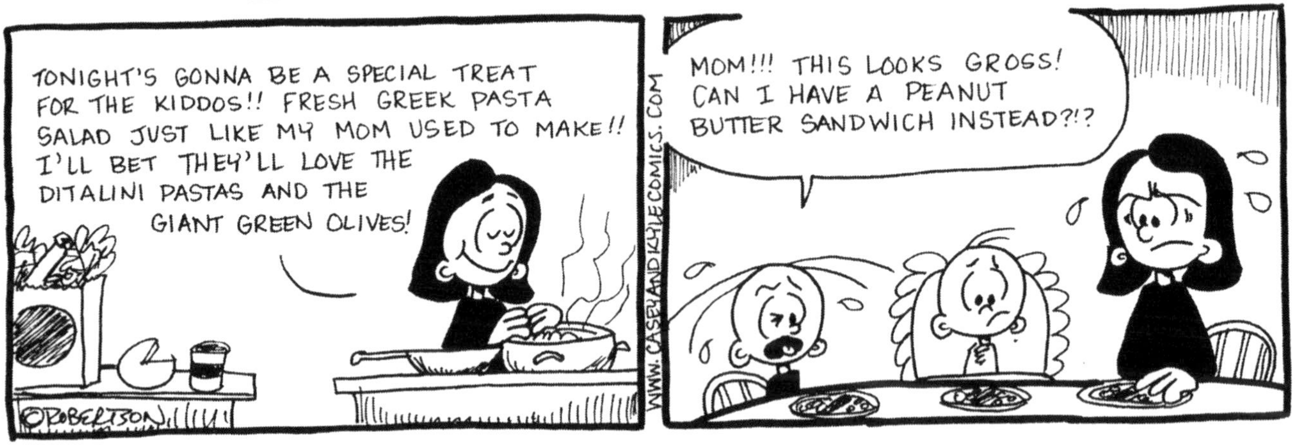
TONIGHT'S GONNA BE A SPECIAL TREAT FOR THE KIDDOS!! FRESH GREEK PASTA SALAD JUST LIKE MY MOM USED TO MAKE!! I'LL BET THEY'LL LOVE THE DITALINI PASTAS AND THE GIANT GREEN OLIVES!
©ROBERTSON
WWW.CASEYANDKYLECOMICS.COM
MOM!!! THIS LOOKS GROSS! CAN I HAVE A PEANUT BUTTER SANDWICH INSTEAD?!?

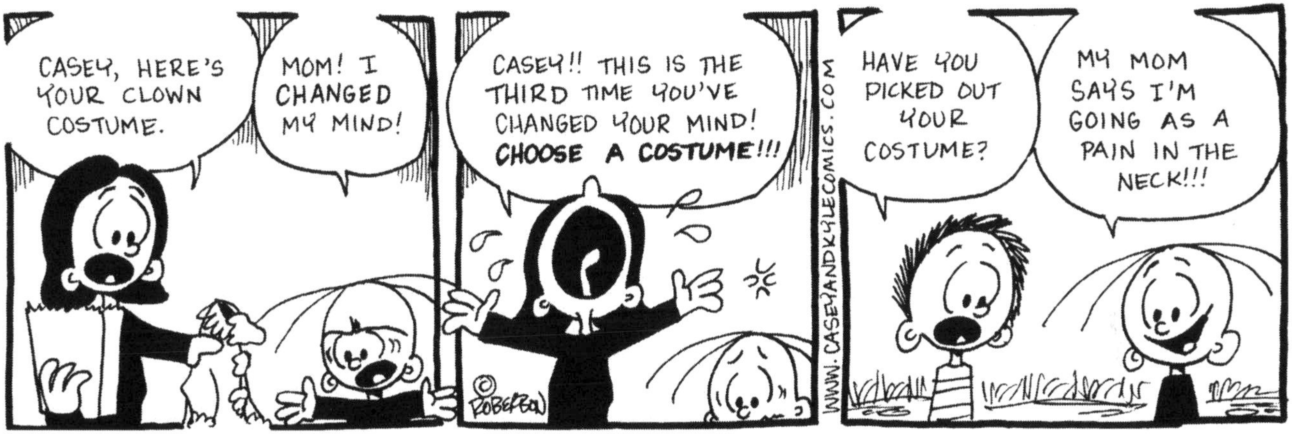
CASEY, HERE'S YOUR CLOWN COSTUME.
MOM! I CHANGED MY MIND!
CASEY!! THIS IS THE THIRD TIME YOU'VE CHANGED YOUR MIND! CHOOSE A COSTUME!!!
WWW.CASEYANDKYLECOMICS.COM
HAVE YOU PICKED OUT YOUR COSTUME?
MY MOM SAYS I'M GOING AS A PAIN IN THE NECK!!!

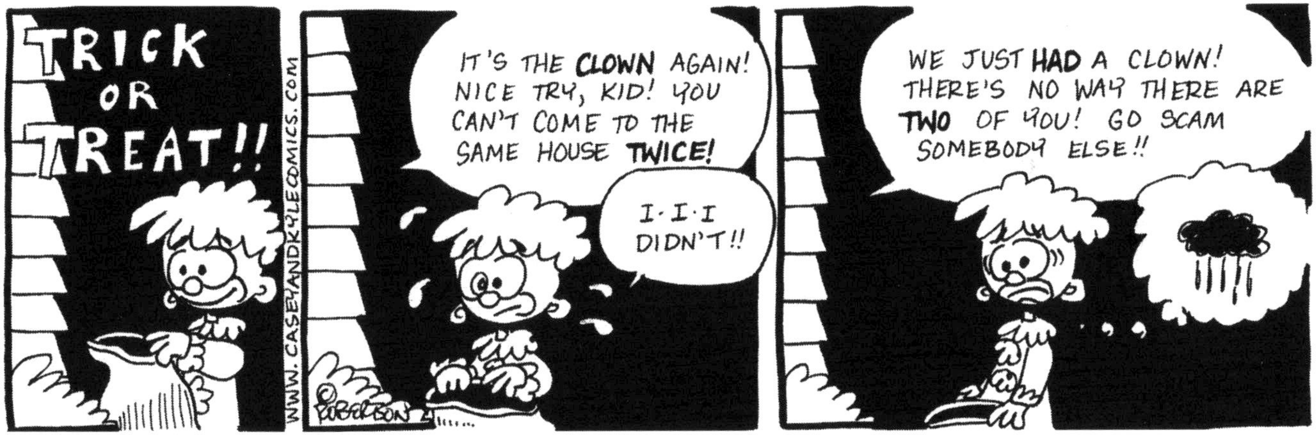
TRICK OR TREAT!!
WWW.CASEYANDKYLECOMICS.COM
IT'S THE CLOWN AGAIN! NICE TRY, KID! YOU CAN'T COME TO THE SAME HOUSE TWICE!
I-I-I DIDN'T!!
WE JUST HAD A CLOWN! THERE'S NO WAY THERE ARE TWO OF YOU! GO SCAM SOMEBODY ELSE!!

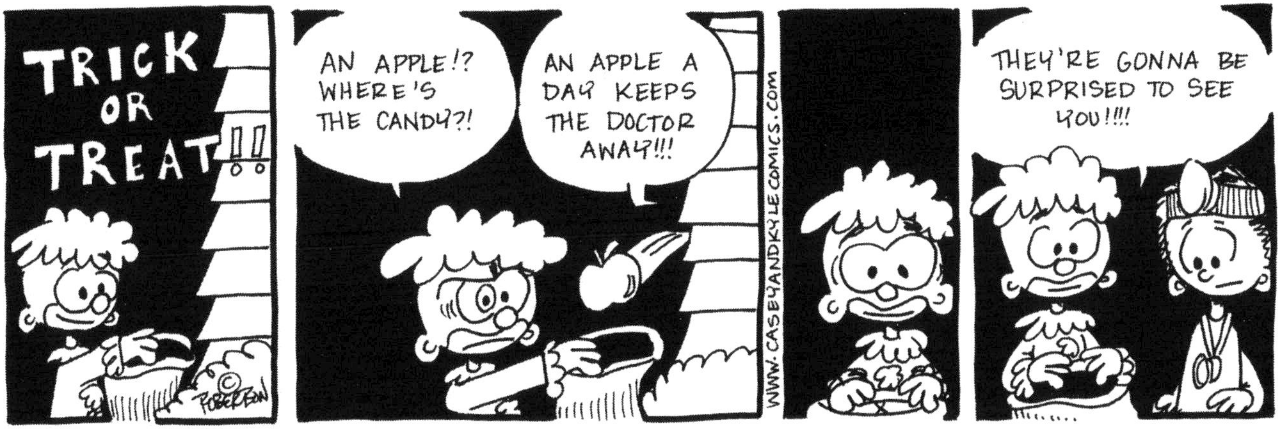
TRICK OR TREAT!!
AN APPLE!? WHERE'S THE CANDY?!
AN APPLE A DAY KEEPS THE DOCTOR AWAY!!!
WWW.CASEYANDKYLECOMICS.COM
THEY'RE GONNA BE SURPRISED TO SEE YOU!!!!

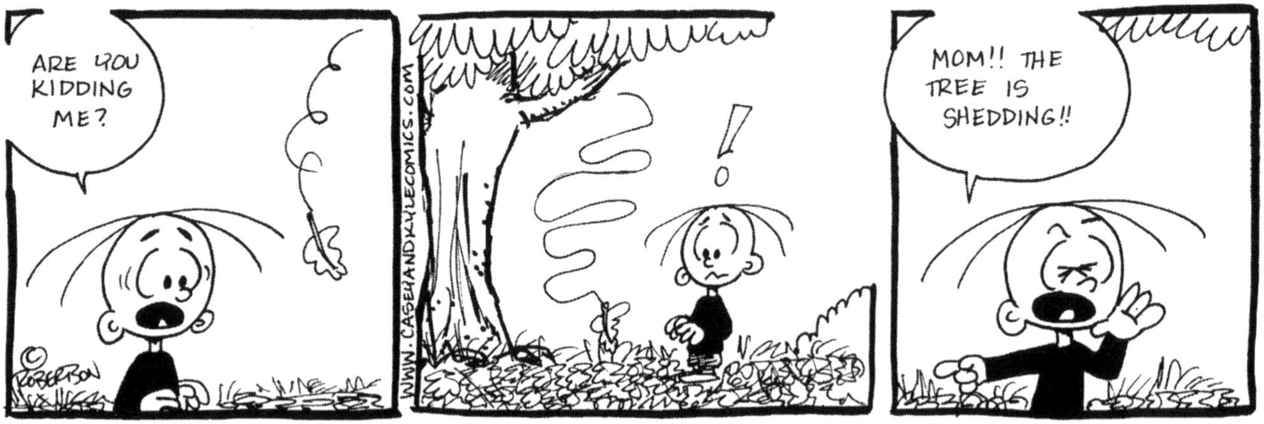
ARE YOU KIDDING ME?
©ROBERTSON
WWW.CASEYANDKYLECOMICS.COM
!
MOM!! THE TREE IS SHEDDING!!

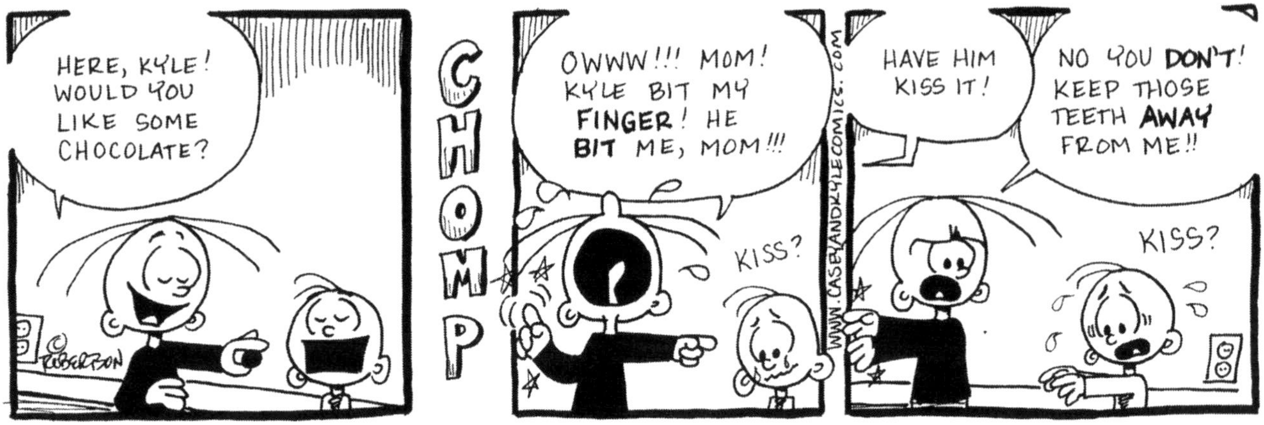
HERE, KYLE! WOULD YOU LIKE SOME CHOCOLATE?
©ROBERTSON
CHOMP
OWWW!!! MOM! KYLE BIT MY FINGER! HE BIT ME, MOM!!!
KISS?
WWW.CASEYANDKYLECOMICS.COM
HAVE HIM KISS IT!
NO YOU DON'T! KEEP THOSE TEETH AWAY FROM ME!!
KISS?

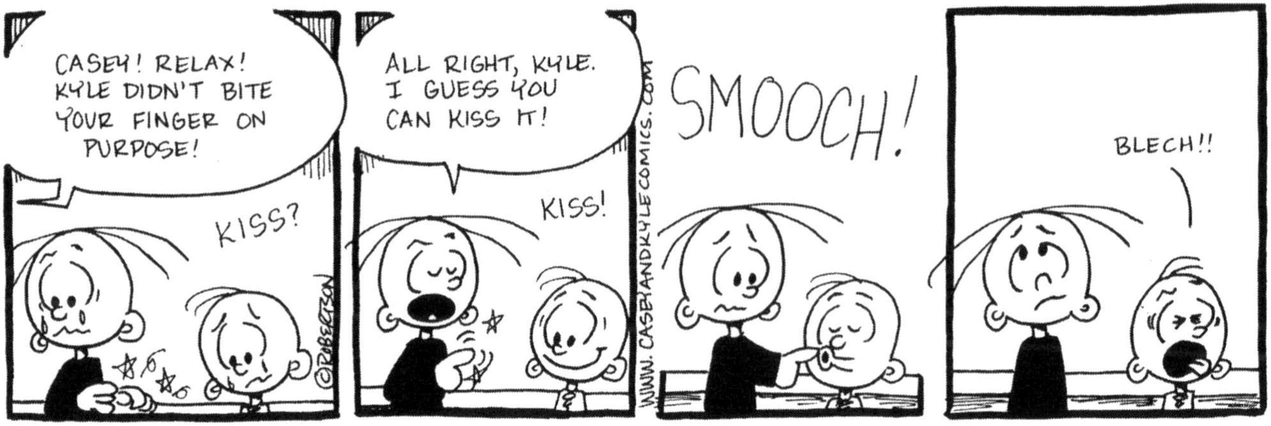
CASEY! RELAX! KYLE DIDN'T BITE YOUR FINGER ON PURPOSE!
KISS?
©ROBERTSON
ALL RIGHT, KYLE. I GUESS YOU CAN KISS IT!
KISS!
WWW.CASEYANDKYLECOMICS.COM
SMOOCH!
BLECH!!

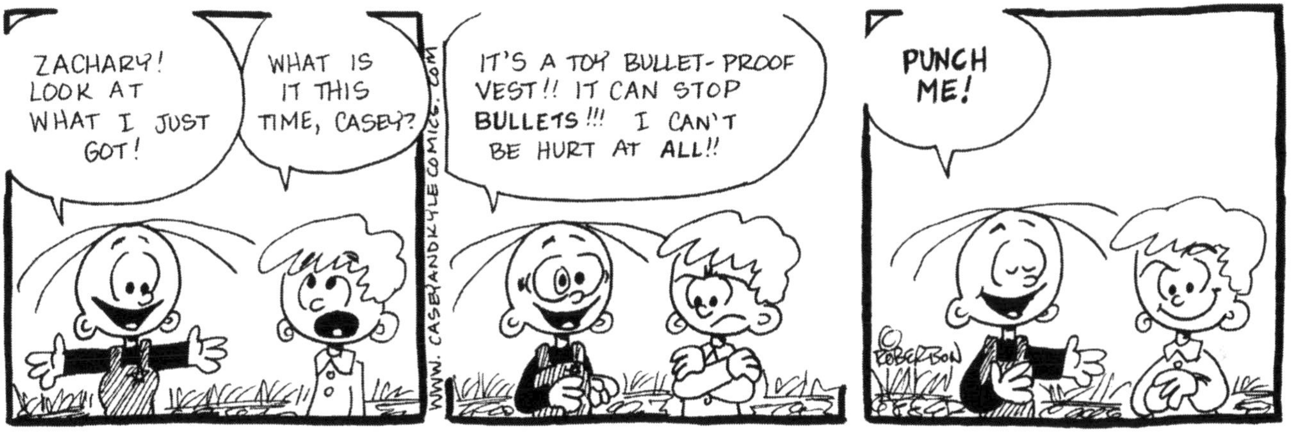
ZACHARY! LOOK AT WHAT I JUST GOT!
WHAT IS IT THIS TIME, CASEY?
WWW.CASEYANDKYLECOMICS.COM
IT'S A TOY BULLET-PROOF VEST!! IT CAN STOP BULLETS!!! I CAN'T BE HURT AT ALL!!
PUNCH ME!
© ROBERTSON

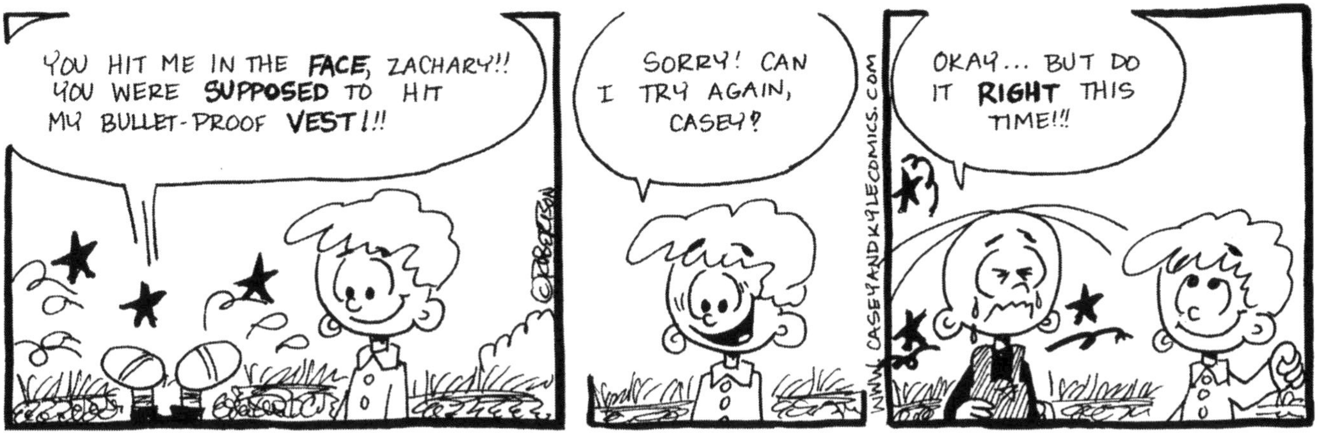
YOU HIT ME IN THE FACE, ZACHARY!! YOU WERE SUPPOSED TO HIT MY BULLET-PROOF VEST!!!
© ROBERTSON
SORRY! CAN I TRY AGAIN, CASEY?
WWW.CASEYANDKYLECOMICS.COM
OKAY... BUT DO IT RIGHT THIS TIME!!!

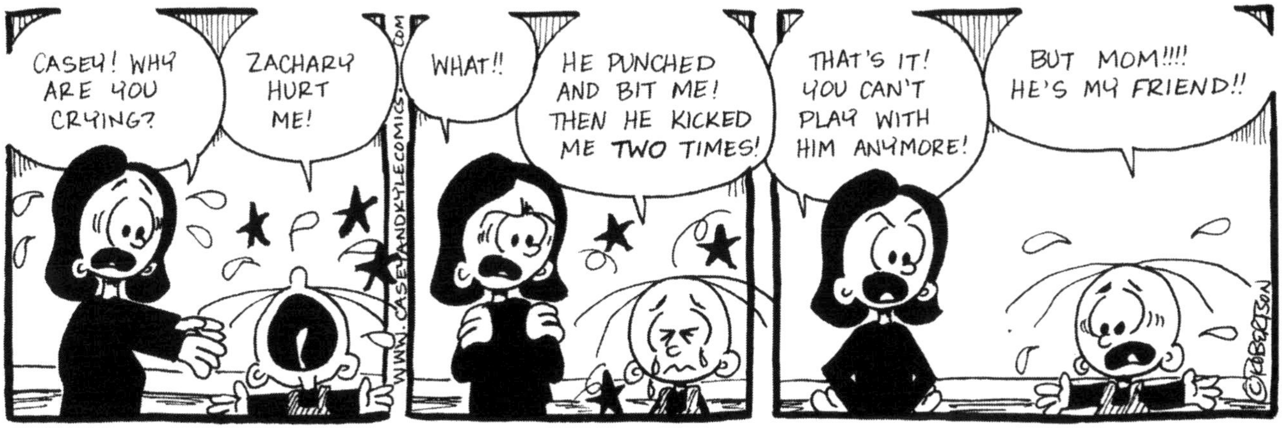
CASEY! WHY ARE YOU CRYING?
ZACHARY HURT ME!
WWW.CASEYANDKYLECOMICS.COM
WHAT!!
HE PUNCHED AND BIT ME! THEN HE KICKED ME TWO TIMES!
THAT'S IT! YOU CAN'T PLAY WITH HIM ANYMORE!
BUT MOM!!!! HE'S MY FRIEND!!
© ROBERTSON

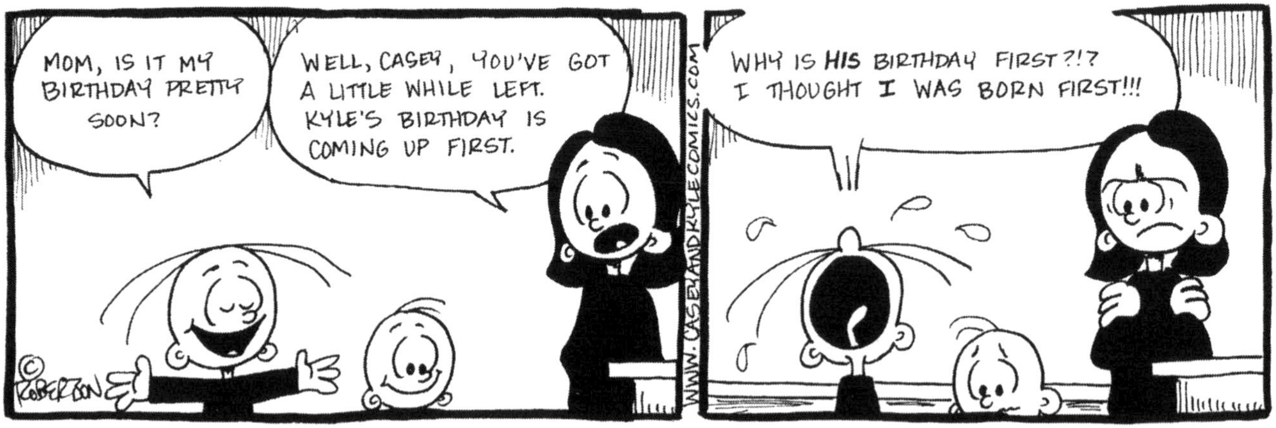
MOM, IS IT MY BIRTHDAY PRETTY SOON?
WELL, CASEY, YOU'VE GOT A LITTLE WHILE LEFT. KYLE'S BIRTHDAY IS COMING UP FIRST.
WWW.CASEYANDKYLECOMICS.COM
WHY IS HIS BIRTHDAY FIRST?!? I THOUGHT I WAS BORN FIRST!!!

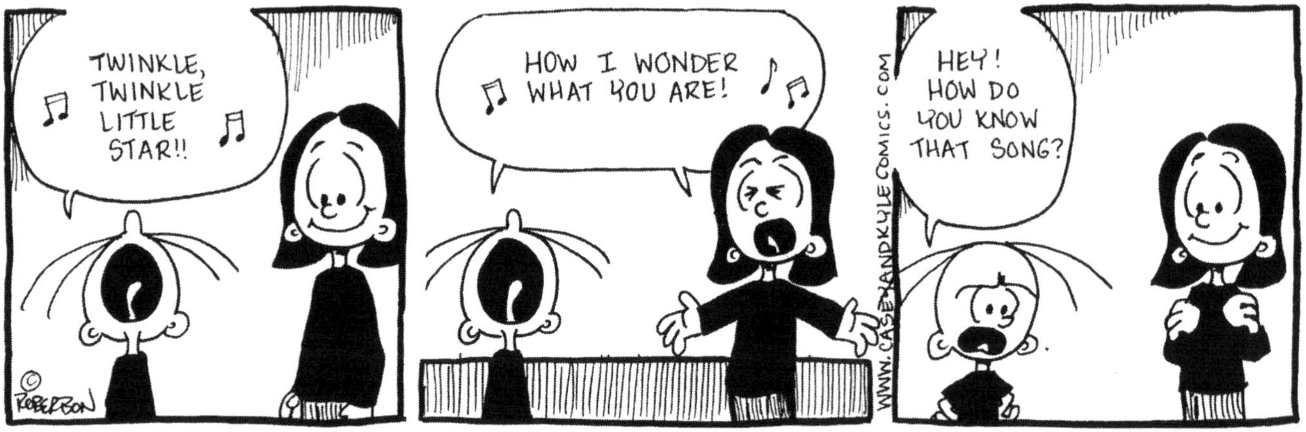
TWINKLE, TWINKLE LITTLE STAR!!
HOW I WONDER WHAT YOU ARE!
WWW.CASEYANDKYLECOMICS.COM
HEY! HOW DO YOU KNOW THAT SONG?

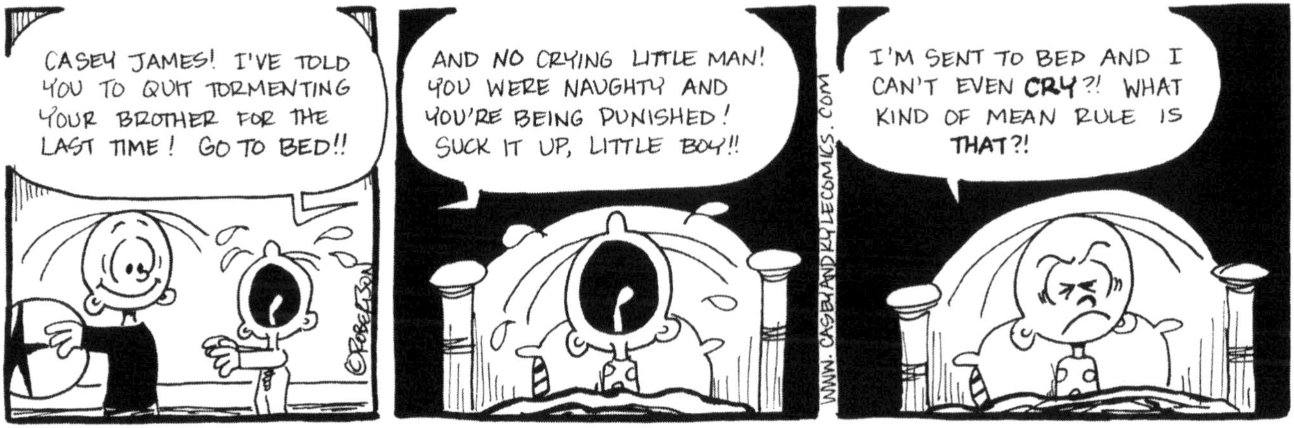
CASEY JAMES! I'VE TOLD YOU TO QUIT TORMENTING YOUR BROTHER FOR THE LAST TIME! GO TO BED!!
AND NO CRYING LITTLE MAN! YOU WERE NAUGHTY AND YOU'RE BEING PUNISHED! SUCK IT UP, LITTLE BOY!!
WWW.CASEYANDKYLECOMICS.COM
I'M SENT TO BED AND I CAN'T EVEN CRY?! WHAT KIND OF MEAN RULE IS THAT?!

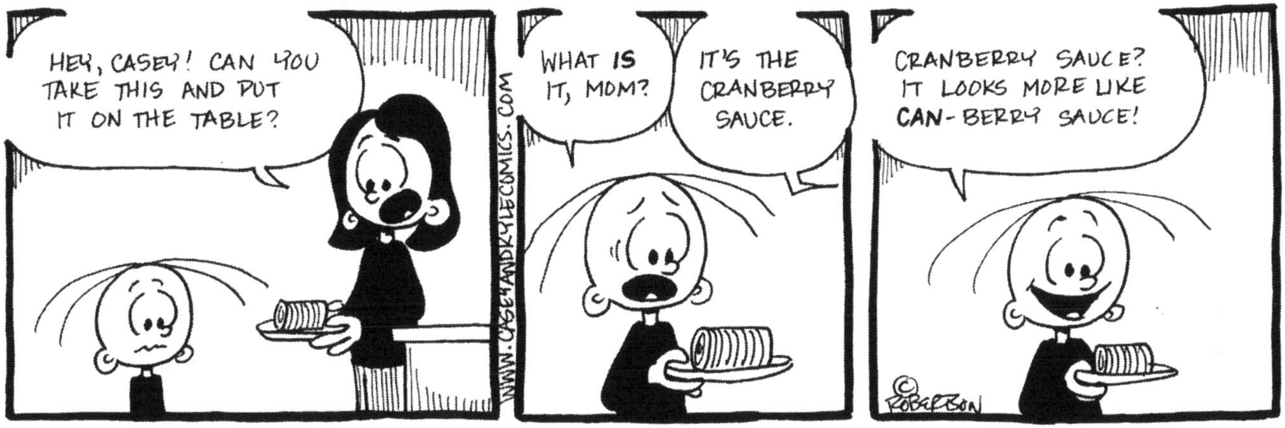
HEY, CASEY! CAN YOU TAKE THIS AND PUT IT ON THE TABLE?
WWW.CASEYANDKYLECOMICS.COM
WHAT IS IT, MOM?
IT'S THE CRANBERRY SAUCE.
CRANBERRY SAUCE? IT LOOKS MORE LIKE CAN-BERRY SAUCE!
© ROBERSON

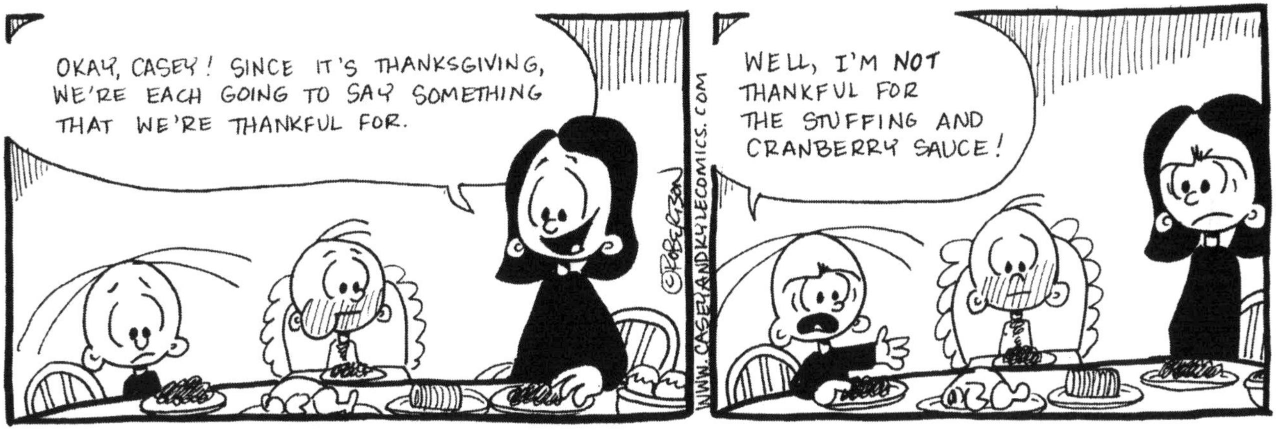
OKAY, CASEY! SINCE IT'S THANKSGIVING, WE'RE EACH GOING TO SAY SOMETHING THAT WE'RE THANKFUL FOR.
© ROBERSON
WWW.CASEYANDKYLECOMICS.COM
WELL, I'M NOT THANKFUL FOR THE STUFFING AND CRANBERRY SAUCE!

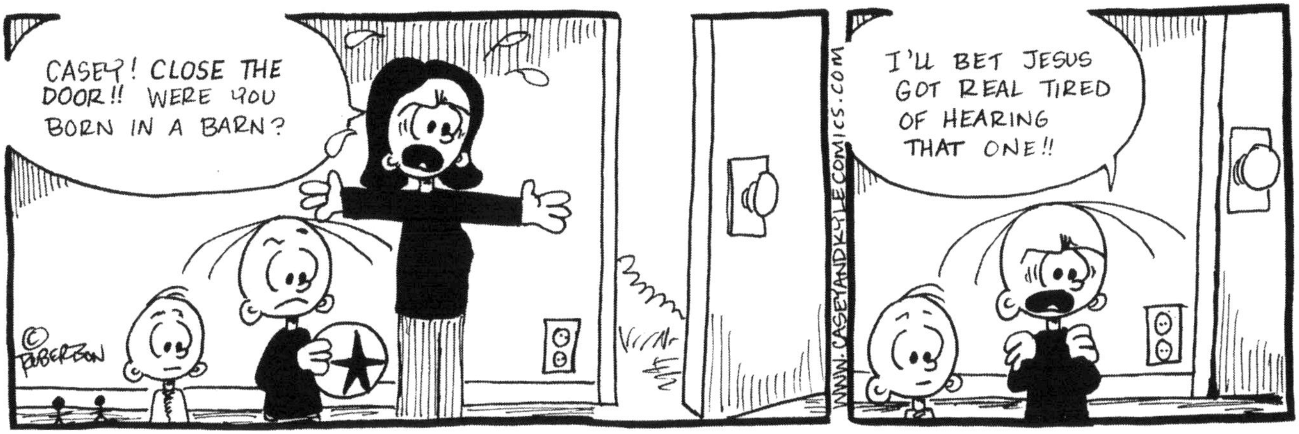
CASEY! CLOSE THE DOOR!! WERE YOU BORN IN A BARN?
© ROBERSON
WWW.CASEYANDKYLECOMICS.COM
I'LL BET JESUS GOT REAL TIRED OF HEARING THAT ONE!!

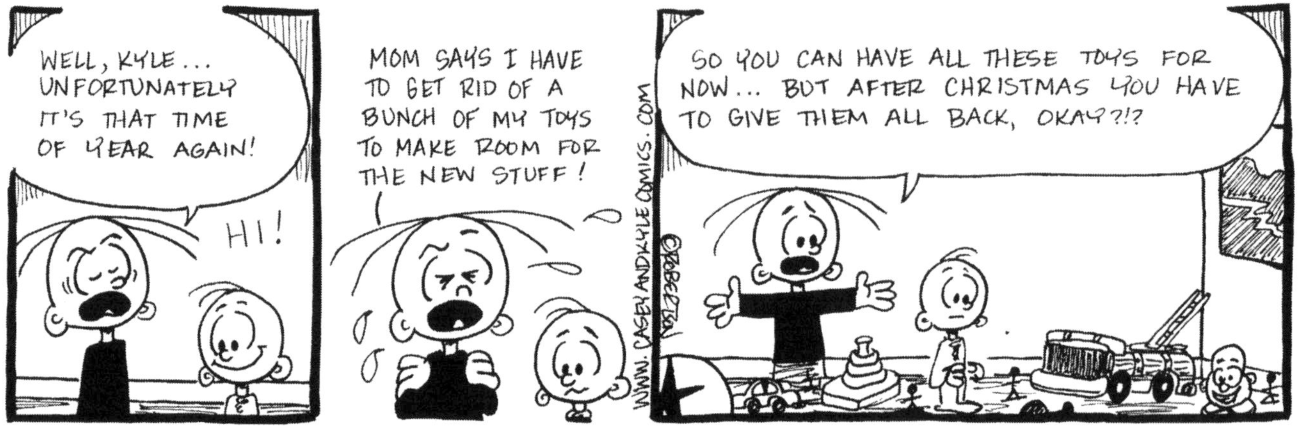
WELL, KYLE... UNFORTUNATELY IT'S THAT TIME OF YEAR AGAIN!
HI!
MOM SAYS I HAVE TO GET RID OF A BUNCH OF MY TOYS TO MAKE ROOM FOR THE NEW STUFF!
WWW.CASEYANDKYLECOMICS.COM
©ROBERTSON
SO YOU CAN HAVE ALL THESE TOYS FOR NOW... BUT AFTER CHRISTMAS YOU HAVE TO GIVE THEM ALL BACK, OKAY?!?

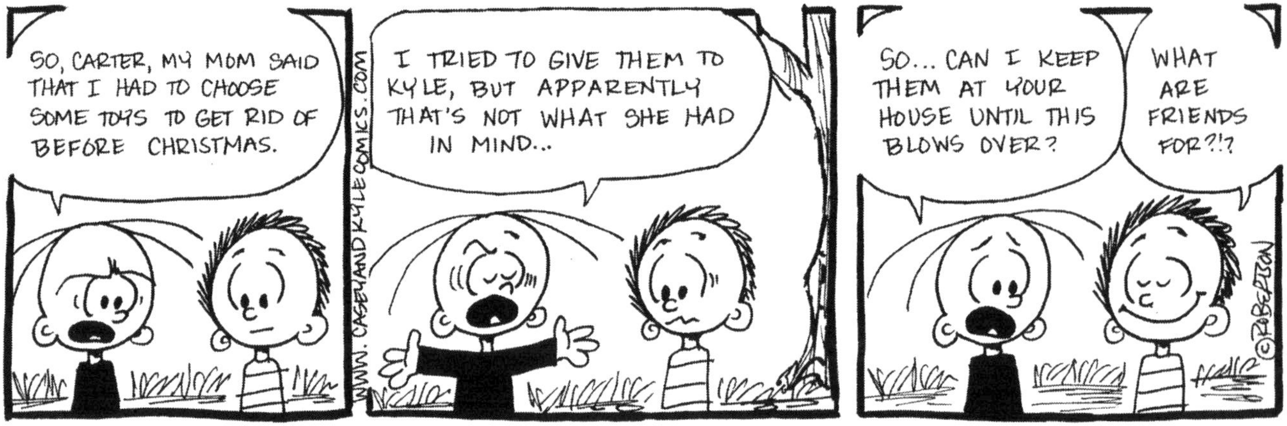
SO, CARTER, MY MOM SAID THAT I HAD TO CHOOSE SOME TOYS TO GET RID OF BEFORE CHRISTMAS.
WWW.CASEYANDKYLECOMICS.COM
I TRIED TO GIVE THEM TO KYLE, BUT APPARENTLY THAT'S NOT WHAT SHE HAD IN MIND...
SO... CAN I KEEP THEM AT YOUR HOUSE UNTIL THIS BLOWS OVER?
WHAT ARE FRIENDS FOR?!?
©ROBERTSON

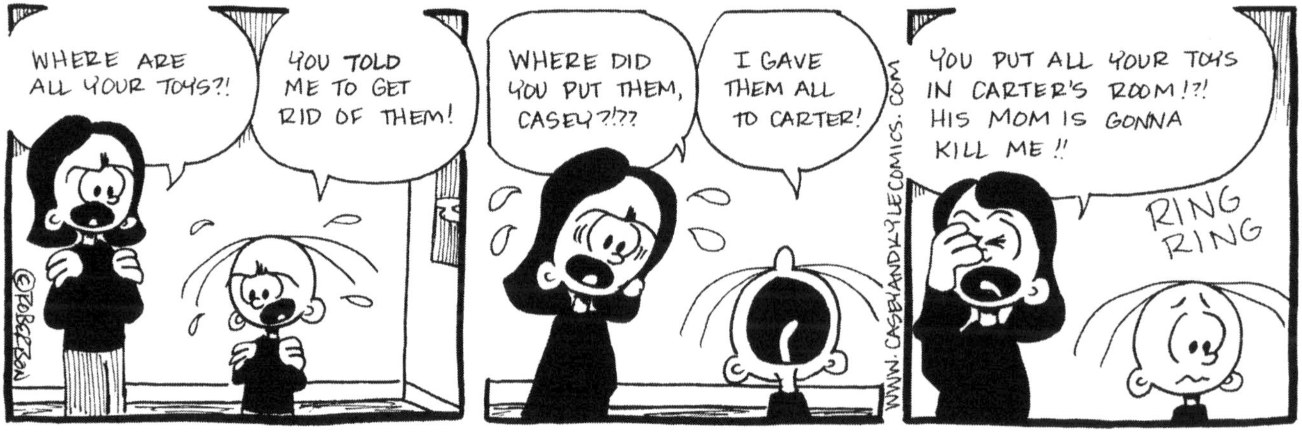
WHERE ARE ALL YOUR TOYS?!
YOU TOLD ME TO GET RID OF THEM!
©ROBERTSON
WHERE DID YOU PUT THEM, CASEY?!??
I GAVE THEM ALL TO CARTER!
WWW.CASEYANDKYLECOMICS.COM
YOU PUT ALL YOUR TOYS IN CARTER'S ROOM!?! HIS MOM IS GONNA KILL ME!!
RING RING

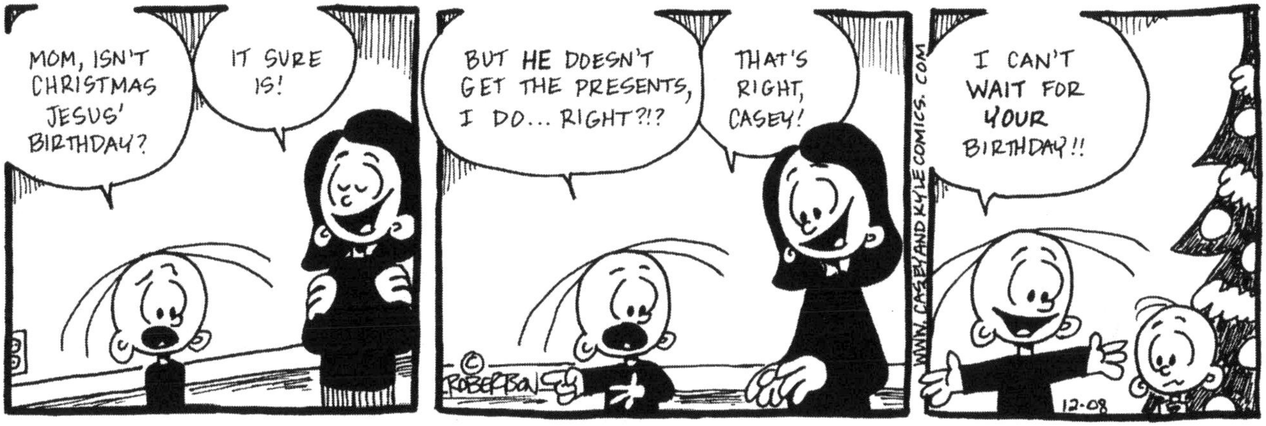
MOM, ISN'T CHRISTMAS JESUS' BIRTHDAY?
IT SURE IS!
BUT HE DOESN'T GET THE PRESENTS, I DO... RIGHT?!?
THAT'S RIGHT, CASEY!
©ROBERTSON
WWW.CASEYANDKYLECOMICS.COM
I CAN'T WAIT FOR YOUR BIRTHDAY!!
12-08

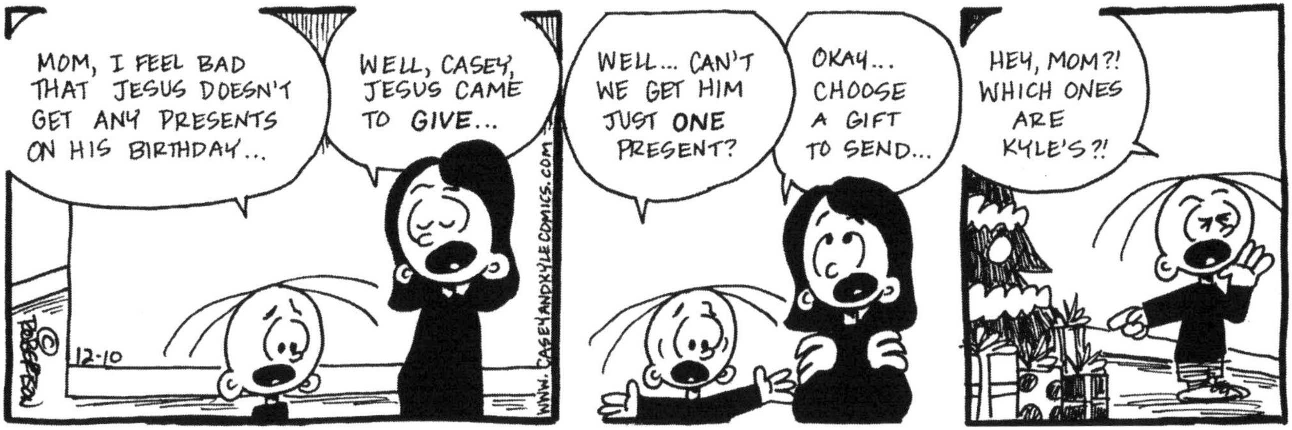
MOM, I FEEL BAD THAT JESUS DOESN'T GET ANY PRESENTS ON HIS BIRTHDAY...
WELL, CASEY, JESUS CAME TO GIVE...
©ROBERTSON
12-10
WWW.CASEYANDKYLECOMICS.COM
WELL... CAN'T WE GET HIM JUST ONE PRESENT?
OKAY... CHOOSE A GIFT TO SEND...
HEY, MOM?! WHICH ONES ARE KYLE'S?!

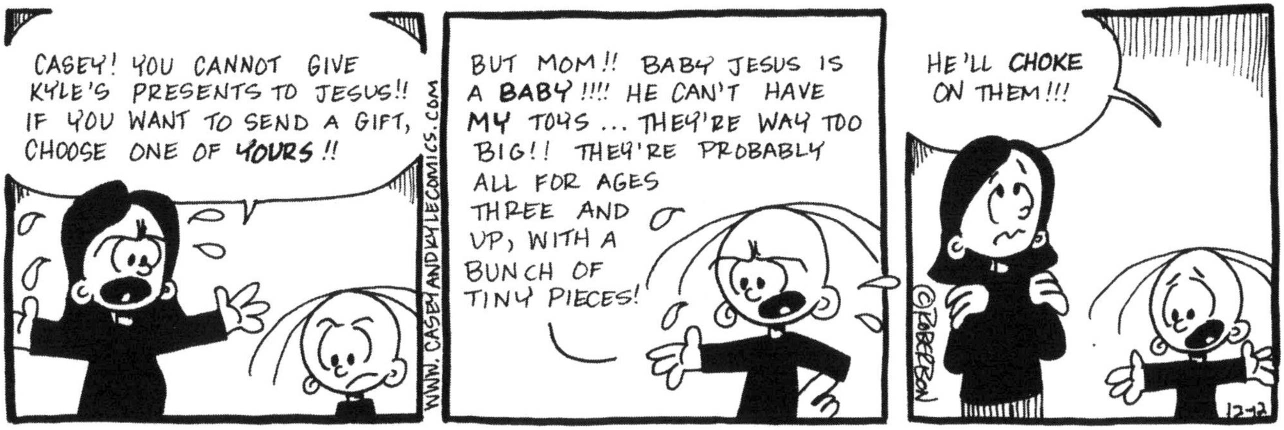
CASEY! YOU CANNOT GIVE KYLE'S PRESENTS TO JESUS!! IF YOU WANT TO SEND A GIFT, CHOOSE ONE OF YOURS!!
WWW.CASEYANDKYLECOMICS.COM
BUT MOM!! BABY JESUS IS A BABY!!!! HE CAN'T HAVE MY TOYS... THEY'RE WAY TOO BIG!! THEY'RE PROBABLY ALL FOR AGES THREE AND UP, WITH A BUNCH OF TINY PIECES!
HE'LL CHOKE ON THEM!!!
©ROBERTSON
12-12

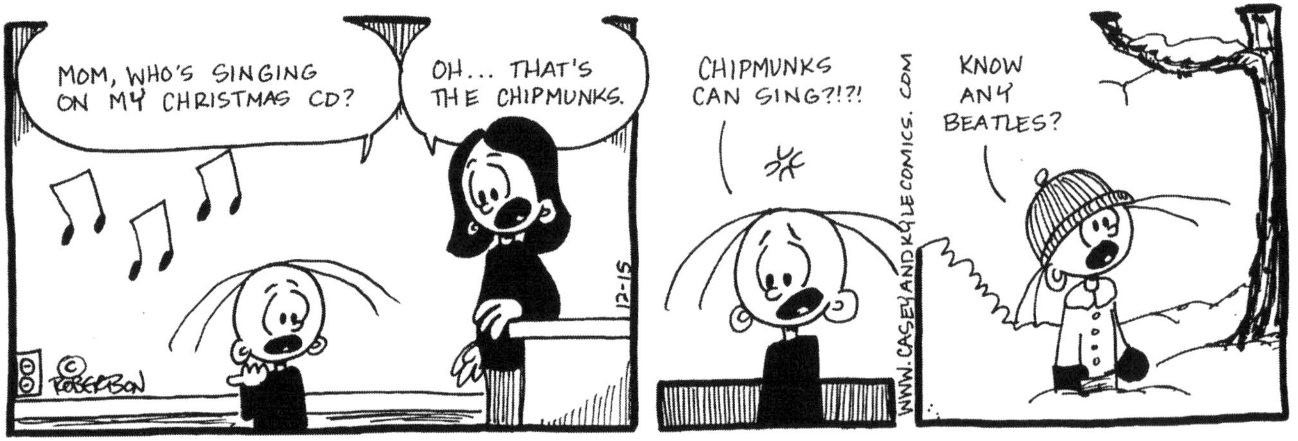
MOM, WHO'S SINGING ON MY CHRISTMAS CD?
OH... THAT'S THE CHIPMUNKS.
12-15
© ROBERSON
CHIPMUNKS CAN SING?!?!
WWW.CASEYANDKYLECOMICS.COM
KNOW ANY BEATLES?

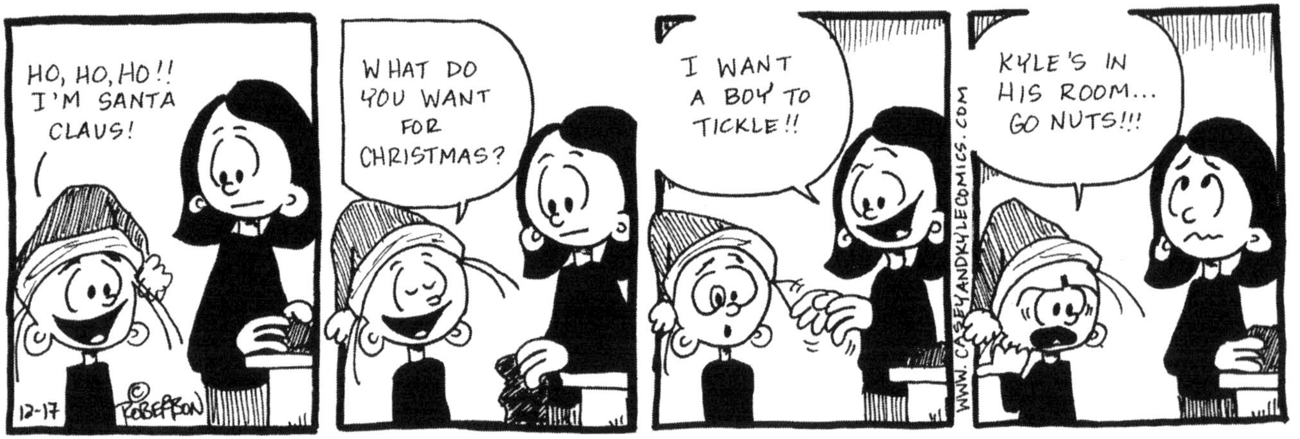
HO, HO, HO!! I'M SANTA CLAUS!
12-17
© ROBERSON
WHAT DO YOU WANT FOR CHRISTMAS?
I WANT A BOY TO TICKLE!!
WWW.CASEYANDKYLECOMICS.COM
KYLE'S IN HIS ROOM... GO NUTS!!!

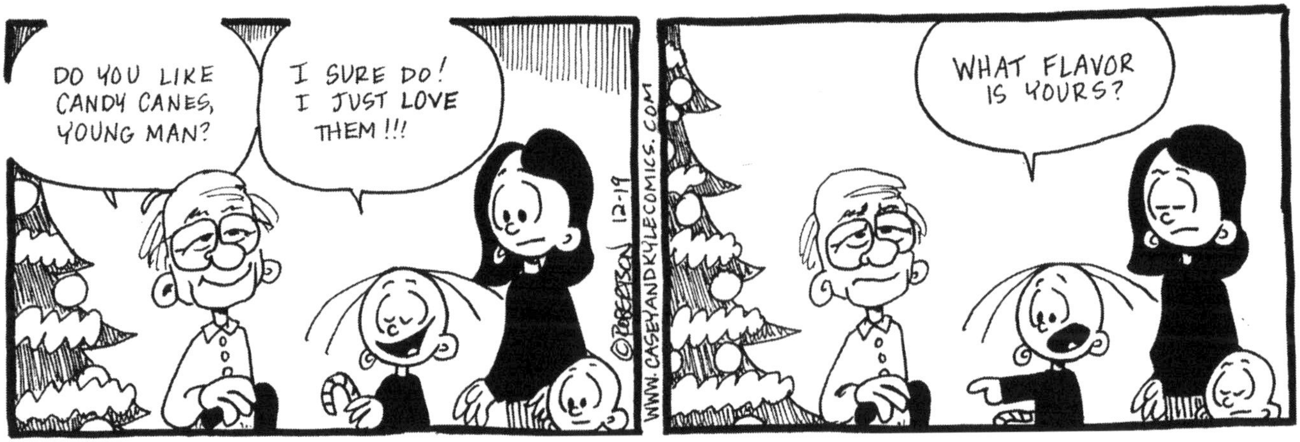
DO YOU LIKE CANDY CANES, YOUNG MAN?
I SURE DO! I JUST LOVE THEM!!!
12-19
© ROBERSON
WWW.CASEYANDKYLECOMICS.COM
WHAT FLAVOR IS YOURS?

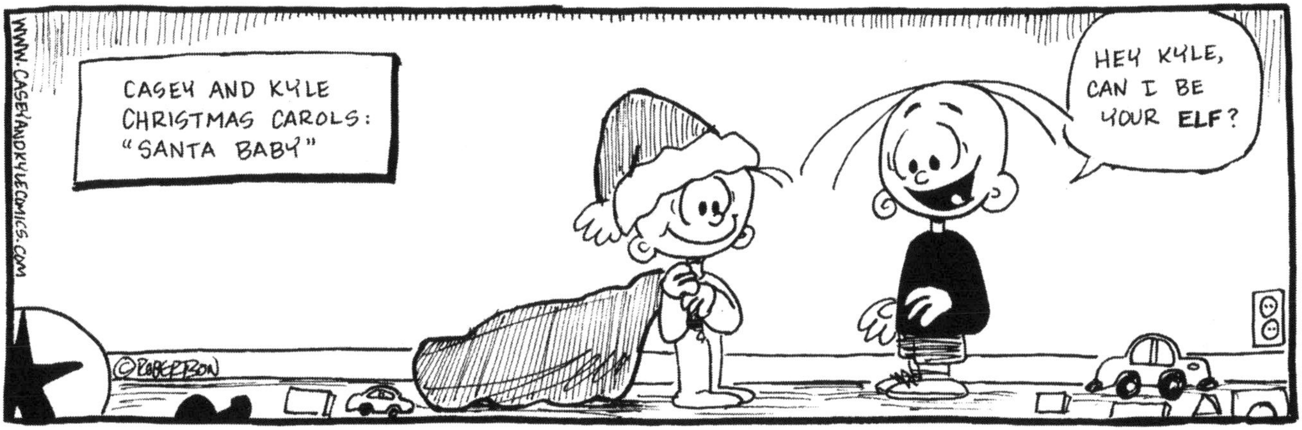
WWW.CASEYANDKYLECOMICS.COM
CASEY AND KYLE CHRISTMAS CAROLS: "SANTA BABY"
HEY KYLE, CAN I BE YOUR ELF?
©ROBERTSON

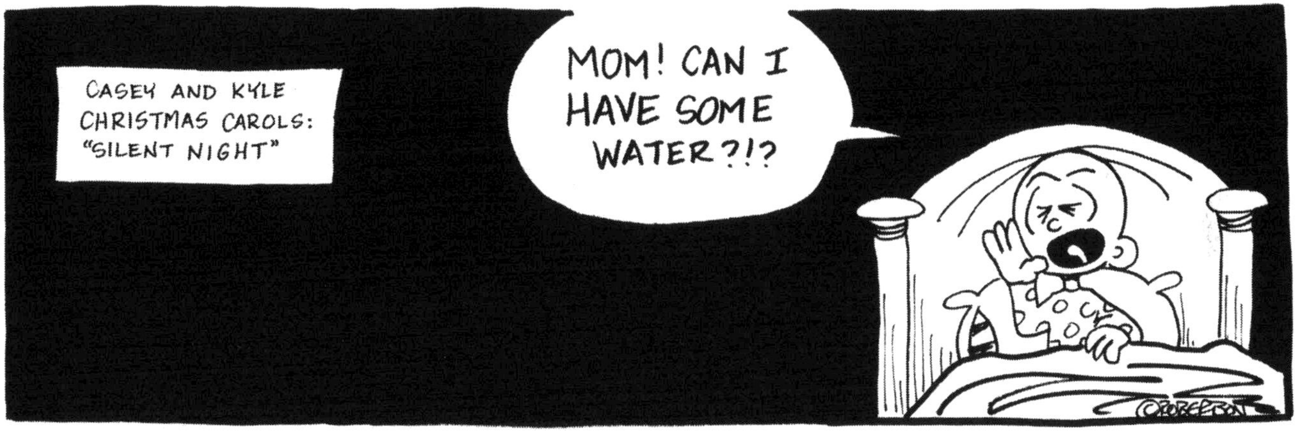
CASEY AND KYLE CHRISTMAS CAROLS: "SILENT NIGHT"
MOM! CAN I HAVE SOME WATER?!?
©ROBERTSON

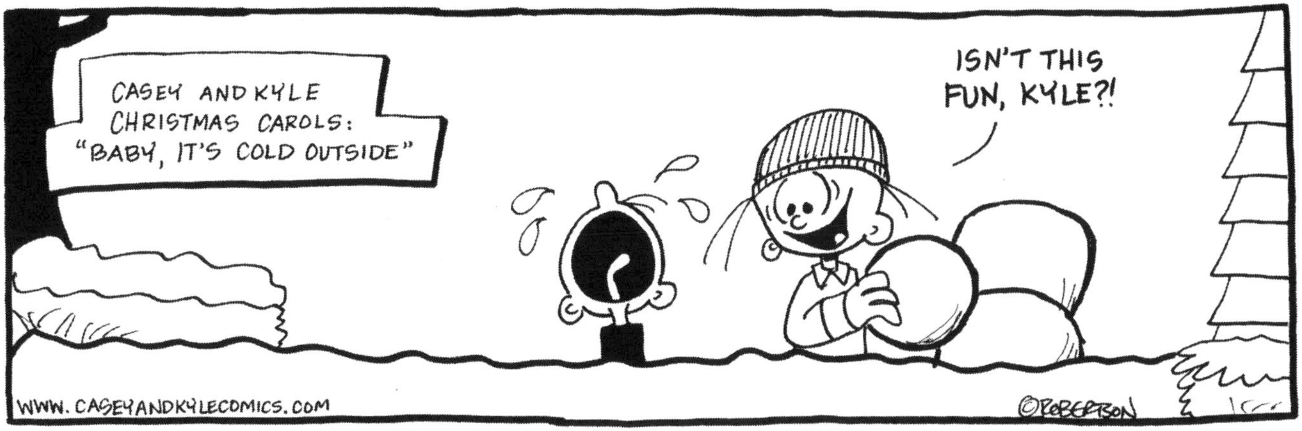
CASEY AND KYLE CHRISTMAS CAROLS: "BABY, IT'S COLD OUTSIDE"
ISN'T THIS FUN, KYLE?!
WWW.CASEYANDKYLECOMICS.COM
©ROBERTSON

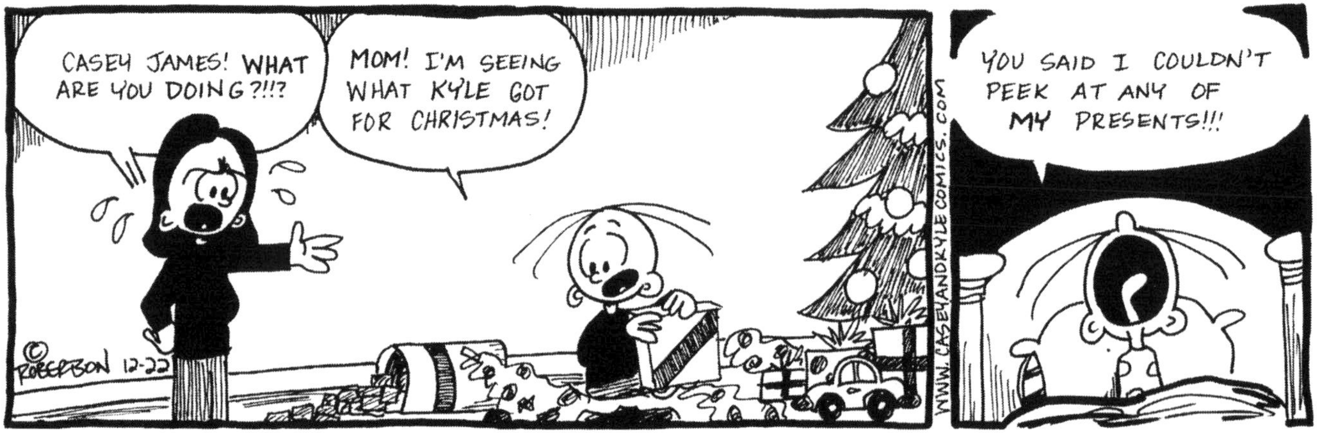
CASEY JAMES! WHAT ARE YOU DOING?!!?
MOM! I'M SEEING WHAT KYLE GOT FOR CHRISTMAS!
YOU SAID I COULDN'T PEEK AT ANY OF MY PRESENTS!!!
© ROBERSON 12-22
WWW.CASEYANDKYLECOMICS.COM

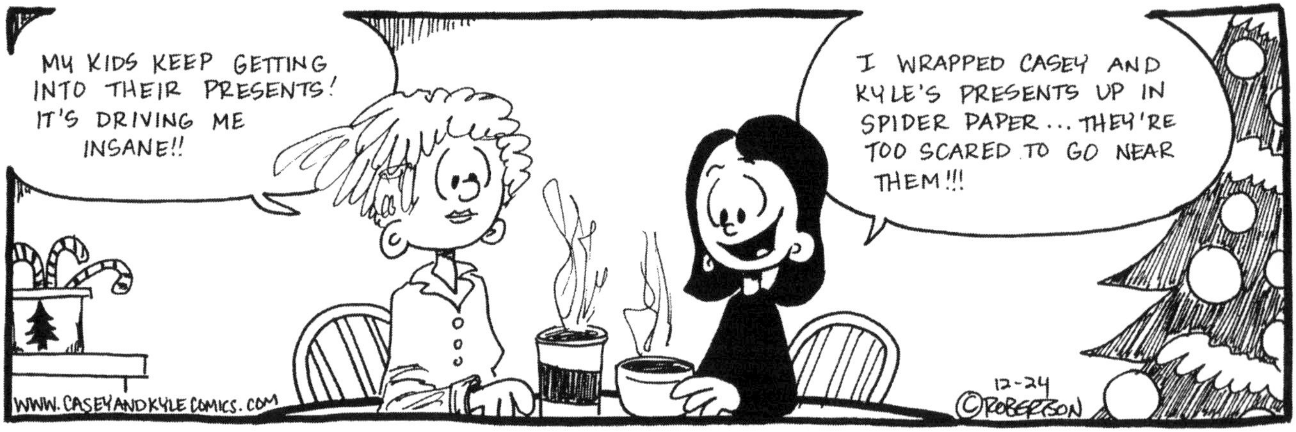
MY KIDS KEEP GETTING INTO THEIR PRESENTS! IT'S DRIVING ME INSANE!!
I WRAPPED CASEY AND KYLE'S PRESENTS UP IN SPIDER PAPER... THEY'RE TOO SCARED TO GO NEAR THEM!!!
WWW.CASEYANDKYLECOMICS.COM
12-24 ©ROBERSON

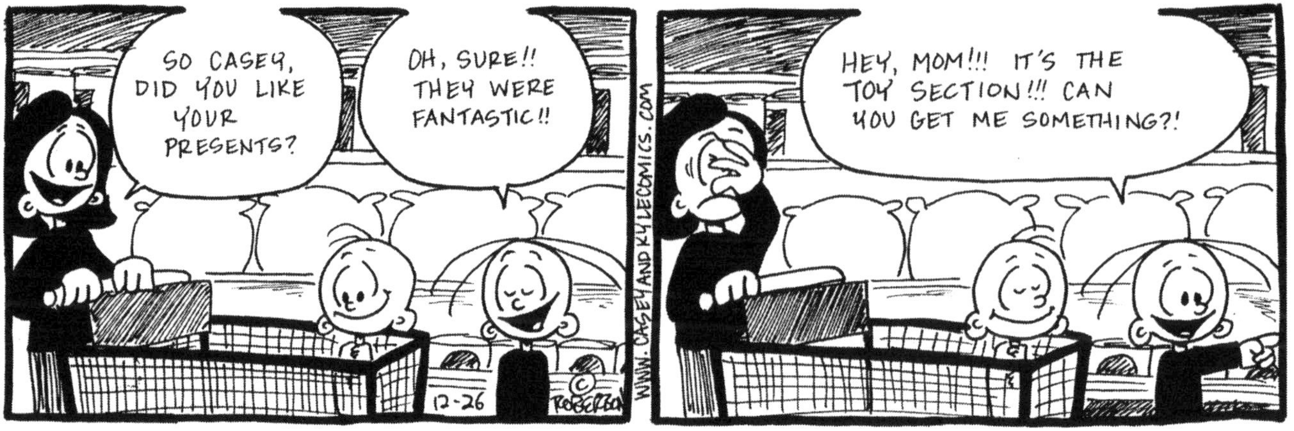
SO CASEY, DID YOU LIKE YOUR PRESENTS?
OH, SURE!! THEY WERE FANTASTIC!!
HEY, MOM!!! IT'S THE TOY SECTION!!! CAN YOU GET ME SOMETHING?!
12-26 © ROBERSON
WWW.CASEYANDKYLECOMICS.COM

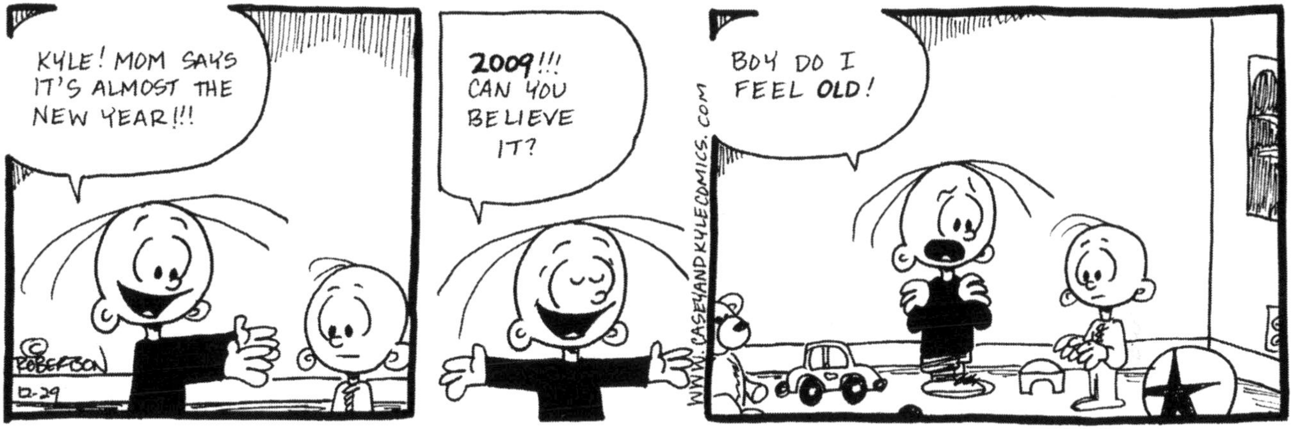
KYLE! MOM SAYS IT'S ALMOST THE NEW YEAR!!!
© ROBERTSON
12-29
2009!!! CAN YOU BELIEVE IT?
WWW.CASEYANDKYLECOMICS.COM
BOY DO I FEEL OLD!

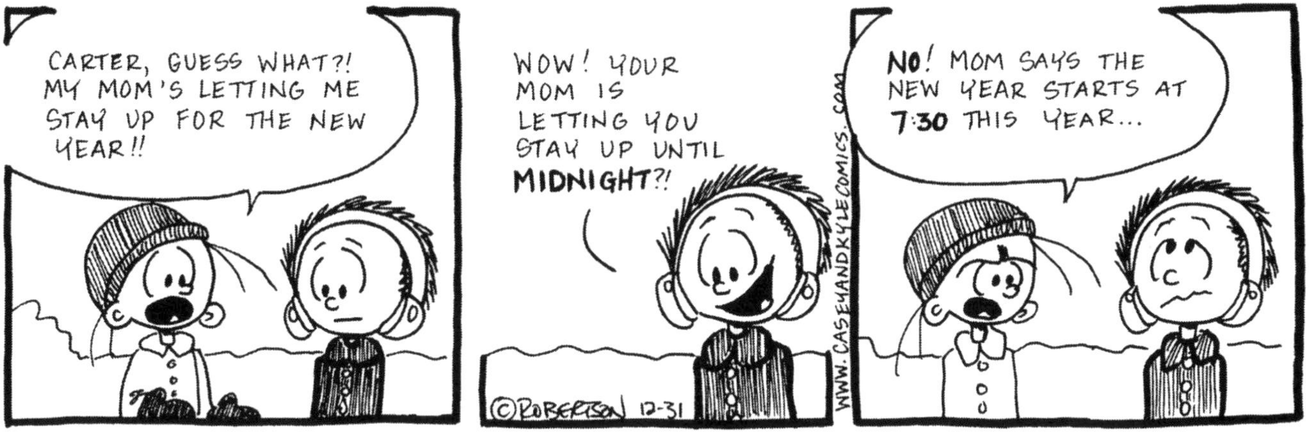
CARTER, GUESS WHAT?! MY MOM'S LETTING ME STAY UP FOR THE NEW YEAR!!
WOW! YOUR MOM IS LETTING YOU STAY UP UNTIL MIDNIGHT?!
©ROBERTSON 12-31
WWW.CASEYANDKYLECOMICS.COM
NO! MOM SAYS THE NEW YEAR STARTS AT 7:30 THIS YEAR...

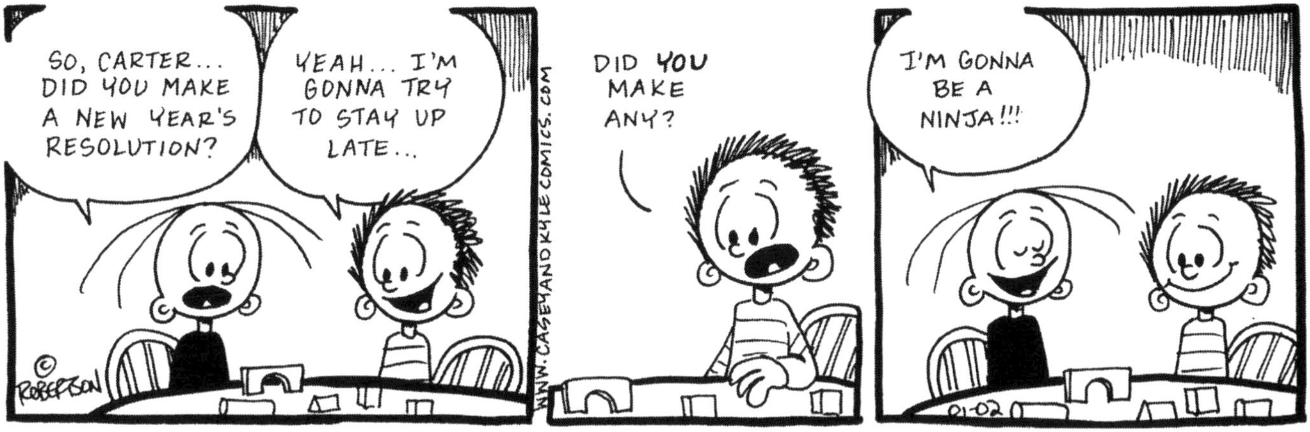
SO, CARTER... DID YOU MAKE A NEW YEAR'S RESOLUTION?
YEAH... I'M GONNA TRY TO STAY UP LATE...
© ROBERTSON
WWW.CASEYANDKYLECOMICS.COM
DID YOU MAKE ANY?
I'M GONNA BE A NINJA!!!
01-02

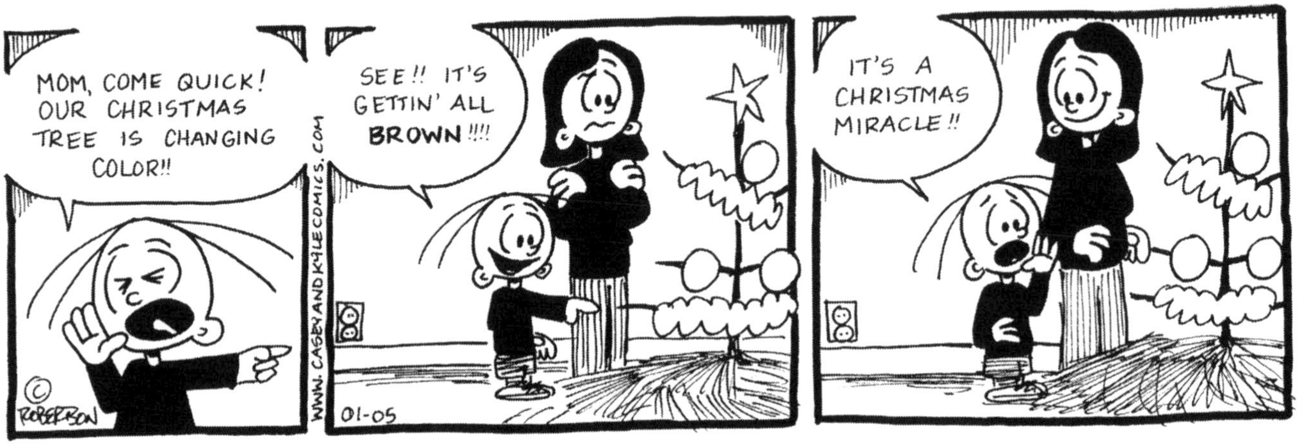
MOM, COME QUICK! OUR CHRISTMAS TREE IS CHANGING COLOR!!
© ROBERTSON
WWW.CASEYANDKYLECOMICS.COM
SEE!! IT'S GETTIN' ALL BROWN!!!!
01-05
IT'S A CHRISTMAS MIRACLE!!

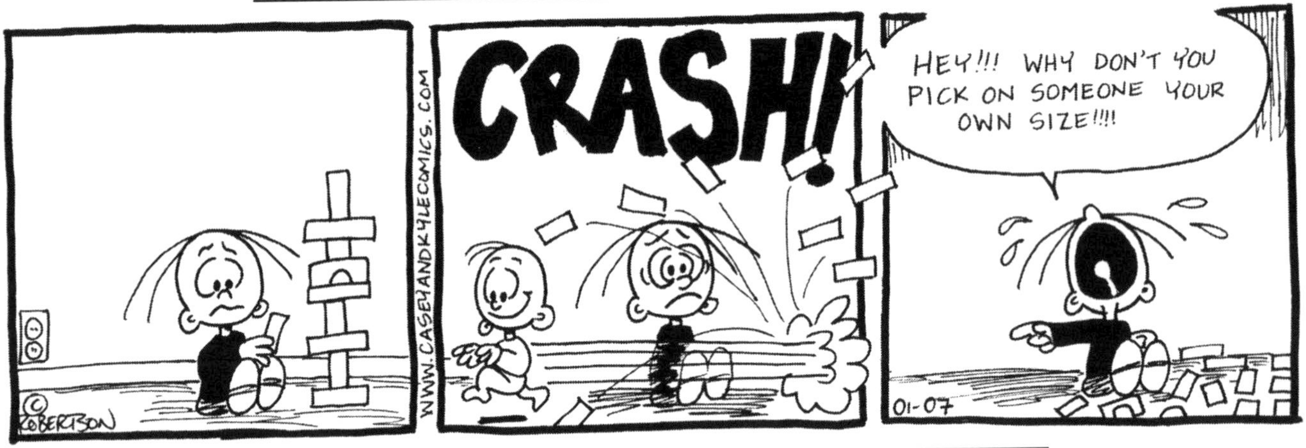
© ROBERTSON
WWW.CASEYANDKYLECOMICS.COM
CRASH!
HEY!!! WHY DON'T YOU PICK ON SOMEONE YOUR OWN SIZE!!!!
01-07

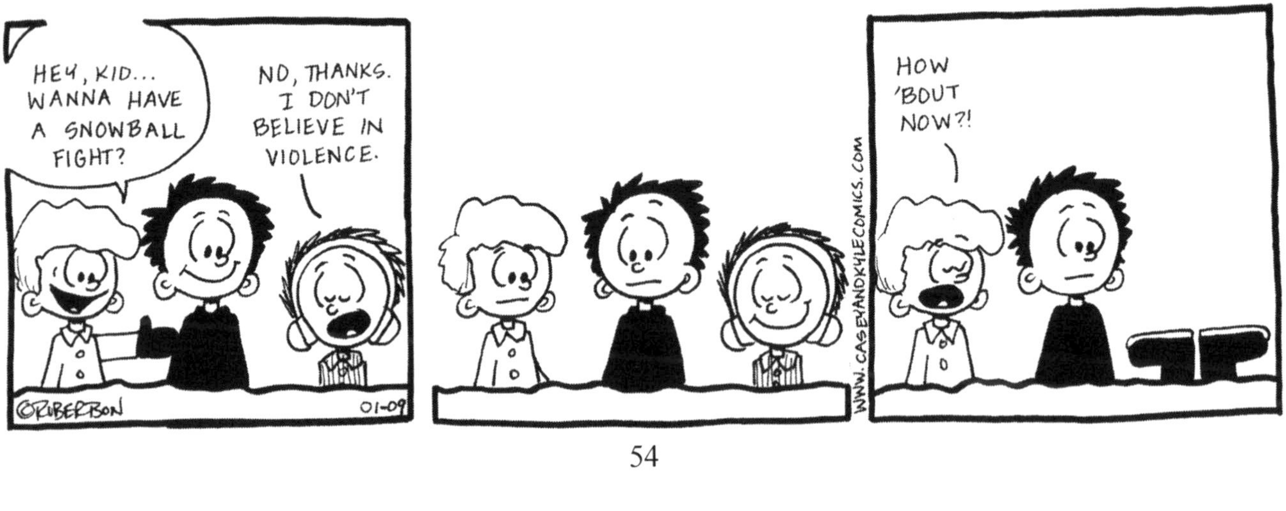
HEY, KID... WANNA HAVE A SNOWBALL FIGHT?
NO, THANKS. I DON'T BELIEVE IN VIOLENCE.
©ROBERTSON
01-09
WWW.CASEYANDKYLECOMICS.COM
HOW 'BOUT NOW?!

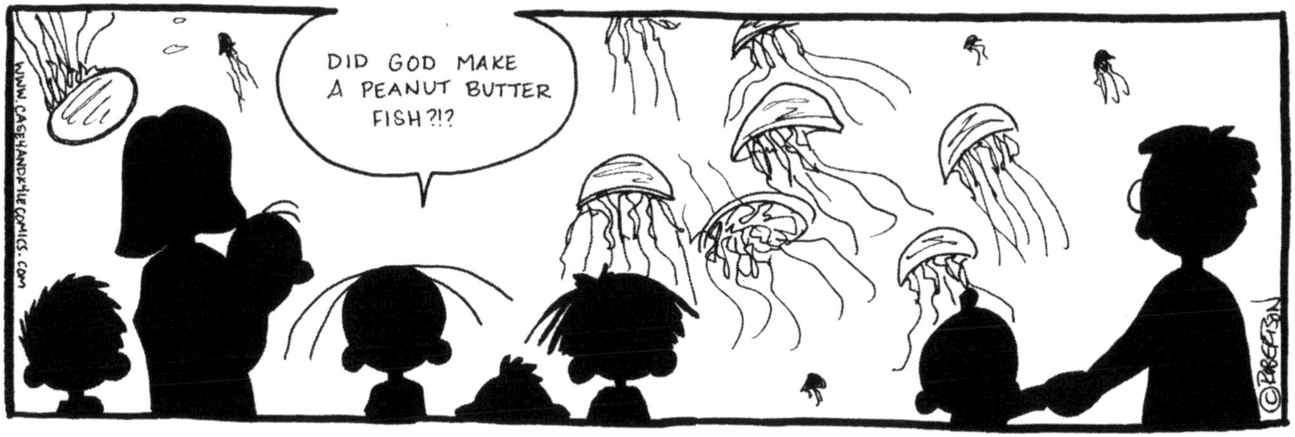
WWW.CASEYANDKYLECOMICS.COM
DID GOD MAKE A PEANUT BUTTER FISH?!?
©ROBERTSON

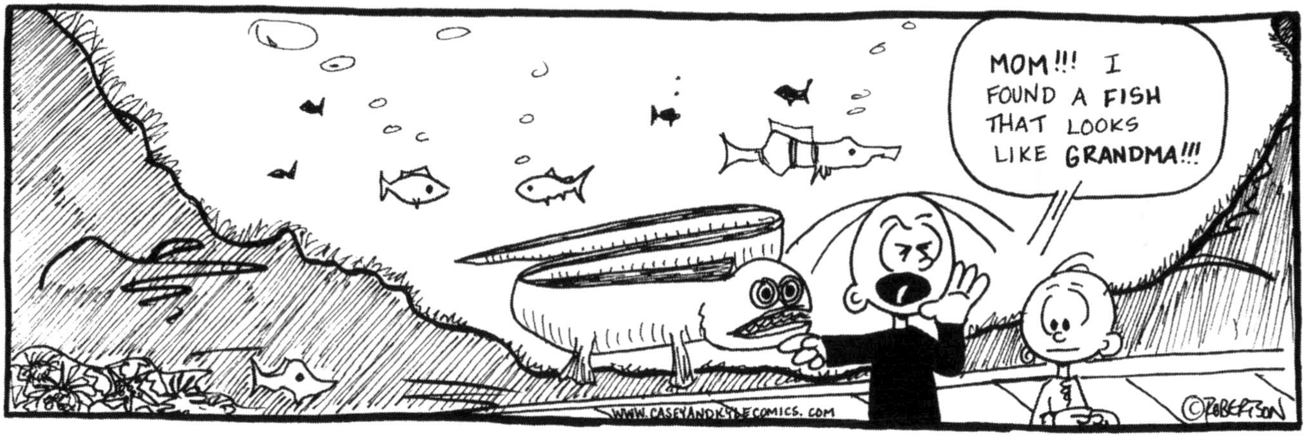
MOM!!! I FOUND A FISH THAT LOOKS LIKE GRANDMA!!!
WWW.CASEYANDKYLECOMICS.COM
©ROBERTSON

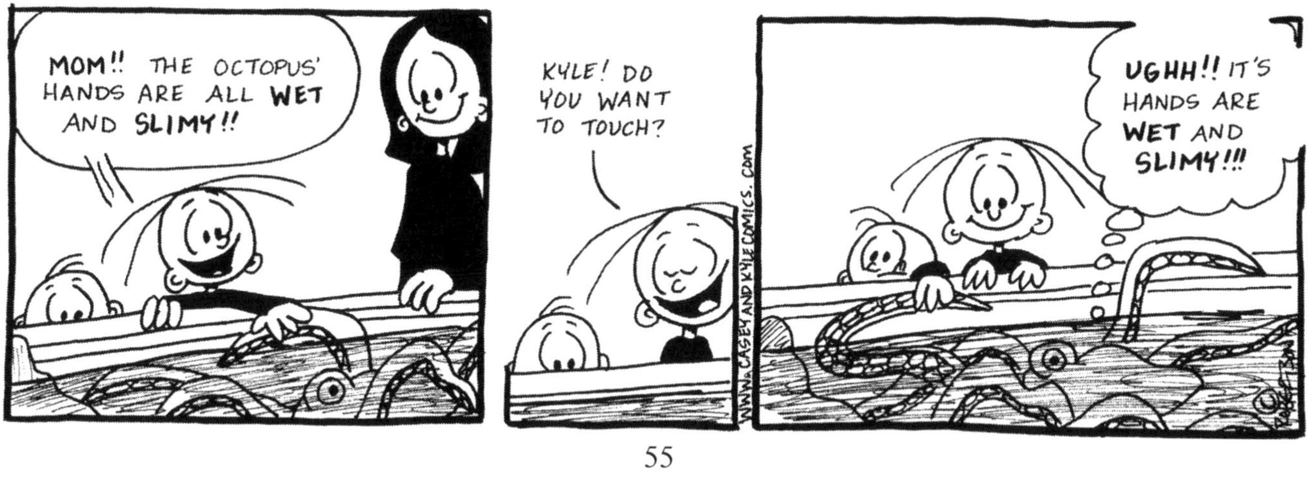
MOM!! THE OCTOPUS' HANDS ARE ALL WET AND SLIMY!!
KYLE! DO YOU WANT TO TOUCH?
WWW.CASEYANDKYLECOMICS.COM
UGHH!! IT'S HANDS ARE WET AND SLIMY!!!
©ROBERTSON

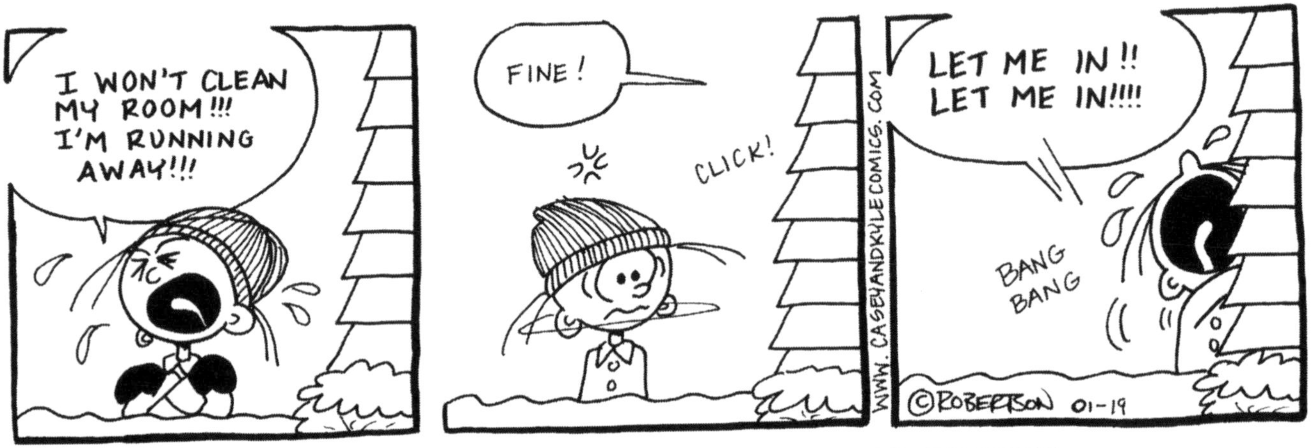
I WON'T CLEAN MY ROOM!!! I'M RUNNING AWAY!!!
FINE!
CLICK!
WWW.CASEYANDKYLECOMICS.COM
LET ME IN!! LET ME IN!!!!
BANG BANG
©ROBERTSON 01-19

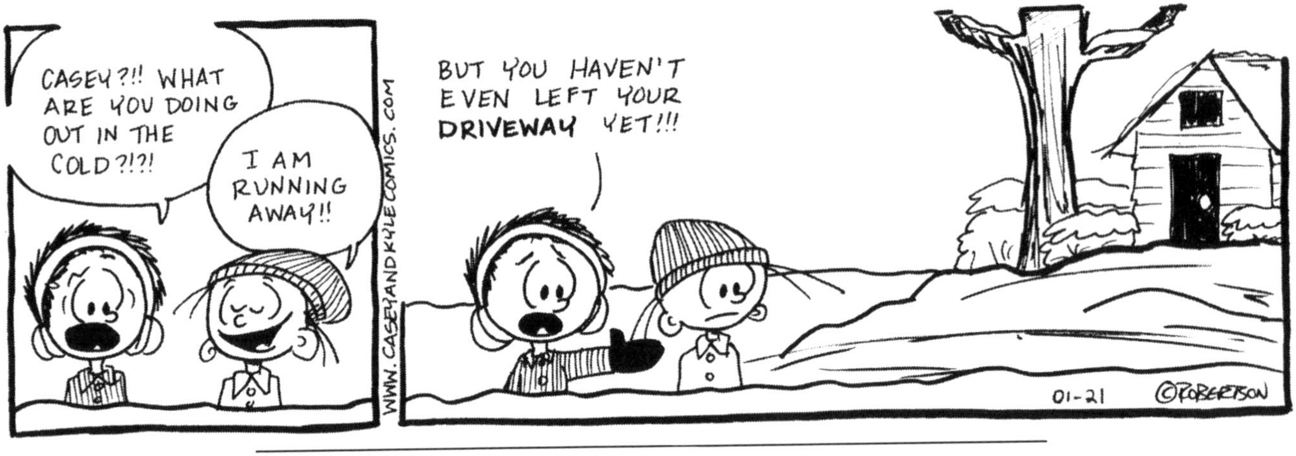
CASEY?!! WHAT ARE YOU DOING OUT IN THE COLD?!?!
I AM RUNNING AWAY!!
WWW.CASEYANDKYLECOMICS.COM
BUT YOU HAVEN'T EVEN LEFT YOUR **DRIVEWAY** YET!!!
01-21 ©ROBERTSON

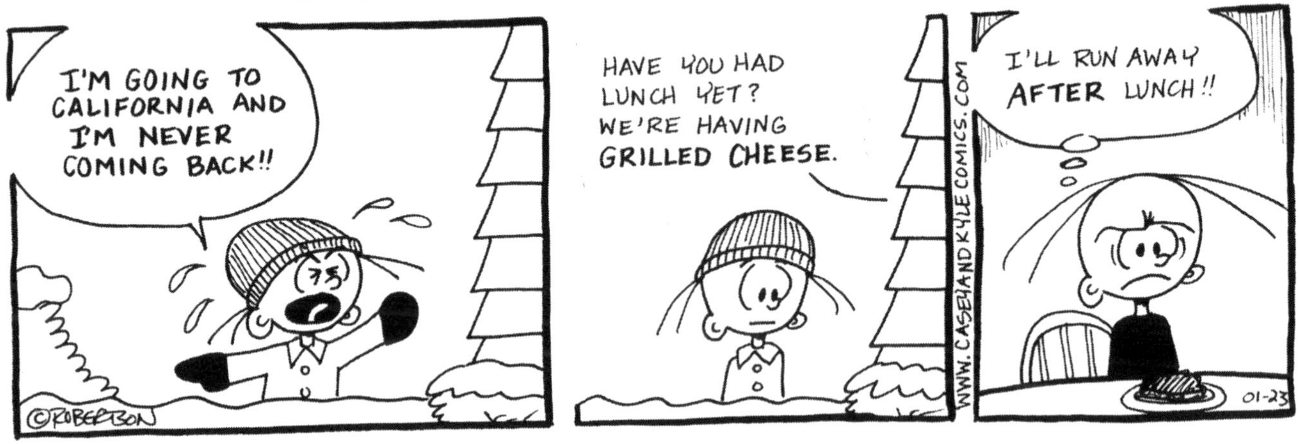
I'M GOING TO CALIFORNIA AND I'M NEVER COMING BACK!!
©ROBERTSON
HAVE YOU HAD LUNCH YET? WE'RE HAVING **GRILLED CHEESE**.
WWW.CASEYANDKYLECOMICS.COM
I'LL RUN AWAY **AFTER** LUNCH!!
01-23

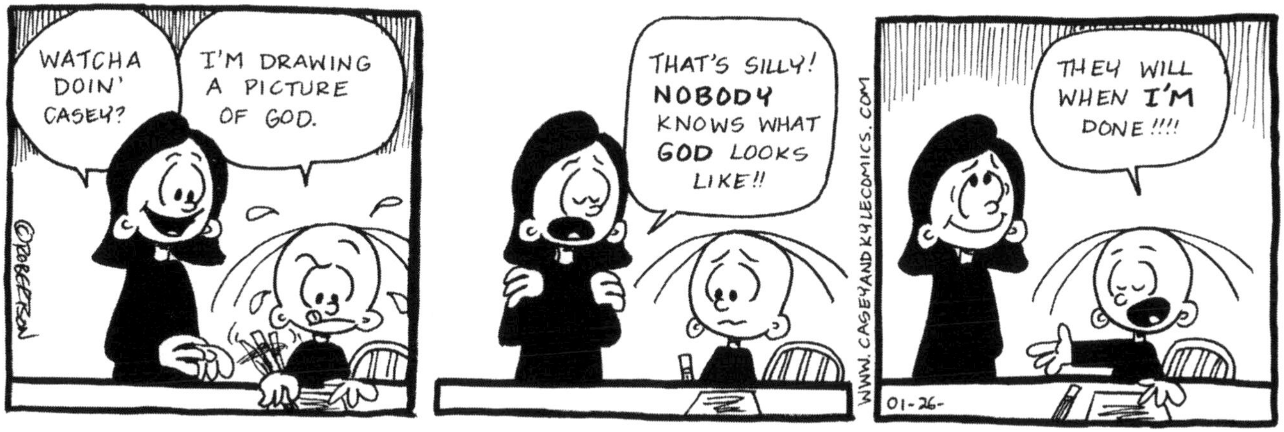
WATCHA DOIN' CASEY?
I'M DRAWING A PICTURE OF GOD.
©ROBERTSON
THAT'S SILLY! NOBODY KNOWS WHAT GOD LOOKS LIKE!!
WWW.CASEYANDKYLECOMICS.COM
THEY WILL WHEN I'M DONE!!!!
01-26-

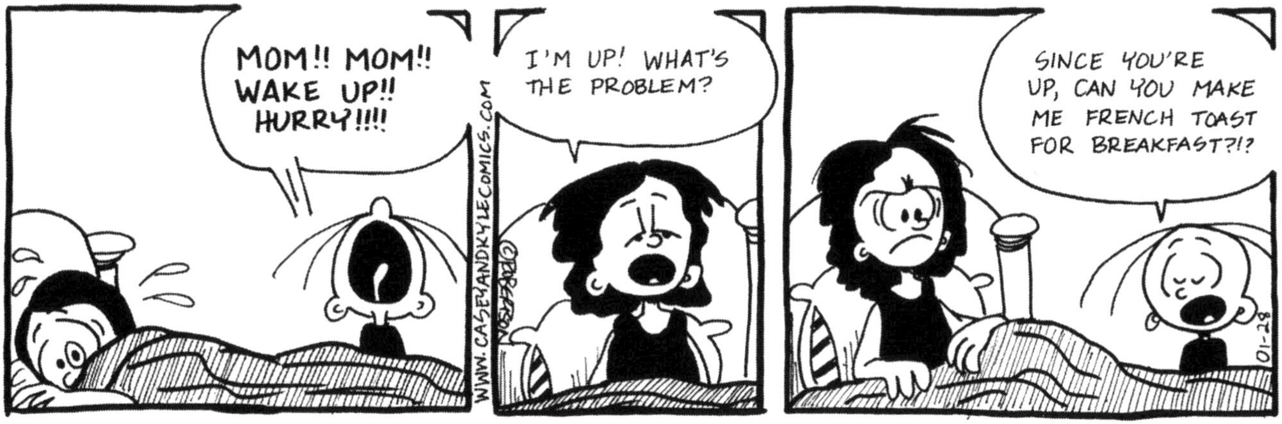
MOM!! MOM!! WAKE UP!! HURRY!!!!
WWW.CASEYANDKYLECOMICS.COM
I'M UP! WHAT'S THE PROBLEM?
©ROBERTSON
SINCE YOU'RE UP, CAN YOU MAKE ME FRENCH TOAST FOR BREAKFAST?!?
01-28

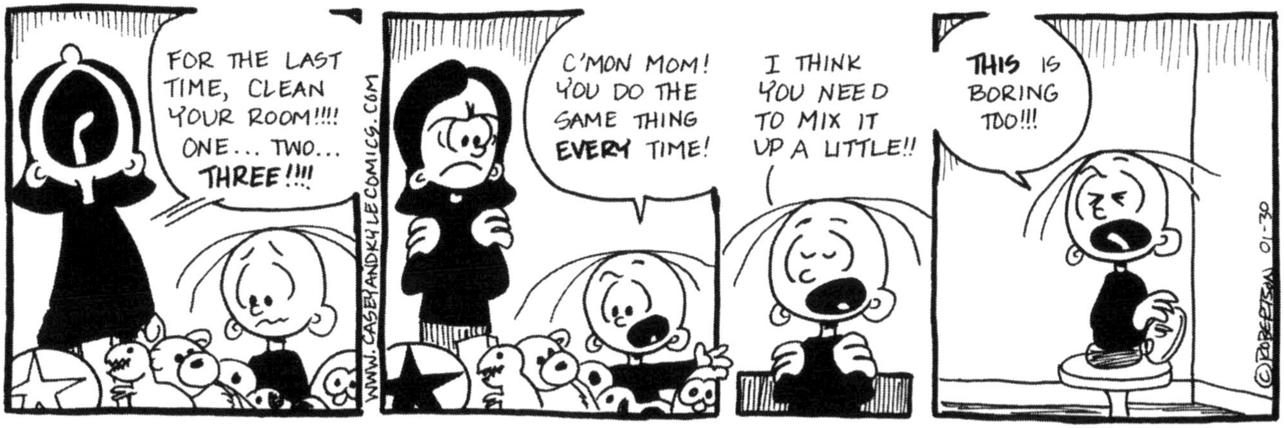
FOR THE LAST TIME, CLEAN YOUR ROOM!!!! ONE... TWO... THREE!!!!
WWW.CASEYANDKYLECOMICS.COM
C'MON MOM! YOU DO THE SAME THING EVERY TIME!
I THINK YOU NEED TO MIX IT UP A LITTLE!!
THIS IS BORING TOO!!!
©ROBERTSON 01-30

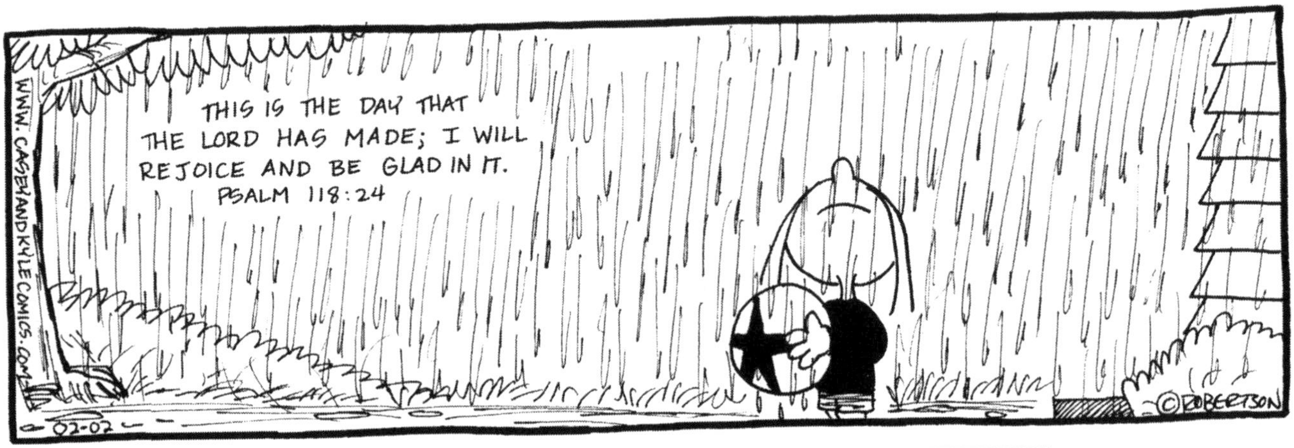
WWW.CASEYANDKYLECOMICS.COM
THIS IS THE DAY THAT THE LORD HAS MADE; I WILL REJOICE AND BE GLAD IN IT.
PSALM 118:24
02-02
©ROBERTSON

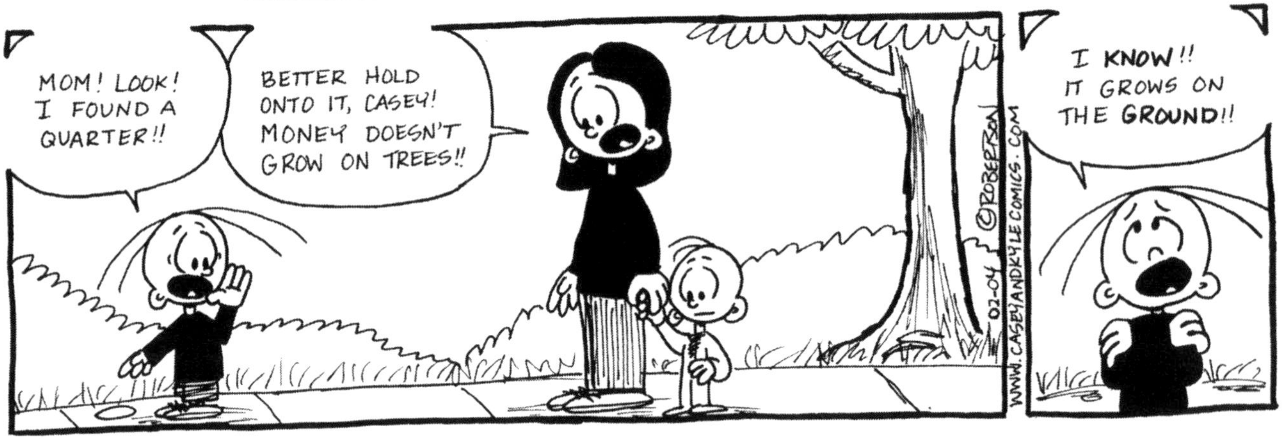
MOM! LOOK! I FOUND A QUARTER!!
BETTER HOLD ONTO IT, CASEY! MONEY DOESN'T GROW ON TREES!!
02-04 ©ROBERTSON
WWW.CASEYANDKYLECOMICS.COM
I **KNOW**!! IT GROWS ON THE **GROUND**!!

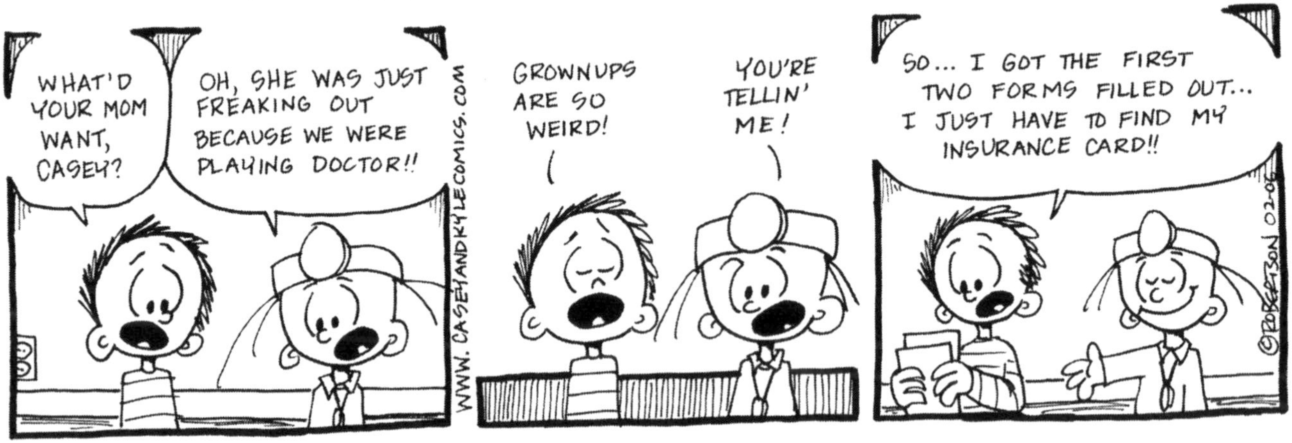
WHAT'D YOUR MOM WANT, CASEY?
OH, SHE WAS JUST FREAKING OUT BECAUSE WE WERE PLAYING DOCTOR!!
WWW.CASEYANDKYLECOMICS.COM
GROWNUPS ARE SO WEIRD!
YOU'RE TELLIN' ME!
SO... I GOT THE FIRST TWO FORMS FILLED OUT... I JUST HAVE TO FIND MY INSURANCE CARD!!
©ROBERTSON 02-06

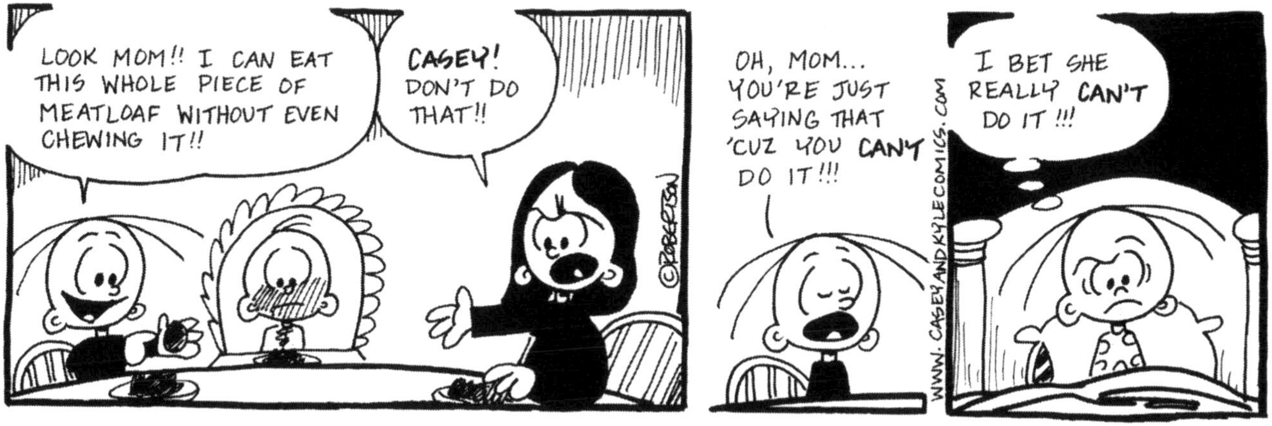
LOOK MOM!! I CAN EAT THIS WHOLE PIECE OF MEATLOAF WITHOUT EVEN CHEWING IT!!
CASEY! DON'T DO THAT!!
©ROBERTSON
OH, MOM... YOU'RE JUST SAYING THAT 'CUZ YOU CAN'T DO IT!!!
WWW.CASEYANDKYLECOMICS.COM
I BET SHE REALLY CAN'T DO IT!!!

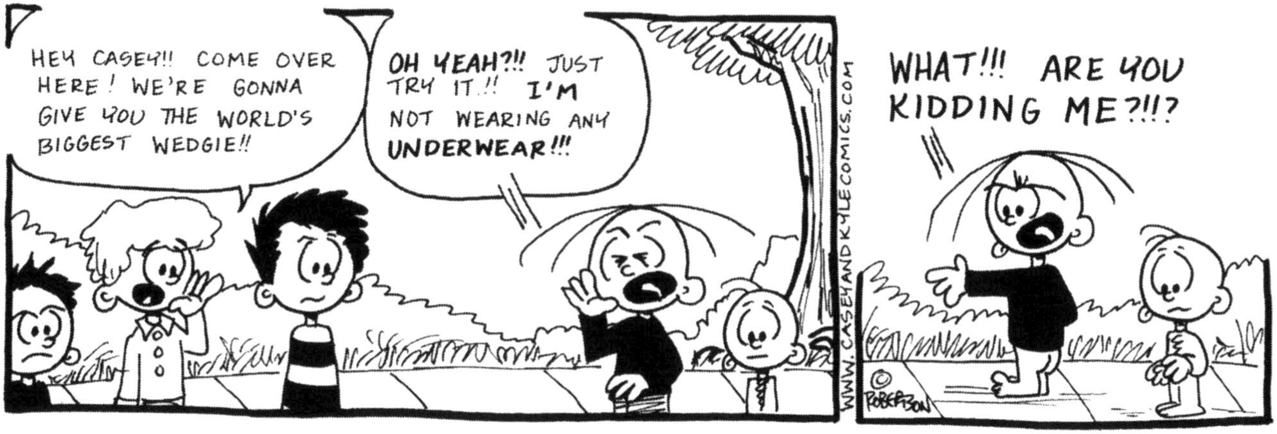
HEY CASEY!! COME OVER HERE! WE'RE GONNA GIVE YOU THE WORLD'S BIGGEST WEDGIE!!
OH YEAH?!! JUST TRY IT!! I'M NOT WEARING ANY UNDERWEAR!!!
WWW.CASEYANDKYLECOMICS.COM
WHAT!!! ARE YOU KIDDING ME?!!?
©ROBERTSON

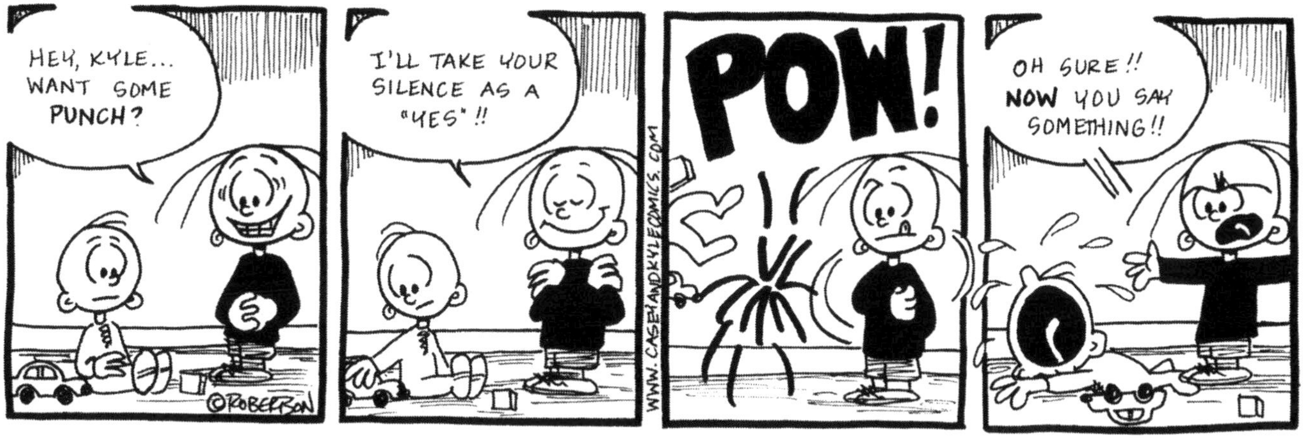
HEY, KYLE... WANT SOME PUNCH?
©ROBERTSON
I'LL TAKE YOUR SILENCE AS A "YES"!!
WWW.CASEYANDKYLECOMICS.COM
POW!
OH SURE!! NOW YOU SAY SOMETHING!!

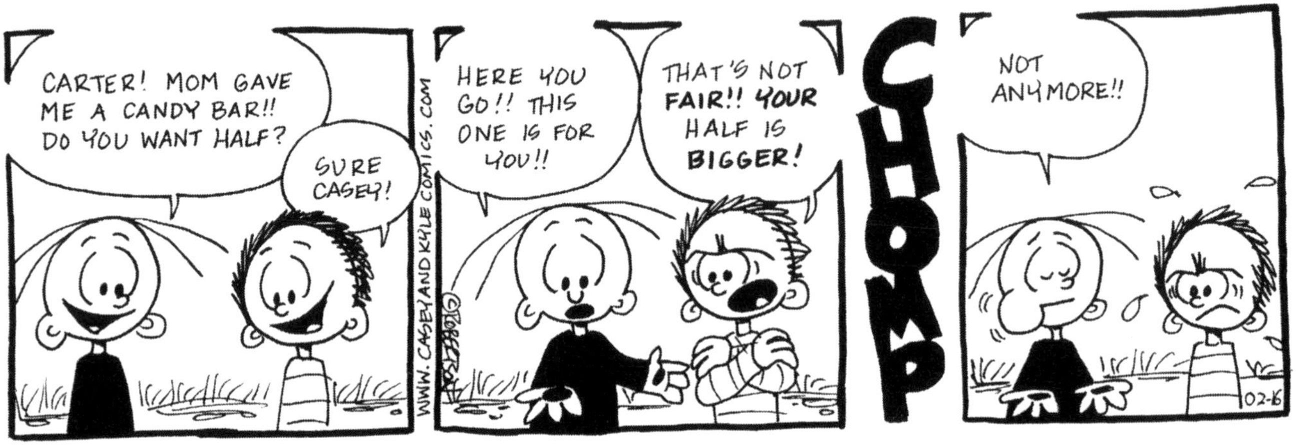
CARTER! MOM GAVE ME A CANDY BAR!! DO YOU WANT HALF?
SURE CASEY!
WWW.CASEYANDKYLECOMICS.COM
©ROBERTSON
HERE YOU GO!! THIS ONE IS FOR YOU!!
THAT'S NOT FAIR!! YOUR HALF IS BIGGER!
CHOMP
NOT ANYMORE!!
02-16

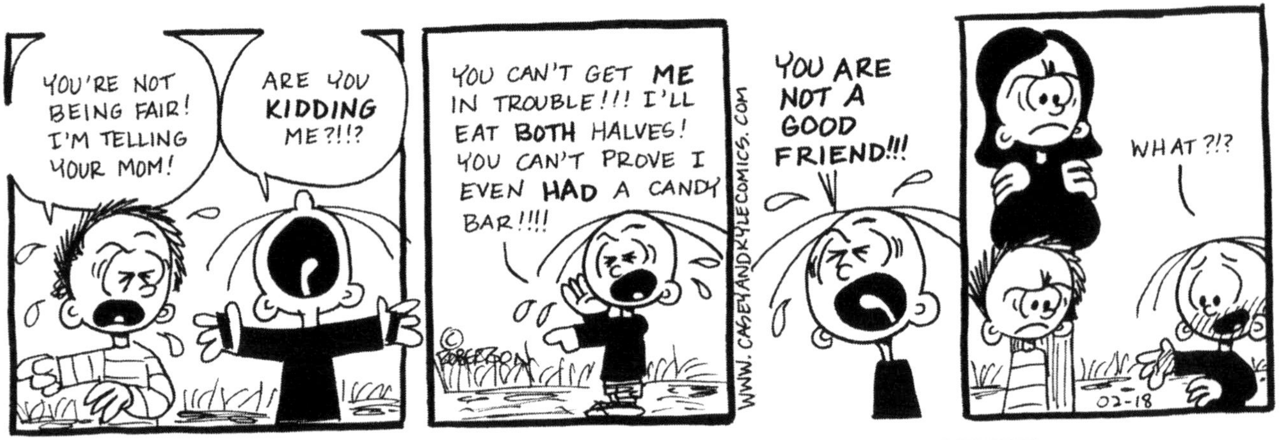
YOU'RE NOT BEING FAIR! I'M TELLING YOUR MOM!
ARE YOU KIDDING ME?!!?
YOU CAN'T GET ME IN TROUBLE!!! I'LL EAT BOTH HALVES! YOU CAN'T PROVE I EVEN HAD A CANDY BAR!!!!
©ROBERTSON
WWW.CASEYANDKYLECOMICS.COM
YOU ARE NOT A GOOD FRIEND!!!
WHAT?!?
02-18

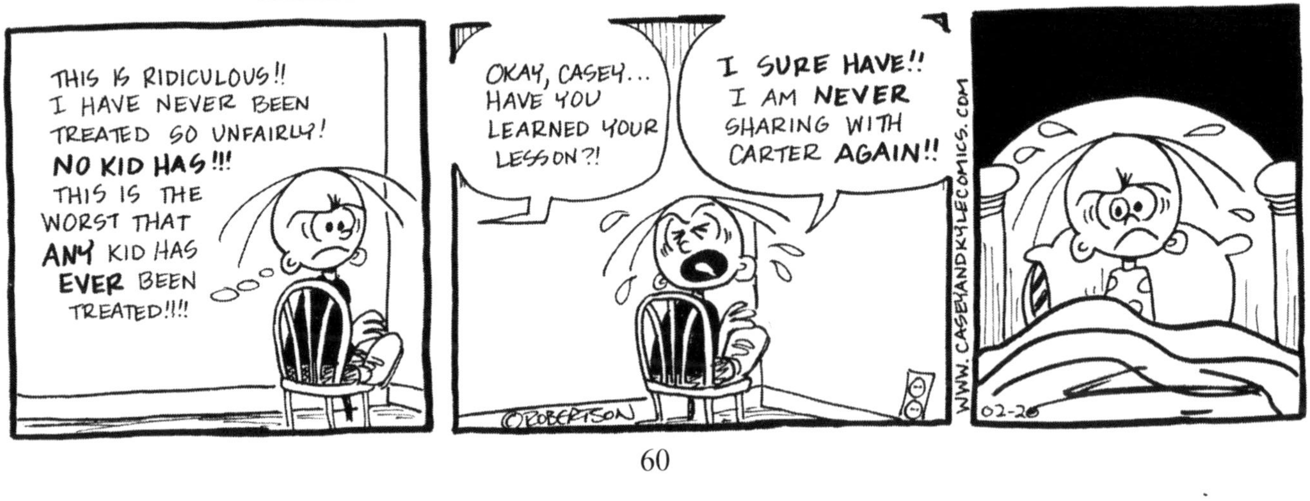
THIS IS RIDICULOUS!! I HAVE NEVER BEEN TREATED SO UNFAIRLY! NO KID HAS!!! THIS IS THE WORST THAT ANY KID HAS EVER BEEN TREATED!!!!
OKAY, CASEY... HAVE YOU LEARNED YOUR LESSON?!
I SURE HAVE!! I AM NEVER SHARING WITH CARTER AGAIN!!
©ROBERTSON
WWW.CASEYANDKYLECOMICS.COM
02-20

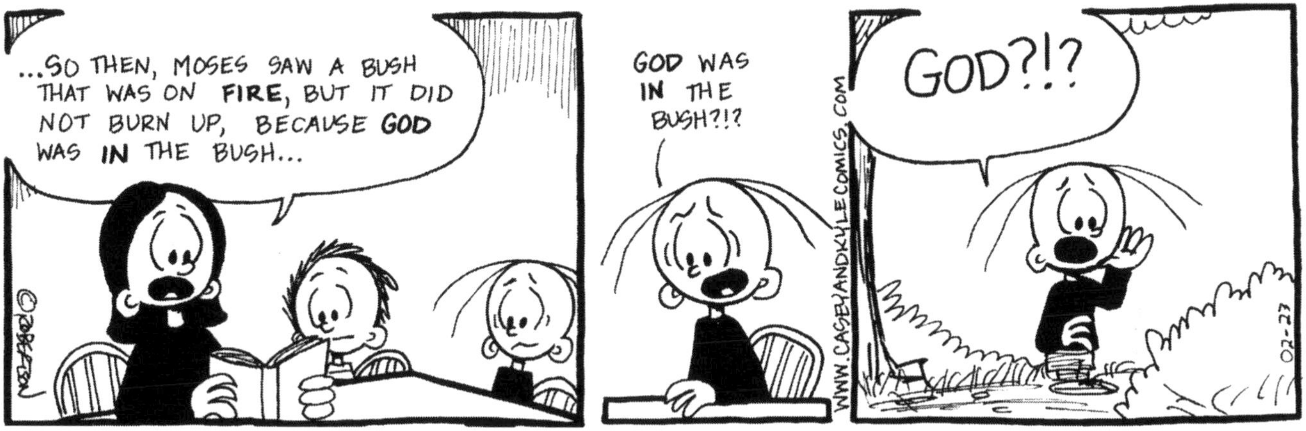
...SO THEN, MOSES SAW A BUSH THAT WAS ON FIRE, BUT IT DID NOT BURN UP, BECAUSE GOD WAS IN THE BUSH...
©ROBERTSON
GOD WAS IN THE BUSH?!?
WWW.CASEYANDKYLECOMICS.COM
GOD?!?
02-23

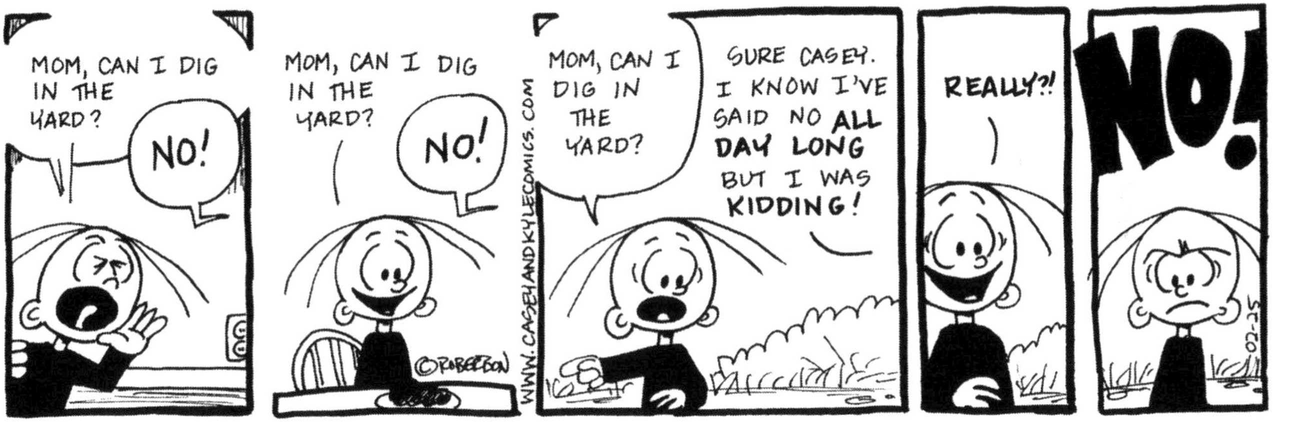
MOM, CAN I DIG IN THE YARD?
NO!
MOM, CAN I DIG IN THE YARD?
NO!
©ROBERTSON
WWW.CASEYANDKYLECOMICS.COM
MOM, CAN I DIG IN THE YARD?
SURE CASEY. I KNOW I'VE SAID NO ALL DAY LONG BUT I WAS KIDDING!
REALLY?!
NO!
02-25

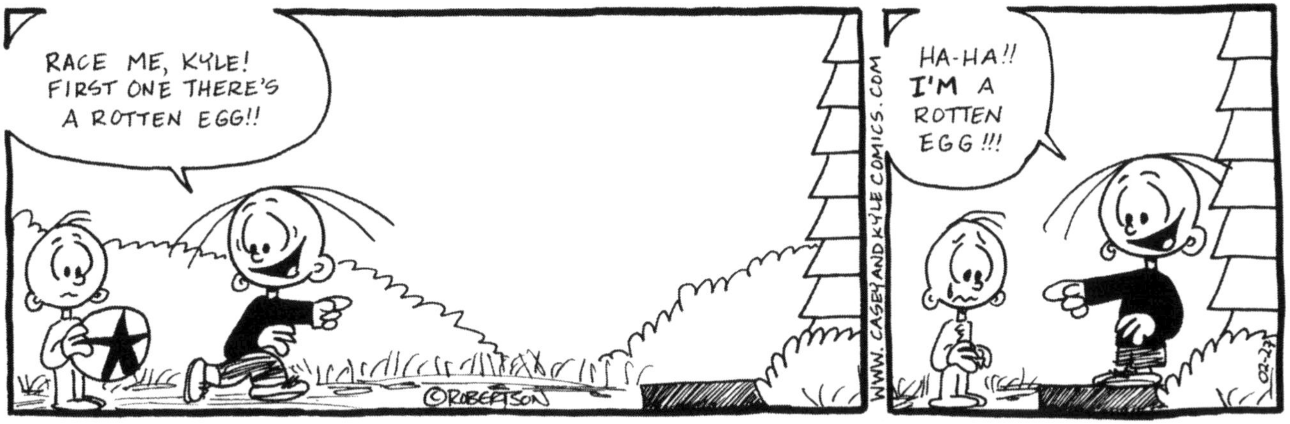
RACE ME, KYLE! FIRST ONE THERE'S A ROTTEN EGG!!
©ROBERTSON
WWW.CASEYANDKYLECOMICS.COM
HA-HA!! I'M A ROTTEN EGG!!!
02-27

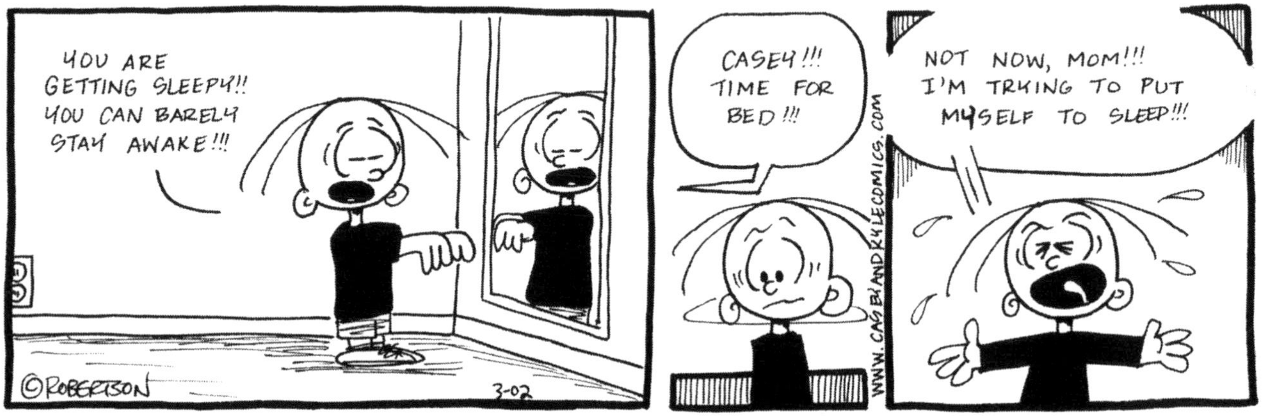
YOU ARE GETTING SLEEPY!! YOU CAN BARELY STAY AWAKE!!!
©ROBERTSON
3-02
CASEY!!! TIME FOR BED!!!
WWW.CASEYANDKYLECOMICS.COM
NOT NOW, MOM!!! I'M TRYING TO PUT MYSELF TO SLEEP!!!

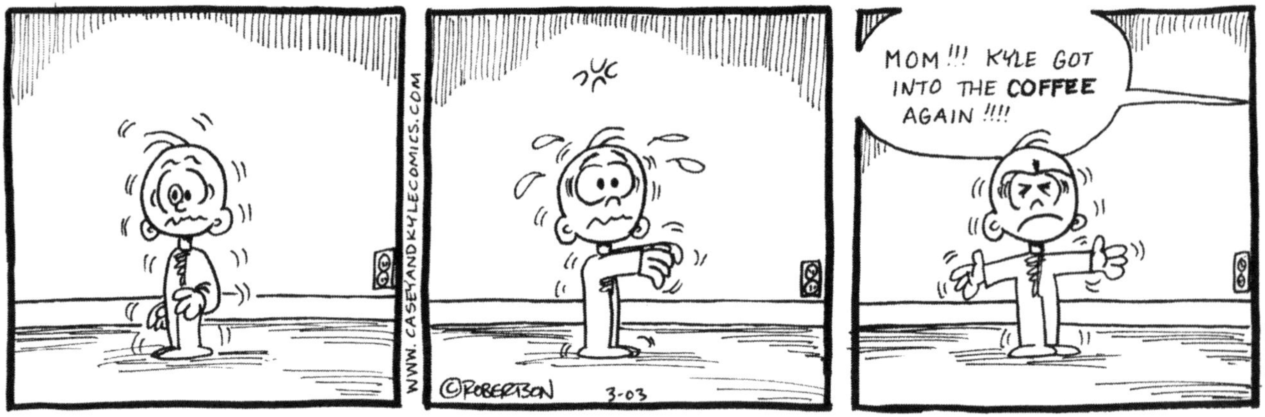
WWW.CASEYANDKYLECOMICS.COM
©ROBERTSON
3-03
MOM!!! KYLE GOT INTO THE COFFEE AGAIN!!!!

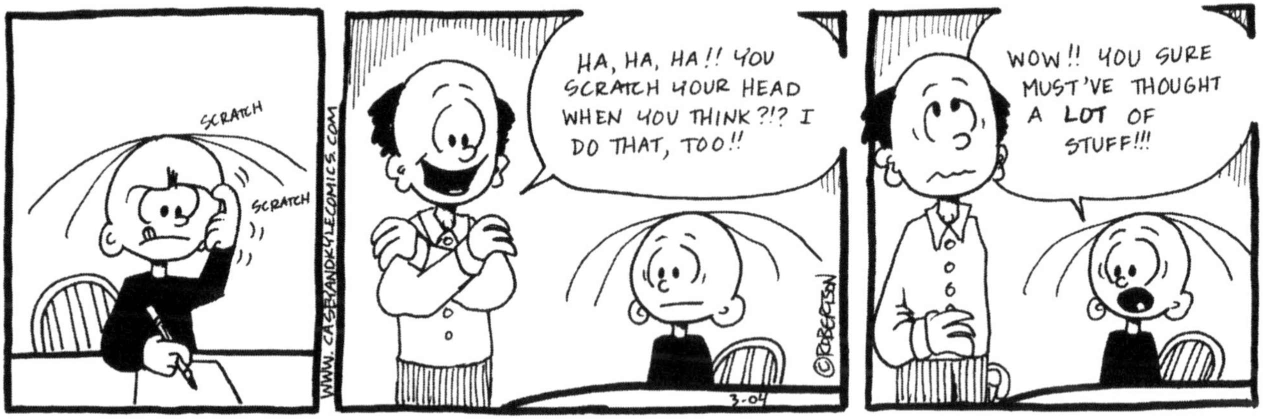
SCRATCH
SCRATCH
WWW.CASEYANDKYLECOMICS.COM
HA, HA, HA!! YOU SCRATCH YOUR HEAD WHEN YOU THINK?!? I DO THAT, TOO!!
©ROBERTSON
3-04
WOW!! YOU SURE MUST'VE THOUGHT A LOT OF STUFF!!!

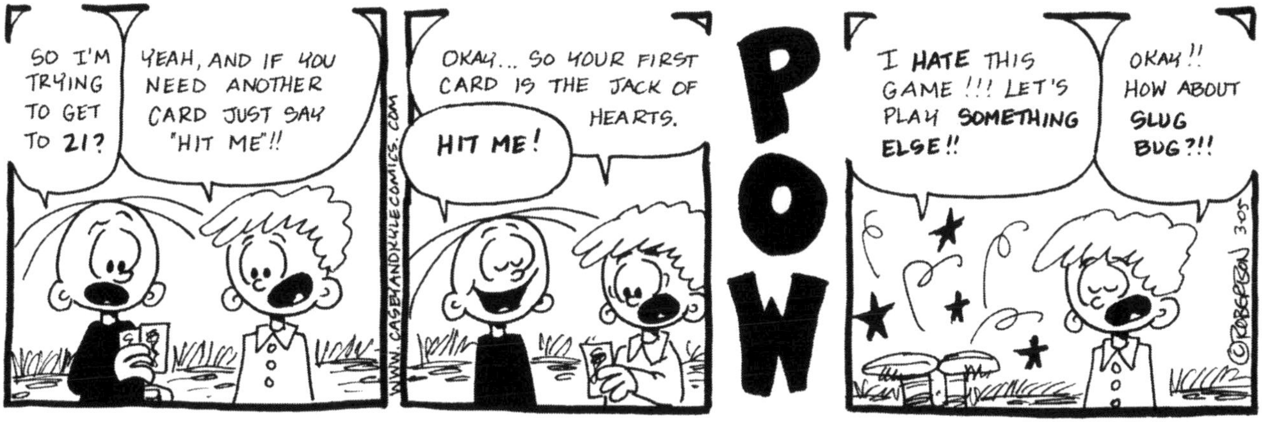
SO I'M TRYING TO GET TO 21?
YEAH, AND IF YOU NEED ANOTHER CARD JUST SAY "HIT ME"!!
WWW.CASEYANDKYLECOMICS.COM
OKAY... SO YOUR FIRST CARD IS THE JACK OF HEARTS.
HIT ME!
POW
I HATE THIS GAME!!! LET'S PLAY SOMETHING ELSE!!
OKAY!! HOW ABOUT SLUG BUG?!!
©ROBERTSON 3-05

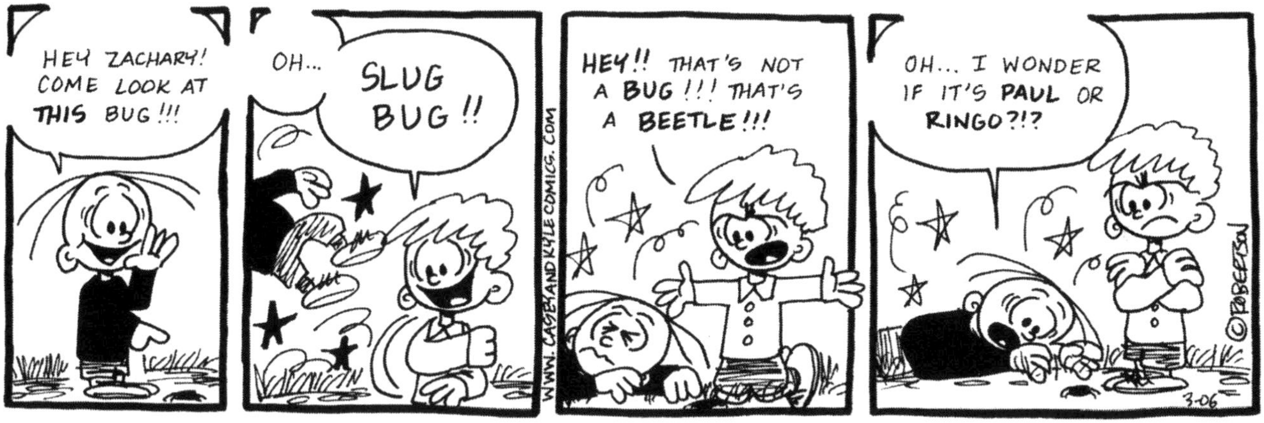
HEY ZACHARY! COME LOOK AT THIS BUG!!!
OH...
SLUG BUG!!
WWW.CASEYANDKYLECOMICS.COM
HEY!! THAT'S NOT A BUG!!! THAT'S A BEETLE!!!
OH... I WONDER IF IT'S PAUL OR RINGO?!?
©ROBERTSON
3-06

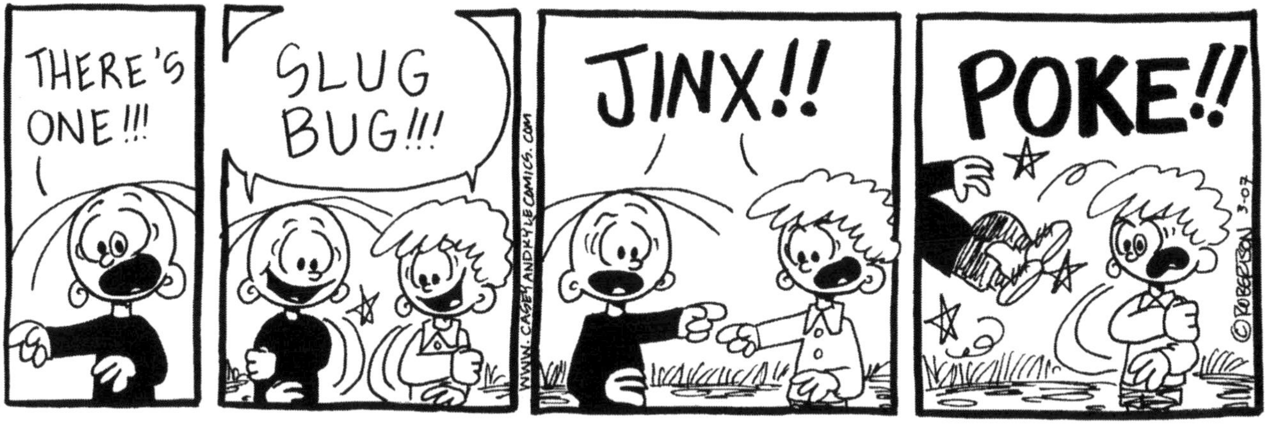
THERE'S ONE!!!
SLUG BUG!!!
WWW.CASEYANDKYLECOMICS.COM
JINX!!
POKE!!
©ROBERTSON 3-07

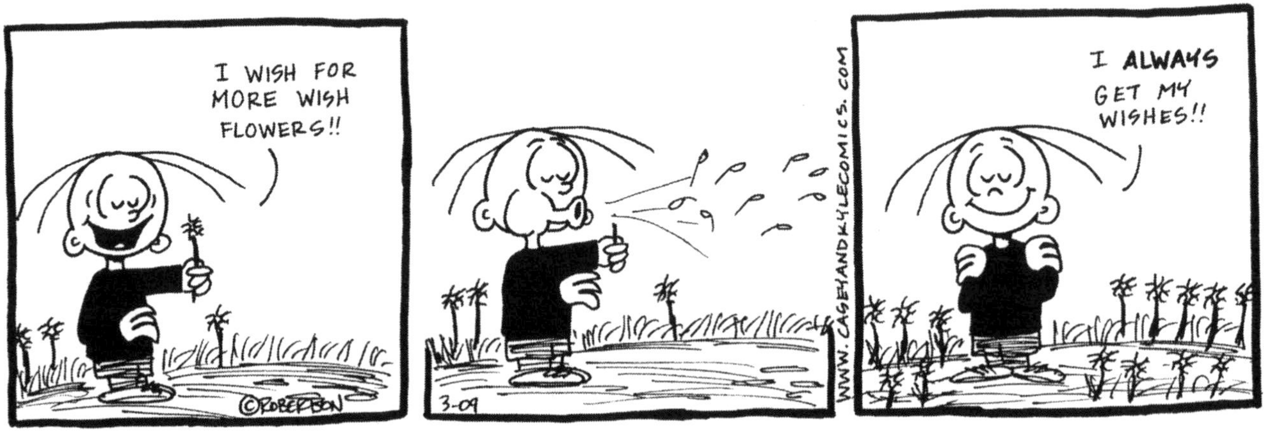
I WISH FOR MORE WISH FLOWERS!!
©ROBERTSON
3-09
WWW.CASEYANDKYLECOMICS.COM
I ALWAYS GET MY WISHES!!

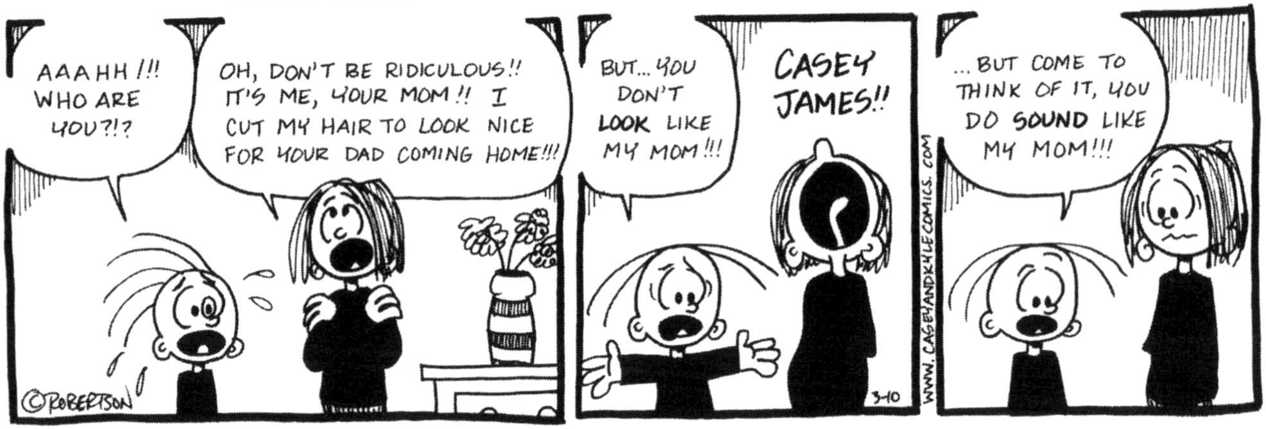
AAAHH!!! WHO ARE YOU?!?
OH, DON'T BE RIDICULOUS!! IT'S ME, YOUR MOM!! I CUT MY HAIR TO LOOK NICE FOR YOUR DAD COMING HOME!!!
©ROBERTSON
BUT... YOU DON'T LOOK LIKE MY MOM!!!
CASEY JAMES!!
3-10
WWW.CASEYANDKYLECOMICS.COM
...BUT COME TO THINK OF IT, YOU DO SOUND LIKE MY MOM!!!

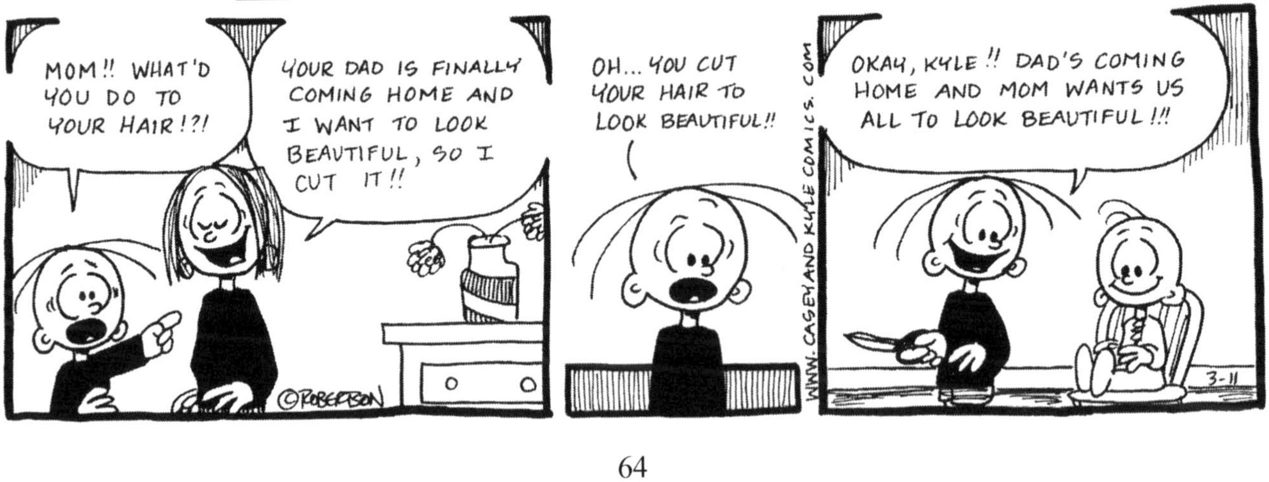
MOM!! WHAT'D YOU DO TO YOUR HAIR!?!
YOUR DAD IS FINALLY COMING HOME AND I WANT TO LOOK BEAUTIFUL, SO I CUT IT!!
©ROBERTSON
OH... YOU CUT YOUR HAIR TO LOOK BEAUTIFUL!!
WWW.CASEYANDKYLECOMICS.COM
OKAY, KYLE!! DAD'S COMING HOME AND MOM WANTS US ALL TO LOOK BEAUTIFUL!!!
3-11

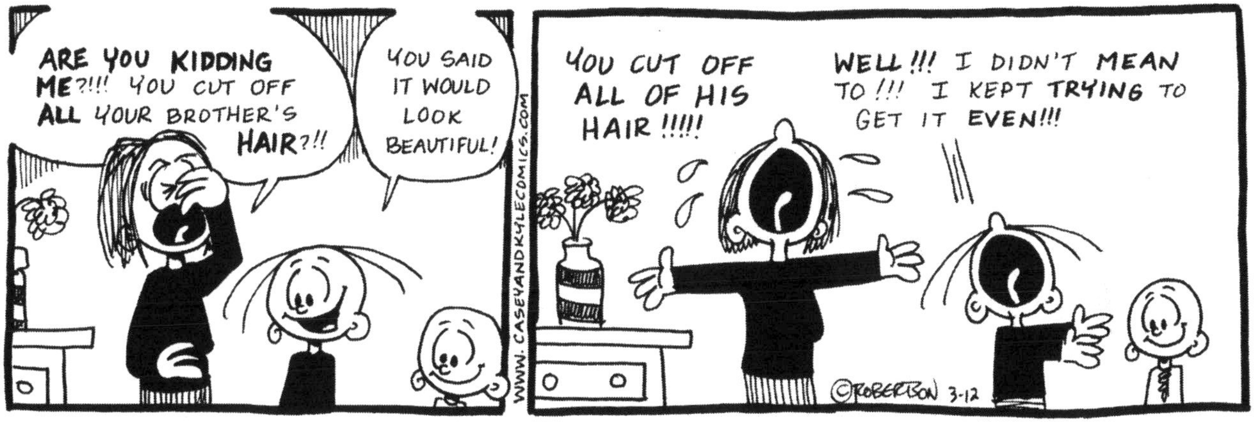
ARE YOU KIDDING ME?!!! YOU CUT OFF ALL YOUR BROTHER'S HAIR?!!
YOU SAID IT WOULD LOOK BEAUTIFUL!
WWW.CASEYANDKYLECOMICS.COM
YOU CUT OFF ALL OF HIS HAIR!!!!!
WELL!!! I DIDN'T MEAN TO!!! I KEPT TRYING TO GET IT EVEN!!!
©ROBERTSON 3-12

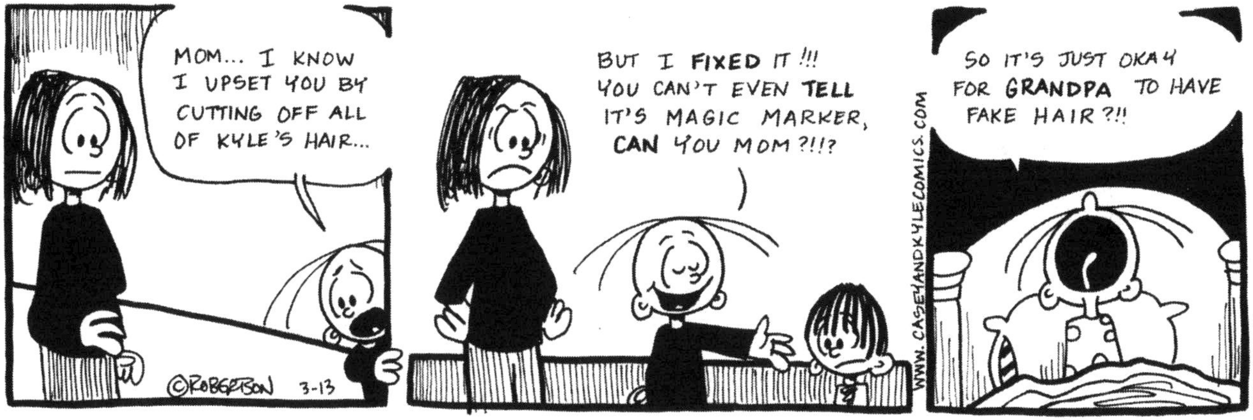
MOM... I KNOW I UPSET YOU BY CUTTING OFF ALL OF KYLE'S HAIR...
©ROBERTSON 3-13
BUT I FIXED IT!!! YOU CAN'T EVEN TELL IT'S MAGIC MARKER, CAN YOU MOM?!!?
WWW.CASEYANDKYLECOMICS.COM
SO IT'S JUST OKAY FOR GRANDPA TO HAVE FAKE HAIR?!!

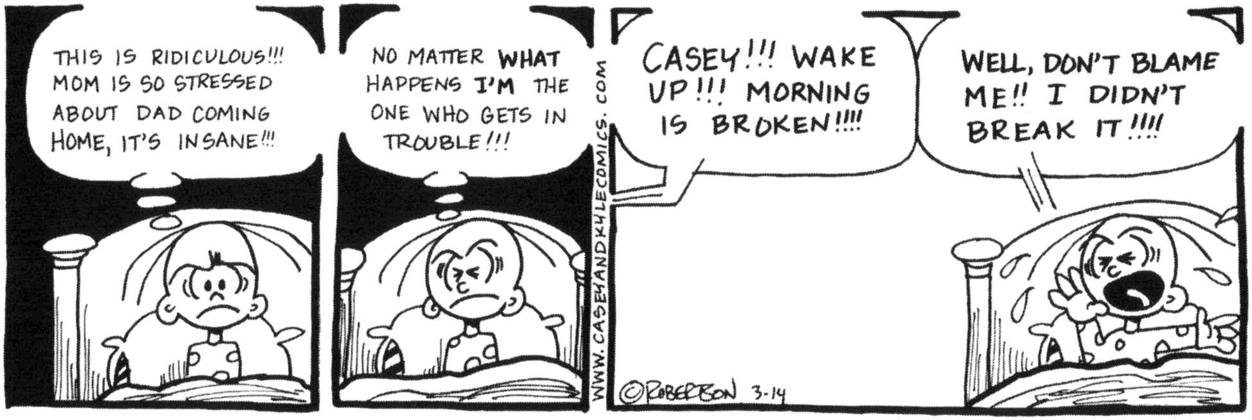
THIS IS RIDICULOUS!!! MOM IS SO STRESSED ABOUT DAD COMING HOME, IT'S INSANE!!!
NO MATTER WHAT HAPPENS I'M THE ONE WHO GETS IN TROUBLE!!!
WWW.CASEYANDKYLECOMICS.COM
CASEY!!! WAKE UP!!! MORNING IS BROKEN!!!!
WELL, DON'T BLAME ME!! I DIDN'T BREAK IT!!!!
©ROBERTSON 3-14

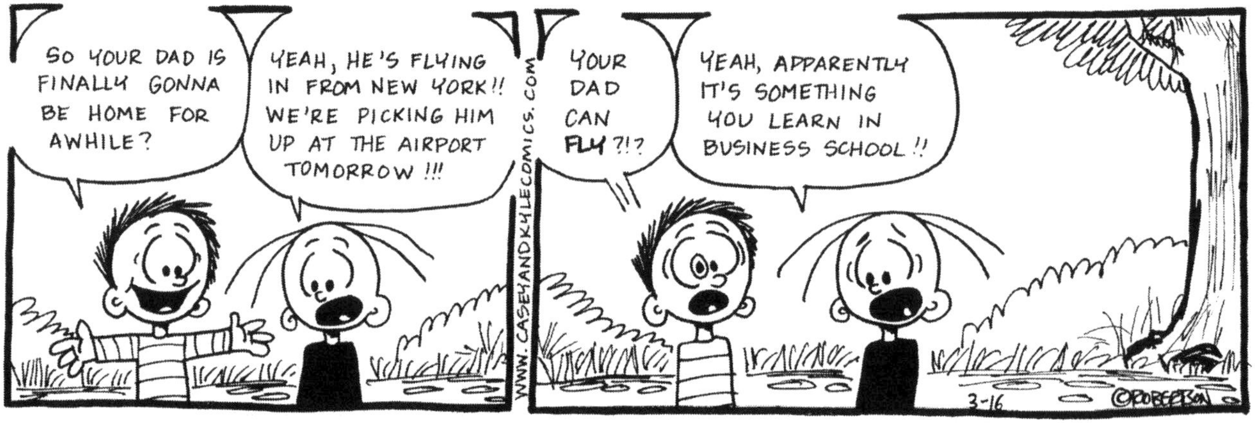
SO YOUR DAD IS FINALLY GONNA BE HOME FOR AWHILE?
YEAH, HE'S FLYING IN FROM NEW YORK!! WE'RE PICKING HIM UP AT THE AIRPORT TOMORROW!!!
WWW.CASEYANDKYLECOMICS.COM
YOUR DAD CAN FLY?!?
YEAH, APPARENTLY IT'S SOMETHING YOU LEARN IN BUSINESS SCHOOL!!
3-16
©ROBERTSON

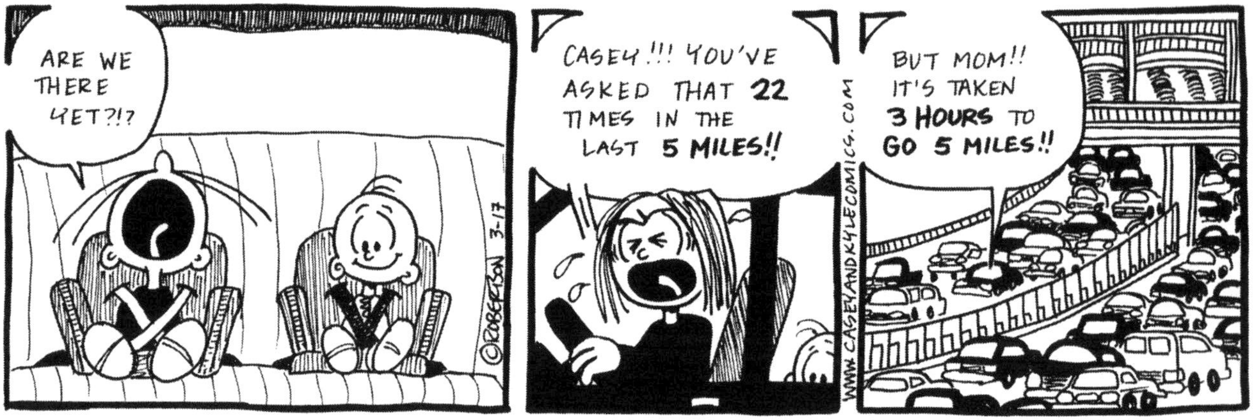
ARE WE THERE YET?!?
©ROBERTSON 3-17
CASEY!!! YOU'VE ASKED THAT 22 TIMES IN THE LAST 5 MILES!!
WWW.CASEYANDKYLECOMICS.COM
BUT MOM!! IT'S TAKEN 3 HOURS TO GO 5 MILES!!

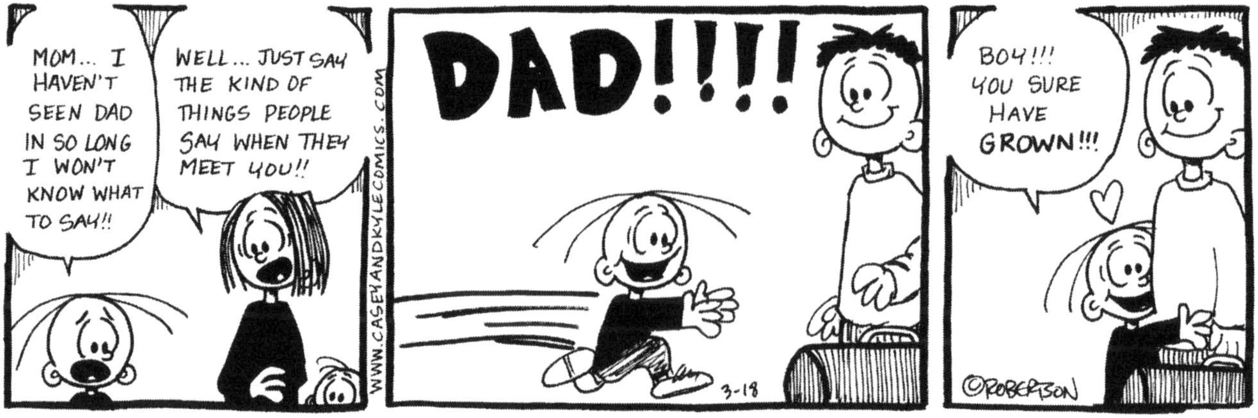
MOM... I HAVEN'T SEEN DAD IN SO LONG I WON'T KNOW WHAT TO SAY!!
WELL... JUST SAY THE KIND OF THINGS PEOPLE SAY WHEN THEY MEET YOU!!
WWW.CASEYANDKYLECOMICS.COM
DAD!!!!
3-18
BOY!!! YOU SURE HAVE GROWN!!!
©ROBERTSON

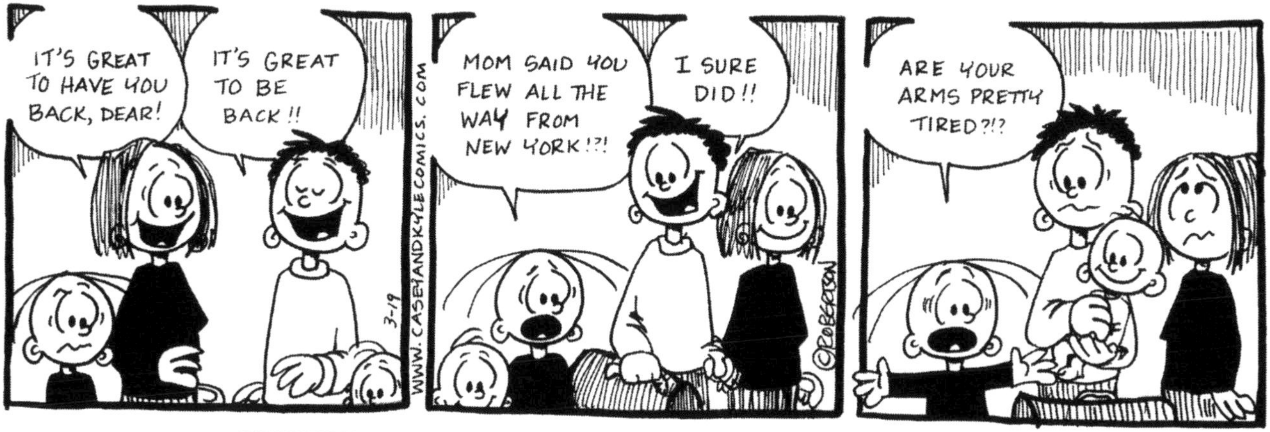
IT'S GREAT TO HAVE YOU BACK, DEAR!
IT'S GREAT TO BE BACK!!
3-19
WWW.CASEYANDKYLECOMICS.COM
MOM SAID YOU FLEW ALL THE WAY FROM NEW YORK!?!
I SURE DID!!
©ROBERTSON
ARE YOUR ARMS PRETTY TIRED?!?

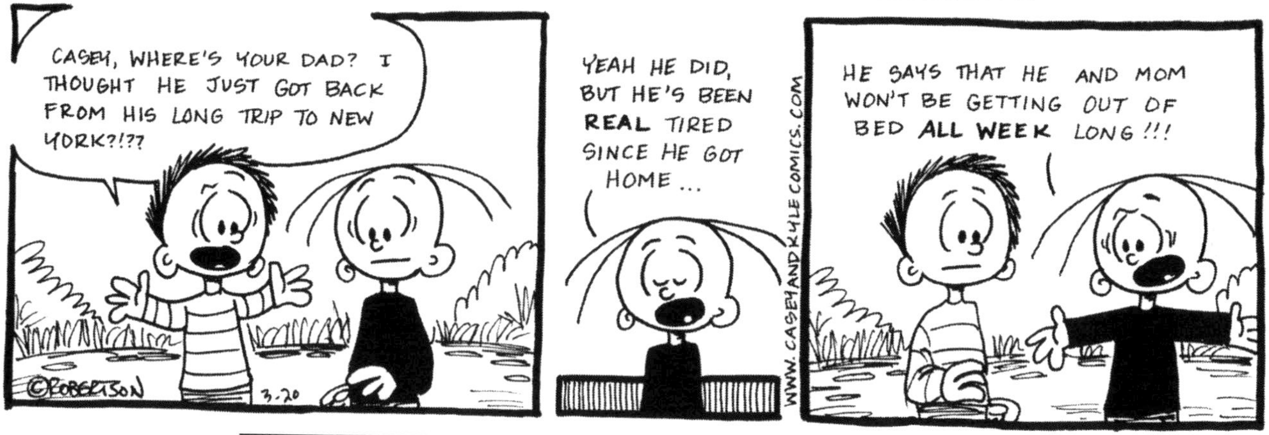
CASEY, WHERE'S YOUR DAD? I THOUGHT HE JUST GOT BACK FROM HIS LONG TRIP TO NEW YORK?!??
©ROBERTSON
3-20
YEAH HE DID, BUT HE'S BEEN REAL TIRED SINCE HE GOT HOME...
WWW.CASEYANDKYLECOMICS.COM
HE SAYS THAT HE AND MOM WON'T BE GETTING OUT OF BED ALL WEEK LONG!!!

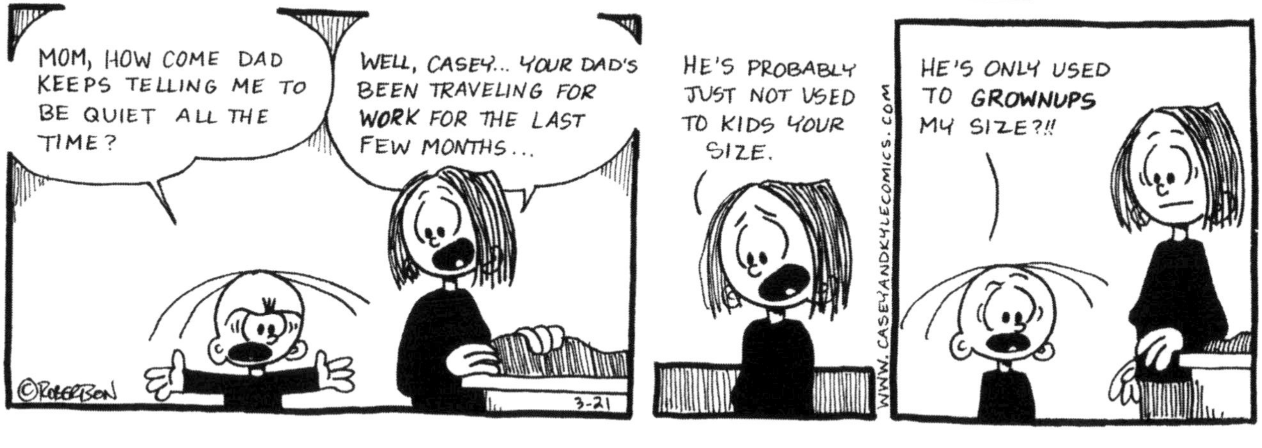
MOM, HOW COME DAD KEEPS TELLING ME TO BE QUIET ALL THE TIME?
WELL, CASEY... YOUR DAD'S BEEN TRAVELING FOR WORK FOR THE LAST FEW MONTHS...
©ROBERTSON
3-21
HE'S PROBABLY JUST NOT USED TO KIDS YOUR SIZE.
WWW.CASEYANDKYLECOMICS.COM
HE'S ONLY USED TO GROWNUPS MY SIZE?!!

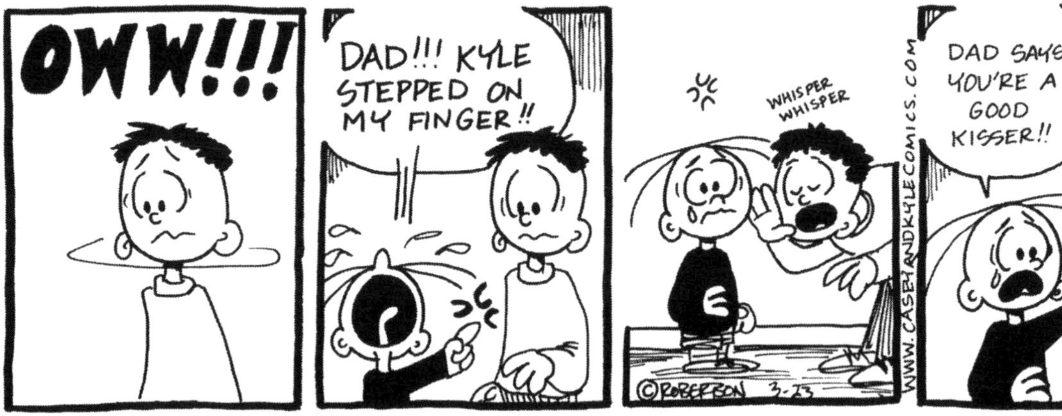
OWW!!!
DAD!!! KYLE STEPPED ON MY FINGER!!
WHISPER WHISPER
©ROBERSON 3-23
WWW.CASEYANDKYLECOMICS.COM
DAD SAYS YOU'RE A GOOD KISSER!!

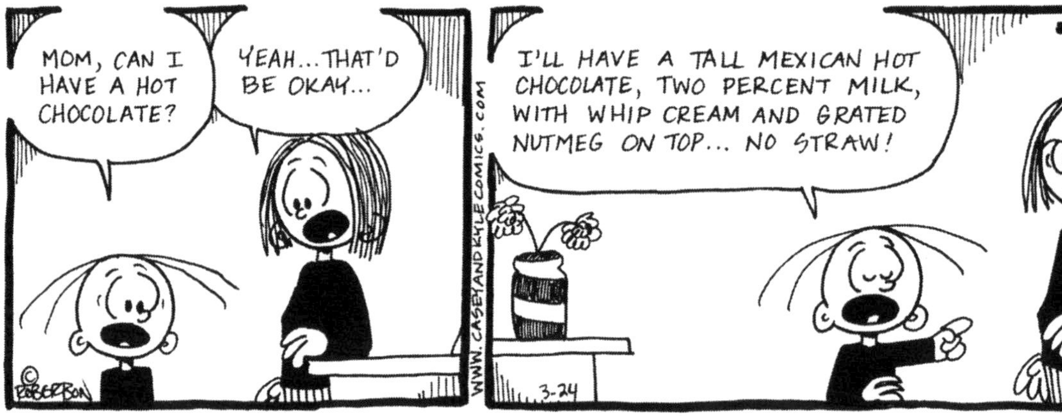
MOM, CAN I HAVE A HOT CHOCOLATE?
YEAH... THAT'D BE OKAY...
©ROBERSON
WWW.CASEYANDKYLECOMICS.COM
I'LL HAVE A TALL MEXICAN HOT CHOCOLATE, TWO PERCENT MILK, WITH WHIP CREAM AND GRATED NUTMEG ON TOP... NO STRAW!
3-24

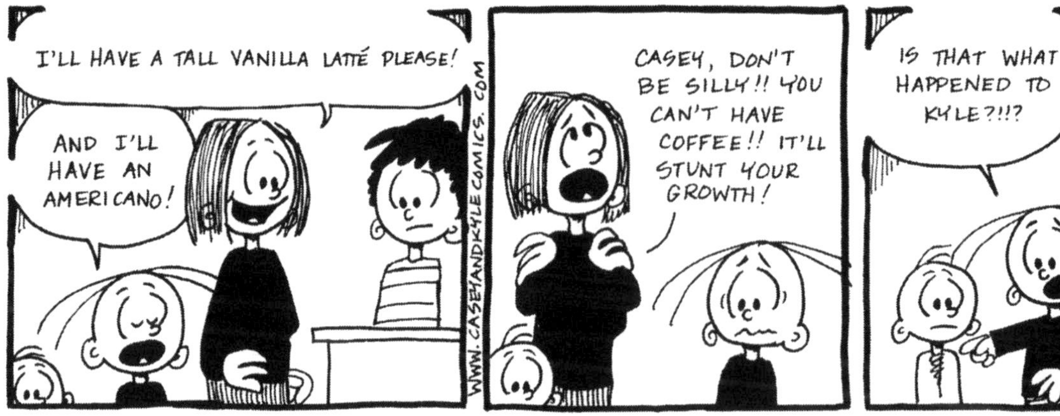
I'LL HAVE A TALL VANILLA LATTÉ PLEASE!
AND I'LL HAVE AN AMERICANO!
WWW.CASEYANDKYLECOMICS.COM
CASEY, DON'T BE SILLY!! YOU CAN'T HAVE COFFEE!! IT'LL STUNT YOUR GROWTH!
IS THAT WHAT HAPPENED TO KYLE?!!?
3-25
©ROBERSON

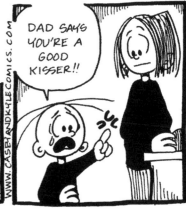

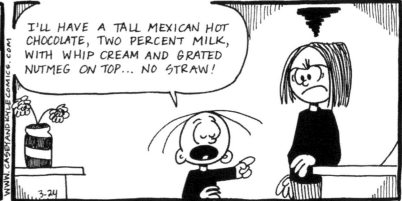

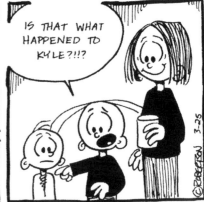

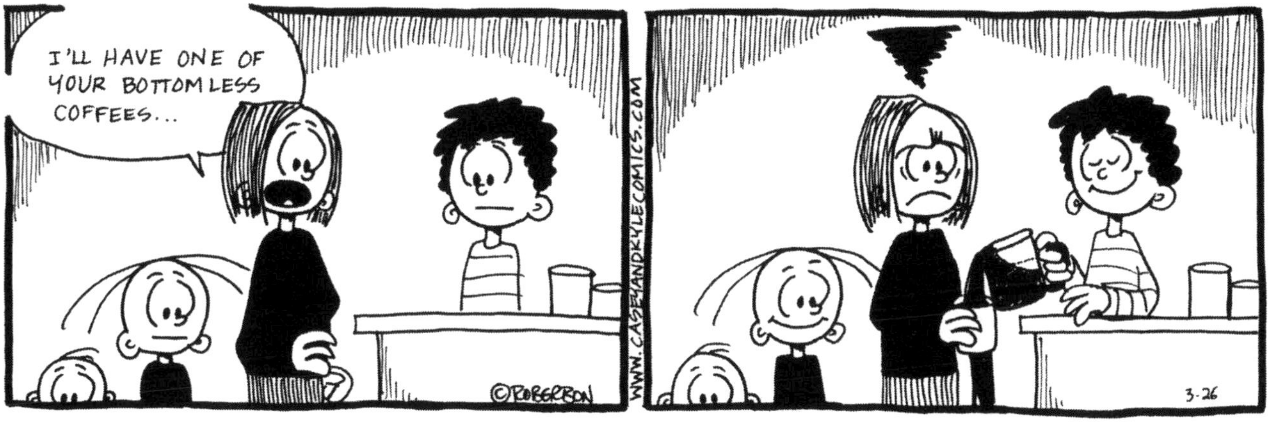
I'LL HAVE ONE OF YOUR BOTTOMLESS COFFEES...
©ROBERSON
WWW.CASEYANDKYLECOMICS.COM
3-26

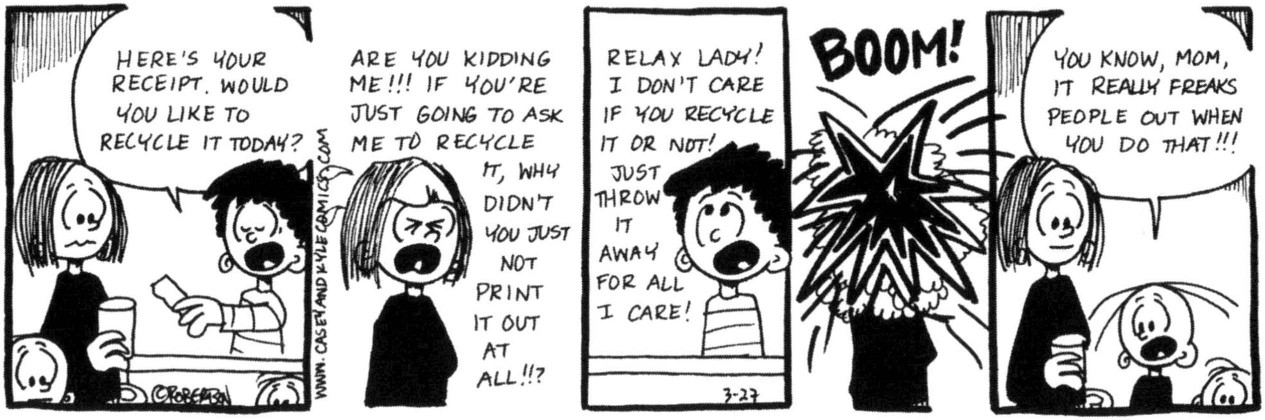
HERE'S YOUR RECEIPT. WOULD YOU LIKE TO RECYCLE IT TODAY?
©ROBERSON
WWW.CASEYANDKYLECOMICS.COM
ARE YOU KIDDING ME!!! IF YOU'RE JUST GOING TO ASK ME TO RECYCLE IT, WHY DIDN'T YOU JUST NOT PRINT IT OUT AT ALL!!?
RELAX LADY! I DON'T CARE IF YOU RECYCLE IT OR NOT! JUST THROW IT AWAY FOR ALL I CARE!
3-27
BOOM!
YOU KNOW, MOM, IT REALLY FREAKS PEOPLE OUT WHEN YOU DO THAT!!!

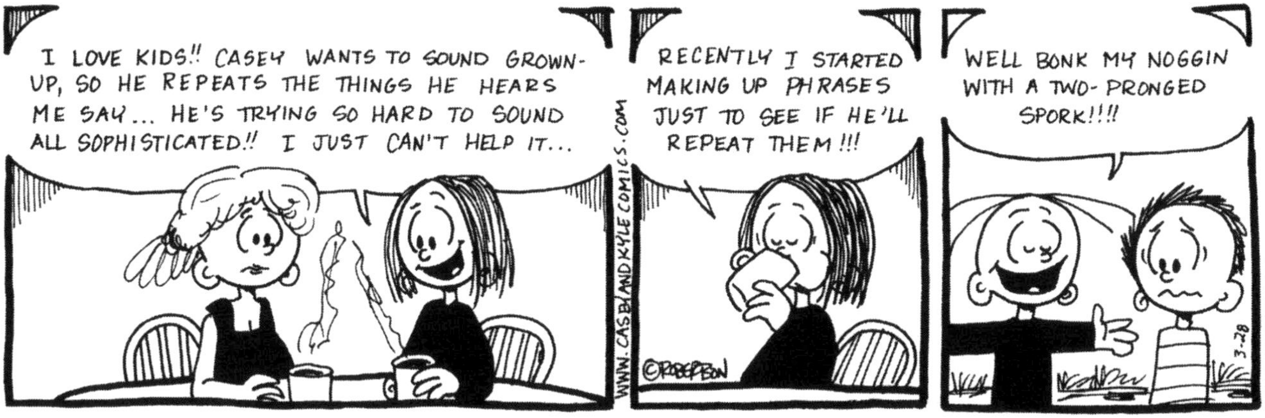
I LOVE KIDS!! CASEY WANTS TO SOUND GROWN-UP, SO HE REPEATS THE THINGS HE HEARS ME SAY... HE'S TRYING SO HARD TO SOUND ALL SOPHISTICATED!! I JUST CAN'T HELP IT...
WWW.CASEYANDKYLECOMICS.COM
RECENTLY I STARTED MAKING UP PHRASES JUST TO SEE IF HE'LL REPEAT THEM!!!
©ROBERSON
WELL BONK MY NOGGIN WITH A TWO-PRONGED SPORK!!!!
3-28

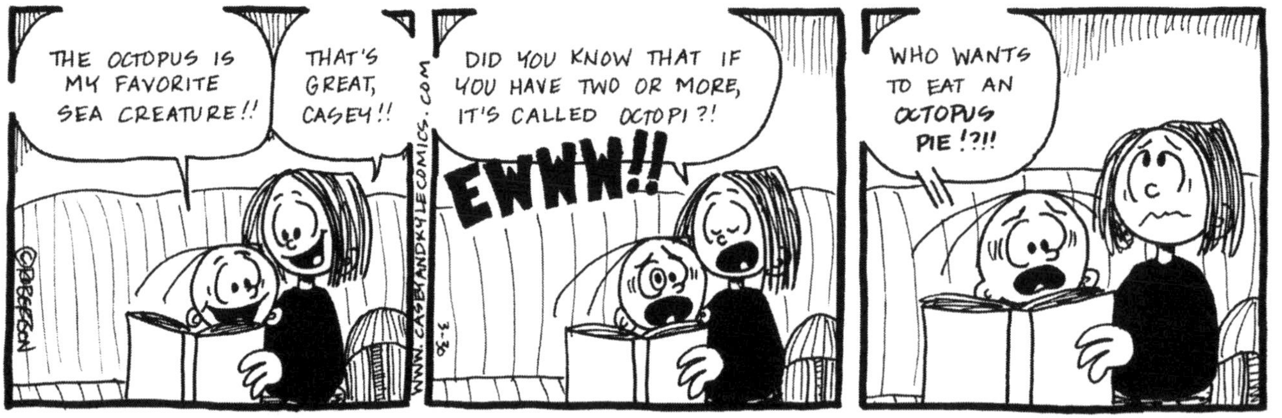
THE OCTOPUS IS MY FAVORITE SEA CREATURE!!
THAT'S GREAT, CASEY!!
WWW.CASEYANDKYLECOMICS.COM
3-30
DID YOU KNOW THAT IF YOU HAVE TWO OR MORE, IT'S CALLED OCTOPI?!
EWWW!!
WHO WANTS TO EAT AN OCTOPUS PIE!?!!

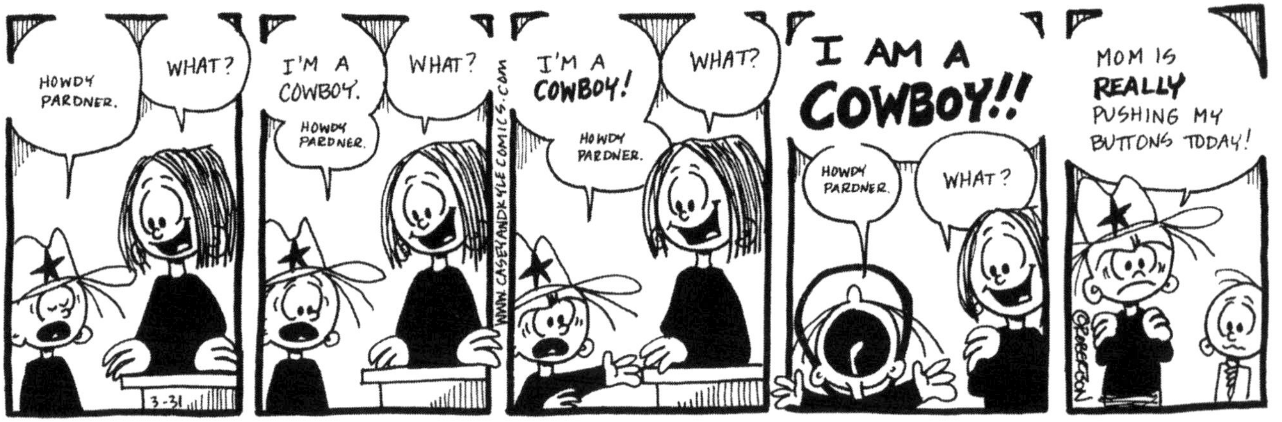
HOWDY PARDNER.
WHAT?
3-31
I'M A COWBOY.
HOWDY PARDNER.
WHAT?
WWW.CASEYANDKYLECOMICS.COM
I'M A COWBOY!
HOWDY PARDNER.
WHAT?
I AM A COWBOY!!
HOWDY PARDNER.
WHAT?
MOM IS REALLY PUSHING MY BUTTONS TODAY!

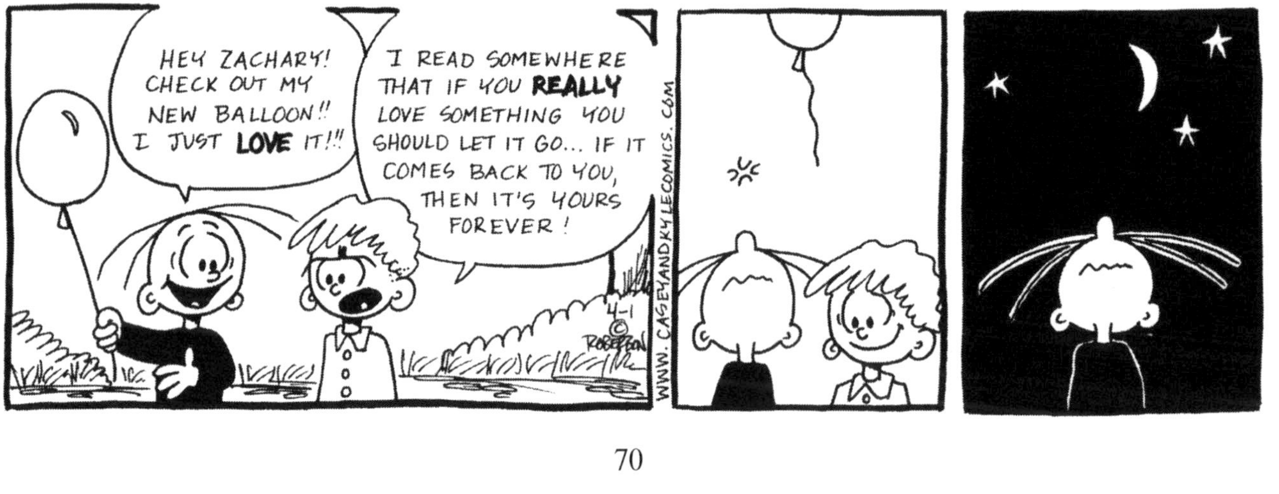
HEY ZACHARY! CHECK OUT MY NEW BALLOON!! I JUST LOVE IT!!!
I READ SOMEWHERE THAT IF YOU REALLY LOVE SOMETHING YOU SHOULD LET IT GO... IF IT COMES BACK TO YOU, THEN IT'S YOURS FOREVER!
4-1
WWW.CASEYANDKYLECOMICS.COM

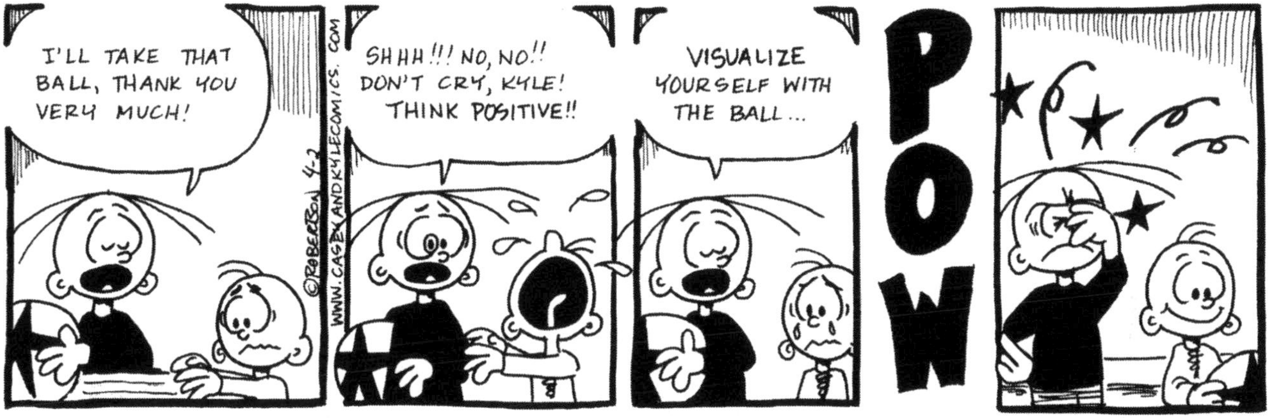
I'LL TAKE THAT BALL, THANK YOU VERY MUCH!
©ROBERTSON 4-2
WWW.CASEYANDKYLECOMICS.COM
SHHH!!! NO, NO!! DON'T CRY, KYLE! THINK POSITIVE!!
VISUALIZE YOURSELF WITH THE BALL...
POW

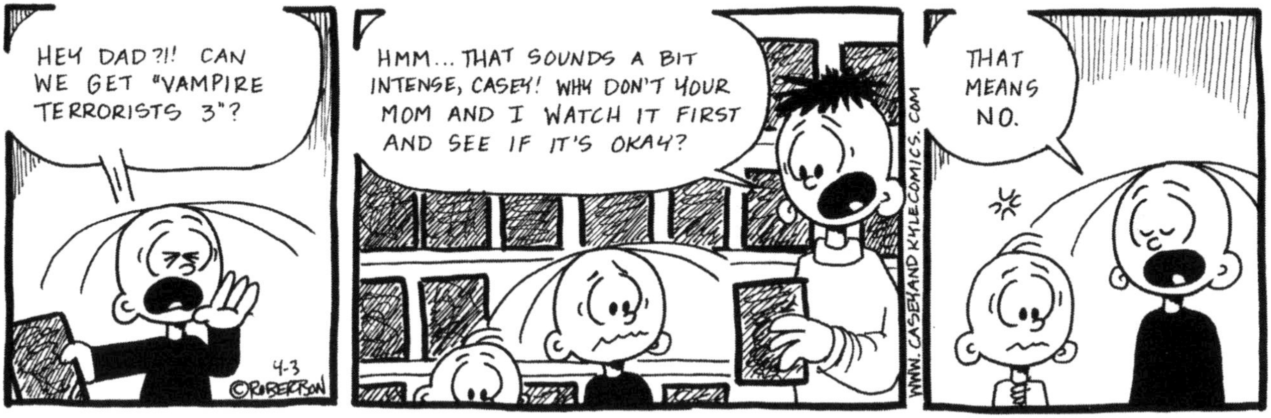
HEY DAD?!! CAN WE GET "VAMPIRE TERRORISTS 3"?
4-3
©ROBERTSON
HMM... THAT SOUNDS A BIT INTENSE, CASEY! WHY DON'T YOUR MOM AND I WATCH IT FIRST AND SEE IF IT'S OKAY?
WWW.CASEYANDKYLECOMICS.COM
THAT MEANS NO.

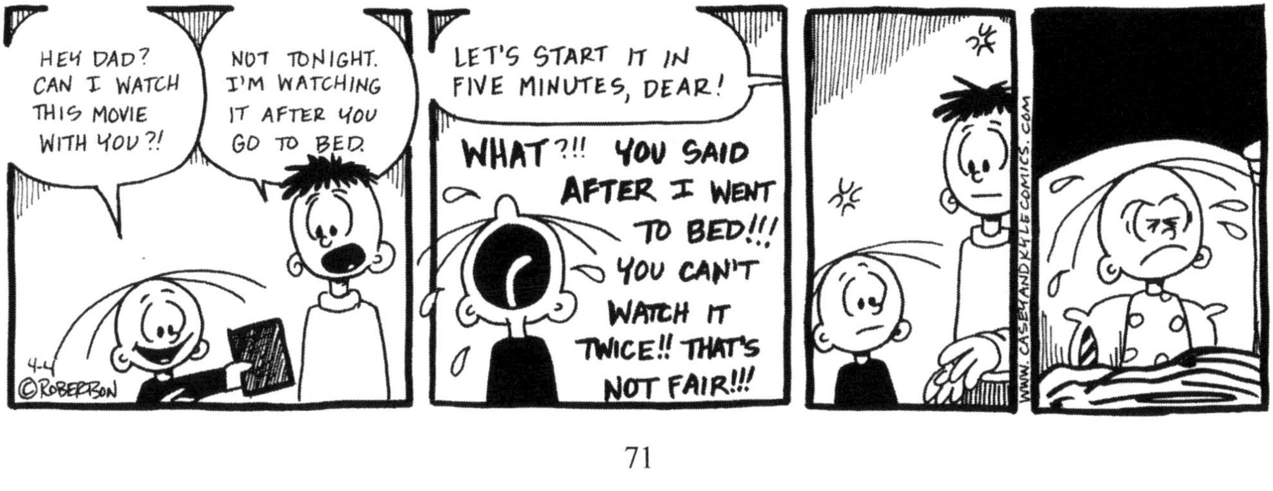
HEY DAD? CAN I WATCH THIS MOVIE WITH YOU?!
NOT TONIGHT. I'M WATCHING IT AFTER YOU GO TO BED.
4-4
©ROBERTSON
LET'S START IT IN FIVE MINUTES, DEAR!
WHAT?!! YOU SAID AFTER I WENT TO BED!!! YOU CAN'T WATCH IT TWICE!! THAT'S NOT FAIR!!!
WWW.CASEYANDKYLECOMICS.COM

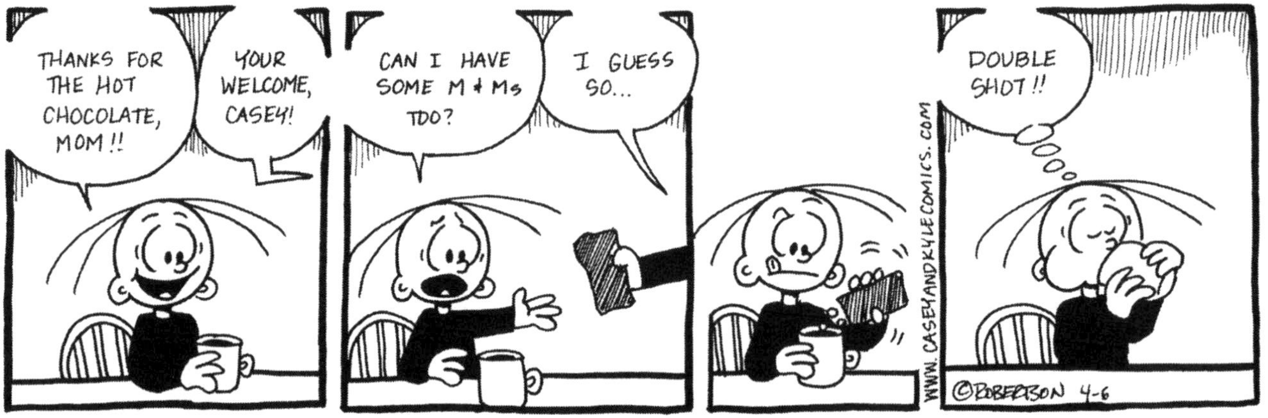
THANKS FOR THE HOT CHOCOLATE, MOM!!
YOUR WELCOME, CASEY!
CAN I HAVE SOME M & Ms TOO?
I GUESS SO...
WWW.CASEYANDKYLECOMICS.COM
DOUBLE SHOT!!
©ROBERTSON 4-6

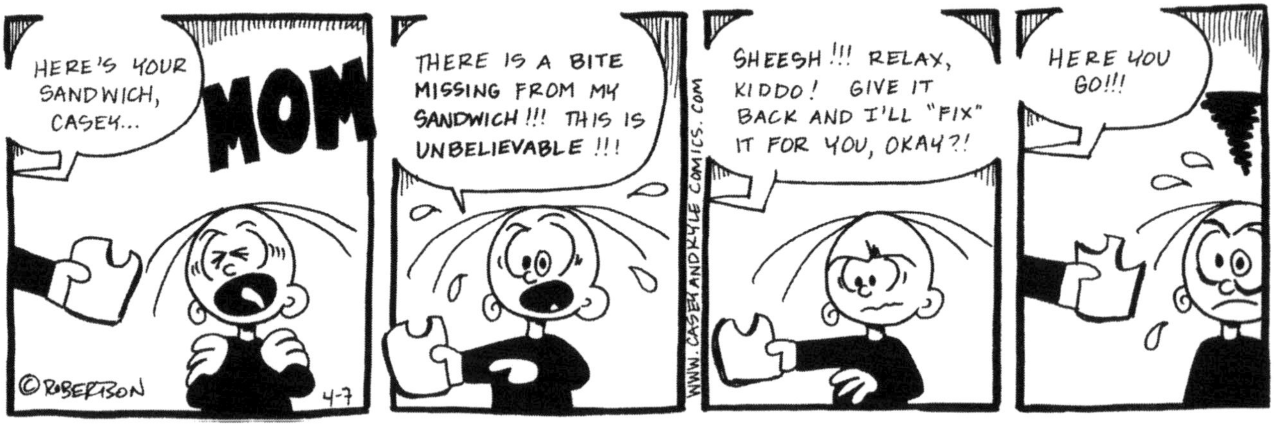
HERE'S YOUR SANDWICH, CASEY...
MOM
©ROBERTSON
4-7
THERE IS A BITE MISSING FROM MY SANDWICH!!! THIS IS UNBELIEVABLE!!!
WWW.CASEYANDKYLECOMICS.COM
SHEESH!!! RELAX, KIDDO! GIVE IT BACK AND I'LL "FIX" IT FOR YOU, OKAY?!
HERE YOU GO!!!

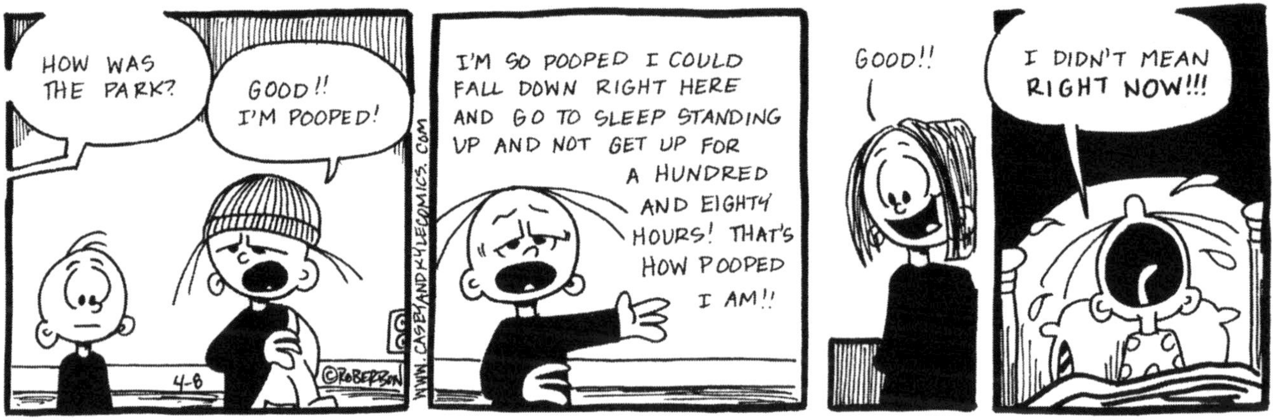
HOW WAS THE PARK?
GOOD!! I'M POOPED!
4-8
©ROBERTSON
WWW.CASEYANDKYLECOMICS.COM
I'M SO POOPED I COULD FALL DOWN RIGHT HERE AND GO TO SLEEP STANDING UP AND NOT GET UP FOR A HUNDRED AND EIGHTY HOURS! THAT'S HOW POOPED I AM!!
GOOD!!
I DIDN'T MEAN RIGHT NOW!!!

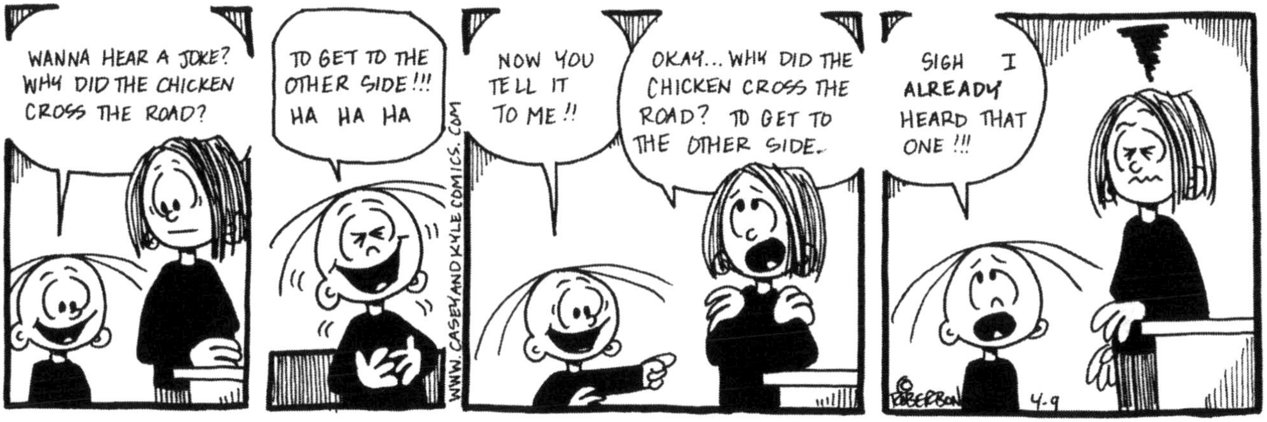
WANNA HEAR A JOKE? WHY DID THE CHICKEN CROSS THE ROAD?
TO GET TO THE OTHER SIDE!!! HA HA HA
WWW.CASEYANDKYLECOMICS.COM
NOW YOU TELL IT TO ME!!
OKAY... WHY DID THE CHICKEN CROSS THE ROAD? TO GET TO THE OTHER SIDE.
SIGH I ALREADY HEARD THAT ONE!!!
©ROBERSON
4-9

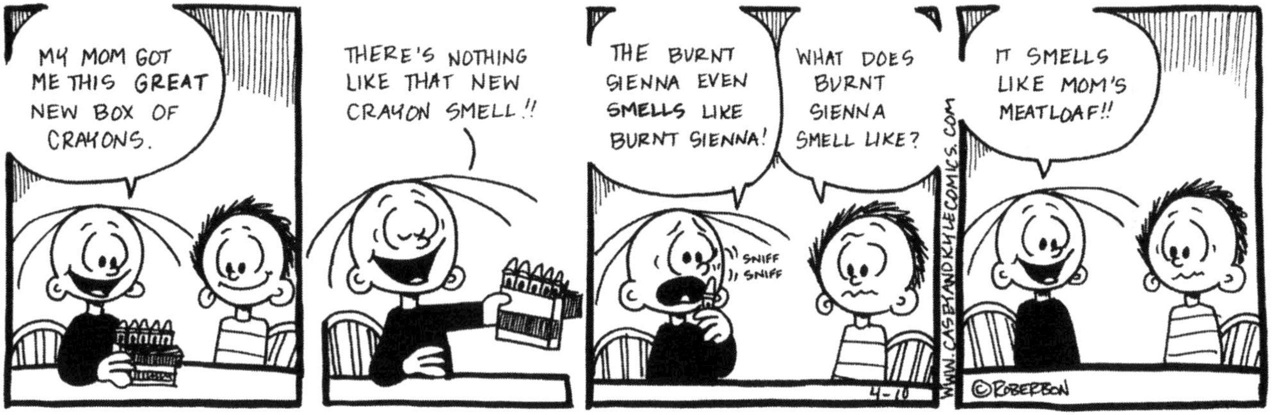
MY MOM GOT ME THIS GREAT NEW BOX OF CRAYONS.
THERE'S NOTHING LIKE THAT NEW CRAYON SMELL!!
THE BURNT SIENNA EVEN SMELLS LIKE BURNT SIENNA!
SNIFF SNIFF
WHAT DOES BURNT SIENNA SMELL LIKE?
4-10
WWW.CASEYANDKYLECOMICS.COM
IT SMELLS LIKE MOM'S MEATLOAF!!
©ROBERSON

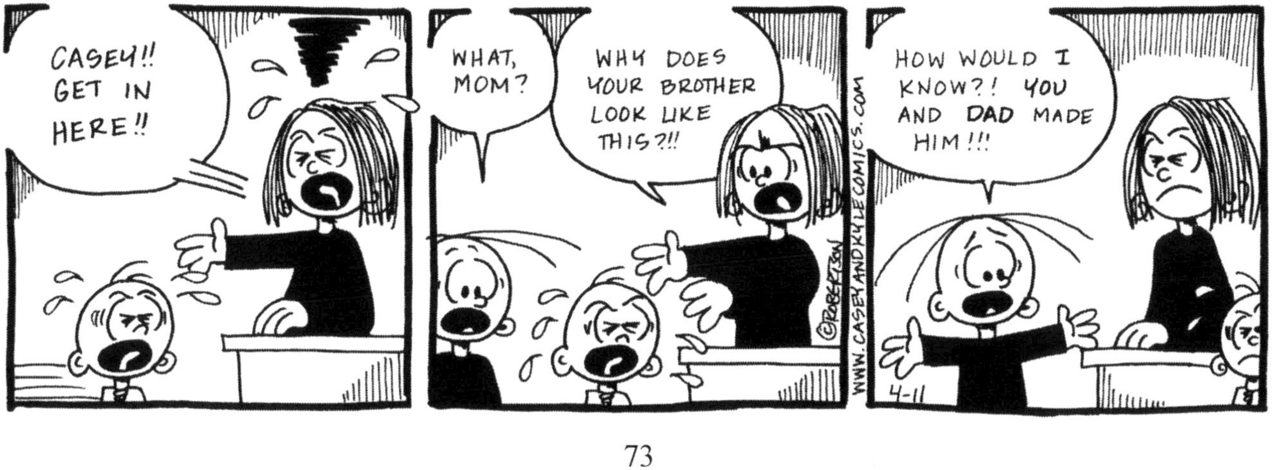
CASEY!! GET IN HERE!!
WHAT, MOM?
WHY DOES YOUR BROTHER LOOK LIKE THIS?!!
©ROBERSON
WWW.CASEYANDKYLECOMICS.COM
HOW WOULD I KNOW?! YOU AND DAD MADE HIM!!!
4-11

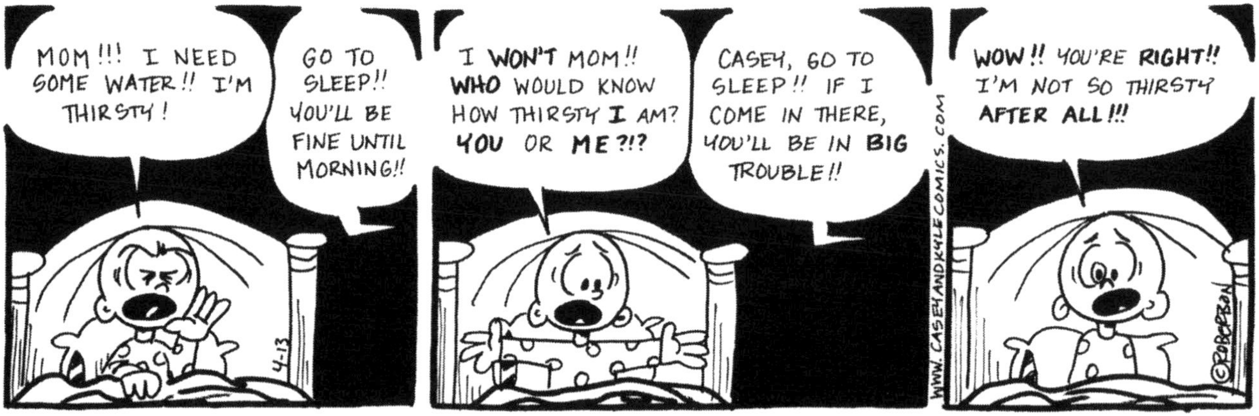
MOM!!! I NEED SOME WATER!! I'M THIRSTY!
GO TO SLEEP!! YOU'LL BE FINE UNTIL MORNING!!
4-13
I WON'T MOM!! WHO WOULD KNOW HOW THIRSTY I AM? YOU OR ME?!?
CASEY, GO TO SLEEP!! IF I COME IN THERE, YOU'LL BE IN BIG TROUBLE!!
WWW.CASEYANDKYLECOMICS.COM
WOW!! YOU'RE RIGHT!! I'M NOT SO THIRSTY AFTER ALL!!!
©ROBERTSON

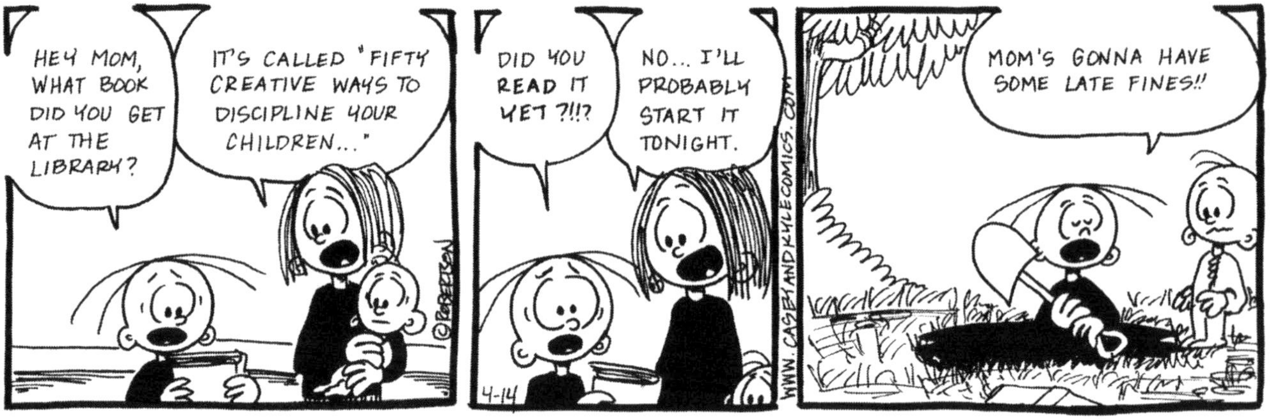
HEY MOM, WHAT BOOK DID YOU GET AT THE LIBRARY?
IT'S CALLED "FIFTY CREATIVE WAYS TO DISCIPLINE YOUR CHILDREN..."
©ROBERTSON
DID YOU READ IT YET?!!?
NO... I'LL PROBABLY START IT TONIGHT.
4-14
WWW.CASEYANDKYLECOMICS.COM
MOM'S GONNA HAVE SOME LATE FINES!!

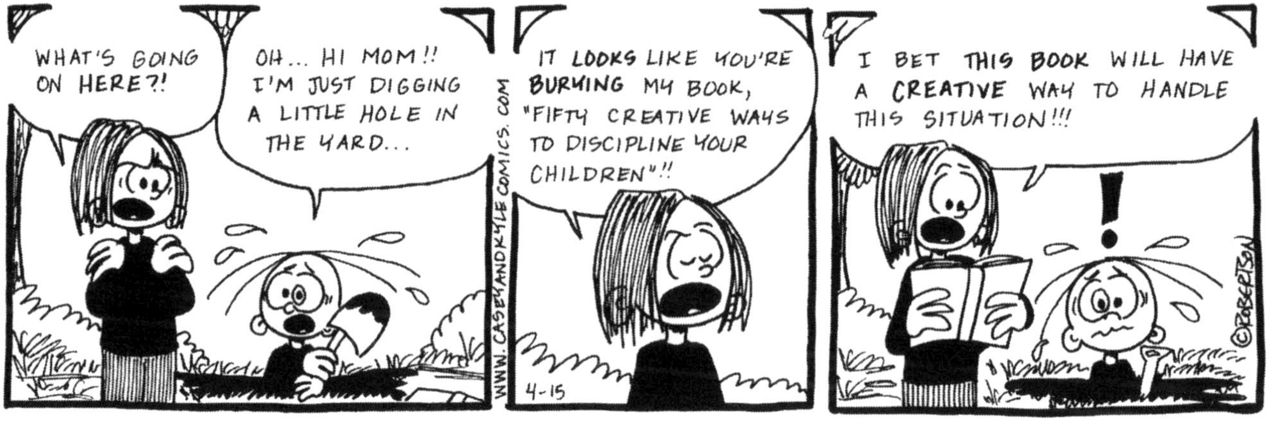
WHAT'S GOING ON HERE?!
OH... HI MOM!! I'M JUST DIGGING A LITTLE HOLE IN THE YARD...
WWW.CASEYANDKYLECOMICS.COM
IT LOOKS LIKE YOU'RE BURYING MY BOOK, "FIFTY CREATIVE WAYS TO DISCIPLINE YOUR CHILDREN"!!
4-15
I BET THIS BOOK WILL HAVE A CREATIVE WAY TO HANDLE THIS SITUATION!!!
!
©ROBERTSON

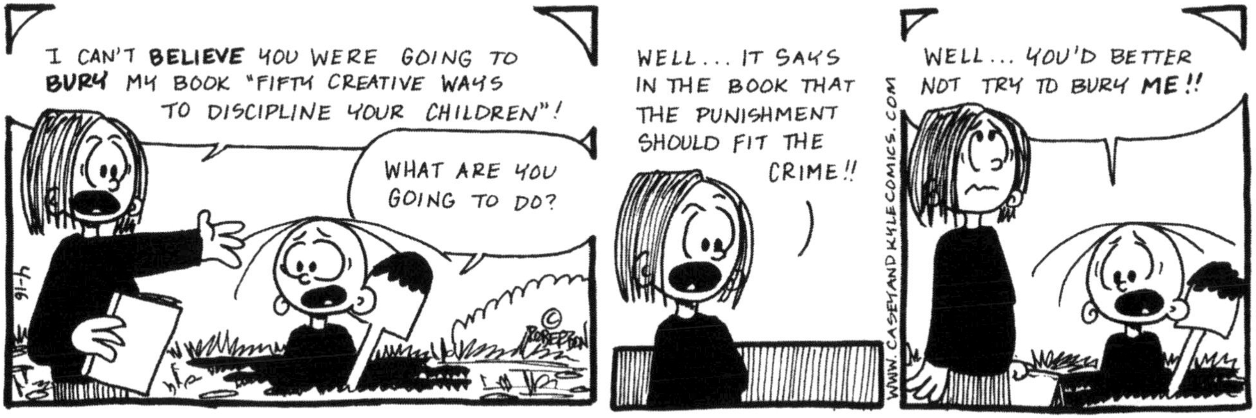
I CAN'T BELIEVE YOU WERE GOING TO BURY MY BOOK "FIFTY CREATIVE WAYS TO DISCIPLINE YOUR CHILDREN"!
WHAT ARE YOU GOING TO DO?
4-16
© ROBERSON
WELL... IT SAYS IN THE BOOK THAT THE PUNISHMENT SHOULD FIT THE CRIME!!
WWW.CASEYANDKYLECOMICS.COM
WELL... YOU'D BETTER NOT TRY TO BURY ME!!

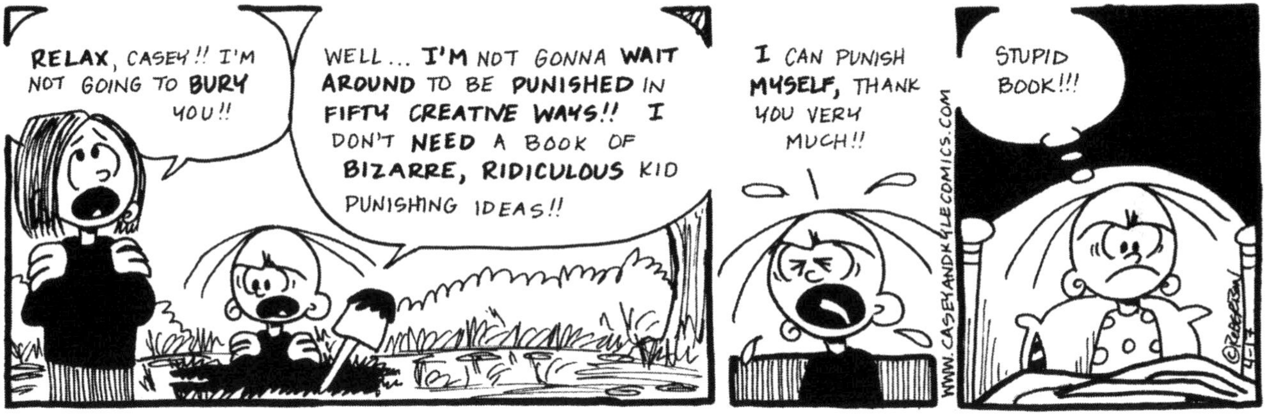
RELAX, CASEY!! I'M NOT GOING TO BURY YOU!!
WELL... I'M NOT GONNA WAIT AROUND TO BE PUNISHED IN FIFTY CREATIVE WAYS!! I DON'T NEED A BOOK OF BIZARRE, RIDICULOUS KID PUNISHING IDEAS!!
I CAN PUNISH MYSELF, THANK YOU VERY MUCH!!
WWW.CASEYANDKYLECOMICS.COM
STUPID BOOK!!!
©ROBERSON 4-17

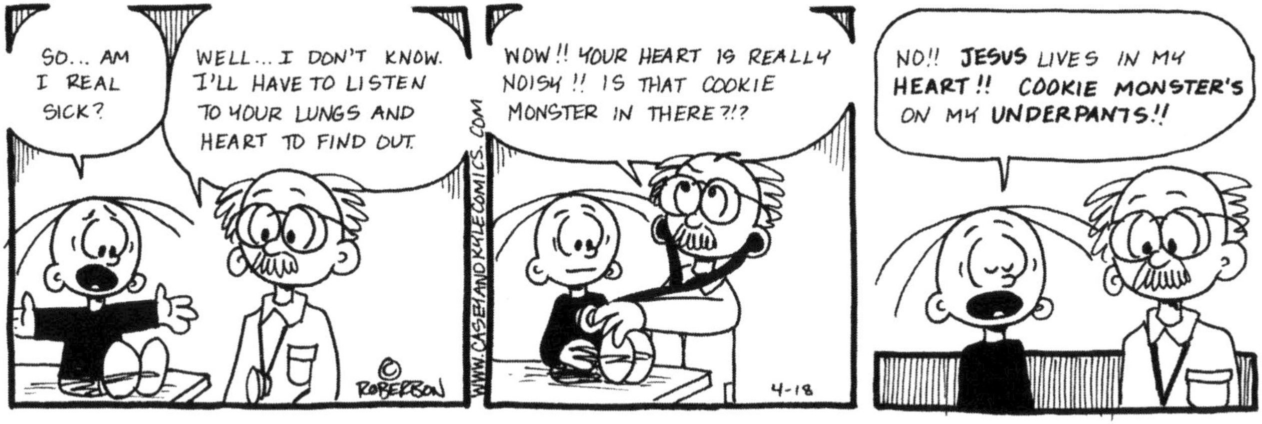
SO... AM I REAL SICK?
WELL... I DON'T KNOW. I'LL HAVE TO LISTEN TO YOUR LUNGS AND HEART TO FIND OUT.
© ROBERSON
WWW.CASEYANDKYLECOMICS.COM
WOW!! YOUR HEART IS REALLY NOISY!! IS THAT COOKIE MONSTER IN THERE?!?
4-18
NO!! JESUS LIVES IN MY HEART!! COOKIE MONSTER'S ON MY UNDERPANTS!!

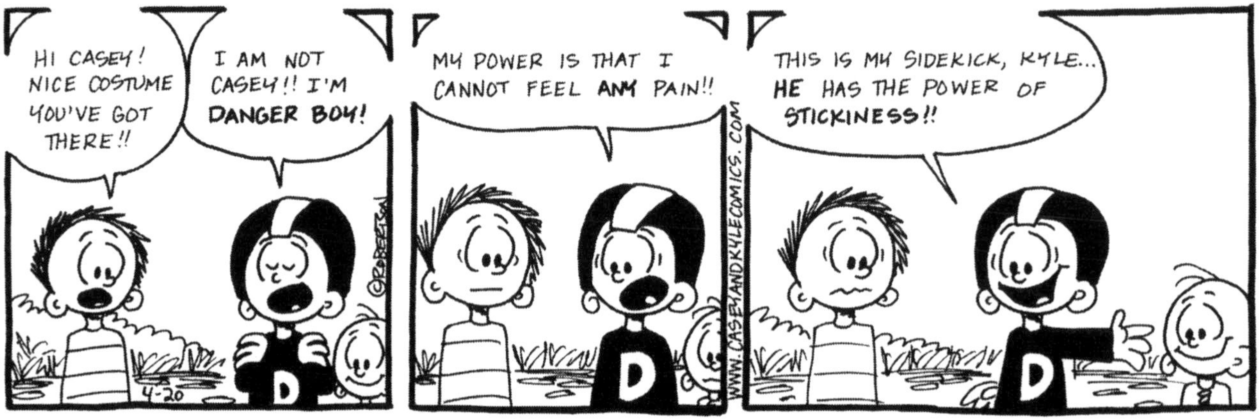
HI CASEY! NICE COSTUME YOU'VE GOT THERE!!
I AM NOT CASEY!! I'M DANGER BOY!
4-20
©ROBERTSON
MY POWER IS THAT I CANNOT FEEL ANY PAIN!!
WWW.CASEYANDKYLECOMICS.COM
THIS IS MY SIDEKICK, KYLE... HE HAS THE POWER OF STICKINESS!!

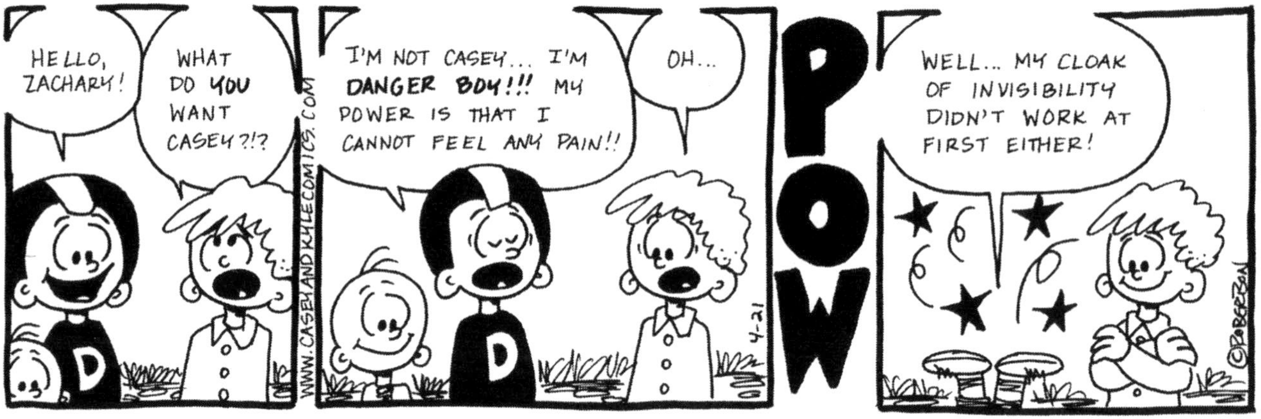
HELLO, ZACHARY!
WHAT DO YOU WANT CASEY?!?
WWW.CASEYANDKYLECOMICS.COM
I'M NOT CASEY... I'M DANGER BOY!!! MY POWER IS THAT I CANNOT FEEL ANY PAIN!!
OH...
4-21
POW
WELL... MY CLOAK OF INVISIBILITY DIDN'T WORK AT FIRST EITHER!
©ROBERTSON

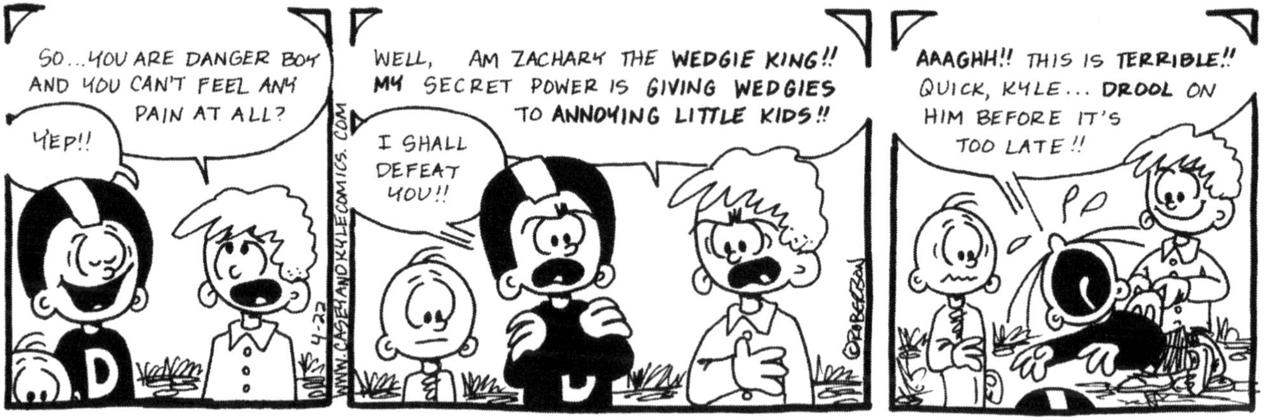
SO...YOU ARE DANGER BOY AND YOU CAN'T FEEL ANY PAIN AT ALL?
YEP!!
4-22
WWW.CASEYANDKYLECOMICS.COM
WELL, AM ZACHARY THE WEDGIE KING!! MY SECRET POWER IS GIVING WEDGIES TO ANNOYING LITTLE KIDS!!
I SHALL DEFEAT YOU!!
©ROBERTSON
AAAGHH!! THIS IS TERRIBLE!! QUICK, KYLE... DROOL ON HIM BEFORE IT'S TOO LATE!!

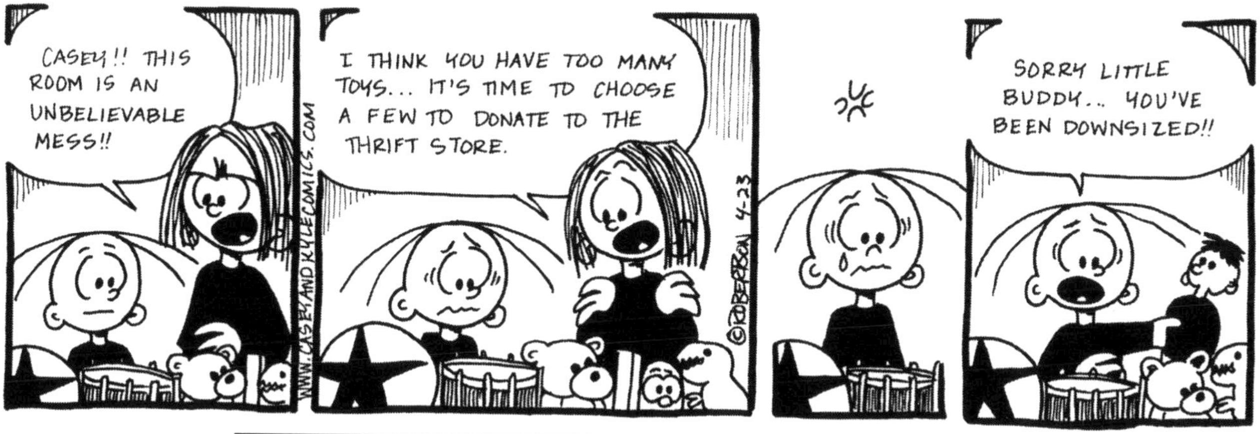
CASEY!! THIS ROOM IS AN UNBELIEVABLE MESS!!
WWW.CASEYANDKYLECOMICS.COM
I THINK YOU HAVE TOO MANY TOYS... IT'S TIME TO CHOOSE A FEW TO DONATE TO THE THRIFT STORE.
©ROBERSON 4-23
SORRY LITTLE BUDDY... YOU'VE BEEN DOWNSIZED!!

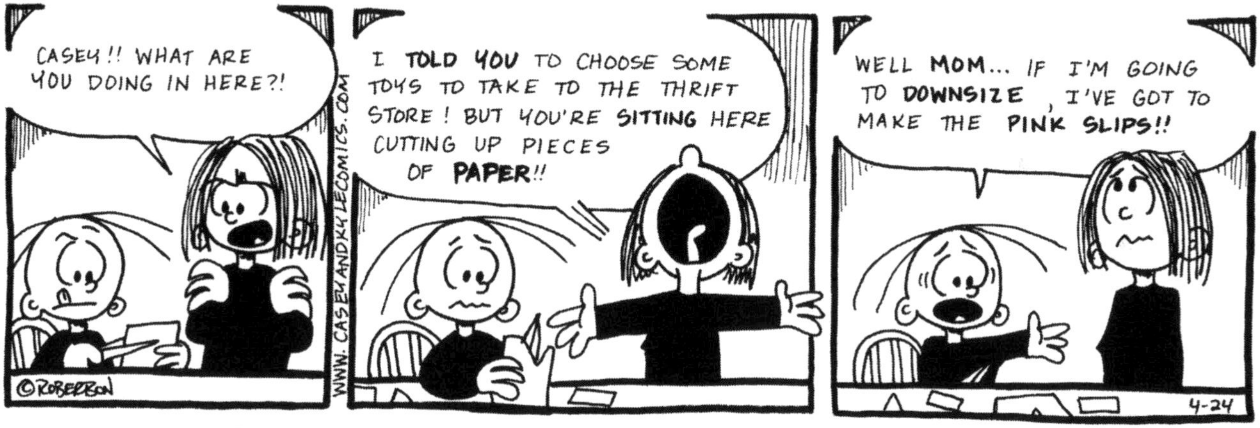
CASEY!! WHAT ARE YOU DOING IN HERE?!
©ROBERSON
WWW.CASEYANDKYLECOMICS.COM
I TOLD YOU TO CHOOSE SOME TOYS TO TAKE TO THE THRIFT STORE! BUT YOU'RE SITTING HERE CUTTING UP PIECES OF PAPER!!
WELL MOM... IF I'M GOING TO DOWNSIZE, I'VE GOT TO MAKE THE PINK SLIPS!!
4-24

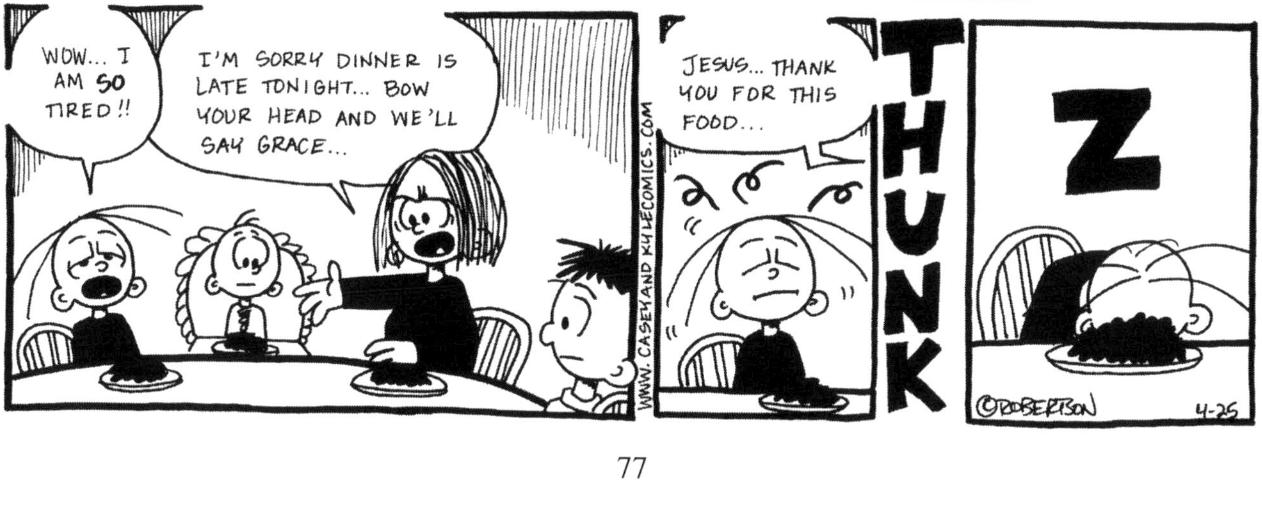
WOW... I AM SO TIRED!!
I'M SORRY DINNER IS LATE TONIGHT... BOW YOUR HEAD AND WE'LL SAY GRACE...
WWW.CASEYANDKYLECOMICS.COM
JESUS... THANK YOU FOR THIS FOOD...
THUNK
Z
©ROBERSON
4-25

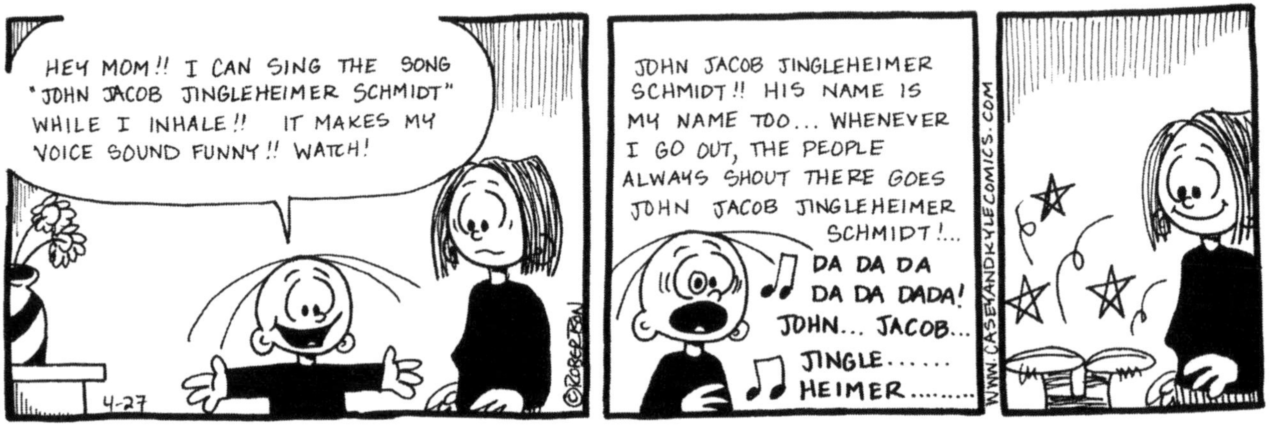
HEY MOM!! I CAN SING THE SONG "JOHN JACOB JINGLEHEIMER SCHMIDT" WHILE I INHALE!! IT MAKES MY VOICE SOUND FUNNY!! WATCH!
4-27
©ROBERTSON
JOHN JACOB JINGLEHEIMER SCHMIDT!! HIS NAME IS MY NAME TOO... WHENEVER I GO OUT, THE PEOPLE ALWAYS SHOUT THERE GOES JOHN JACOB JINGLEHEIMER SCHMIDT!...
DA DA DA DA DA DADA! JOHN... JACOB... JINGLE...... HEIMER........
WWW.CASEYANDKYLECOMICS.COM

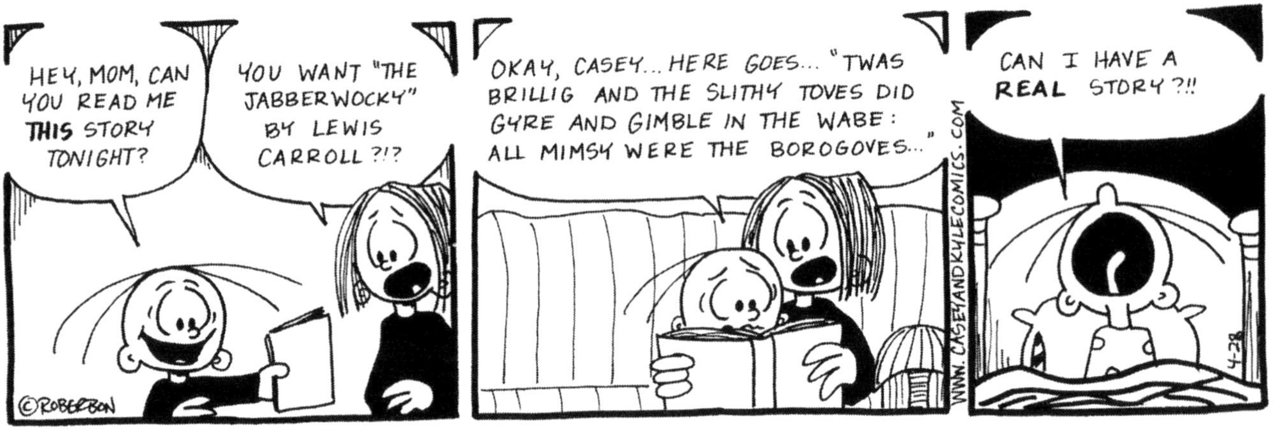
HEY, MOM, CAN YOU READ ME THIS STORY TONIGHT?
YOU WANT "THE JABBERWOCKY" BY LEWIS CARROLL ?!?
©ROBERTSON
OKAY, CASEY... HERE GOES... "TWAS BRILLIG AND THE SLITHY TOVES DID GYRE AND GIMBLE IN THE WABE: ALL MIMSY WERE THE BOROGOVES..."
WWW.CASEYANDKYLECOMICS.COM
CAN I HAVE A REAL STORY?!!
4-28

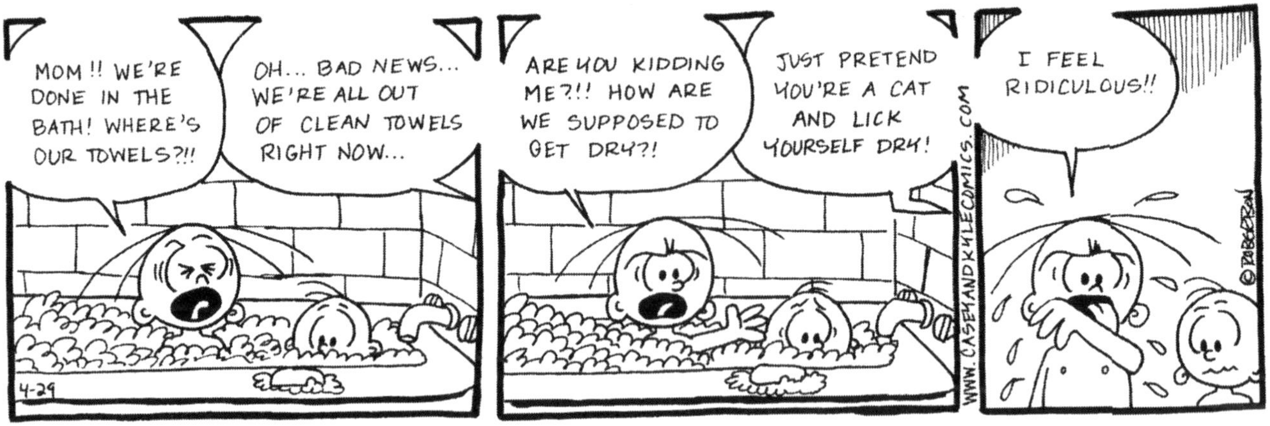
MOM!! WE'RE DONE IN THE BATH! WHERE'S OUR TOWELS?!!
OH... BAD NEWS... WE'RE ALL OUT OF CLEAN TOWELS RIGHT NOW...
4-29
ARE YOU KIDDING ME?!! HOW ARE WE SUPPOSED TO GET DRY?!
JUST PRETEND YOU'RE A CAT AND LICK YOURSELF DRY!
WWW.CASEYANDKYLECOMICS.COM
I FEEL RIDICULOUS!!
©ROBERTSON

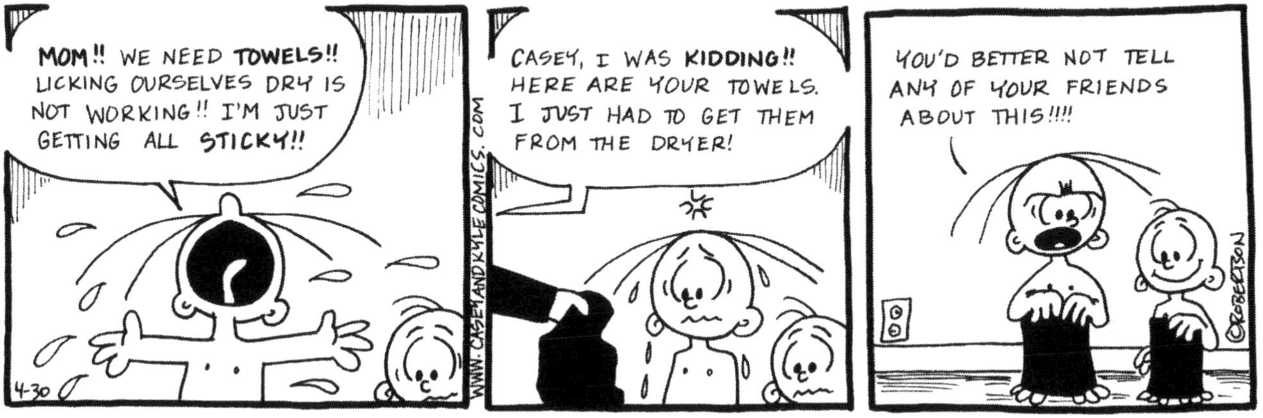
MOM!! WE NEED TOWELS!! LICKING OURSELVES DRY IS NOT WORKING!! I'M JUST GETTING ALL STICKY!!
4-30
WWW.CASEYANDKYLECOMICS.COM
CASEY, I WAS KIDDING!! HERE ARE YOUR TOWELS. I JUST HAD TO GET THEM FROM THE DRYER!
YOU'D BETTER NOT TELL ANY OF YOUR FRIENDS ABOUT THIS!!!!
©ROBERTSON

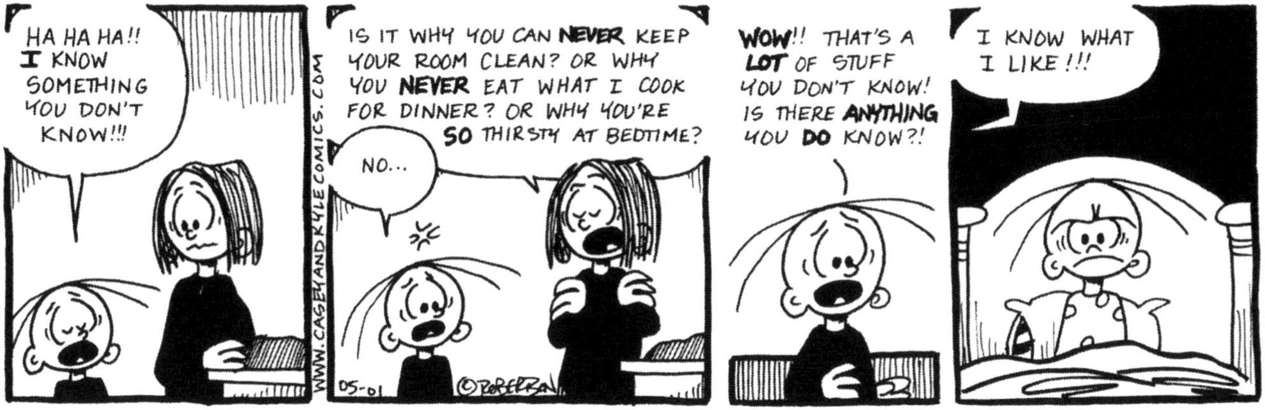
HA HA HA!! I KNOW SOMETHING YOU DON'T KNOW!!!
WWW.CASEYANDKYLECOMICS.COM
NO...
IS IT WHY YOU CAN NEVER KEEP YOUR ROOM CLEAN? OR WHY YOU NEVER EAT WHAT I COOK FOR DINNER? OR WHY YOU'RE SO THIRSTY AT BEDTIME?
05-01
©ROBERTSON
WOW!! THAT'S A LOT OF STUFF YOU DON'T KNOW! IS THERE ANYTHING YOU DO KNOW?!
I KNOW WHAT I LIKE!!!

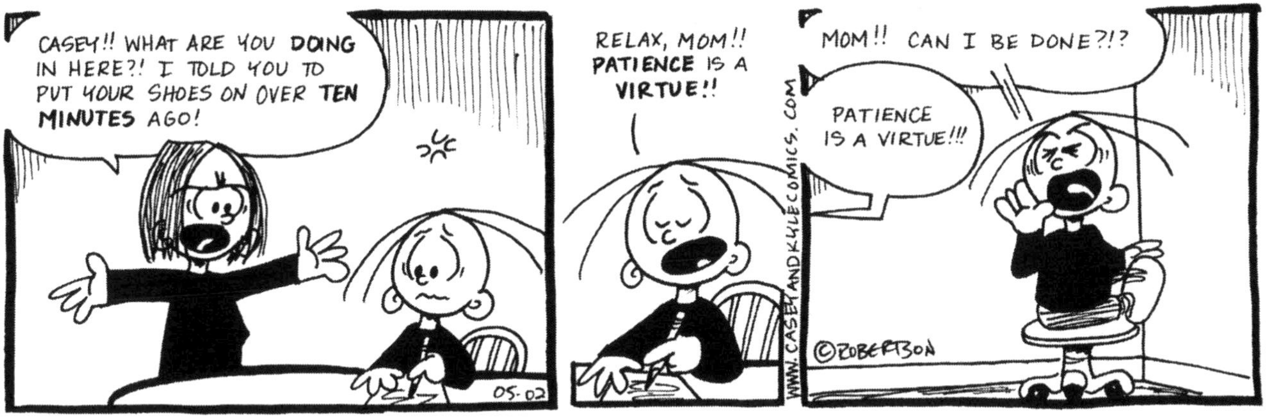
CASEY!! WHAT ARE YOU DOING IN HERE?! I TOLD YOU TO PUT YOUR SHOES ON OVER TEN MINUTES AGO!
05-02
RELAX, MOM!! PATIENCE IS A VIRTUE!!
WWW.CASEYANDKYLECOMICS.COM
MOM!! CAN I BE DONE?!?
PATIENCE IS A VIRTUE!!!
©ROBERTSON

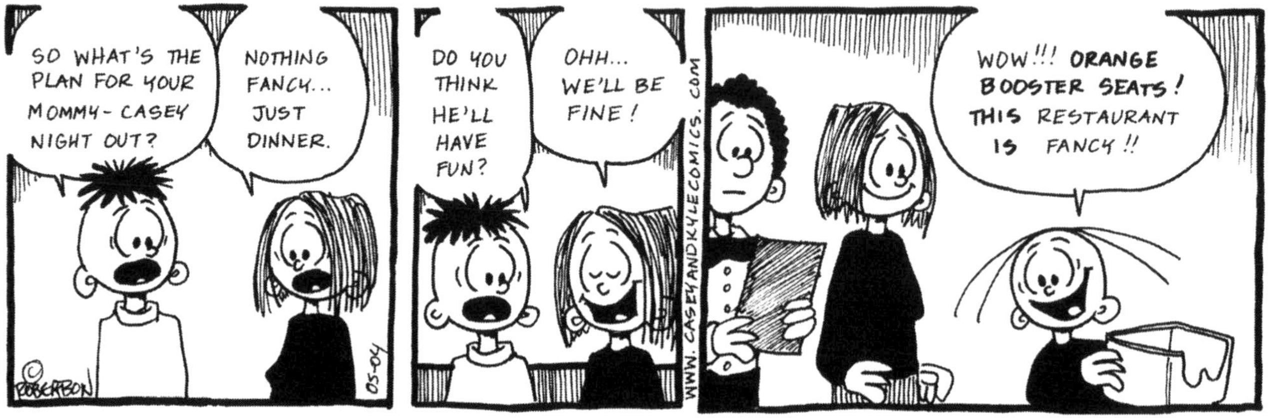
SO WHAT'S THE PLAN FOR YOUR MOMMY-CASEY NIGHT OUT?
NOTHING FANCY... JUST DINNER.
© ROBERTSON
05-04
DO YOU THINK HE'LL HAVE FUN?
OHH... WE'LL BE FINE!
WWW.CASEYANDKYLECOMICS.COM
WOW!!! ORANGE BOOSTER SEATS! THIS RESTAURANT IS FANCY!!

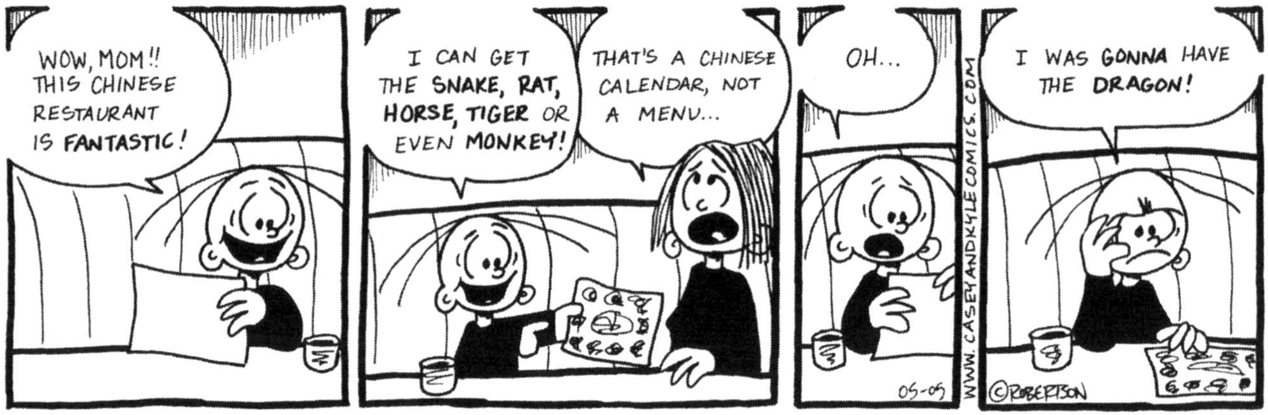
WOW, MOM!! THIS CHINESE RESTAURANT IS FANTASTIC!
I CAN GET THE SNAKE, RAT, HORSE, TIGER OR EVEN MONKEY!
THAT'S A CHINESE CALENDAR, NOT A MENU...
OH...
05-05
WWW.CASEYANDKYLECOMICS.COM
I WAS GONNA HAVE THE DRAGON!
©ROBERTSON

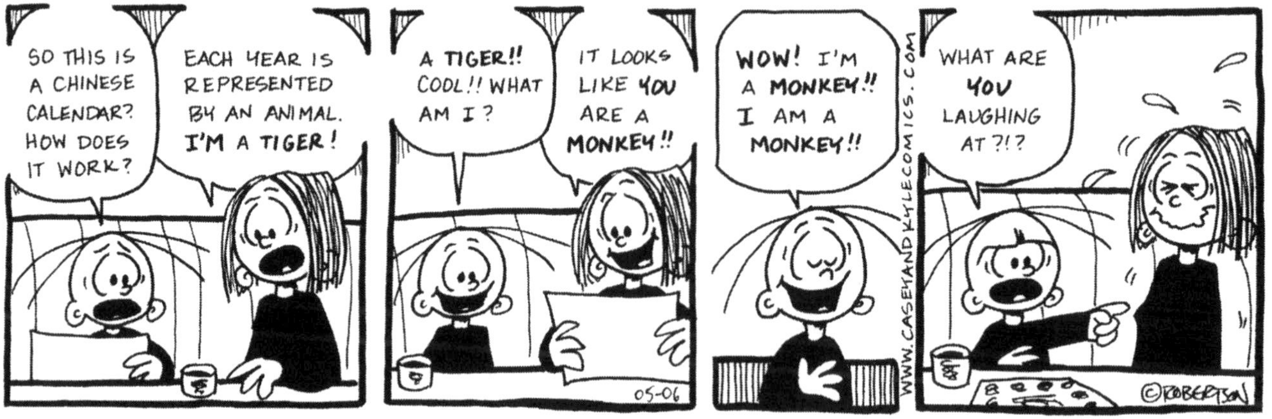
SO THIS IS A CHINESE CALENDAR? HOW DOES IT WORK?
EACH YEAR IS REPRESENTED BY AN ANIMAL. I'M A TIGER!
A TIGER!! COOL!! WHAT AM I?
IT LOOKS LIKE YOU ARE A MONKEY!!
05-06
WOW! I'M A MONKEY!! I AM A MONKEY!!
WWW.CASEYANDKYLECOMICS.COM
WHAT ARE YOU LAUGHING AT?!?
©ROBERTSON

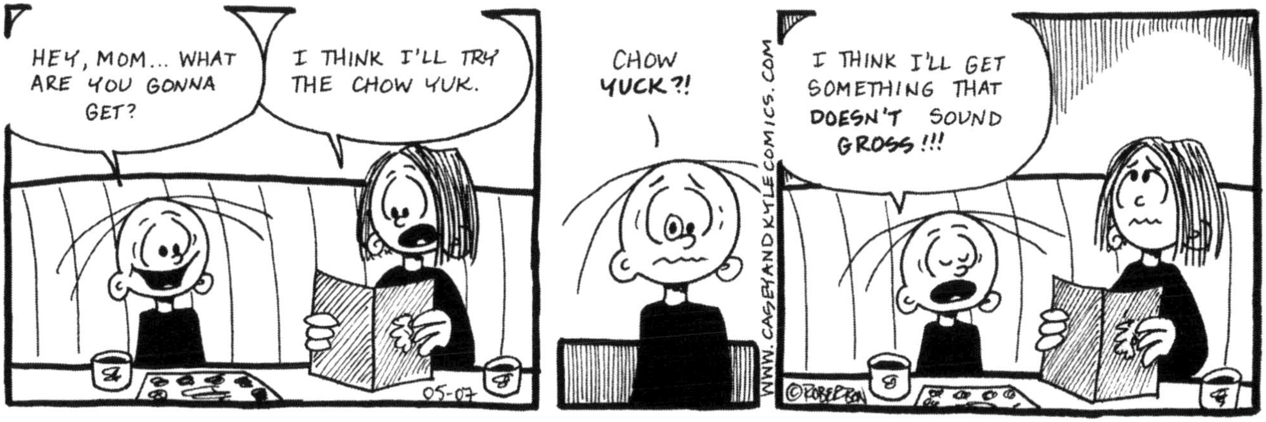
HEY, MOM... WHAT ARE YOU GONNA GET?
I THINK I'LL TRY THE CHOW YUK.
05-07
CHOW **YUCK**?!
WWW.CASEYANDKYLECOMICS.COM
I THINK I'LL GET SOMETHING THAT **DOESN'T** SOUND **GROSS**!!!

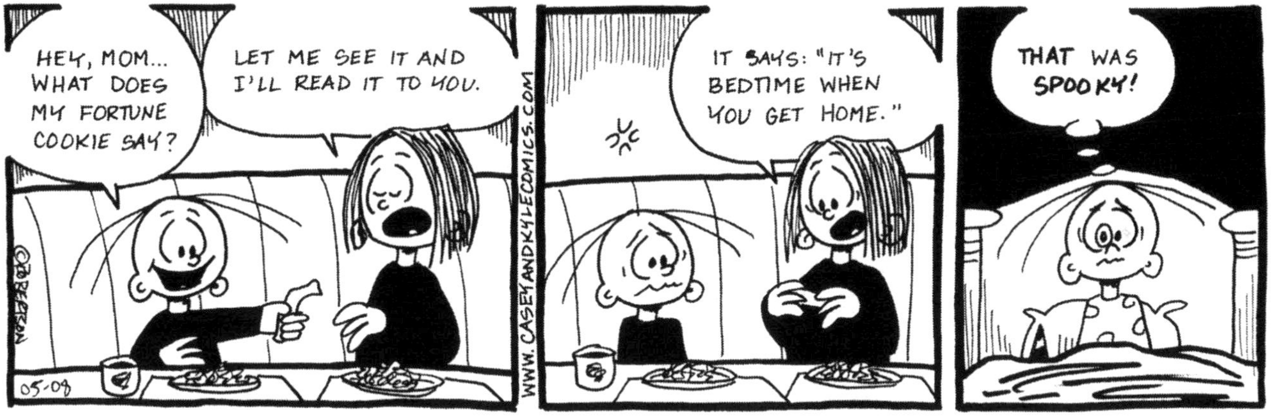
HEY, MOM... WHAT DOES MY FORTUNE COOKIE SAY?
LET ME SEE IT AND I'LL READ IT TO YOU.
05-08
WWW.CASEYANDKYLECOMICS.COM
IT SAYS: "IT'S BEDTIME WHEN YOU GET HOME."
THAT WAS **SPOOKY**!

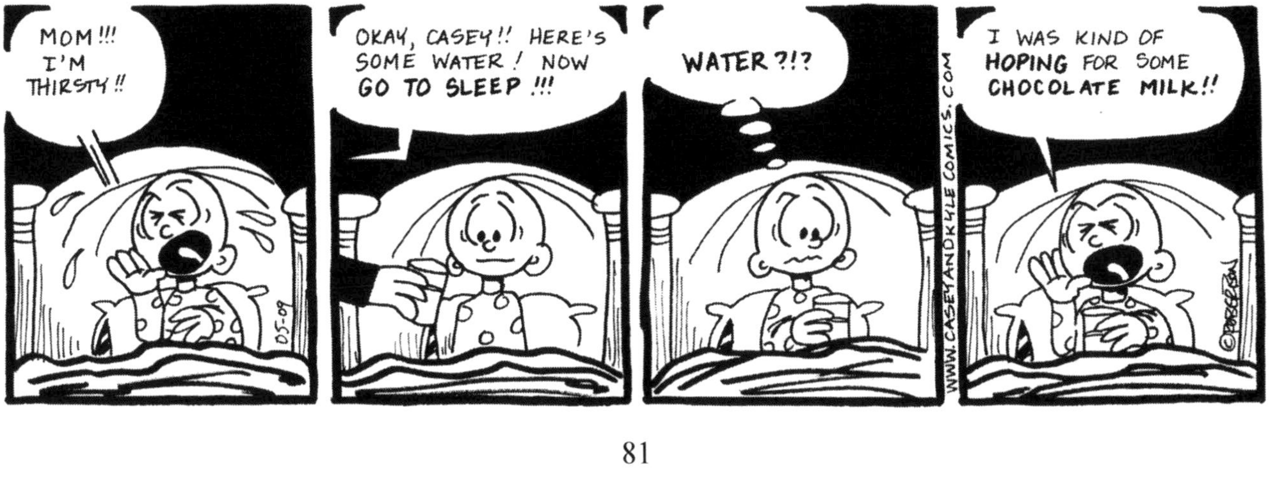
MOM!!! I'M THIRSTY!!
05-09
OKAY, CASEY!! HERE'S SOME WATER! NOW **GO TO SLEEP**!!!
WATER?!?
WWW.CASEYANDKYLECOMICS.COM
I WAS KIND OF **HOPING** FOR SOME **CHOCOLATE MILK**!!

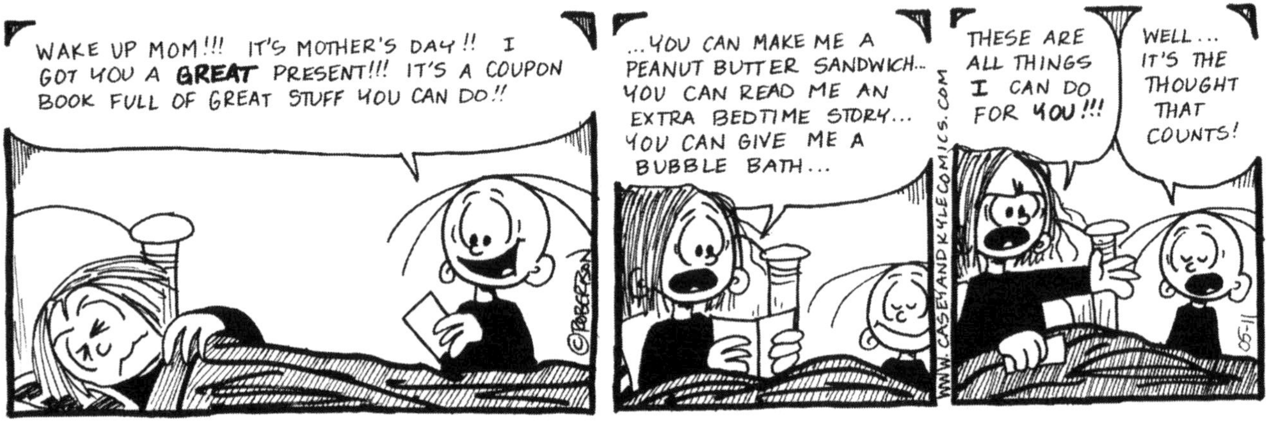
WAKE UP MOM!!! IT'S MOTHER'S DAY!! I GOT YOU A GREAT PRESENT!!! IT'S A COUPON BOOK FULL OF GREAT STUFF YOU CAN DO!!
©ROBERTSON
...YOU CAN MAKE ME A PEANUT BUTTER SANDWICH... YOU CAN READ ME AN EXTRA BEDTIME STORY... YOU CAN GIVE ME A BUBBLE BATH...
WWW.CASEYANDKYLECOMICS.COM
THESE ARE ALL THINGS I CAN DO FOR YOU!!!
WELL... IT'S THE THOUGHT THAT COUNTS!
05-11

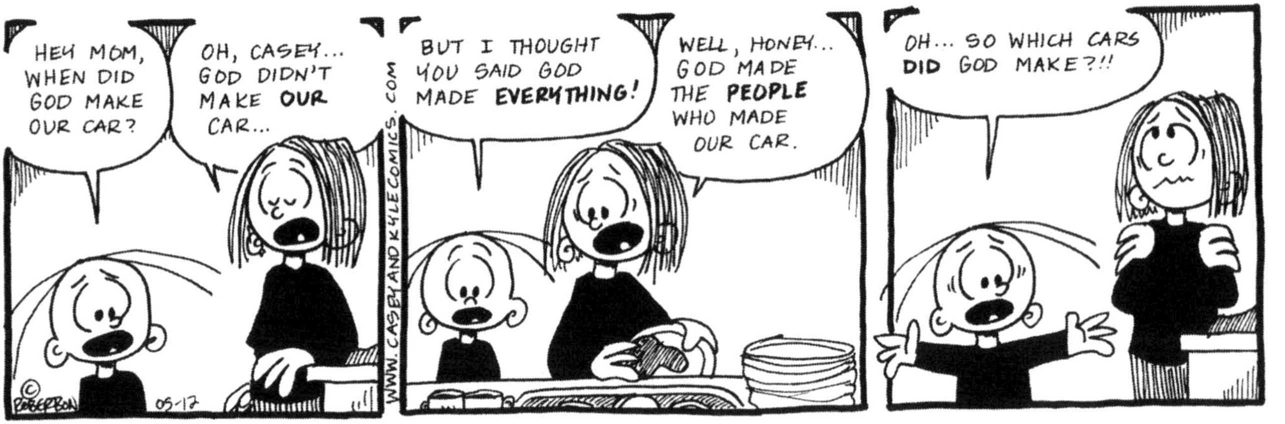
HEY MOM, WHEN DID GOD MAKE OUR CAR?
OH, CASEY... GOD DIDN'T MAKE OUR CAR...
© ROBERTSON
05-12
WWW.CASEYANDKYLECOMICS.COM
BUT I THOUGHT YOU SAID GOD MADE EVERYTHING!
WELL, HONEY... GOD MADE THE PEOPLE WHO MADE OUR CAR.
OH... SO WHICH CARS DID GOD MAKE?!!

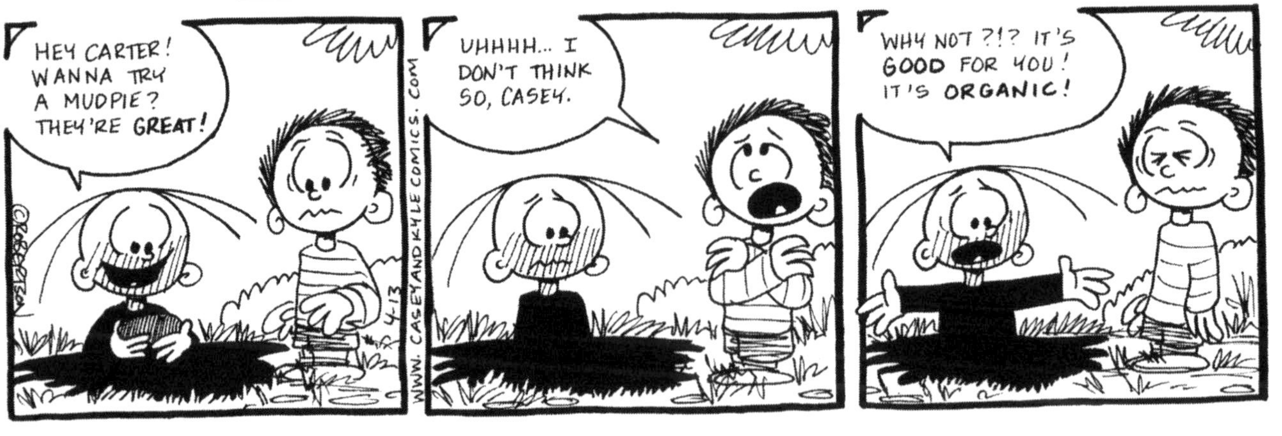
HEY CARTER! WANNA TRY A MUDPIE? THEY'RE GREAT!
©ROBERTSON
4-13
WWW.CASEYANDKYLECOMICS.COM
UHHHH... I DON'T THINK SO, CASEY.
WHY NOT?!? IT'S GOOD FOR YOU! IT'S ORGANIC!

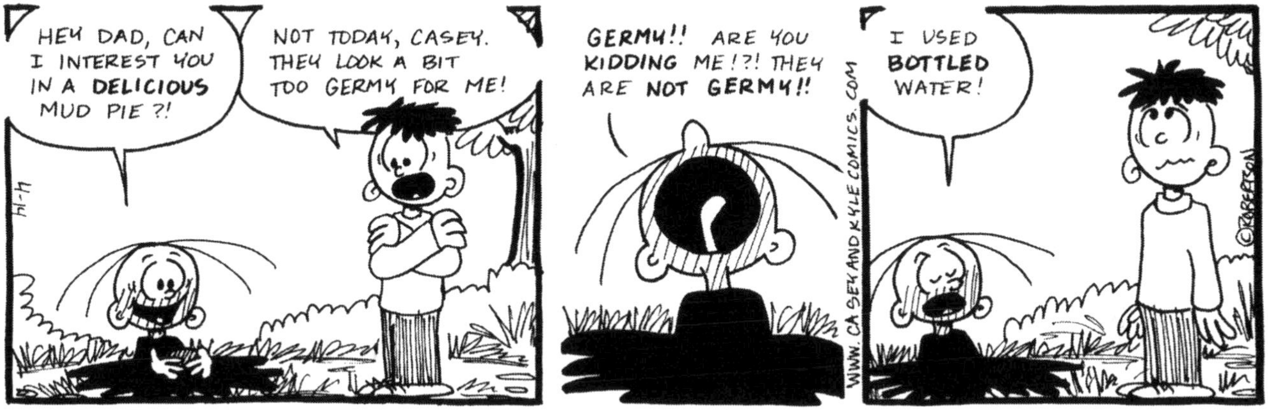
HEY DAD, CAN I INTEREST YOU IN A **DELICIOUS** MUD PIE?!
NOT TODAY, CASEY. THEY LOOK A BIT TOO GERMY FOR ME!
4-14
GERMY!! ARE YOU **KIDDING** ME!?! THEY ARE **NOT GERMY!!**
WWW.CASEYANDKYLECOMICS.COM
I USED **BOTTLED** WATER!
©ROBERTSON

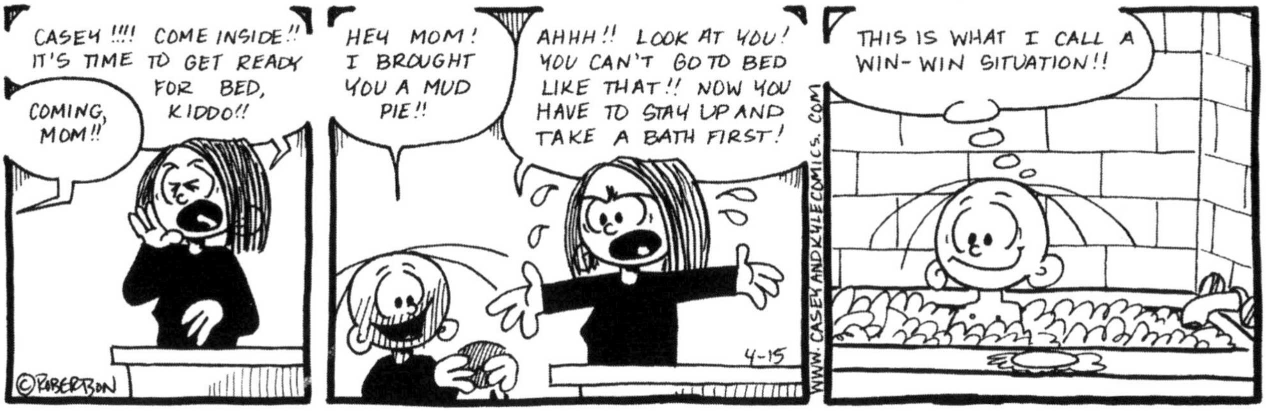
CASEY!!!! COME INSIDE!! IT'S TIME TO GET READY FOR BED, KIDDO!!
COMING, MOM!!
©ROBERTSON
HEY MOM! I BROUGHT YOU A MUD PIE!!
AHHH!! LOOK AT YOU! YOU CAN'T GO TO BED LIKE THAT!! NOW YOU HAVE TO STAY UP AND TAKE A BATH FIRST!
4-15
WWW.CASEYANDKYLECOMICS.COM
THIS IS WHAT I CALL A WIN-WIN SITUATION!!

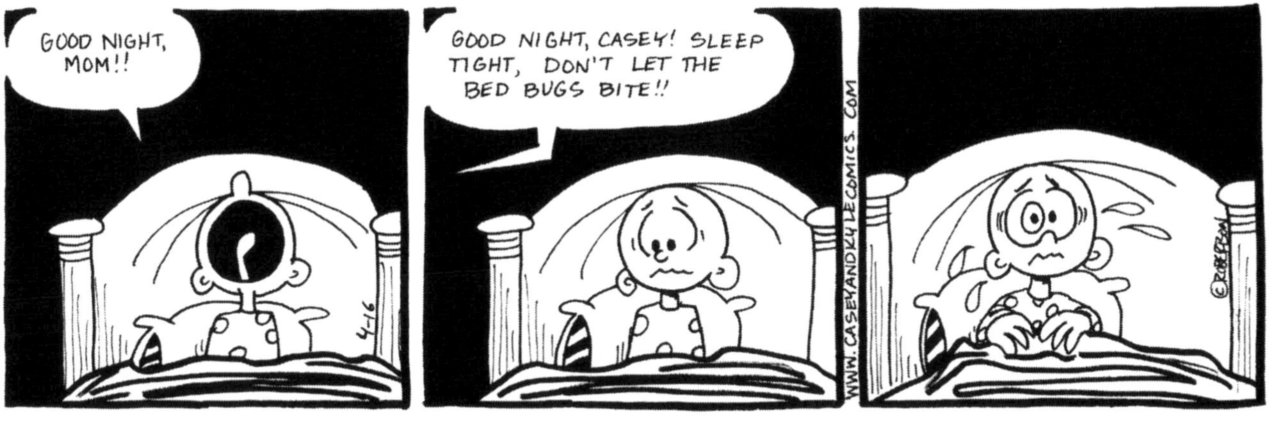
GOOD NIGHT, MOM!!
4-16
GOOD NIGHT, CASEY! SLEEP TIGHT, DON'T LET THE BED BUGS BITE!!
WWW.CASEYANDKYLECOMICS.COM
©ROBERTSON

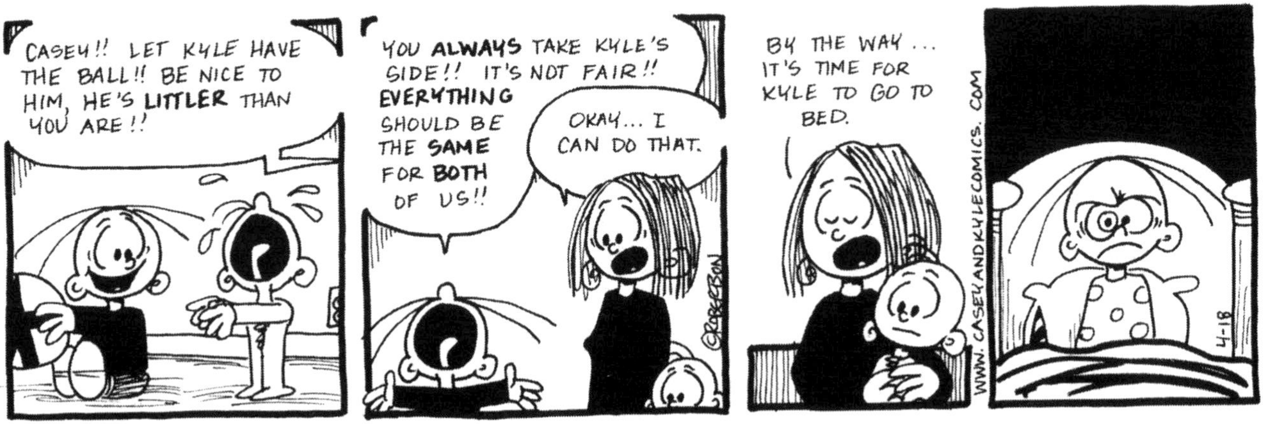
CASEY!! LET KYLE HAVE THE BALL!! BE NICE TO HIM, HE'S **LITTLER** THAN YOU ARE!!
YOU **ALWAYS** TAKE KYLE'S SIDE!! IT'S NOT FAIR!! **EVERYTHING** SHOULD BE THE **SAME** FOR **BOTH** OF US!!
OKAY... I CAN DO THAT.
©ROBERTSON
BY THE WAY... IT'S TIME FOR KYLE TO GO TO BED.
WWW.CASEYANDKYLECOMICS.COM
4-18

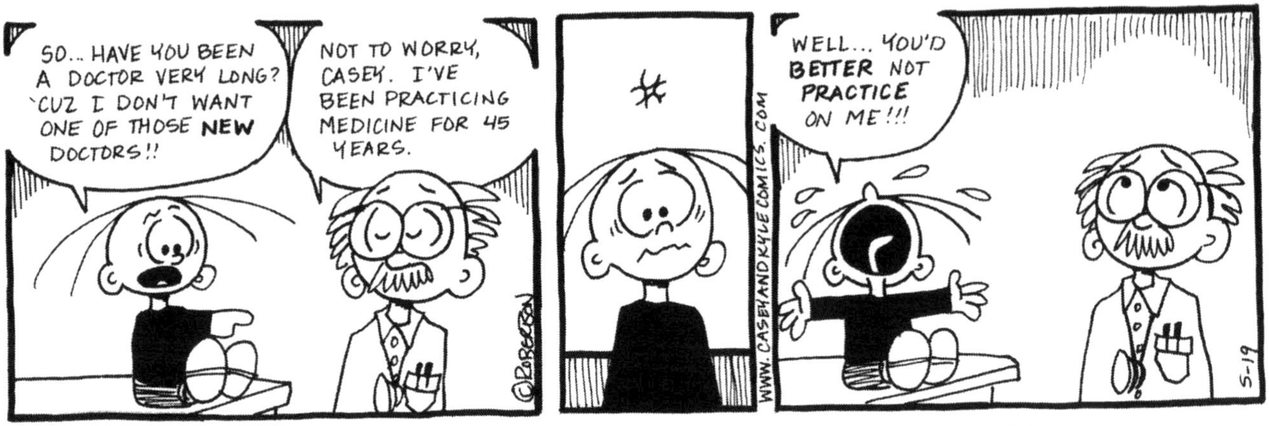
SO... HAVE YOU BEEN A DOCTOR VERY LONG? 'CUZ I DON'T WANT ONE OF THOSE **NEW** DOCTORS!!
NOT TO WORRY, CASEY. I'VE BEEN PRACTICING MEDICINE FOR 45 YEARS.
©ROBERTSON
WWW.CASEYANDKYLECOMICS.COM
WELL... YOU'D **BETTER** NOT **PRACTICE** ON ME!!!
5-19

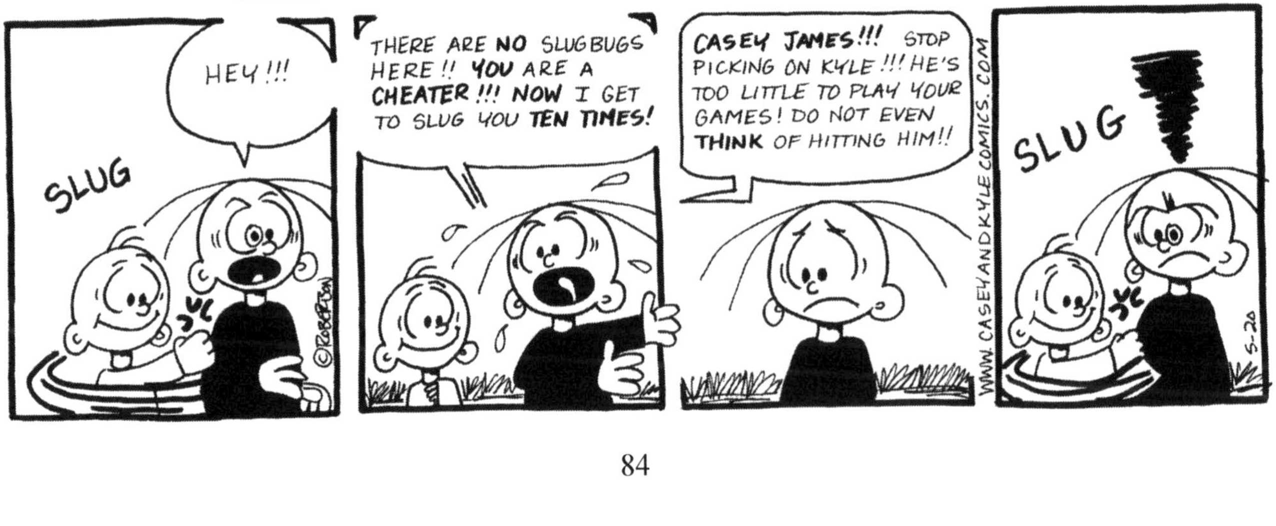
HEY!!!
SLUG
©ROBERTSON
THERE ARE **NO** SLUGBUGS HERE!! **YOU** ARE A **CHEATER**!!! **NOW** I GET TO SLUG YOU **TEN TIMES**!
CASEY JAMES!!! STOP PICKING ON KYLE!!! HE'S TOO LITTLE TO PLAY YOUR GAMES! DO NOT EVEN **THINK** OF HITTING HIM!!
WWW.CASEYANDKYLECOMICS.COM
SLUG
5-20

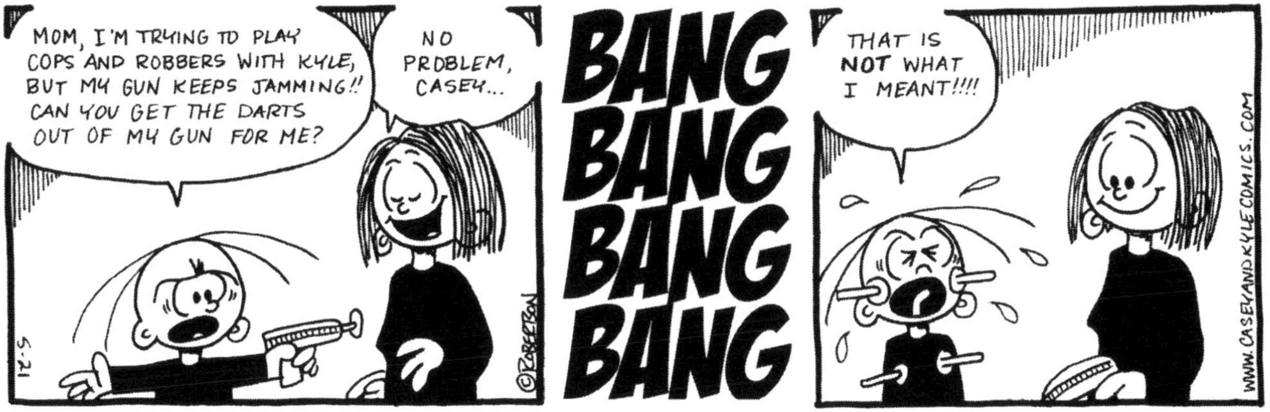
MOM, I'M TRYING TO PLAY COPS AND ROBBERS WITH KYLE, BUT MY GUN KEEPS JAMMING!! CAN YOU GET THE DARTS OUT OF MY GUN FOR ME?
NO PROBLEM, CASEY...
BANG BANG BANG BANG
THAT IS NOT WHAT I MEANT!!!!
WWW.CASEYANDKYLECOMICS.COM

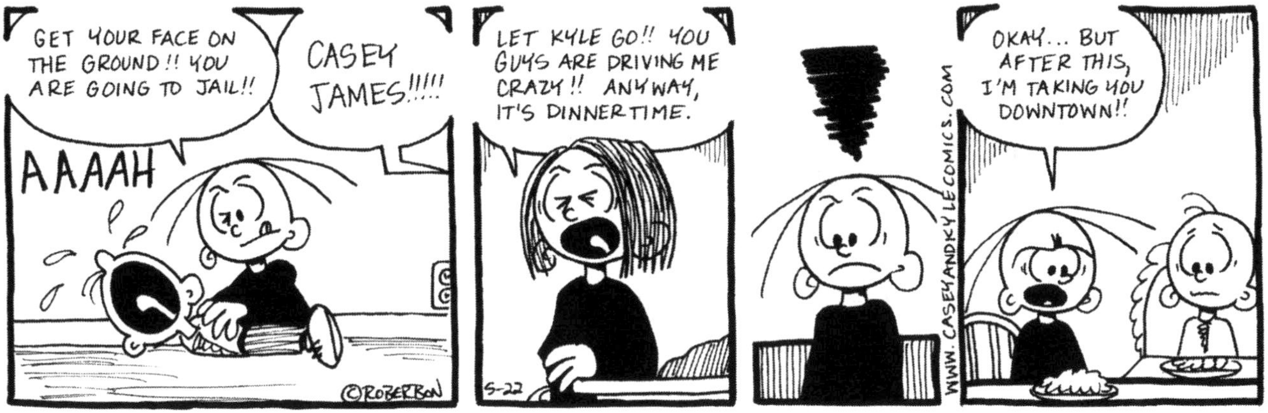
GET YOUR FACE ON THE GROUND!! YOU ARE GOING TO JAIL!!
CASEY JAMES!!!!!
AAAAH
LET KYLE GO!! YOU GUYS ARE DRIVING ME CRAZY!! ANYWAY, IT'S DINNERTIME.
OKAY... BUT AFTER THIS, I'M TAKING YOU DOWNTOWN!!
WWW.CASEYANDKYLECOMICS.COM

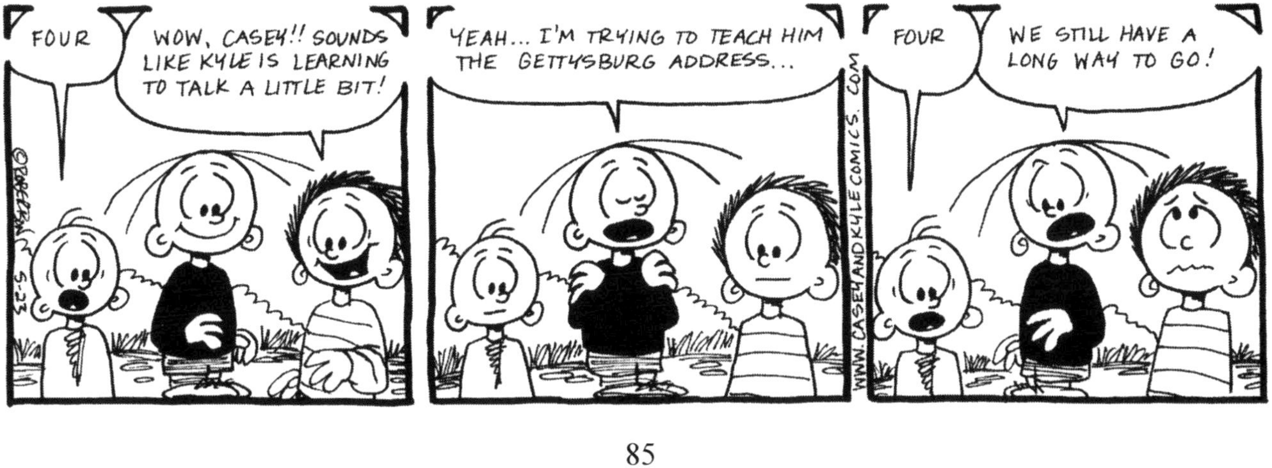
FOUR
WOW, CASEY!! SOUNDS LIKE KYLE IS LEARNING TO TALK A LITTLE BIT!
YEAH... I'M TRYING TO TEACH HIM THE GETTYSBURG ADDRESS...
FOUR
WE STILL HAVE A LONG WAY TO GO!
WWW.CASEYANDKYLECOMICS.COM

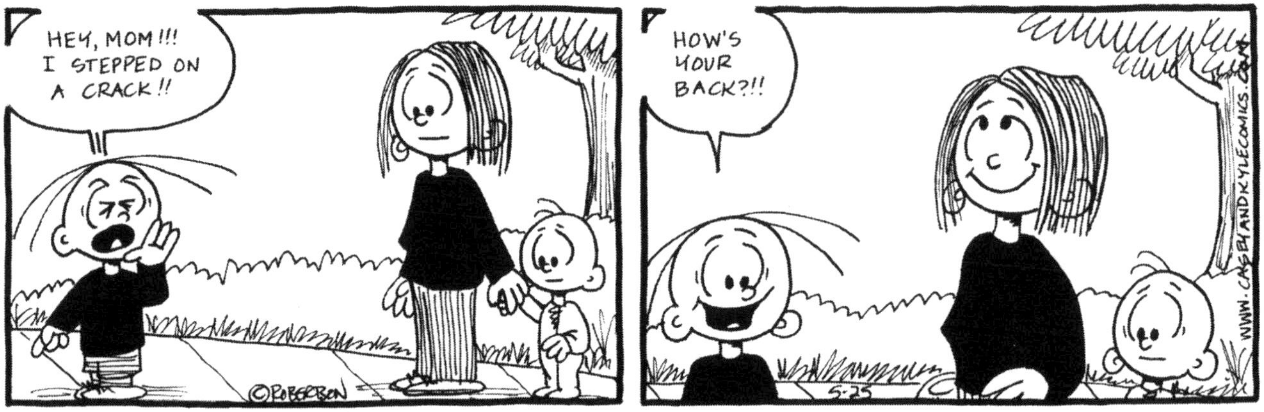
HEY, MOM!!! I STEPPED ON A CRACK!!
©ROBERTSON
HOW'S YOUR BACK?!!
5-25
WWW.CASEYANDKYLECOMICS.COM

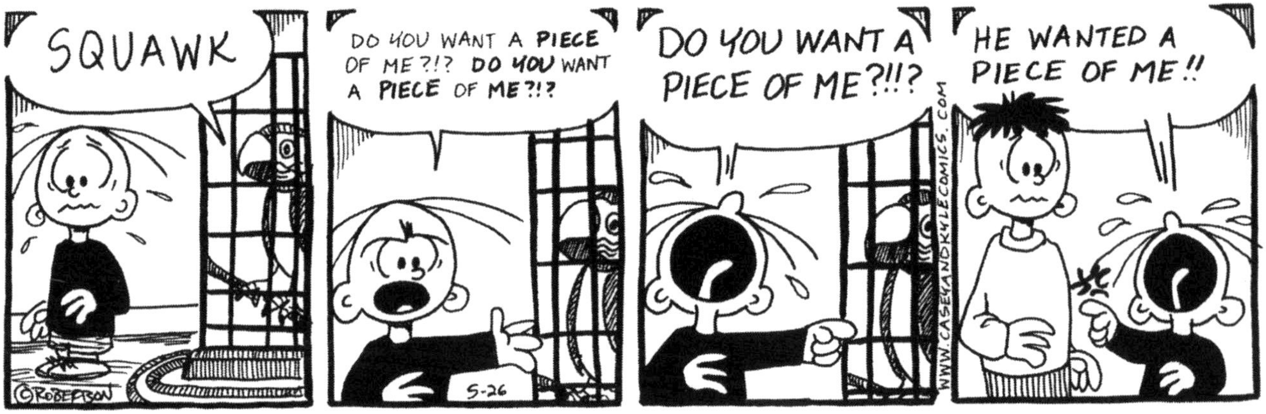
SQUAWK
©ROBERTSON
DO YOU WANT A **PIECE** OF ME?!? **DO YOU** WANT A **PIECE** OF **ME**?!?
5-26
DO YOU WANT A PIECE OF ME?!!?
WWW.CASEYANDKYLECOMICS.COM
HE WANTED A PIECE OF ME!!

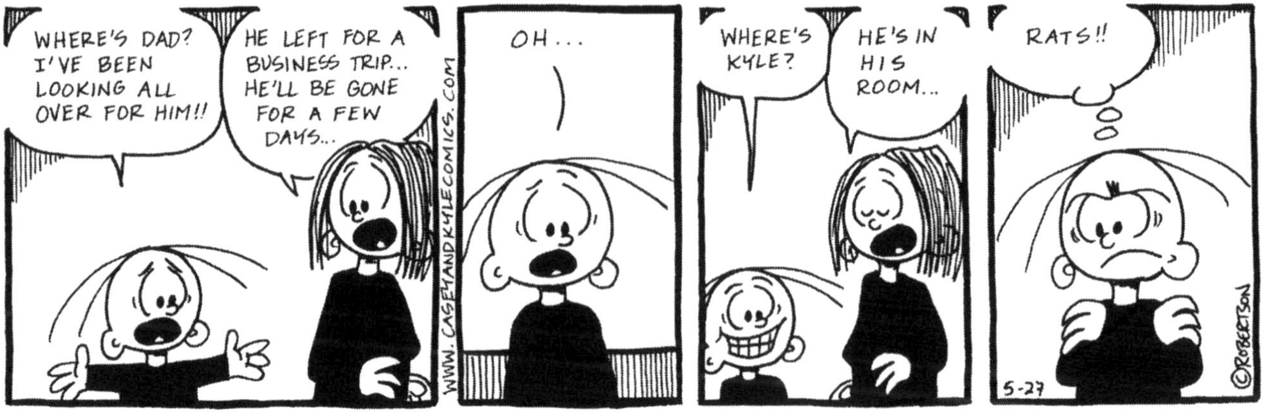
WHERE'S DAD? I'VE BEEN LOOKING ALL OVER FOR HIM!!
HE LEFT FOR A BUSINESS TRIP... HE'LL BE GONE FOR A FEW DAYS...
WWW.CASEYANDKYLECOMICS.COM
OH...
WHERE'S KYLE?
HE'S IN HIS ROOM...
RATS!!
©ROBERTSON
5-27

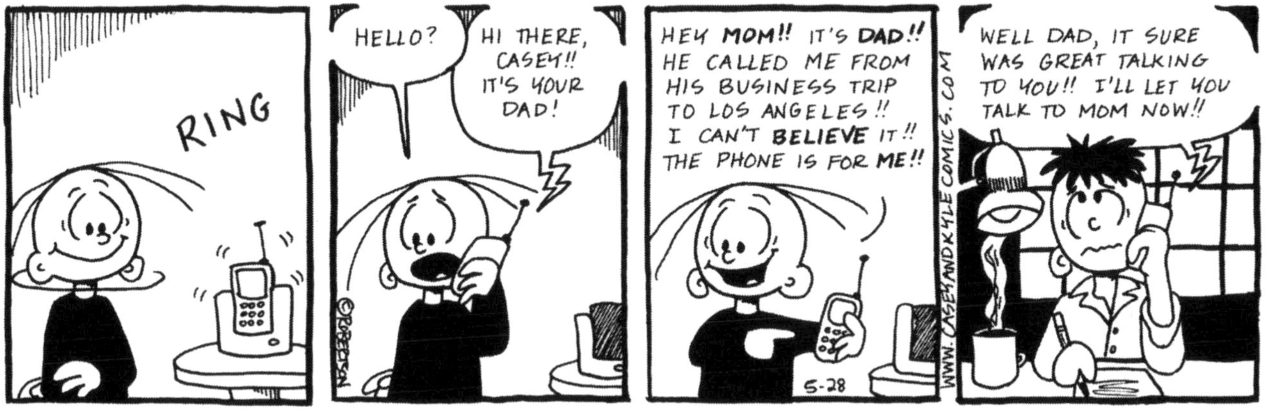
RING
HELLO?
HI THERE, CASEY!! IT'S YOUR DAD!
©ROBERTSON
HEY MOM!! IT'S DAD!! HE CALLED ME FROM HIS BUSINESS TRIP TO LOS ANGELES!! I CAN'T BELIEVE IT!! THE PHONE IS FOR ME!!
5-28
WWW.CASEYANDKYLECOMICS.COM
WELL DAD, IT SURE WAS GREAT TALKING TO YOU!! I'LL LET YOU TALK TO MOM NOW!!

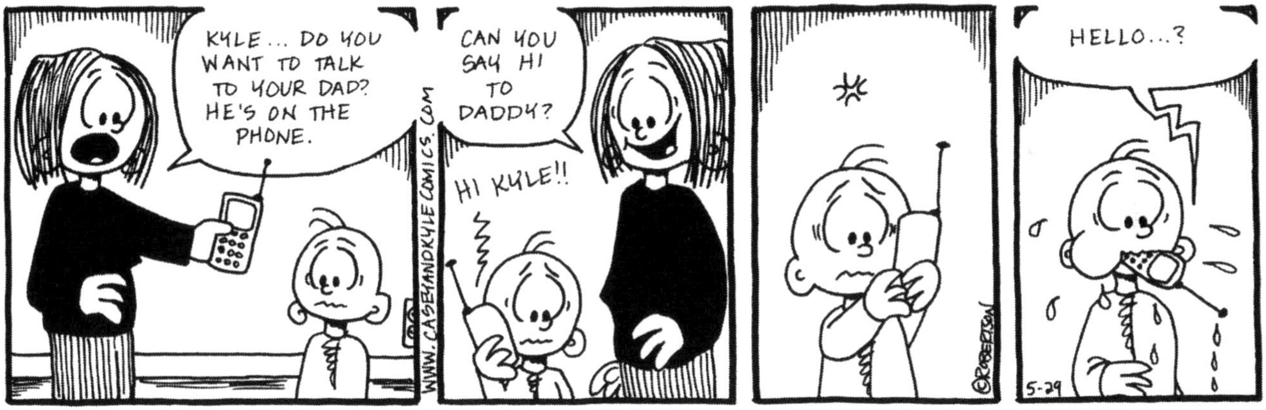
KYLE... DO YOU WANT TO TALK TO YOUR DAD? HE'S ON THE PHONE.
WWW.CASEYANDKYLECOMICS.COM
CAN YOU SAY HI TO DADDY?
HI KYLE!!
©ROBERTSON
HELLO...?
5-29

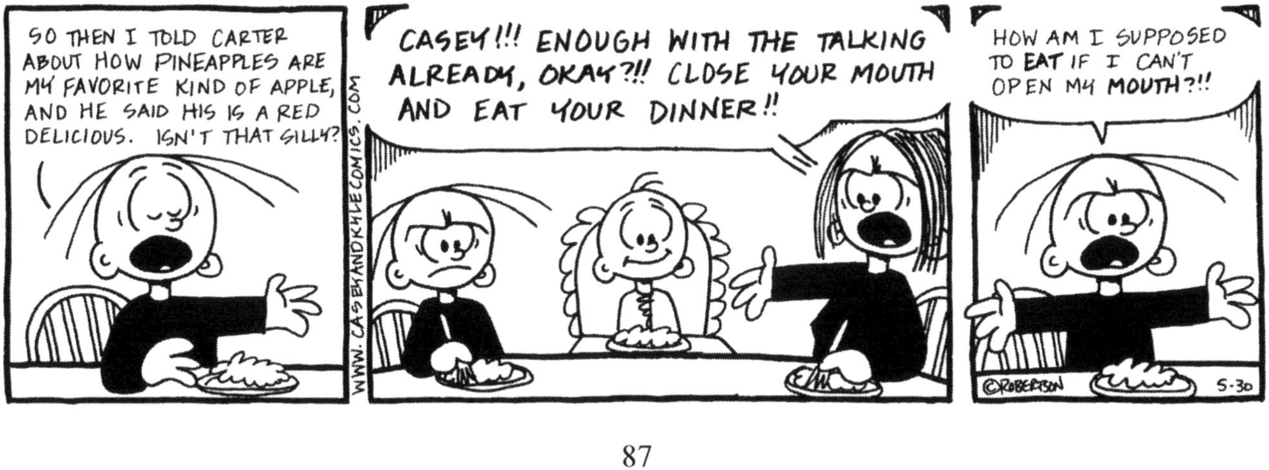
SO THEN I TOLD CARTER ABOUT HOW PINEAPPLES ARE MY FAVORITE KIND OF APPLE, AND HE SAID HIS IS A RED DELICIOUS. ISN'T THAT SILLY?
WWW.CASEYANDKYLECOMICS.COM
CASEY!!! ENOUGH WITH THE TALKING ALREADY, OKAY?!! CLOSE YOUR MOUTH AND EAT YOUR DINNER!!
HOW AM I SUPPOSED TO EAT IF I CAN'T OPEN MY MOUTH?!!
©ROBERTSON
5-30

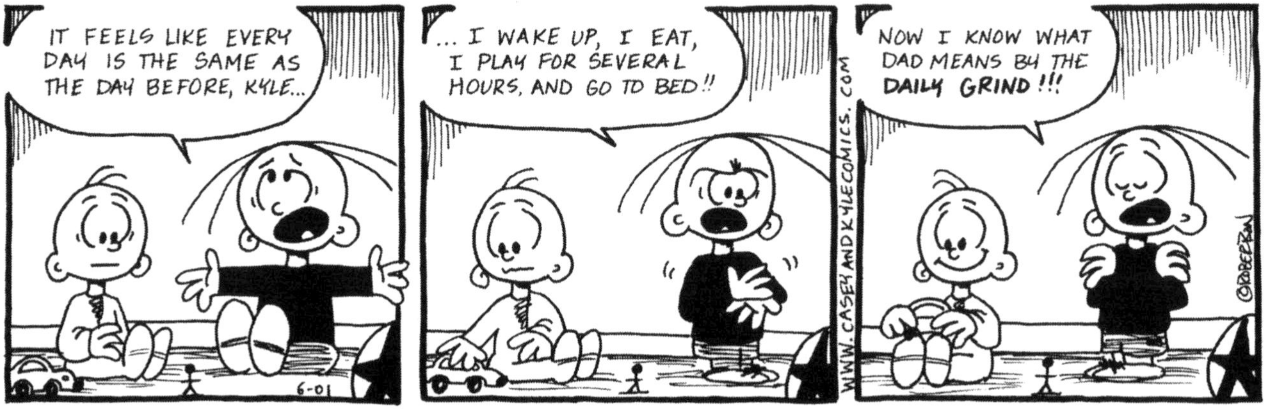
IT FEELS LIKE EVERY DAY IS THE SAME AS THE DAY BEFORE, KYLE...
6-01
... I WAKE UP, I EAT, I PLAY FOR SEVERAL HOURS, AND GO TO BED!!
WWW.CASEYANDKYLECOMICS.COM
NOW I KNOW WHAT DAD MEANS BY THE DAILY GRIND!!!
©ROBERTSON

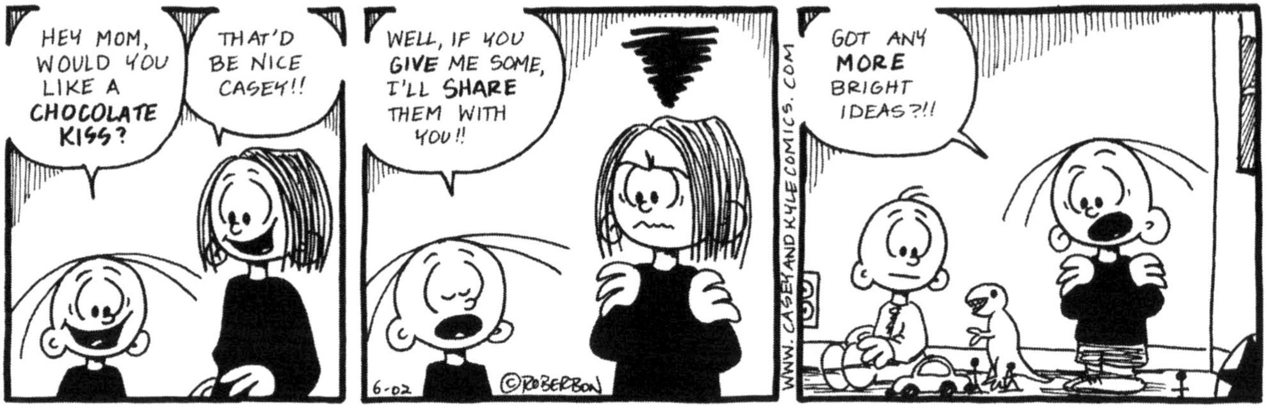
HEY MOM, WOULD YOU LIKE A CHOCOLATE KISS?
THAT'D BE NICE CASEY!!
WELL, IF YOU GIVE ME SOME, I'LL SHARE THEM WITH YOU!!
6-02
©ROBERTSON
WWW.CASEYANDKYLECOMICS.COM
GOT ANY MORE BRIGHT IDEAS?!!

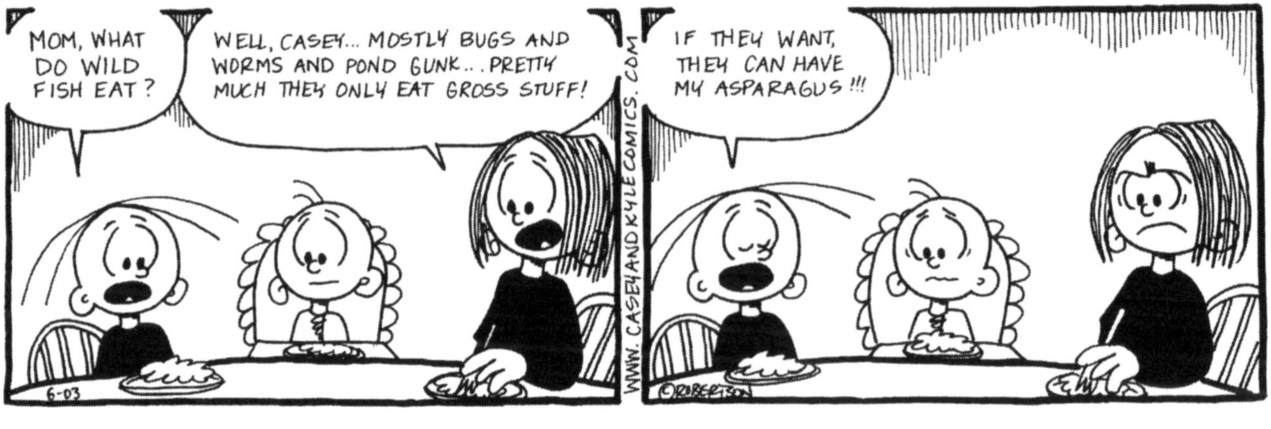
MOM, WHAT DO WILD FISH EAT?
WELL, CASEY... MOSTLY BUGS AND WORMS AND POND GUNK... PRETTY MUCH THEY ONLY EAT GROSS STUFF!
6-03
WWW.CASEYANDKYLECOMICS.COM
IF THEY WANT, THEY CAN HAVE MY ASPARAGUS!!!
©ROBERTSON

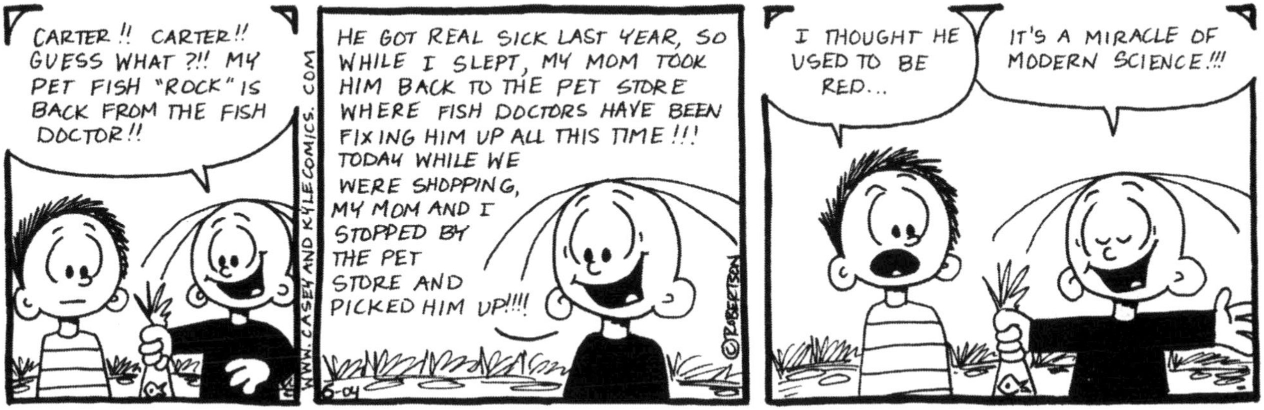
CARTER!! CARTER!! GUESS WHAT?!! MY PET FISH "ROCK" IS BACK FROM THE FISH DOCTOR!!
WWW.CASEYANDKYLECOMICS.COM
HE GOT REAL SICK LAST YEAR, SO WHILE I SLEPT, MY MOM TOOK HIM BACK TO THE PET STORE WHERE FISH DOCTORS HAVE BEEN FIXING HIM UP ALL THIS TIME!!! TODAY WHILE WE WERE SHOPPING, MY MOM AND I STOPPED BY THE PET STORE AND PICKED HIM UP!!!!
6-04
©ROBERTSON
I THOUGHT HE USED TO BE RED...
IT'S A MIRACLE OF MODERN SCIENCE!!!

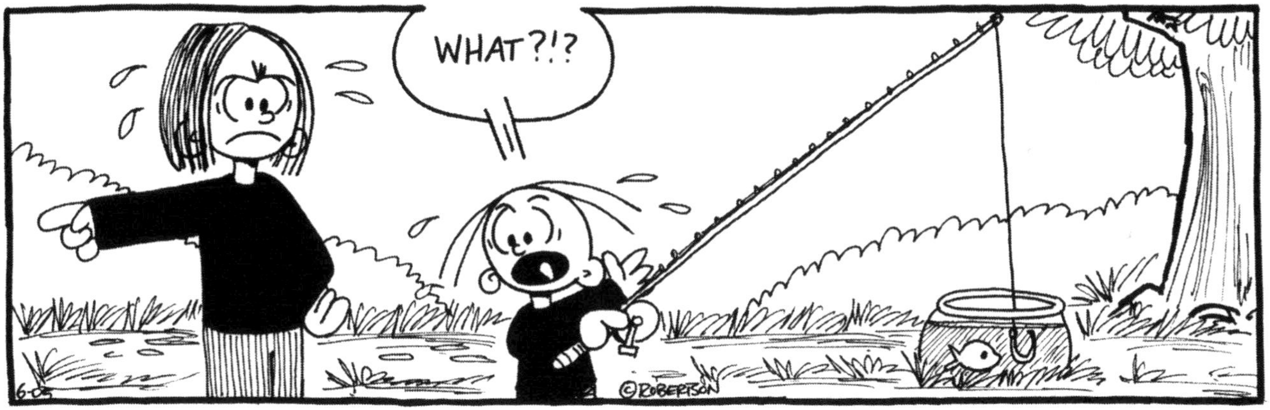
WHAT?!?
©ROBERTSON

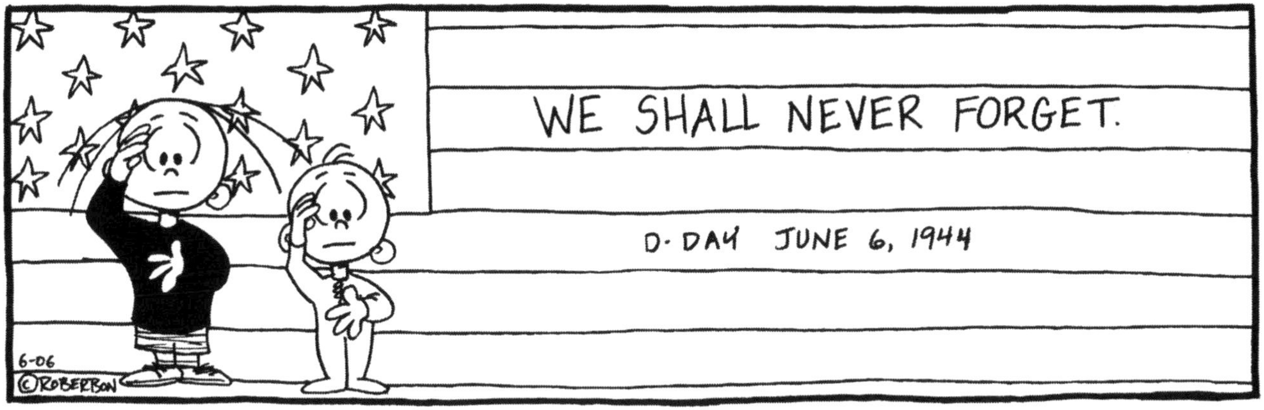
WE SHALL NEVER FORGET.
D-DAY JUNE 6, 1944
6-06

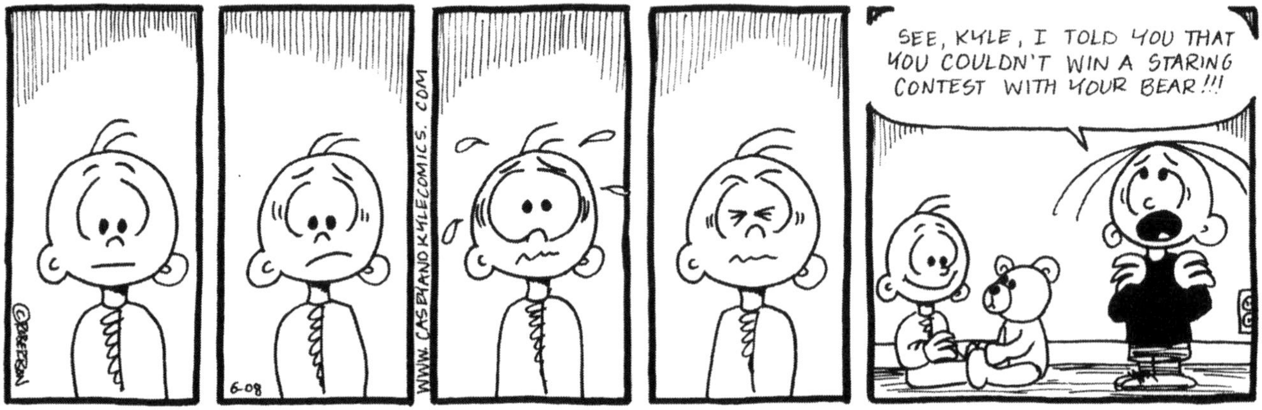
©ROBERTSON
6-08
WWW.CASEYANDKYLECOMICS.COM
SEE, KYLE, I TOLD YOU THAT YOU COULDN'T WIN A STARING CONTEST WITH YOUR BEAR!!!

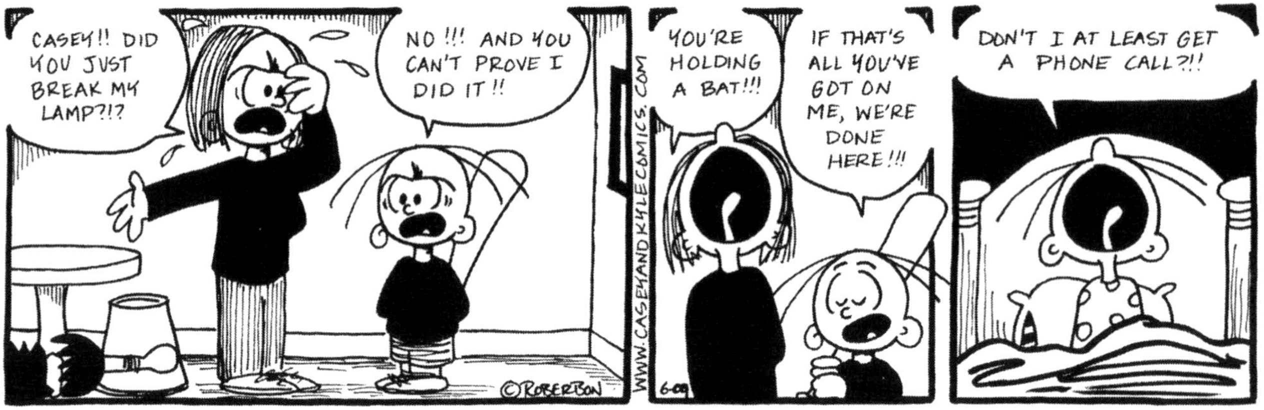
CASEY!! DID YOU JUST BREAK MY LAMP?!?
NO!!! AND YOU CAN'T PROVE I DID IT!!
©ROBERTSON
WWW.CASEYANDKYLECOMICS.COM
6-09
YOU'RE HOLDING A BAT!!!
IF THAT'S ALL YOU'VE GOT ON ME, WE'RE DONE HERE!!!
DON'T I AT LEAST GET A PHONE CALL?!!

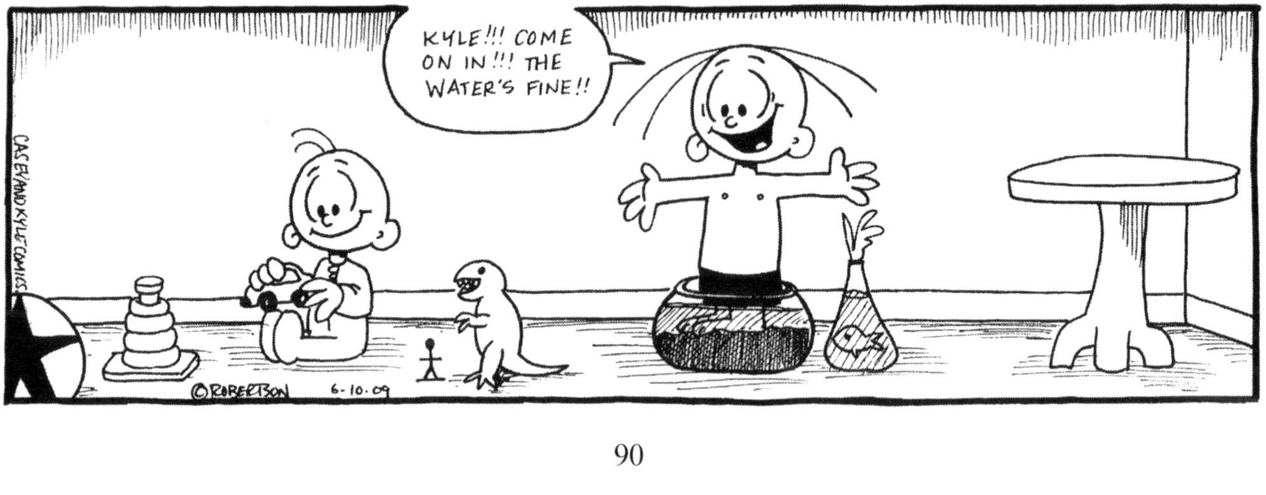
CASEYANDKYLECOMICS
KYLE!!! COME ON IN!!! THE WATER'S FINE!!
©ROBERTSON
6-10-09

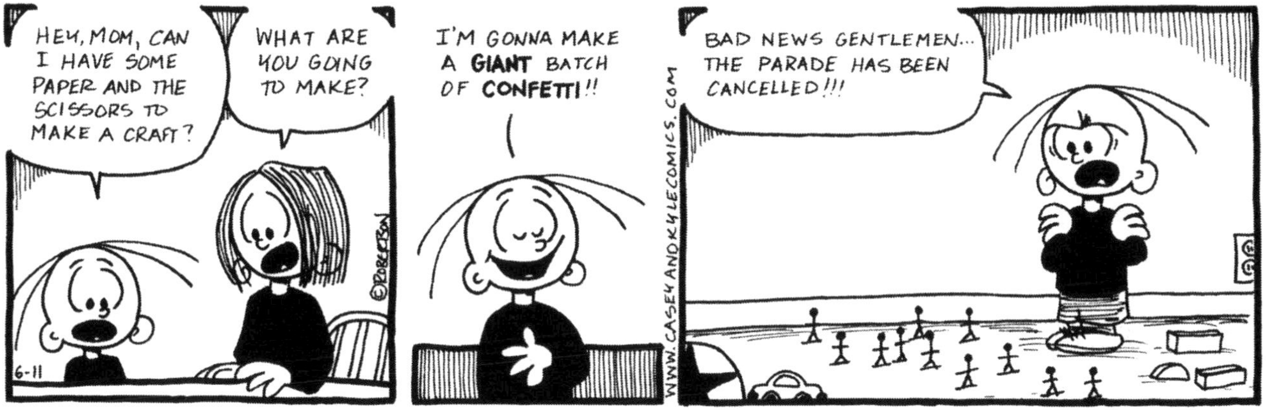
HEY, MOM, CAN I HAVE SOME PAPER AND THE SCISSORS TO MAKE A CRAFT?
WHAT ARE YOU GOING TO MAKE?
©ROBERTSON
6-11
I'M GONNA MAKE A GIANT BATCH OF CONFETTI!!
WWW.CASEYANDKYLECOMICS.COM
BAD NEWS GENTLEMEN... THE PARADE HAS BEEN CANCELLED!!!

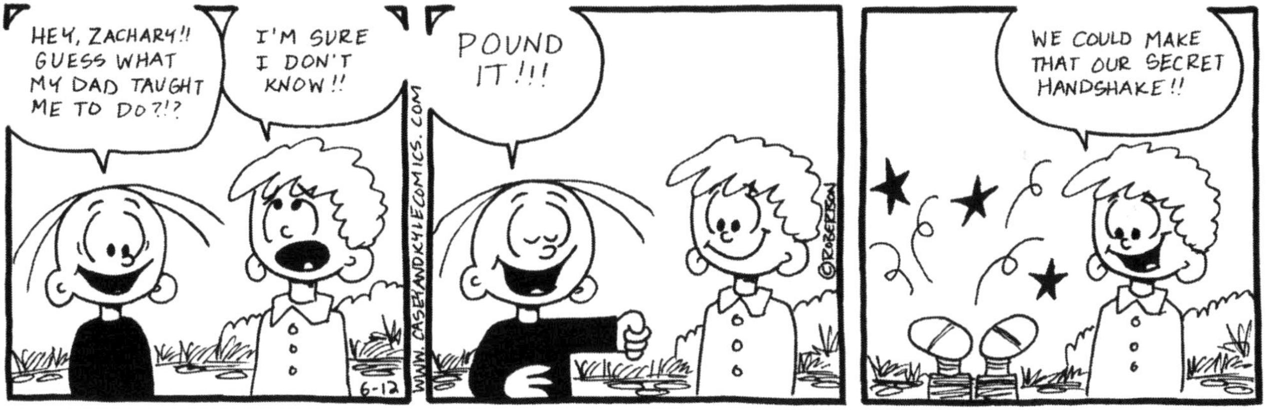
HEY, ZACHARY!! GUESS WHAT MY DAD TAUGHT ME TO DO?!?
I'M SURE I DON'T KNOW!!
6-12
WWW.CASEYANDKYLECOMICS.COM
POUND IT!!!
©ROBERTSON
WE COULD MAKE THAT OUR SECRET HANDSHAKE!!

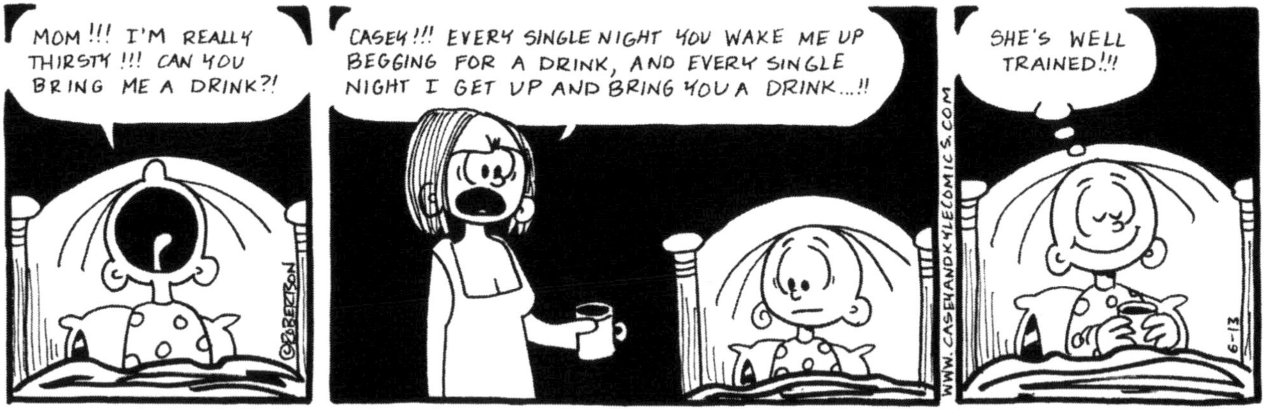
MOM!!! I'M REALLY THIRSTY!!! CAN YOU BRING ME A DRINK?!
©ROBERTSON
CASEY!!! EVERY SINGLE NIGHT YOU WAKE ME UP BEGGING FOR A DRINK, AND EVERY SINGLE NIGHT I GET UP AND BRING YOU A DRINK...!!
WWW.CASEYANDKYLECOMICS.COM
SHE'S WELL TRAINED!!!
6-13

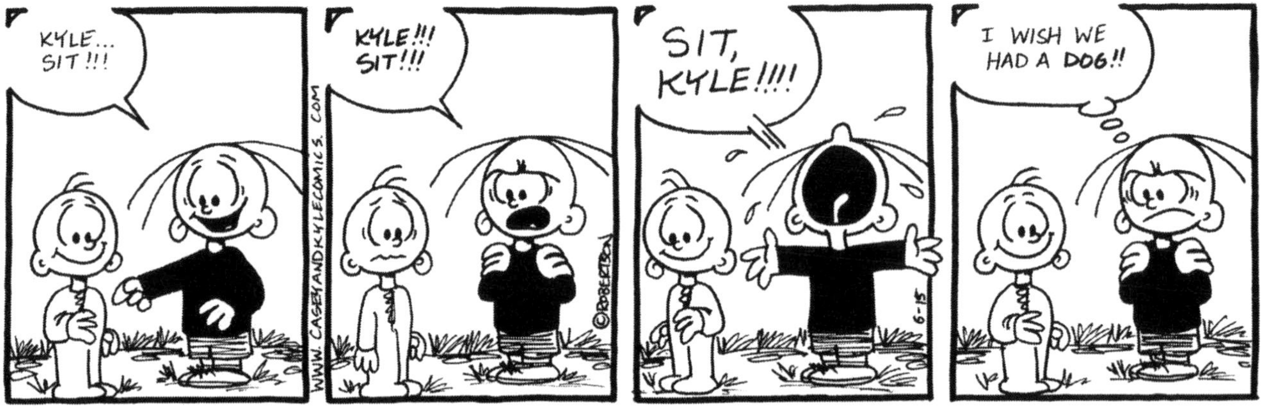
KYLE...
SIT!!!
KYLE!!!
SIT!!!
WWW.CASEYANDKYLECOMICS.COM
©ROBERTSON
SIT,
KYLE!!!!
6-15
I WISH WE
HAD A DOG!!

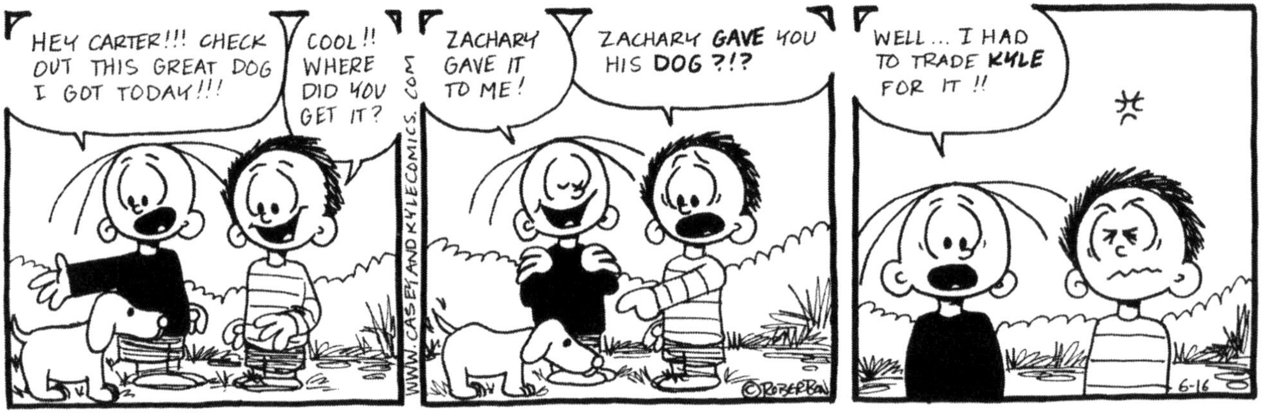
HEY CARTER!!! CHECK OUT THIS GREAT DOG I GOT TODAY!!!
COOL!! WHERE DID YOU GET IT?
WWW.CASEYANDKYLECOMICS.COM
ZACHARY GAVE IT TO ME!
ZACHARY GAVE YOU HIS DOG?!?
©ROBERTSON
WELL... I HAD TO TRADE KYLE FOR IT!!
6-16

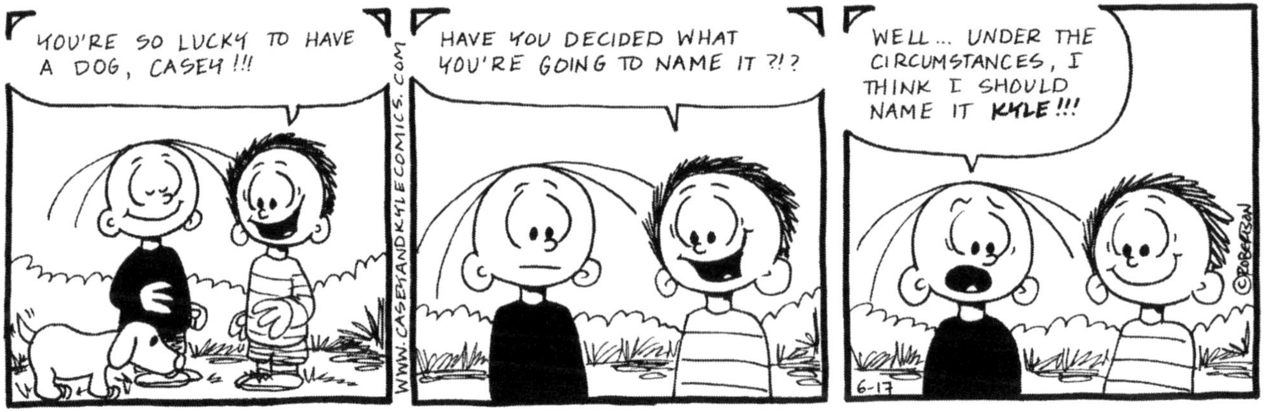
YOU'RE SO LUCKY TO HAVE A DOG, CASEY!!!
WWW.CASEYANDKYLECOMICS.COM
HAVE YOU DECIDED WHAT YOU'RE GOING TO NAME IT?!?
6-17
WELL... UNDER THE CIRCUMSTANCES, I THINK I SHOULD NAME IT KYLE!!!
©ROBERTSON

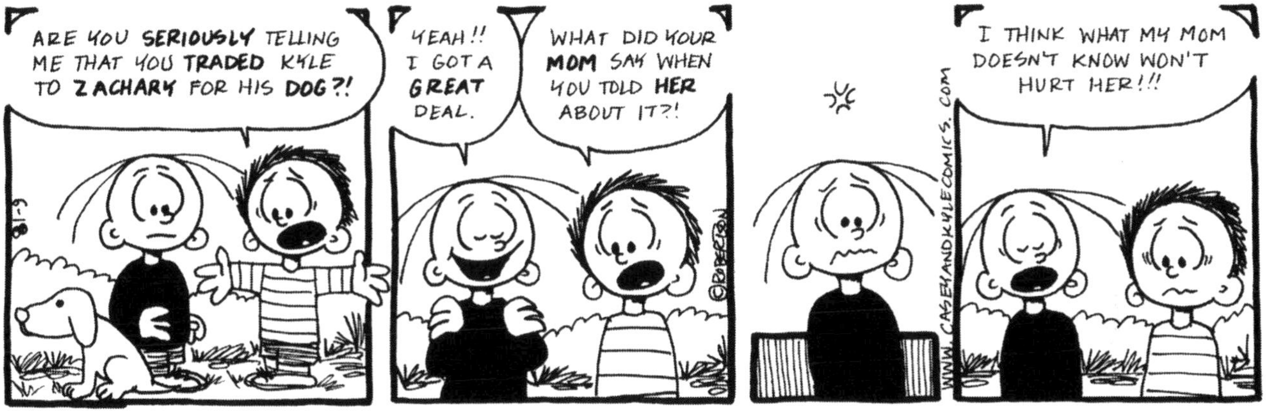
ARE YOU SERIOUSLY TELLING ME THAT YOU TRADED KYLE TO ZACHARY FOR HIS DOG?!
YEAH!! I GOT A GREAT DEAL.
WHAT DID YOUR MOM SAY WHEN YOU TOLD HER ABOUT IT?!
I THINK WHAT MY MOM DOESN'T KNOW WON'T HURT HER!!!
©ROBERTSON
WWW.CASEYANDKYLECOMICS.COM

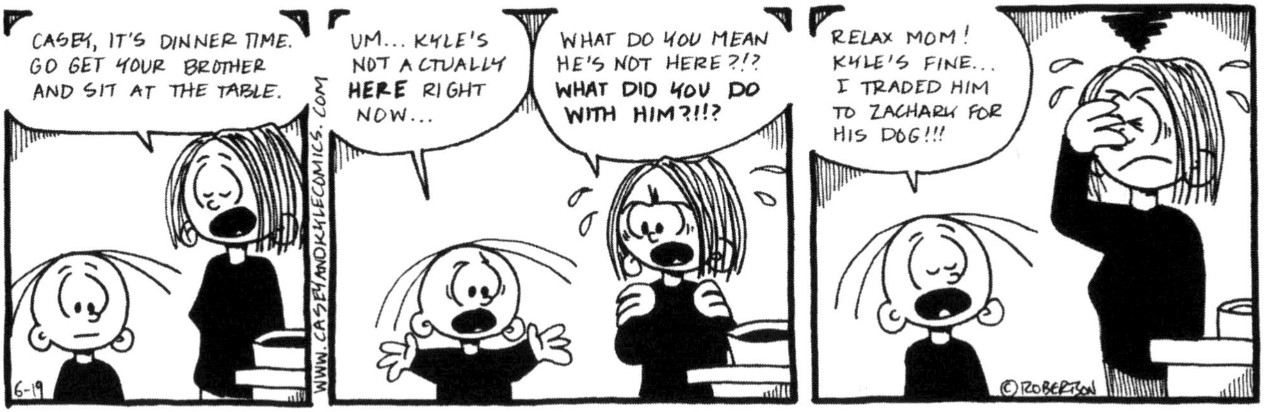
CASEY, IT'S DINNER TIME. GO GET YOUR BROTHER AND SIT AT THE TABLE.
6-19
WWW.CASEYANDKYLECOMICS.COM
UM... KYLE'S NOT ACTUALLY HERE RIGHT NOW...
WHAT DO YOU MEAN HE'S NOT HERE?!? WHAT DID YOU DO WITH HIM?!!?
RELAX MOM! KYLE'S FINE... I TRADED HIM TO ZACHARY FOR HIS DOG!!!
©ROBERTSON

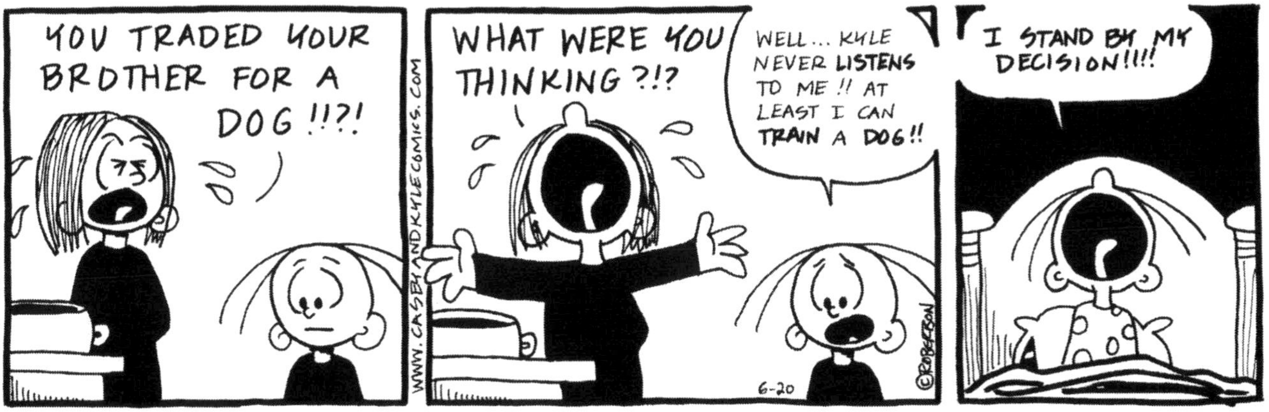
YOU TRADED YOUR BROTHER FOR A DOG!!?!
WWW.CASEYANDKYLECOMICS.COM
WHAT WERE YOU THINKING?!?
WELL... KYLE NEVER LISTENS TO ME!! AT LEAST I CAN TRAIN A DOG!!
6-20
©ROBERTSON
I STAND BY MY DECISION!!!!

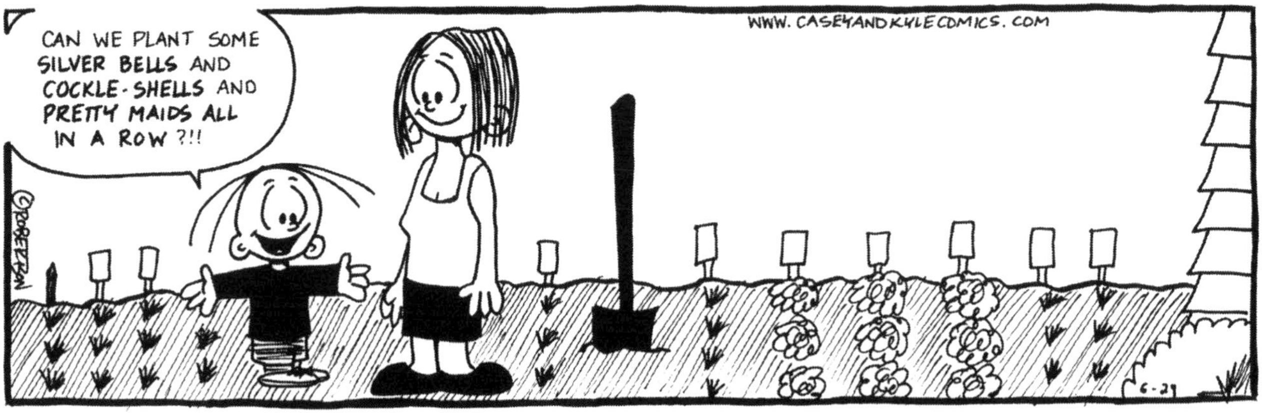
CAN WE PLANT SOME SILVER BELLS AND COCKLE-SHELLS AND PRETTY MAIDS ALL IN A ROW ?!!
WWW. CASEYANDKYLECOMICS. COM
©ROBERTSON
6-29

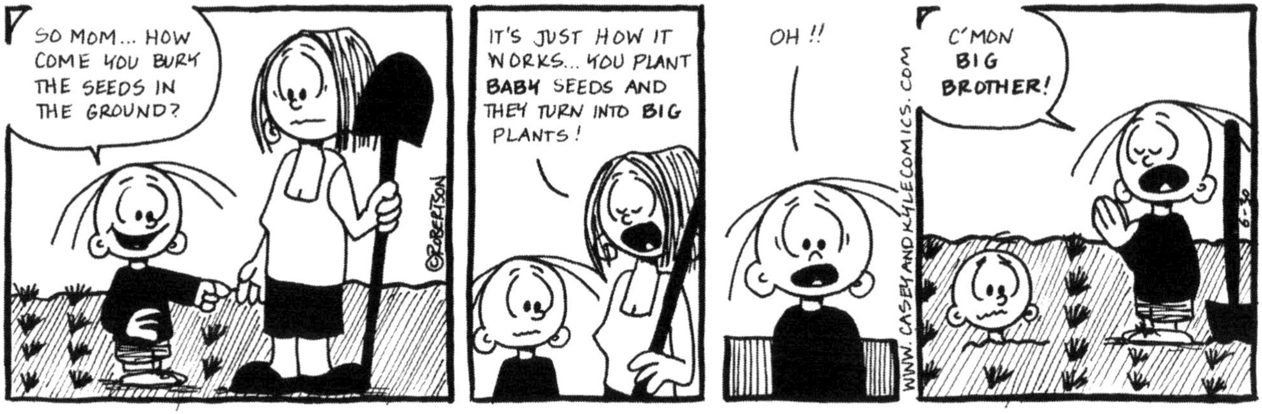
SO MOM... HOW COME YOU BURY THE SEEDS IN THE GROUND?
©ROBERTSON
IT'S JUST HOW IT WORKS... YOU PLANT BABY SEEDS AND THEY TURN INTO BIG PLANTS!
OH !!
WWW. CASEYANDKYLECOMICS. COM
C'MON BIG BROTHER!
6-30

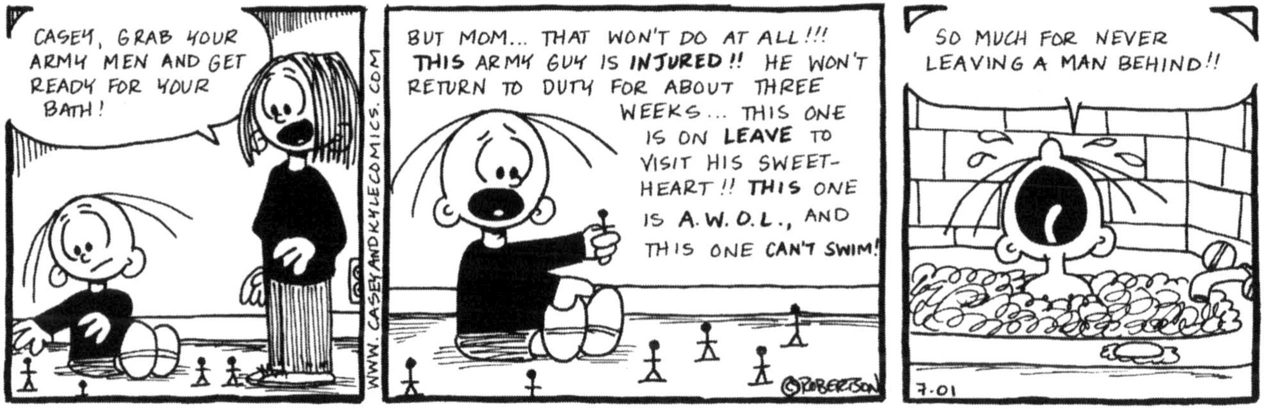
CASEY, GRAB YOUR ARMY MEN AND GET READY FOR YOUR BATH!
WWW. CASEYANDKYLECOMICS. COM
BUT MOM... THAT WON'T DO AT ALL!!! THIS ARMY GUY IS INJURED!! HE WON'T RETURN TO DUTY FOR ABOUT THREE WEEKS... THIS ONE IS ON LEAVE TO VISIT HIS SWEETHEART!! THIS ONE IS A.W.O.L., AND THIS ONE CAN'T SWIM!
©ROBERTSON
SO MUCH FOR NEVER LEAVING A MAN BEHIND!!
7-01

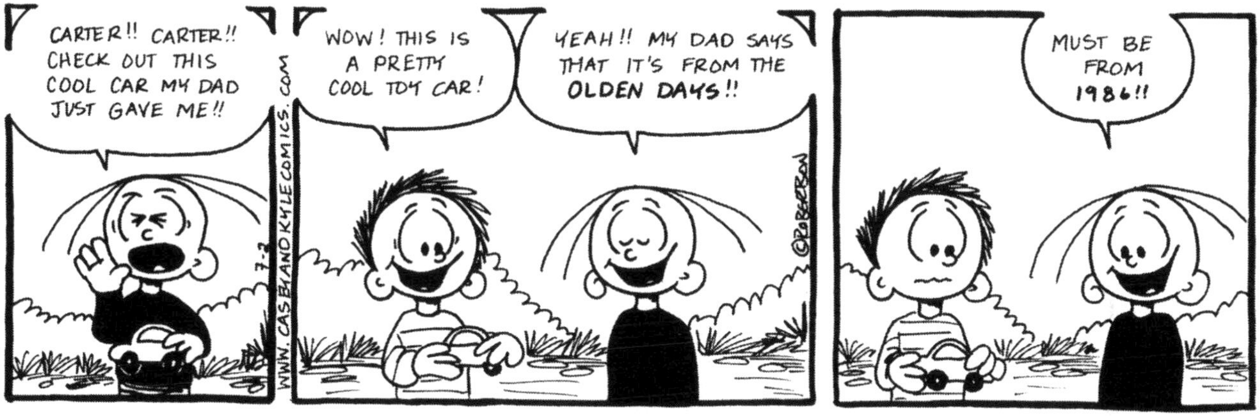
CARTER!! CARTER!! CHECK OUT THIS COOL CAR MY DAD JUST GAVE ME!!
WWW.CASEYANDKYLECOMICS.COM
7-2
WOW! THIS IS A PRETTY COOL TOY CAR!
YEAH!! MY DAD SAYS THAT IT'S FROM THE OLDEN DAYS!!
©ROBERTSON
MUST BE FROM 1986!!

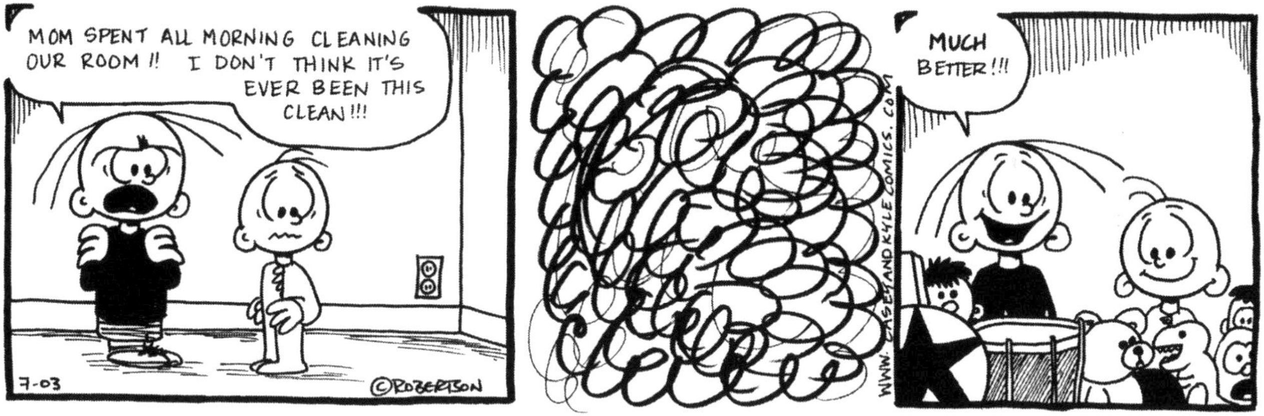
MOM SPENT ALL MORNING CLEANING OUR ROOM!! I DON'T THINK IT'S EVER BEEN THIS CLEAN!!!
7-03
©ROBERTSON
WWW.CASEYANDKYLECOMICS.COM
MUCH BETTER!!!

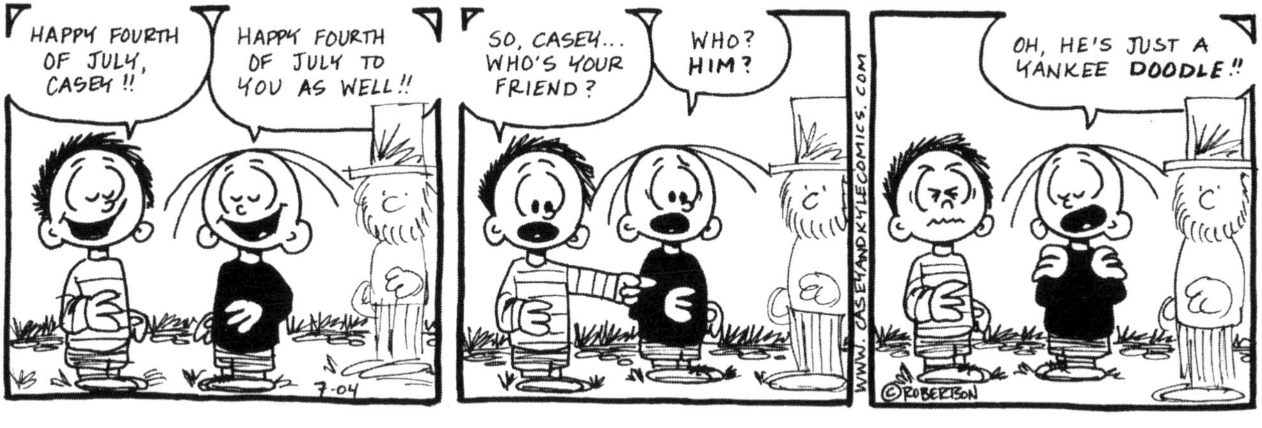
HAPPY FOURTH OF JULY, CASEY!!
HAPPY FOURTH OF JULY TO YOU AS WELL!!
7-04
SO, CASEY... WHO'S YOUR FRIEND?
WHO? HIM?
WWW.CASEYANDKYLECOMICS.COM
OH, HE'S JUST A YANKEE DOODLE!!
©ROBERTSON

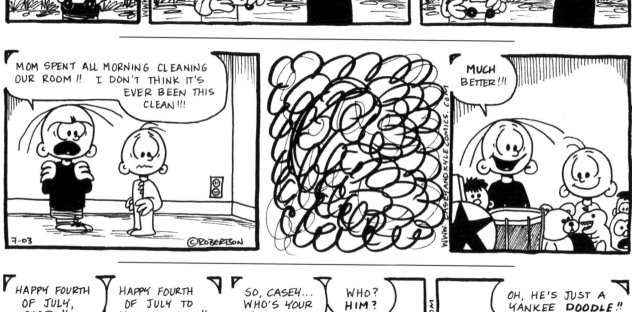

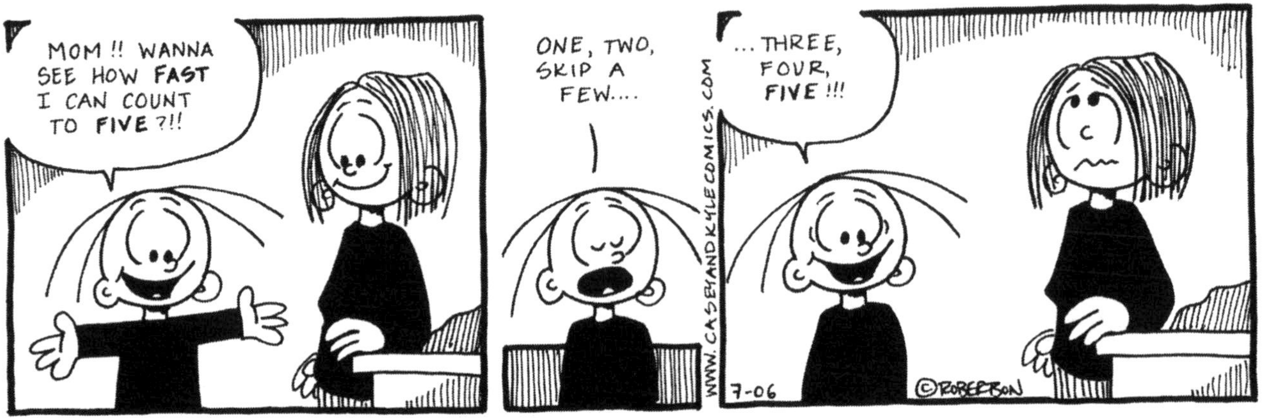
MOM!! WANNA SEE HOW FAST I CAN COUNT TO FIVE?!!
ONE, TWO, SKIP A FEW....
WWW.CASEYANDKYLECOMICS.COM
...THREE, FOUR, FIVE!!!
7-06
©ROBERTSON

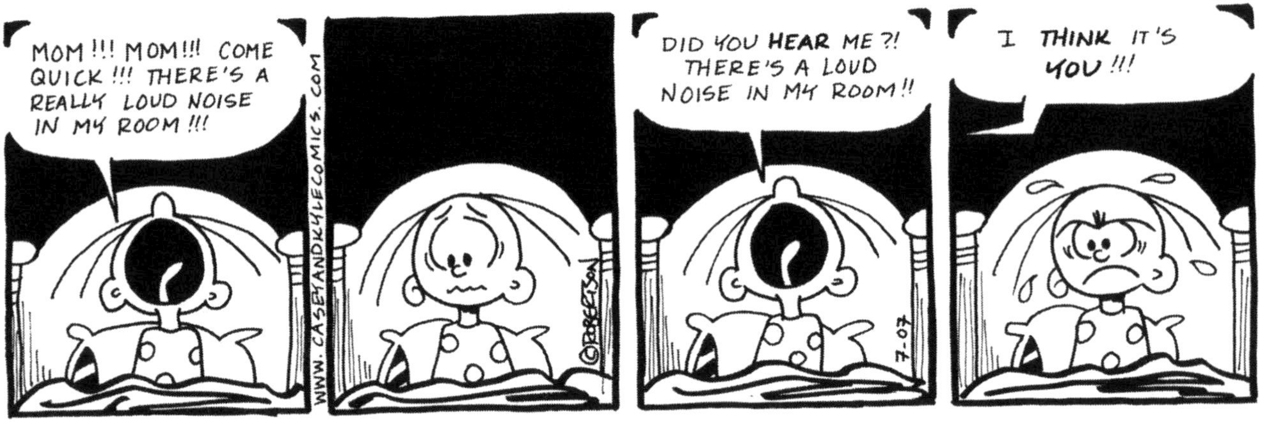
MOM!!! MOM!!! COME QUICK!!! THERE'S A REALLY LOUD NOISE IN MY ROOM!!!
WWW.CASEYANDKYLECOMICS.COM
©ROBERTSON
DID YOU HEAR ME?! THERE'S A LOUD NOISE IN MY ROOM!!
7-07
I THINK IT'S YOU!!!

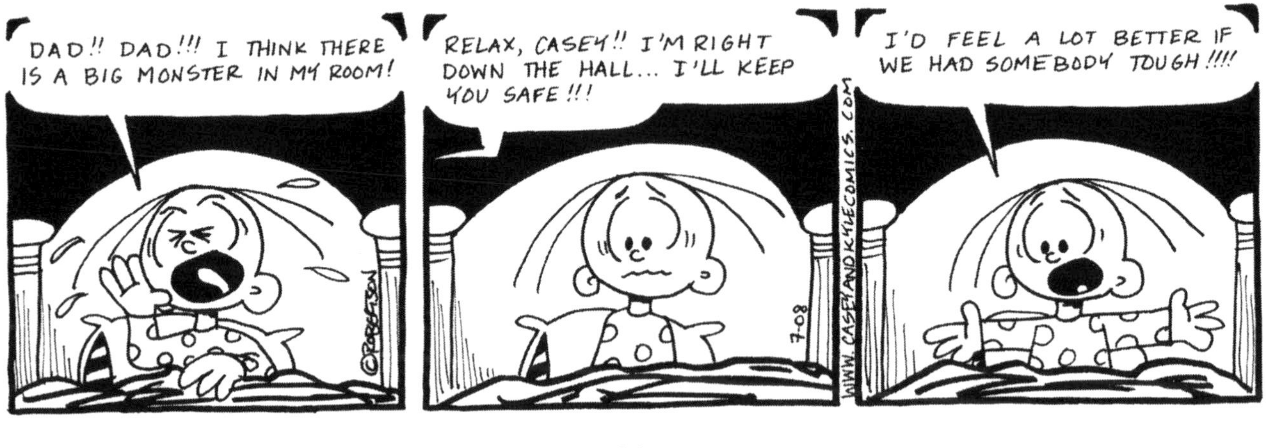
DAD!! DAD!!! I THINK THERE IS A BIG MONSTER IN MY ROOM!
©ROBERTSON
RELAX, CASEY!! I'M RIGHT DOWN THE HALL... I'LL KEEP YOU SAFE!!!
7-08
WWW.CASEYANDKYLECOMICS.COM
I'D FEEL A LOT BETTER IF WE HAD SOMEBODY TOUGH!!!!

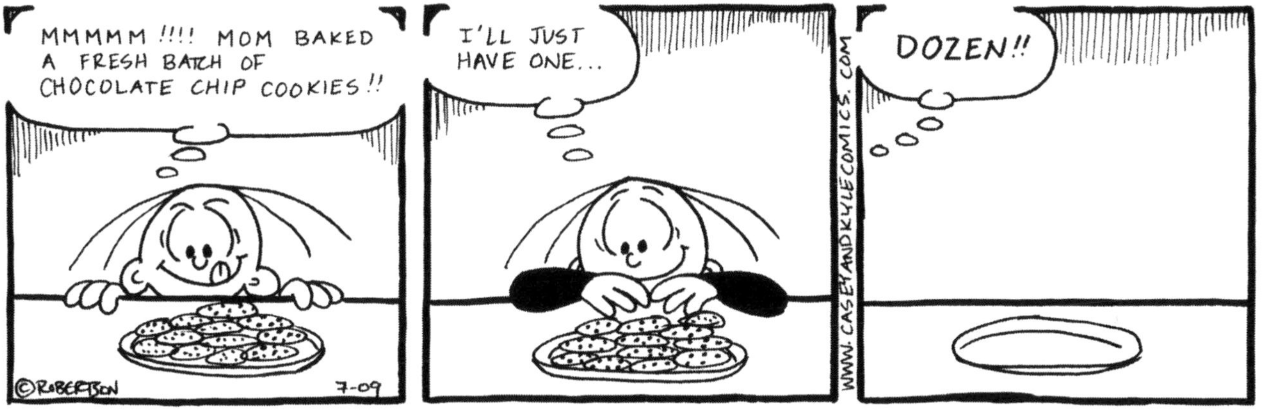
MMMMM!!!! MOM BAKED A FRESH BATCH OF CHOCOLATE CHIP COOKIES!!
©ROBERTSON
7-09
I'LL JUST HAVE ONE...
WWW.CASEYANDKYLECOMICS.COM
DOZEN!!

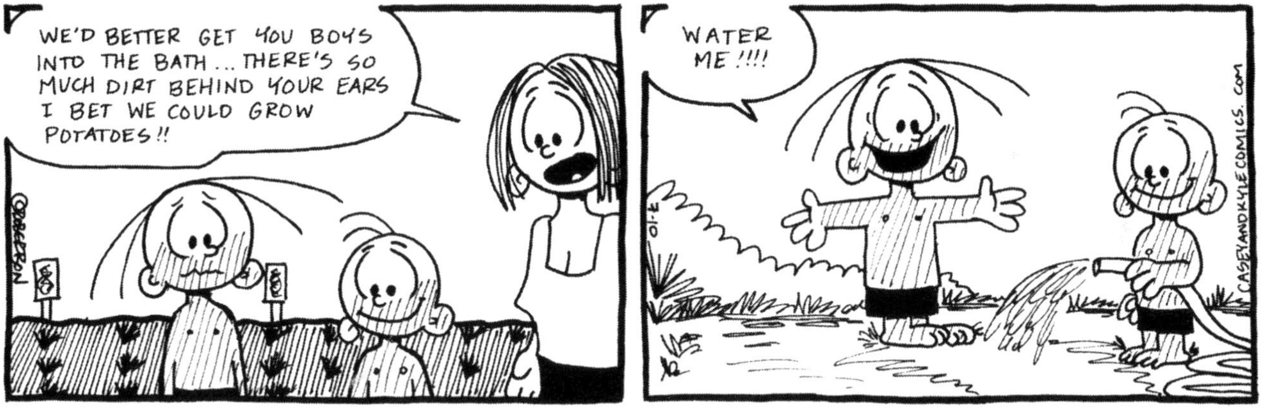
WE'D BETTER GET YOU BOYS INTO THE BATH... THERE'S SO MUCH DIRT BEHIND YOUR EARS I BET WE COULD GROW POTATOES!!
©ROBERTSON
WATER ME!!!!
7-10
CASEYANDKYLECOMICS.COM

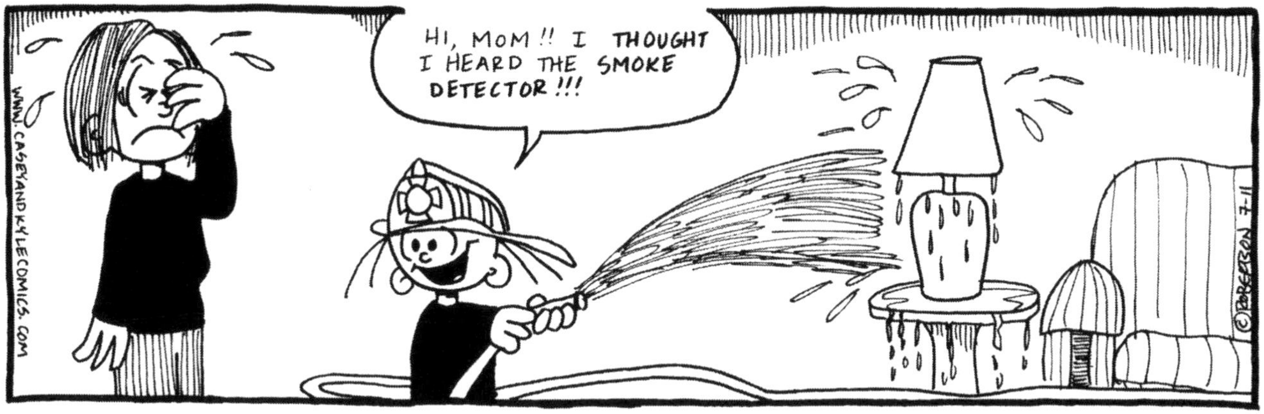
WWW.CASEYANDKYLECOMICS.COM
HI, MOM!! I THOUGHT I HEARD THE SMOKE DETECTOR!!!
©ROBERTSON 7-11

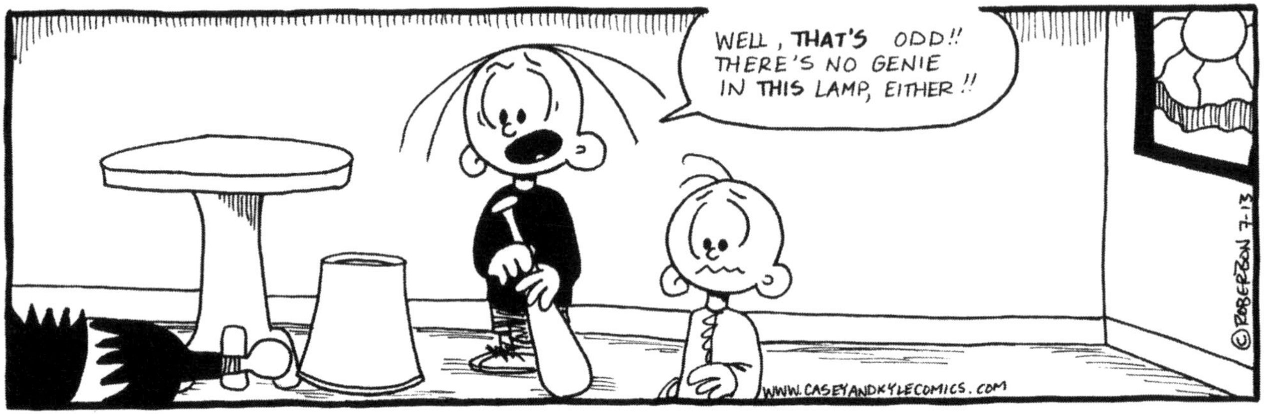
WELL, THAT'S ODD!! THERE'S NO GENIE IN THIS LAMP, EITHER!!
©ROBERSON 7-13
WWW.CASEYANDKYLECOMICS.COM

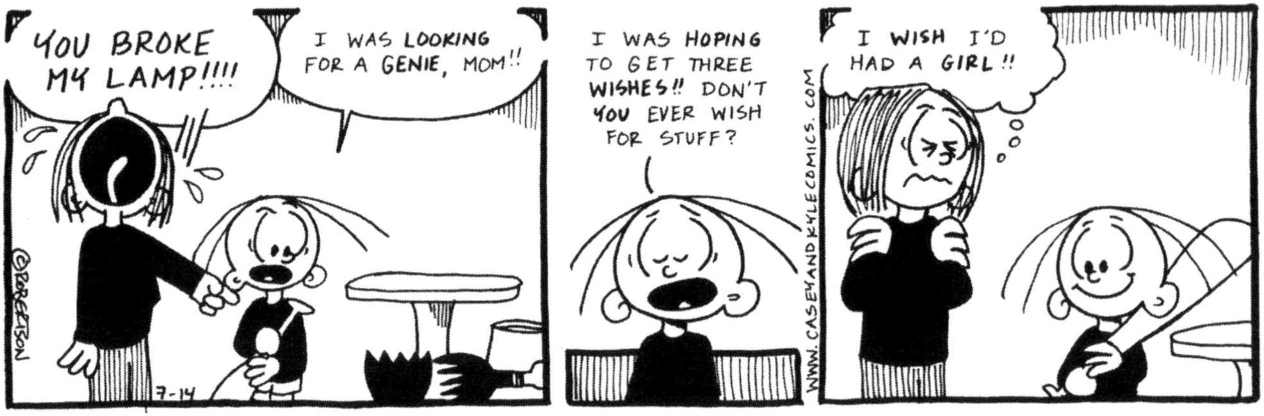
YOU BROKE MY LAMP!!!!
I WAS LOOKING FOR A GENIE, MOM!!
©ROBERSON
7-14
I WAS HOPING TO GET THREE WISHES!! DON'T YOU EVER WISH FOR STUFF?
WWW.CASEYANDKYLECOMICS.COM
I WISH I'D HAD A GIRL!!

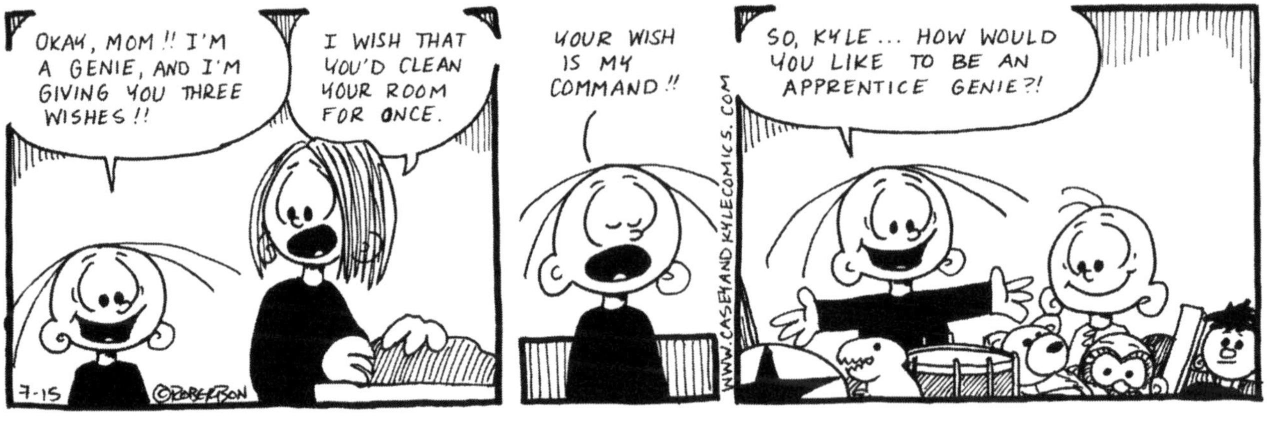
OKAY, MOM!! I'M A GENIE, AND I'M GIVING YOU THREE WISHES!!
I WISH THAT YOU'D CLEAN YOUR ROOM FOR ONCE.
7-15
©ROBERSON
YOUR WISH IS MY COMMAND!!
WWW.CASEYANDKYLECOMICS.COM
SO, KYLE... HOW WOULD YOU LIKE TO BE AN APPRENTICE GENIE?!

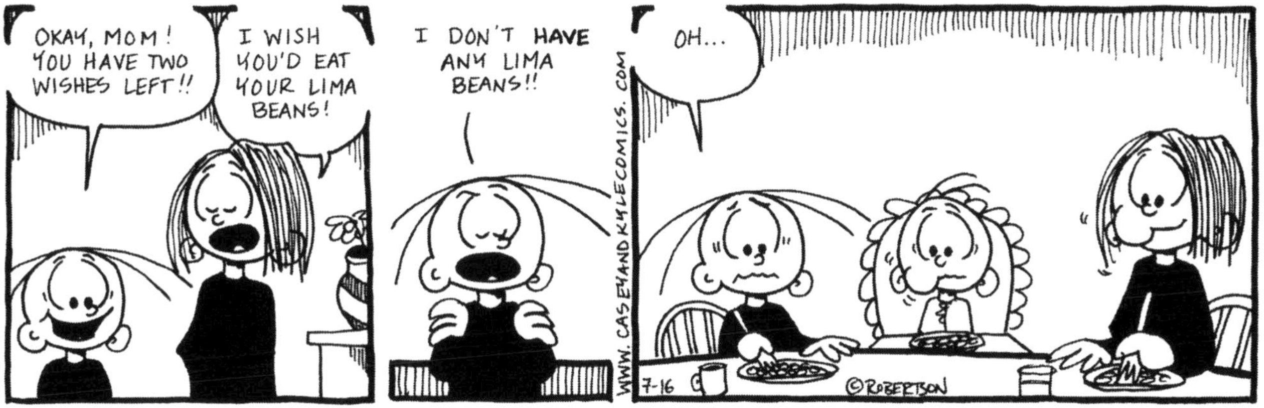
OKAY, MOM! YOU HAVE TWO WISHES LEFT!!
I WISH YOU'D EAT YOUR LIMA BEANS!
I DON'T **HAVE** ANY LIMA BEANS!!
WWW.CASEYANDKYLECOMICS.COM
OH...
7-16
©ROBERTSON

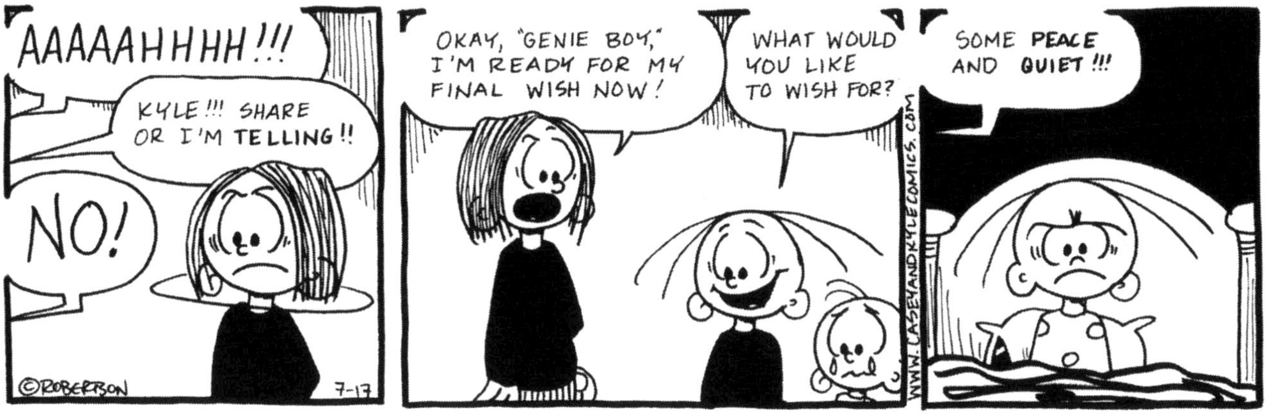
AAAAAHHHH!!!
KYLE!!! SHARE OR I'M **TELLING**!!
NO!
©ROBERTSON
7-17
OKAY, "GENIE BOY," I'M READY FOR MY FINAL WISH NOW!
WHAT WOULD YOU LIKE TO WISH FOR?
WWW.CASEYANDKYLECOMICS.COM
SOME **PEACE** AND **QUIET**!!!

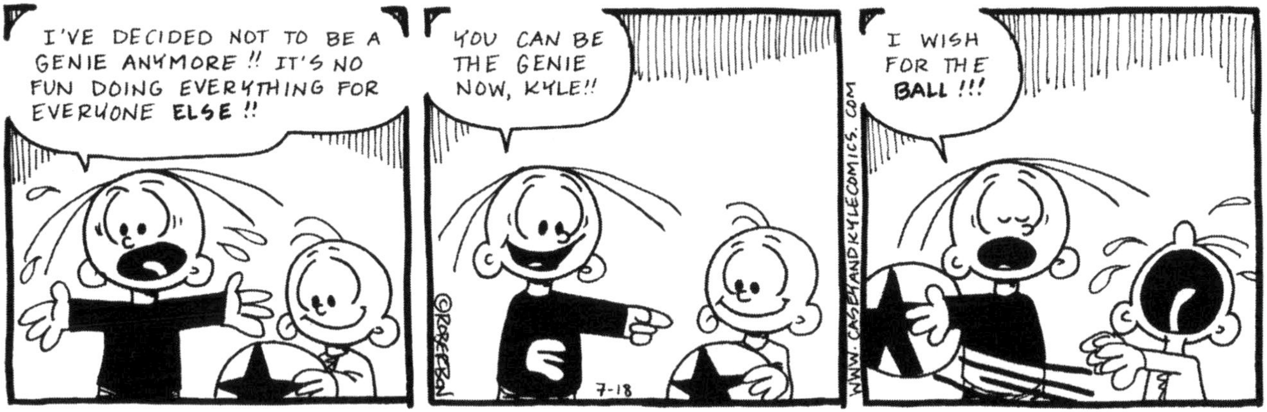
I'VE DECIDED NOT TO BE A GENIE ANYMORE!! IT'S NO FUN DOING EVERYTHING FOR EVERYONE **ELSE**!!
YOU CAN BE THE GENIE NOW, KYLE!!
©ROBERTSON
7-18
WWW.CASEYANDKYLECOMICS.COM
I WISH FOR THE **BALL**!!!

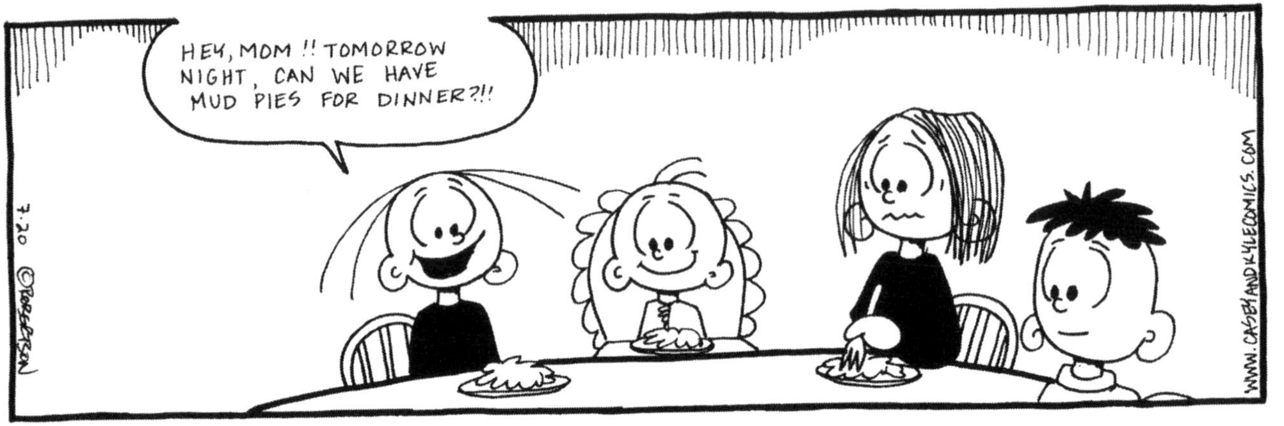
HEY, MOM !! TOMORROW NIGHT, CAN WE HAVE MUD PIES FOR DINNER?!!
7-20 ©ROBERSON
WWW.CASEYANDKYLECOMICS.COM

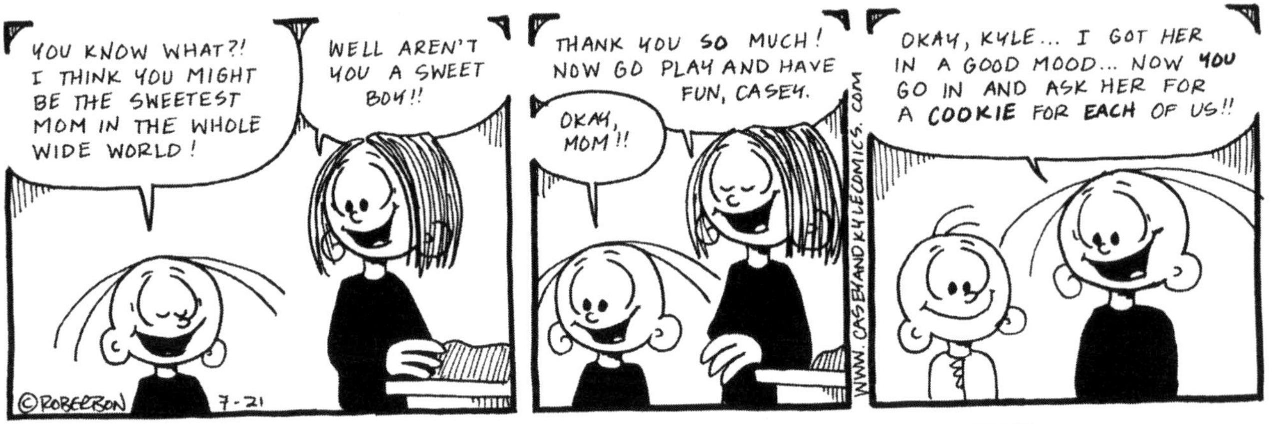
YOU KNOW WHAT?! I THINK YOU MIGHT BE THE SWEETEST MOM IN THE WHOLE WIDE WORLD!
WELL AREN'T YOU A SWEET BOY!!
©ROBERSON 7-21
THANK YOU SO MUCH! NOW GO PLAY AND HAVE FUN, CASEY.
OKAY, MOM!!
WWW.CASEYANDKYLECOMICS.COM
OKAY, KYLE... I GOT HER IN A GOOD MOOD... NOW YOU GO IN AND ASK HER FOR A COOKIE FOR EACH OF US!!

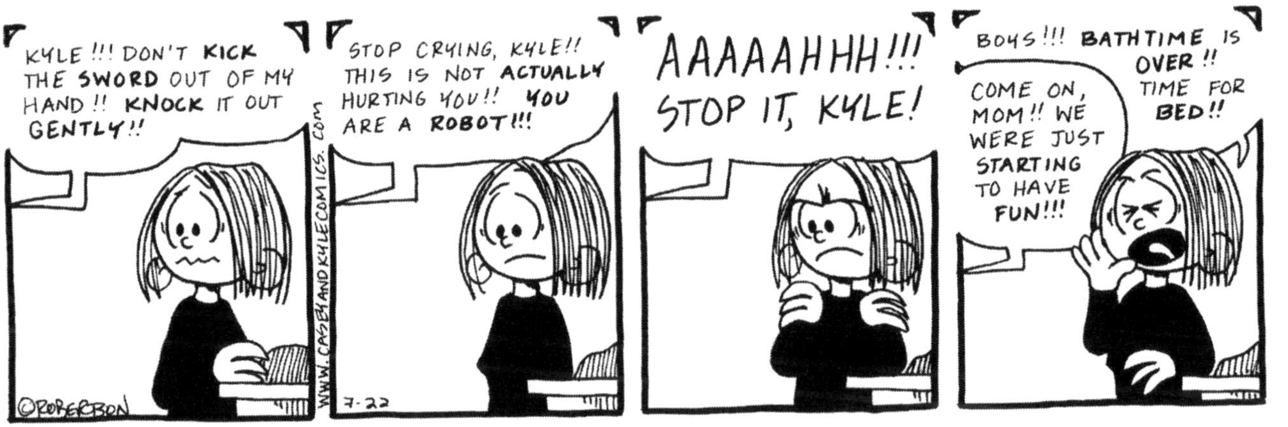
KYLE!!! DON'T KICK THE SWORD OUT OF MY HAND!! KNOCK IT OUT GENTLY!!
©ROBERSON
WWW.CASEYANDKYLECOMICS.COM
STOP CRYING, KYLE!! THIS IS NOT ACTUALLY HURTING YOU!! YOU ARE A ROBOT!!!
7-22
AAAAAHHH!!! STOP IT, KYLE!
BOYS!!! BATHTIME IS OVER!! TIME FOR BED!!
COME ON, MOM!! WE WERE JUST STARTING TO HAVE FUN!!!

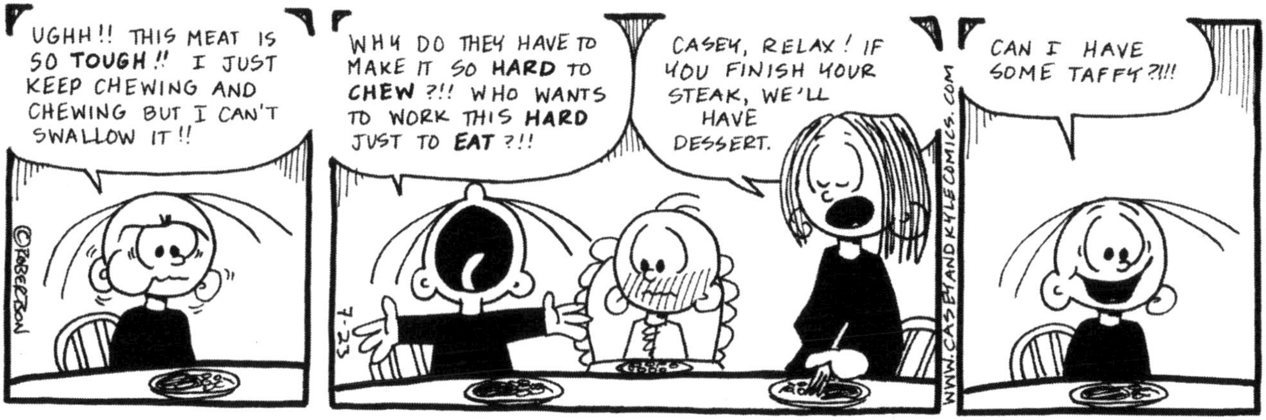
UGHH!! THIS MEAT IS SO TOUGH!! I JUST KEEP CHEWING AND CHEWING BUT I CAN'T SWALLOW IT!!
©ROBERTSON
WHY DO THEY HAVE TO MAKE IT SO HARD TO CHEW?!! WHO WANTS TO WORK THIS HARD JUST TO EAT?!!
7-23
CASEY, RELAX! IF YOU FINISH YOUR STEAK, WE'LL HAVE DESSERT.
WWW.CASEYANDKYLECOMICS.COM
CAN I HAVE SOME TAFFY?!!!

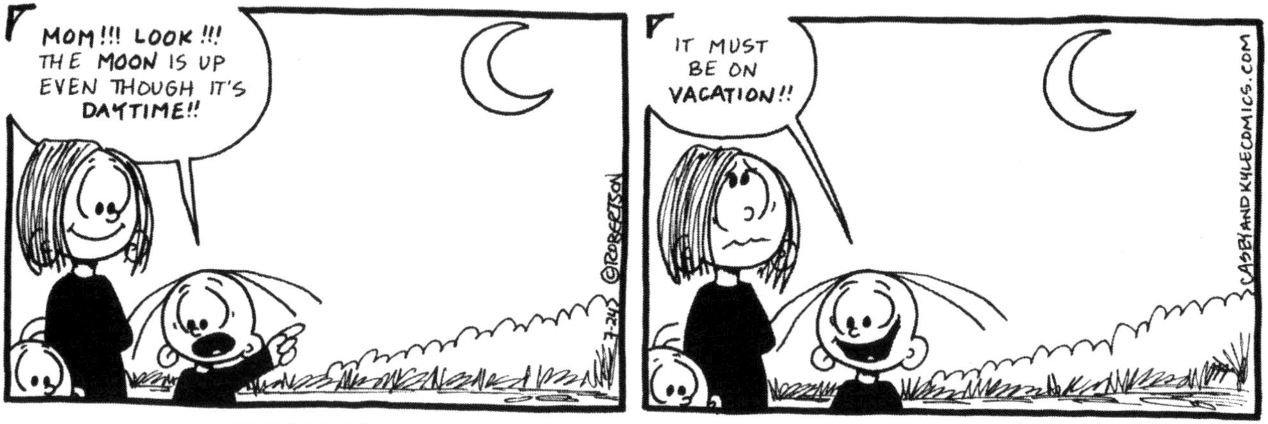
MOM!!! LOOK!!! THE MOON IS UP EVEN THOUGH IT'S DAYTIME!!
©ROBERTSON
7-24
IT MUST BE ON VACATION!!
CASEYANDKYLECOMICS.COM

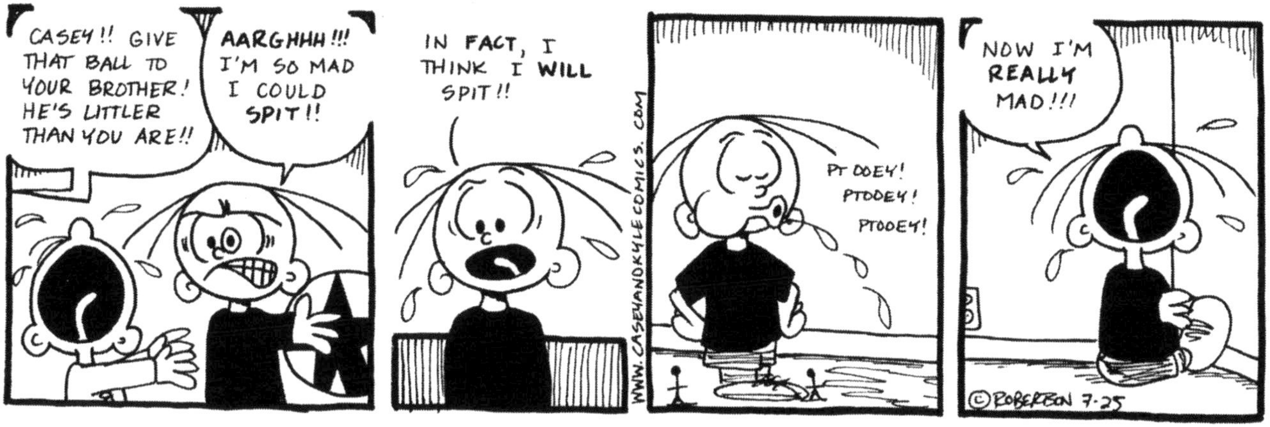
CASEY!! GIVE THAT BALL TO YOUR BROTHER! HE'S LITTLER THAN YOU ARE!!
AARGHHH!!! I'M SO MAD I COULD SPIT!!
IN FACT, I THINK I WILL SPIT!!
WWW.CASEYANDKYLECOMICS.COM
PTOOEY! PTOOEY! PTOOEY!
NOW I'M REALLY MAD!!!
©ROBERTSON 7-25

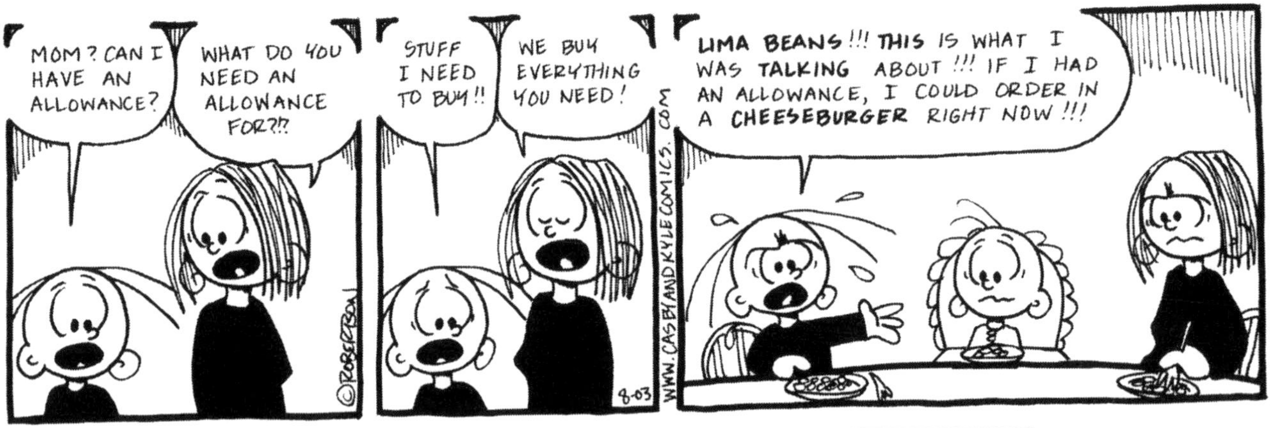
MOM? CAN I HAVE AN ALLOWANCE?
WHAT DO YOU NEED AN ALLOWANCE FOR?!?
©ROBERTSON
STUFF I NEED TO BUY!!
WE BUY EVERYTHING YOU NEED!
8-03
WWW.CASEYANDKYLECOMICS.COM
LIMA BEANS!!! THIS IS WHAT I WAS TALKING ABOUT!!! IF I HAD AN ALLOWANCE, I COULD ORDER IN A CHEESEBURGER RIGHT NOW!!!

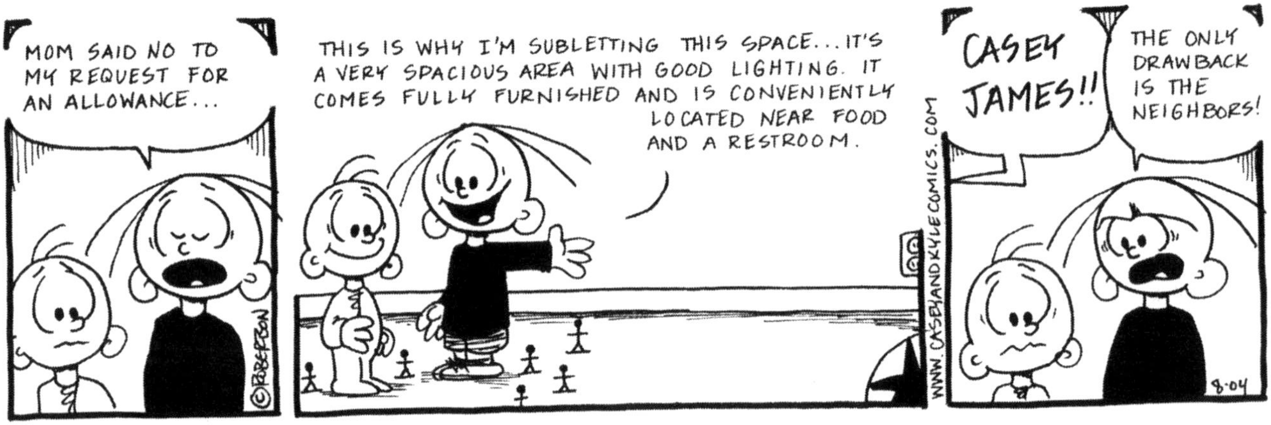
MOM SAID NO TO MY REQUEST FOR AN ALLOWANCE...
©ROBERTSON
THIS IS WHY I'M SUBLETTING THIS SPACE... IT'S A VERY SPACIOUS AREA WITH GOOD LIGHTING. IT COMES FULLY FURNISHED AND IS CONVENIENTLY LOCATED NEAR FOOD AND A RESTROOM.
WWW.CASEYANDKYLECOMICS.COM
CASEY JAMES!!
THE ONLY DRAWBACK IS THE NEIGHBORS!
8-04

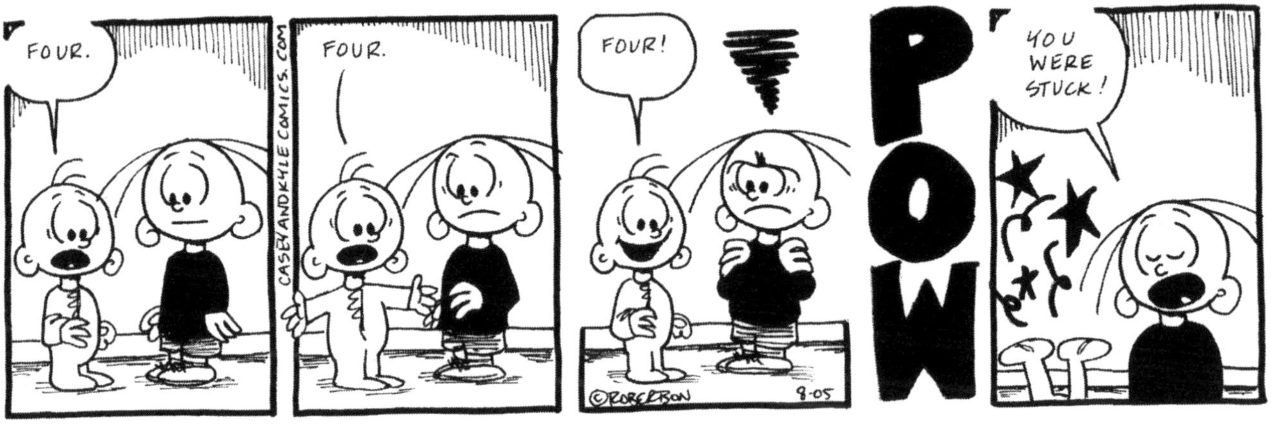
FOUR.
CASEYANDKYLECOMICS.COM
FOUR.
FOUR!
©ROBERTSON
8-05
POW
YOU WERE STUCK!

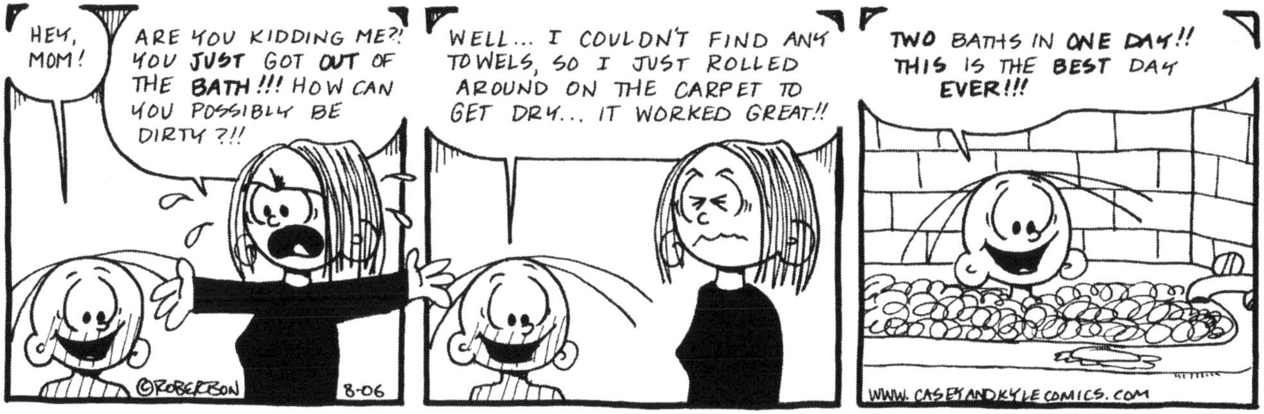
HEY, MOM!
ARE YOU KIDDING ME?! YOU JUST GOT OUT OF THE BATH!!! HOW CAN YOU POSSIBLY BE DIRTY?!!
©ROBERTSON
8-06
WELL... I COULDN'T FIND ANY TOWELS, SO I JUST ROLLED AROUND ON THE CARPET TO GET DRY... IT WORKED GREAT!!
TWO BATHS IN ONE DAY!! THIS IS THE BEST DAY EVER!!!
WWW.CASEYANDKYLECOMICS.COM

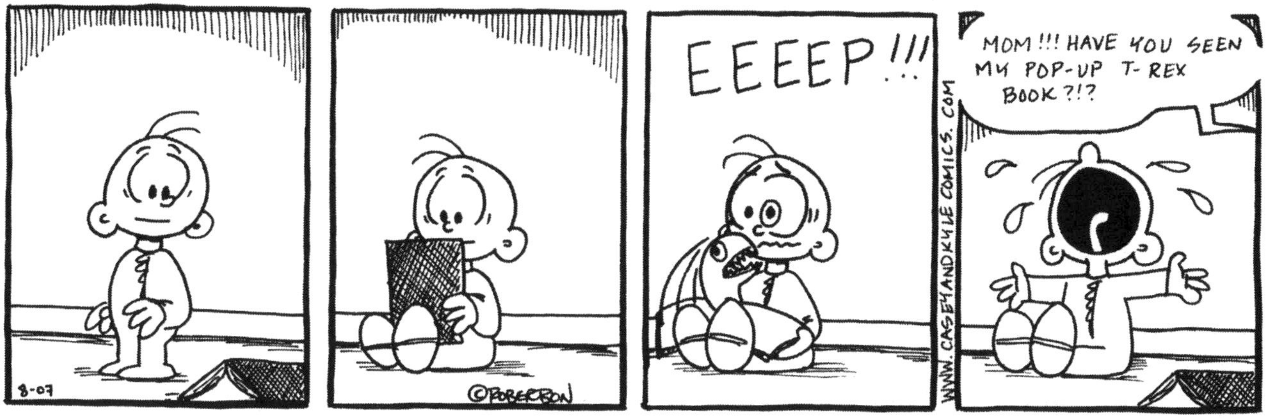
8-07
©ROBERTSON
EEEEP!!!
WWW.CASEYANDKYLECOMICS.COM
MOM!!! HAVE YOU SEEN MY POP-UP T-REX BOOK?!?

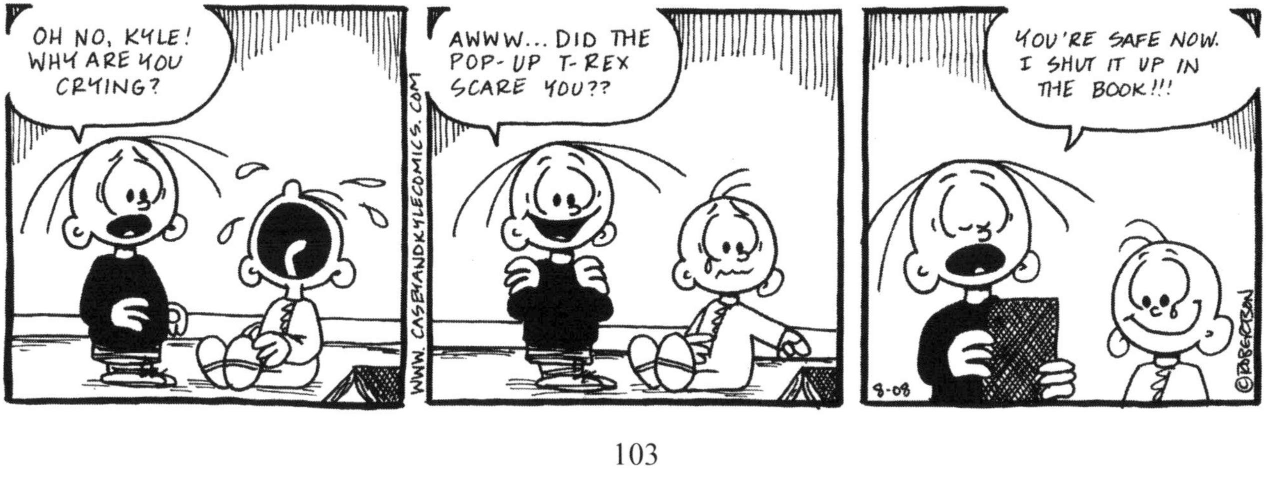
OH NO, KYLE! WHY ARE YOU CRYING?
WWW.CASEYANDKYLECOMICS.COM
AWWW... DID THE POP-UP T-REX SCARE YOU??
YOU'RE SAFE NOW. I SHUT IT UP IN THE BOOK!!!
8-08
©ROBERTSON

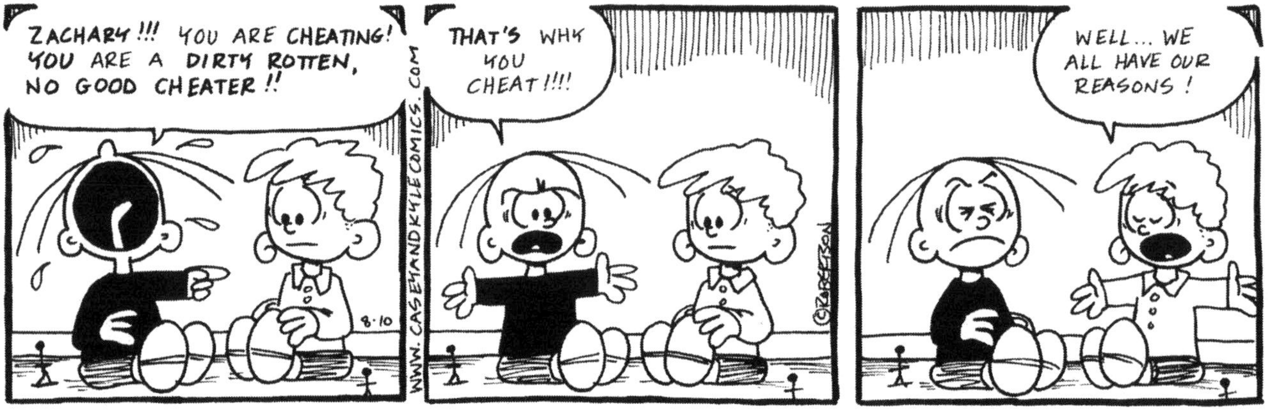
ZACHARY!!! YOU ARE CHEATING! YOU ARE A DIRTY ROTTEN, NO GOOD CHEATER!!
8-10
WWW.CASEYANDKYLECOMICS.COM
THAT'S WHY YOU CHEAT!!!!
©ROBERTSON
WELL... WE ALL HAVE OUR REASONS!

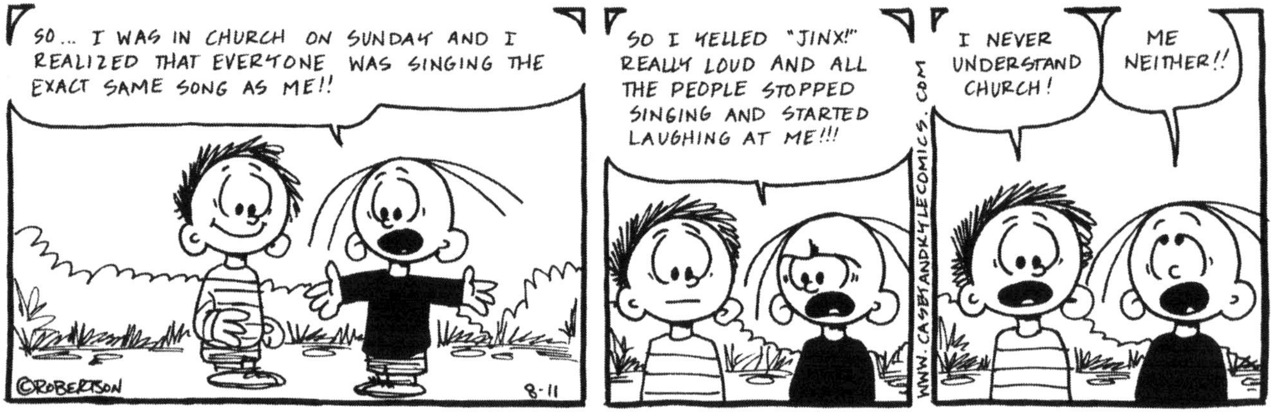
SO... I WAS IN CHURCH ON SUNDAY AND I REALIZED THAT EVERYONE WAS SINGING THE EXACT SAME SONG AS ME!!
©ROBERTSON
8-11
SO I YELLED "JINX!" REALLY LOUD AND ALL THE PEOPLE STOPPED SINGING AND STARTED LAUGHING AT ME!!!
WWW.CASEYANDKYLECOMICS.COM
I NEVER UNDERSTAND CHURCH!
ME NEITHER!!

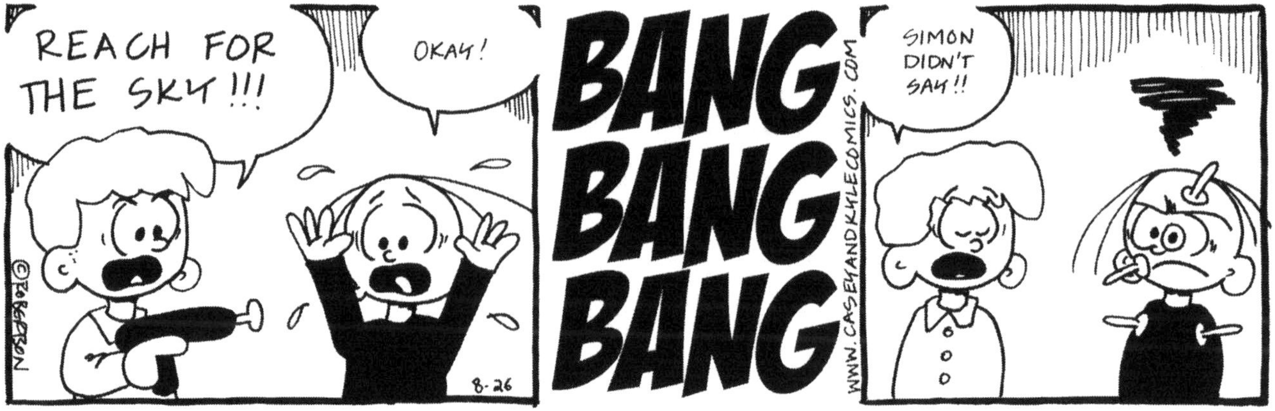
REACH FOR THE SKY!!!
OKAY!
©ROBERTSON
8-26
BANG
BANG
BANG
WWW.CASEYANDKYLECOMICS.COM
SIMON DIDN'T SAY!!

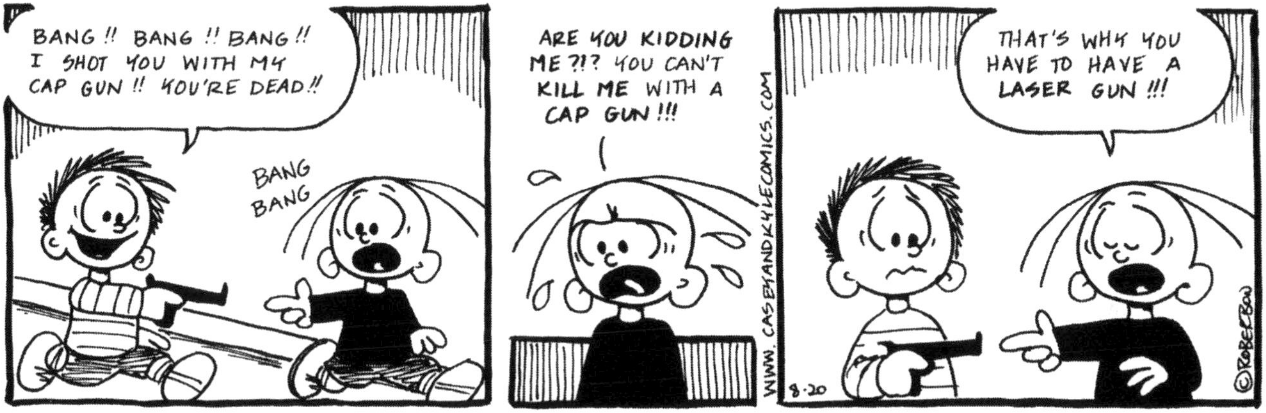
BANG!! BANG!! BANG!! I SHOT YOU WITH MY CAP GUN!! YOU'RE DEAD!!
BANG BANG
ARE YOU KIDDING ME?!? YOU CAN'T KILL ME WITH A CAP GUN!!!
WWW.CASEYANDKYLECOMICS.COM
8·20
THAT'S WHY YOU HAVE TO HAVE A LASER GUN!!!
©ROBERTSON

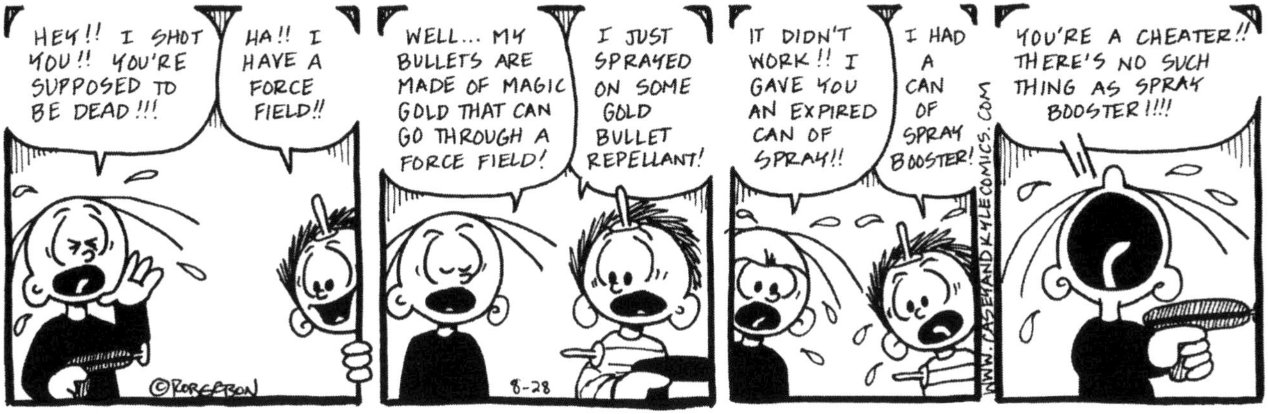
HEY!! I SHOT YOU!! YOU'RE SUPPOSED TO BE DEAD!!!
HA!! I HAVE A FORCE FIELD!!
©ROBERTSON
WELL... MY BULLETS ARE MADE OF MAGIC GOLD THAT CAN GO THROUGH A FORCE FIELD!
I JUST SPRAYED ON SOME GOLD BULLET REPELLANT!
8-28
IT DIDN'T WORK!! I GAVE YOU AN EXPIRED CAN OF SPRAY!!
I HAD A CAN OF SPRAY BOOSTER!
WWW.CASEYANDKYLECOMICS.COM
YOU'RE A CHEATER!! THERE'S NO SUCH THING AS SPRAY BOOSTER!!!!

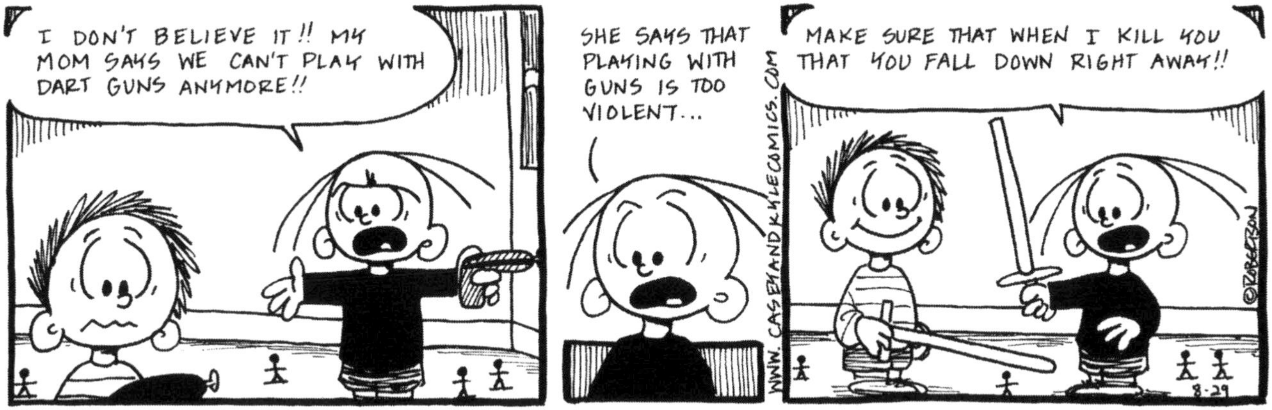
I DON'T BELIEVE IT!! MY MOM SAYS WE CAN'T PLAY WITH DART GUNS ANYMORE!!
SHE SAYS THAT PLAYING WITH GUNS IS TOO VIOLENT...
WWW.CASEYANDKYLECOMICS.COM
MAKE SURE THAT WHEN I KILL YOU THAT YOU FALL DOWN RIGHT AWAY!!
©ROBERTSON
8-29

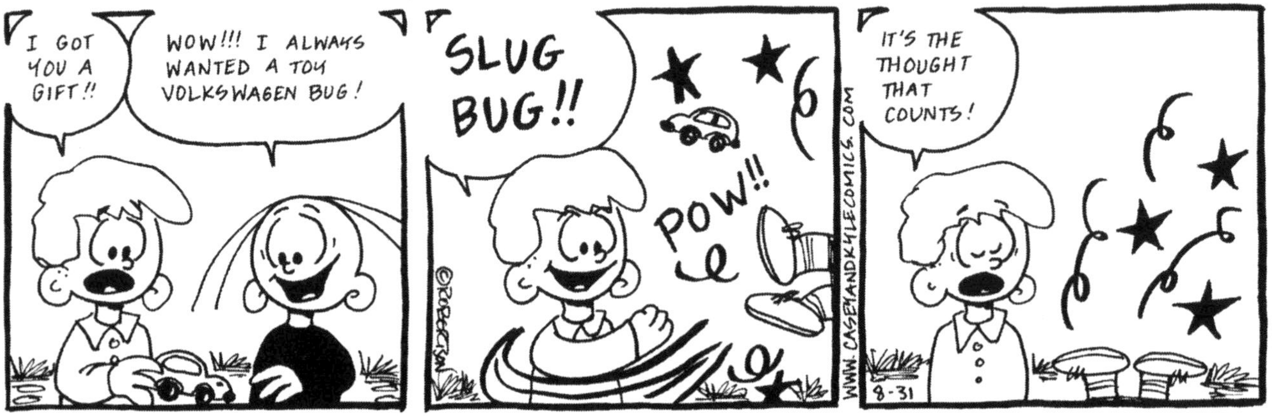
I GOT YOU A GIFT!!
WOW!!! I ALWAYS WANTED A TOY VOLKSWAGEN BUG!
SLUG BUG!!
POW!!
©ROBERTSON
WWW.CASEYANDKYLECOMICS.COM
IT'S THE THOUGHT THAT COUNTS!
8-31

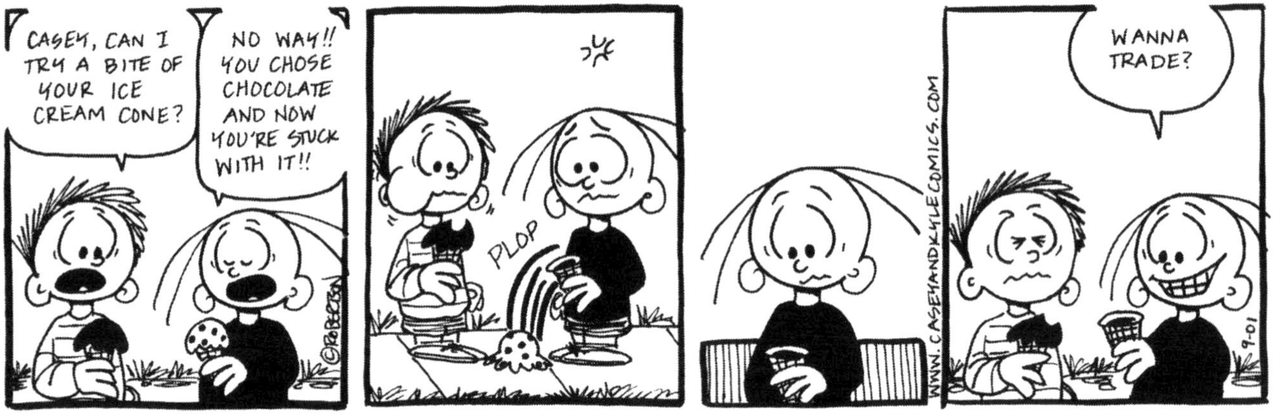
CASEY, CAN I TRY A BITE OF YOUR ICE CREAM CONE?
NO WAY!! YOU CHOSE CHOCOLATE AND NOW YOU'RE STUCK WITH IT!!
©ROBERTSON
PLOP
WWW.CASEYANDKYLECOMICS.COM
WANNA TRADE?
9-01

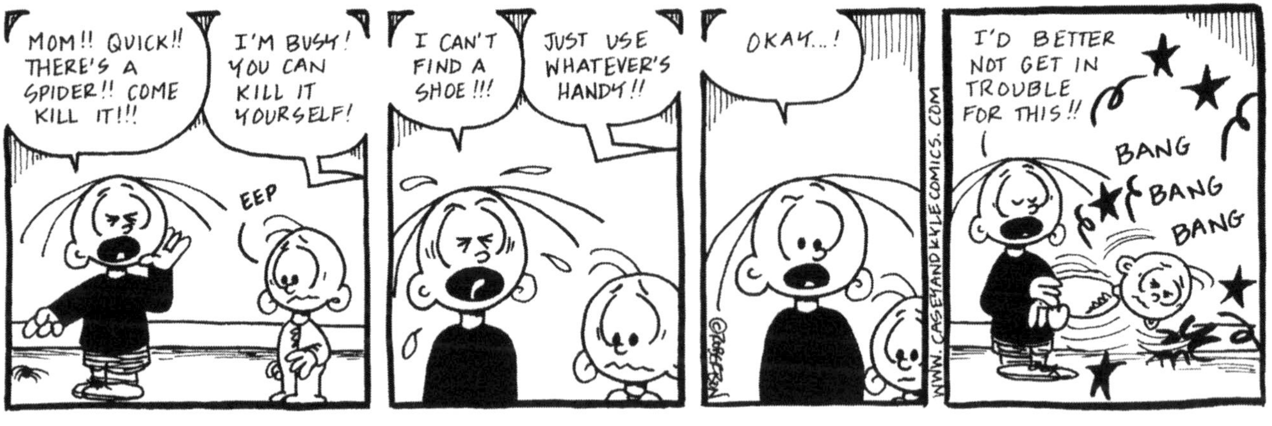
MOM!! QUICK!! THERE'S A SPIDER!! COME KILL IT!!!
I'M BUSY! YOU CAN KILL IT YOURSELF!
EEP
I CAN'T FIND A SHOE!!!
JUST USE WHATEVER'S HANDY!!
OKAY...!
©ROBERTSON
WWW.CASEYANDKYLECOMICS.COM
I'D BETTER NOT GET IN TROUBLE FOR THIS!!
BANG
BANG
BANG

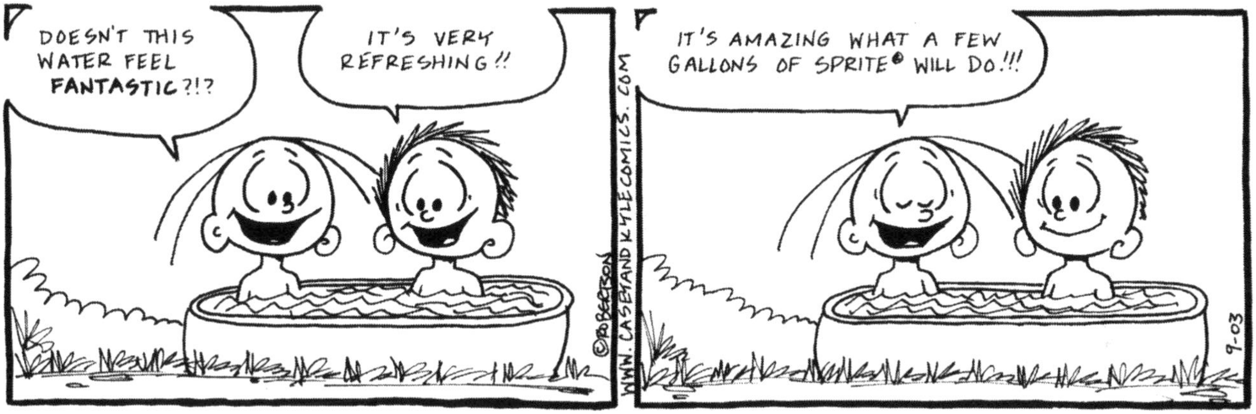
DOESN'T THIS WATER FEEL **FANTASTIC**?!?
IT'S VERY REFRESHING!!
©ROBERTSON
WWW.CASEYANDKYLECOMICS.COM
IT'S AMAZING WHAT A FEW GALLONS OF SPRITE® WILL DO!!!
9-03

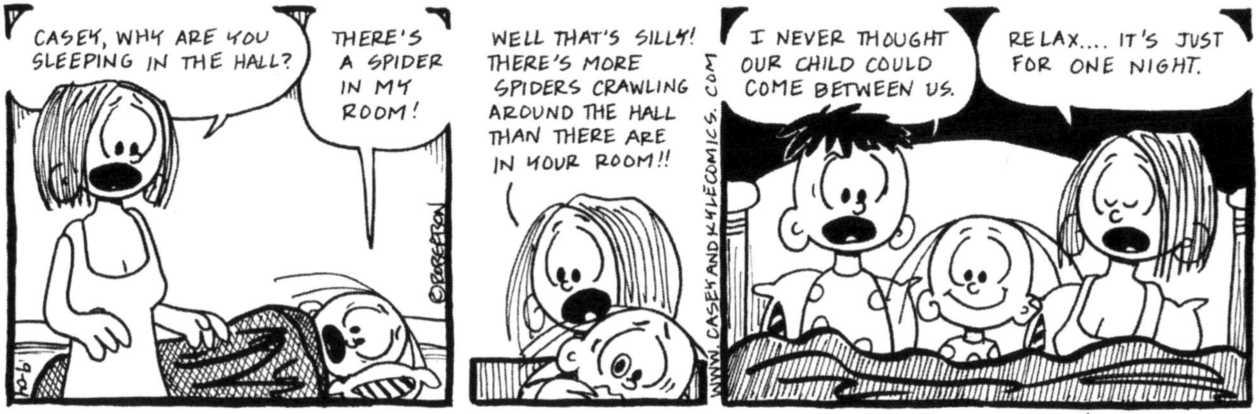
CASEY, WHY ARE YOU SLEEPING IN THE HALL?
THERE'S A SPIDER IN MY ROOM!
9-04
©ROBERTSON
WELL THAT'S SILLY! THERE'S MORE SPIDERS CRAWLING AROUND THE HALL THAN THERE ARE IN YOUR ROOM!!
WWW.CASEYANDKYLECOMICS.COM
I NEVER THOUGHT OUR CHILD COULD COME BETWEEN US.
RELAX.... IT'S JUST FOR ONE NIGHT.

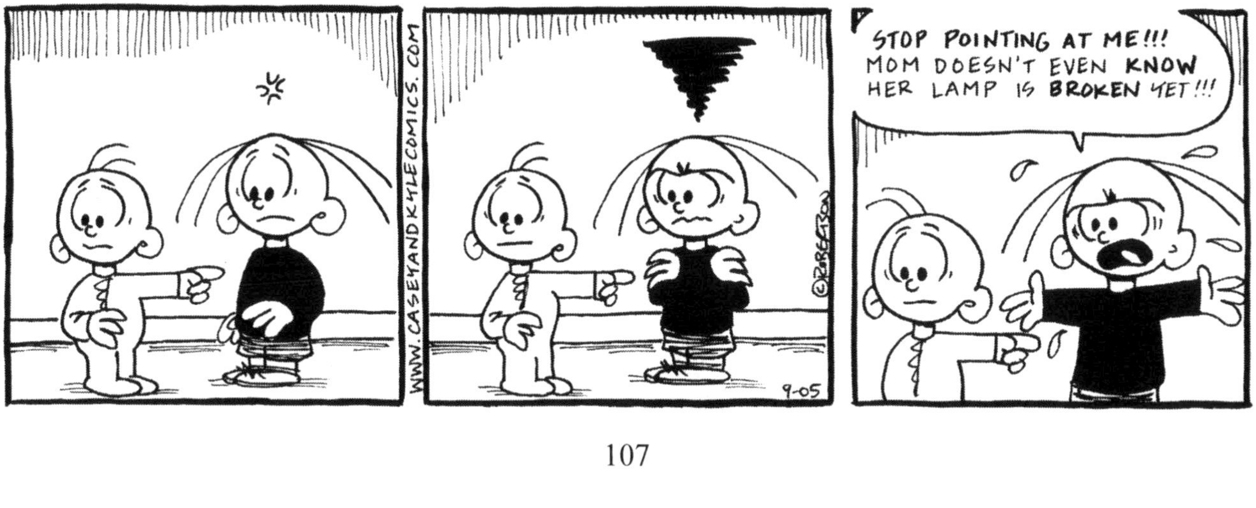
WWW.CASEYANDKYLECOMICS.COM
©ROBERTSON
9-05
STOP POINTING AT ME!!! MOM DOESN'T EVEN **KNOW** HER LAMP IS **BROKEN** YET!!!

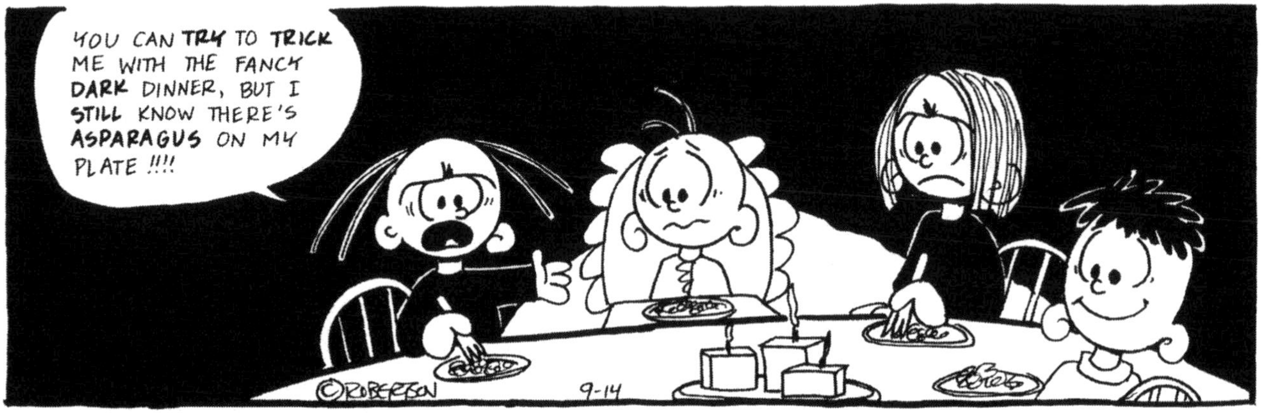
YOU CAN TRY TO TRICK ME WITH THE FANCY DARK DINNER, BUT I STILL KNOW THERE'S ASPARAGUS ON MY PLATE !!!!
©ROBERTSON
9-14

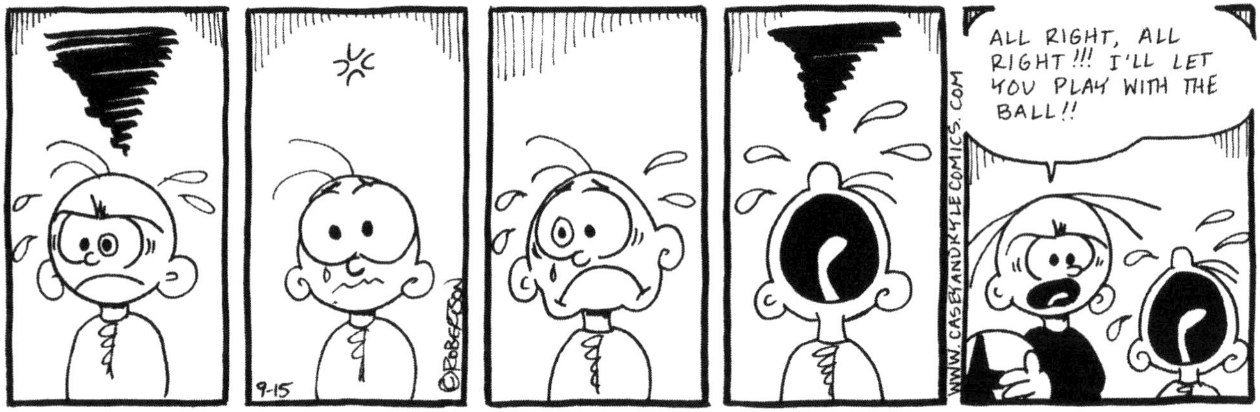
9-15
©ROBERTSON
WWW.CASEYANDKYLECOMICS.COM
ALL RIGHT, ALL RIGHT!!! I'LL LET YOU PLAY WITH THE BALL!!

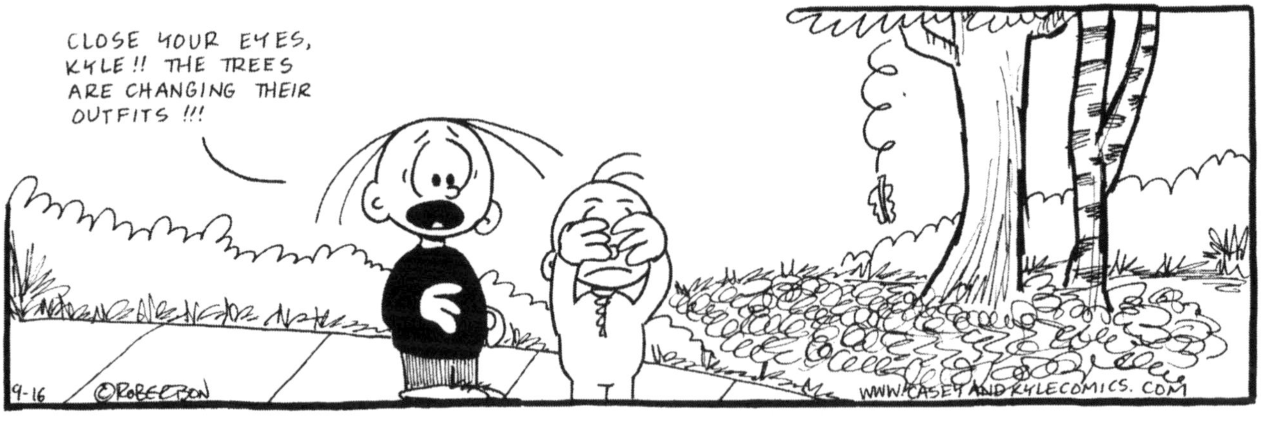
CLOSE YOUR EYES, KYLE!! THE TREES ARE CHANGING THEIR OUTFITS !!!
9-16
©ROBERTSON
WWW.CASEYANDKYLECOMICS.COM

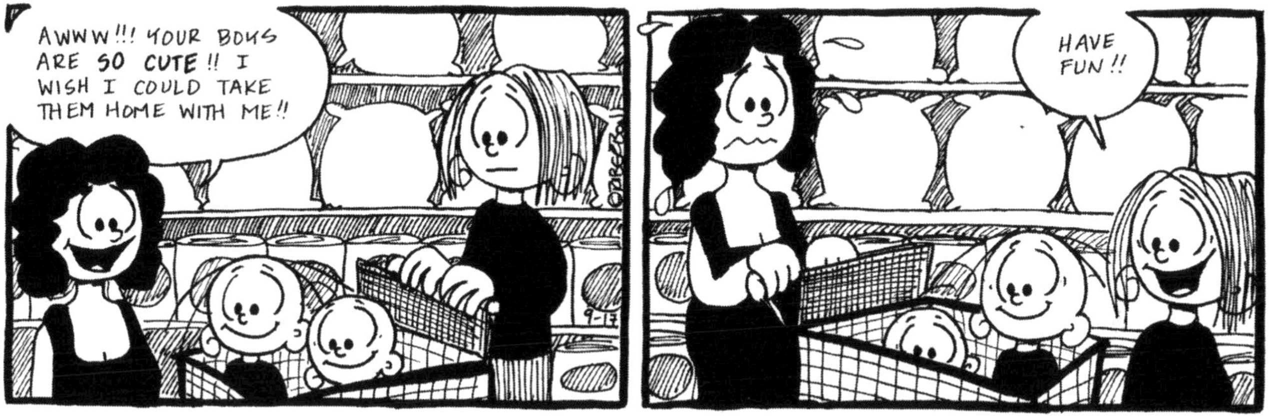
AWWW!!! YOUR BOYS ARE SO CUTE!! I WISH I COULD TAKE THEM HOME WITH ME!!
HAVE FUN!!

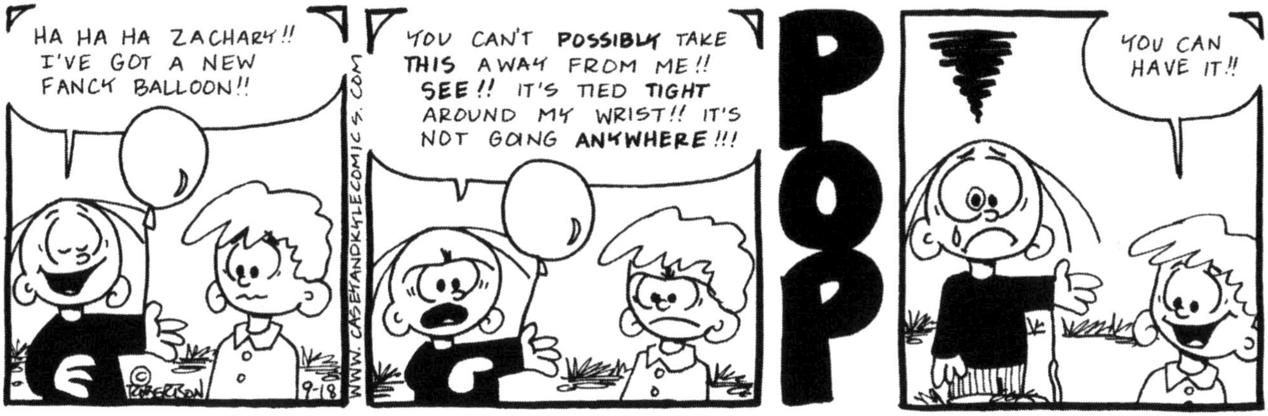
HA HA HA ZACHARY!! I'VE GOT A NEW FANCY BALLOON!!
WWW.CASEYANDKYLECOMICS.COM
YOU CAN'T POSSIBLY TAKE THIS AWAY FROM ME!! SEE!! IT'S TIED TIGHT AROUND MY WRIST!! IT'S NOT GOING ANYWHERE!!!
POP
YOU CAN HAVE IT!!

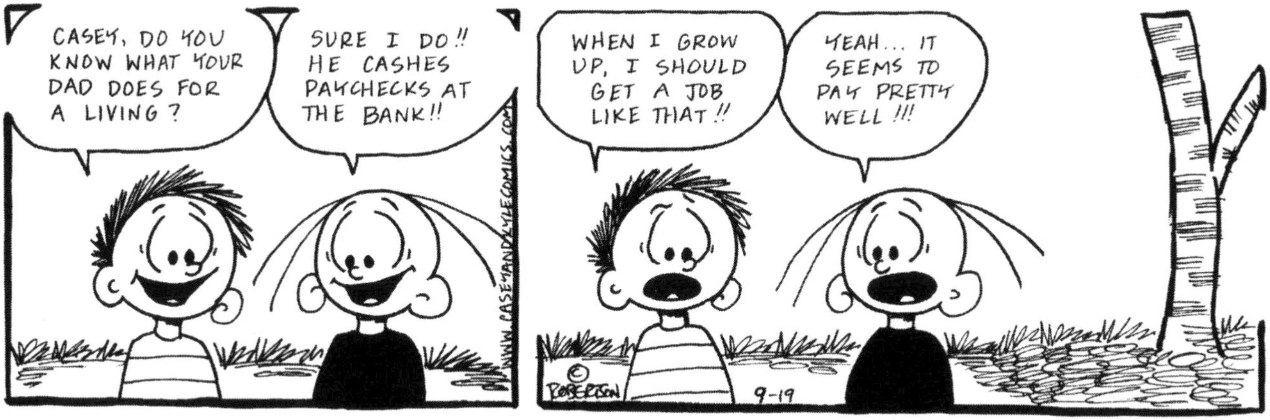
CASEY, DO YOU KNOW WHAT YOUR DAD DOES FOR A LIVING?
SURE I DO!! HE CASHES PAYCHECKS AT THE BANK!!
WWW.CASEYANDKYLECOMICS.COM
WHEN I GROW UP, I SHOULD GET A JOB LIKE THAT!!
YEAH... IT SEEMS TO PAY PRETTY WELL!!!

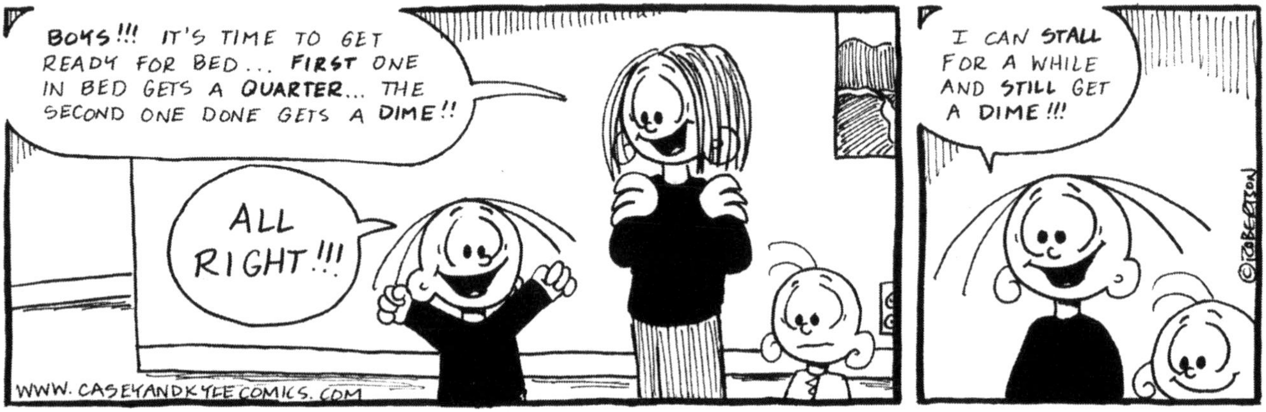
BOYS!!! IT'S TIME TO GET READY FOR BED... FIRST ONE IN BED GETS A QUARTER... THE SECOND ONE DONE GETS A DIME!!
ALL RIGHT!!!
I CAN STALL FOR A WHILE AND STILL GET A DIME!!!
WWW.CASEYANDKYLECOMICS.COM
©ROBERTSON

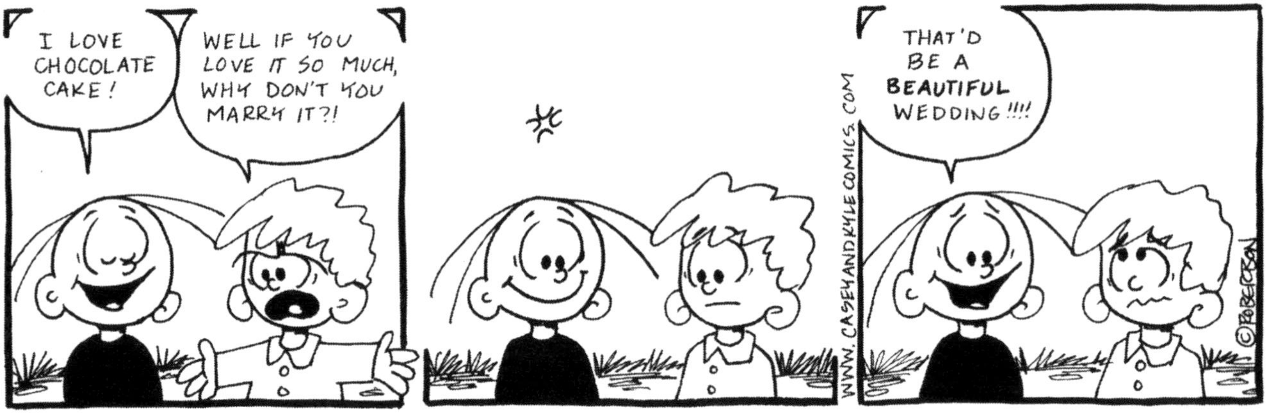
I LOVE CHOCOLATE CAKE!
WELL IF YOU LOVE IT SO MUCH, WHY DON'T YOU MARRY IT?!
THAT'D BE A BEAUTIFUL WEDDING!!!!
WWW.CASEYANDKYLECOMICS.COM
©ROBERTSON

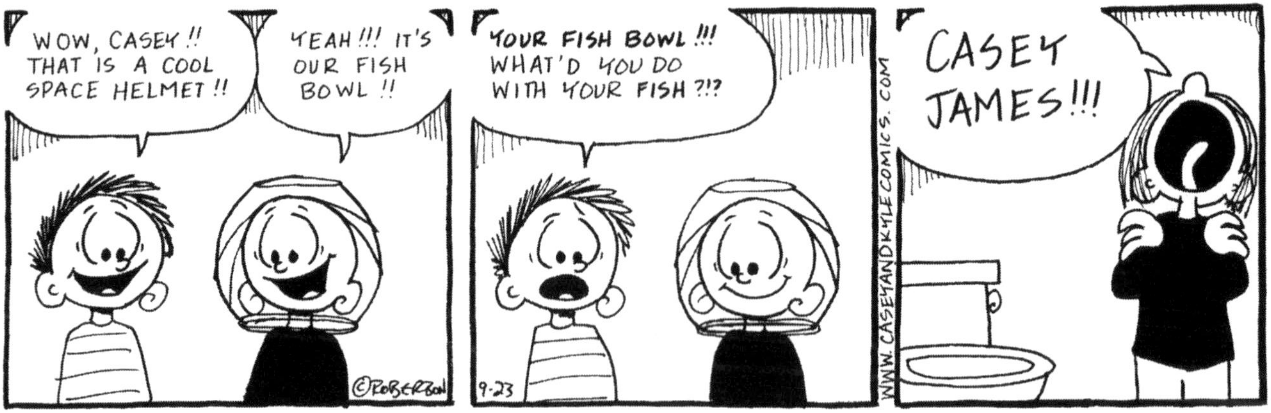
WOW, CASEY!! THAT IS A COOL SPACE HELMET!!
YEAH!!! IT'S OUR FISH BOWL!!
YOUR FISH BOWL!!! WHAT'D YOU DO WITH YOUR FISH?!?
CASEY JAMES!!!
©ROBERTSON
9-23
WWW.CASEYANDKYLECOMICS.COM

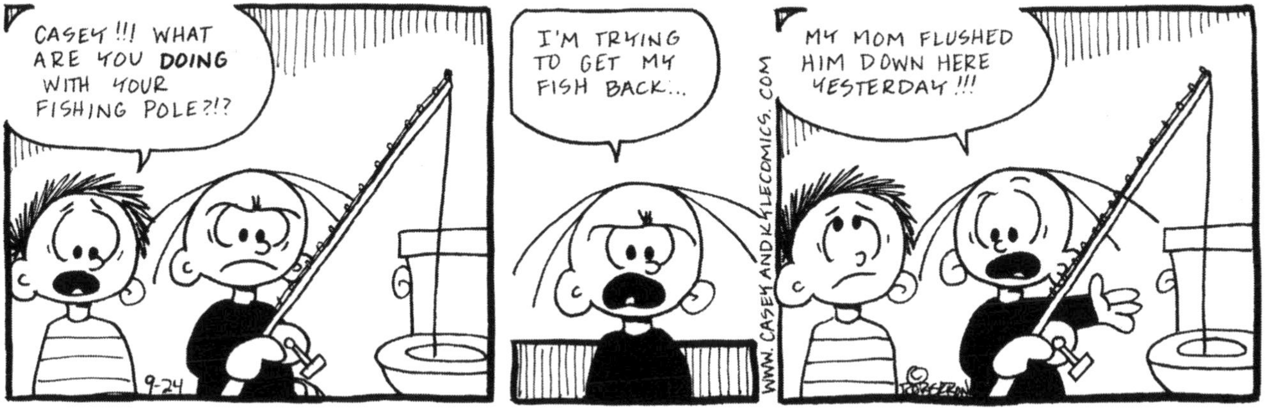
CASEY!!! WHAT ARE YOU DOING WITH YOUR FISHING POLE?!?
I'M TRYING TO GET MY FISH BACK...
MY MOM FLUSHED HIM DOWN HERE YESTERDAY!!!
9-24
WWW.CASEYANDKYLECOMICS.COM

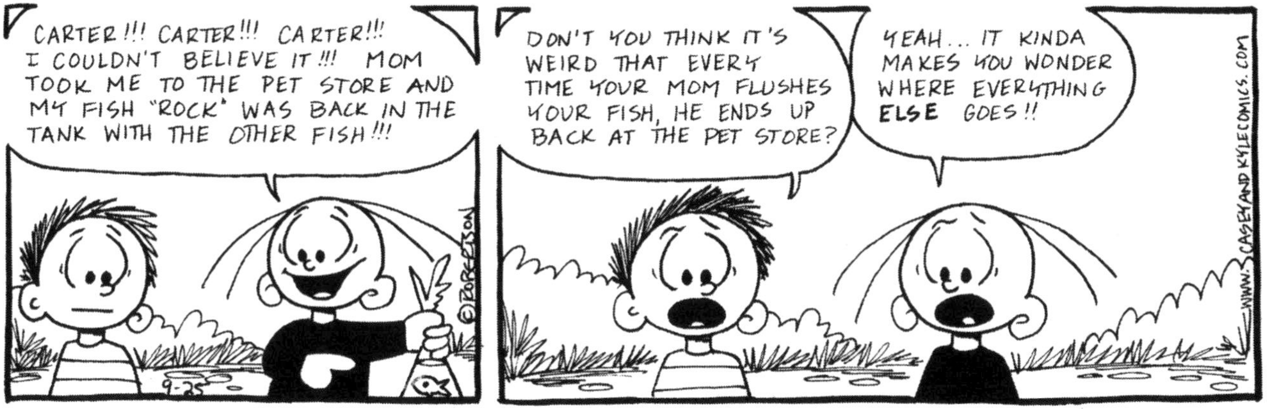
CARTER!!! CARTER!!! CARTER!!! I COULDN'T BELIEVE IT!!! MOM TOOK ME TO THE PET STORE AND MY FISH "ROCK" WAS BACK IN THE TANK WITH THE OTHER FISH!!!
DON'T YOU THINK IT'S WEIRD THAT EVERY TIME YOUR MOM FLUSHES YOUR FISH, HE ENDS UP BACK AT THE PET STORE?
YEAH... IT KINDA MAKES YOU WONDER WHERE EVERYTHING ELSE GOES!!
9-25
WWW.CASEYANDKYLECOMICS.COM

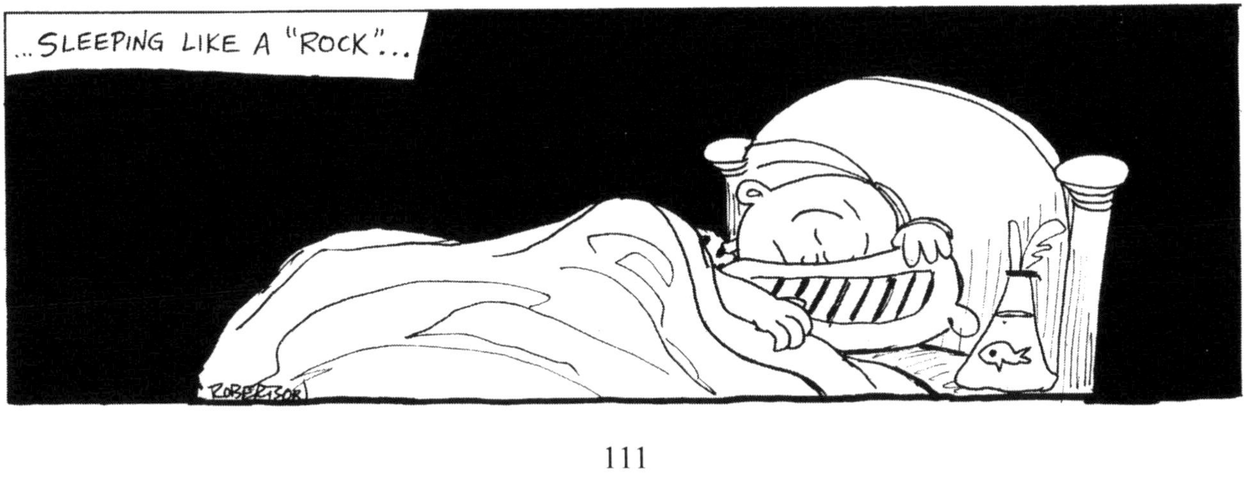
...SLEEPING LIKE A "ROCK"...

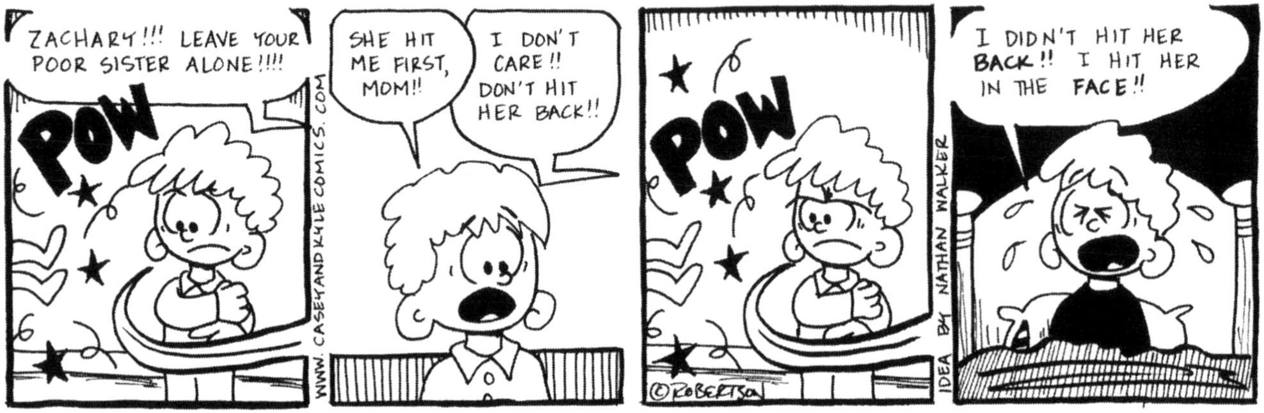
ZACHARY!!! LEAVE YOUR POOR SISTER ALONE!!!!
POW
WWW.CASEYANDKYLECOMICS.COM
SHE HIT ME FIRST, MOM!!
I DON'T CARE!! DON'T HIT HER BACK!!
POW
©ROBERTSON
IDEA BY NATHAN WALKER
I DIDN'T HIT HER BACK!! I HIT HER IN THE FACE!!

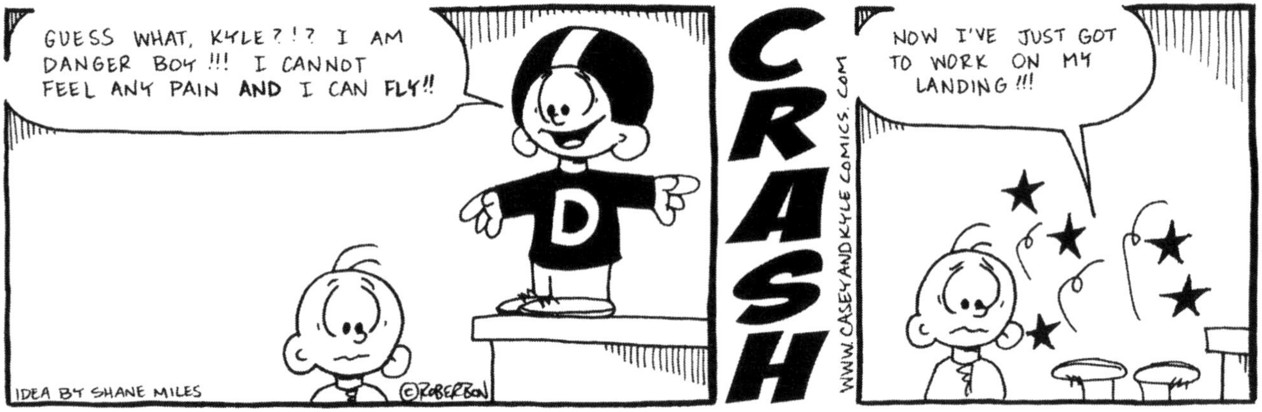
GUESS WHAT, KYLE?!? I AM DANGER BOY!!! I CANNOT FEEL ANY PAIN AND I CAN FLY!!
D
IDEA BY SHANE MILES
©ROBERTSON
CRASH
WWW.CASEYANDKYLECOMICS.COM
NOW I'VE JUST GOT TO WORK ON MY LANDING!!!

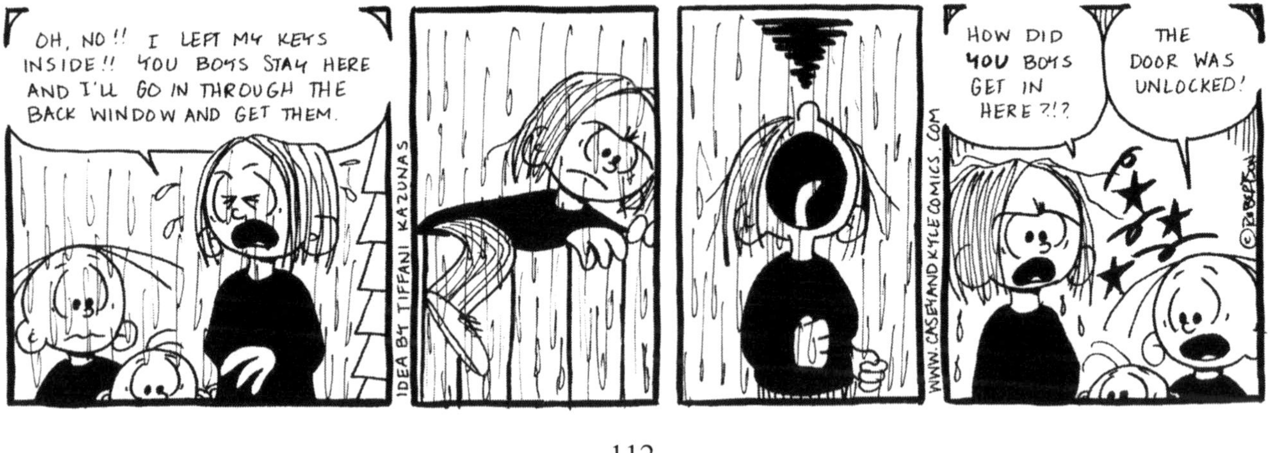
OH, NO!! I LEFT MY KEYS INSIDE!! YOU BOYS STAY HERE AND I'LL GO IN THROUGH THE BACK WINDOW AND GET THEM.
IDEA BY TIFFANI KAZUNAS
WWW.CASEYANDKYLECOMICS.COM
HOW DID YOU BOYS GET IN HERE?!?
THE DOOR WAS UNLOCKED!
©ROBERTSON

Made in the USA
Charleston, SC
25 January 2011